Reimagining Politics after the Terror

Reimagining Politics after the Terror

The Republican Origins of French Liberalism

Andrew Jainchill

Cornell University Press
Ithaca and London

First published 2008 by Cornell University Press

Printed in the United States of America

Library of Congress Cataloging-in-Publication Data

Jainchill, Andrew J. S.
Reimagining politics after the Terror : the republican origins of French liberalism / Andrew Jainchill.
p. cm.
Includes bibliographical references and index.
ISBN 978-0-8014-4669-6 (cloth : alk. paper)
1. France—History—First Republic, 1792–1804. 2. Political culture—France—History. 3. Liberalism—France—History. 4. Republicanism—France—History. I. Title.

DC192.J35 2008
944.04—dc22

2008016675

Cornell University Press strives to use environmentally responsible suppliers and materials to the fullest extent possible in the publishing of its books. Such materials include vegetable-based, low-VOC inks and acid-free papers that are recycled, totally chlorine-free, or partly composed of nonwood fibers. For further information, visit our website at www.cornellpress.cornell.edu.

Cloth printing 10 9 8 7 6 5 4 3 2 1

Contents

Acknowledgments

This project began at the University of California, Berkeley, and it is a pleasure to acknowledge the debts accumulated there. First and foremost, I thank Carla Hesse and Martin Jay, model mentors and advisers throughout graduate school and since. I am particularly grateful for their intellectual rigor and demanding standards. I owe a special thanks to Carla, who consistently pushed me to hone my arguments and refine my claims. I add an extra thanks to Marty, whose astonishing breadth of knowledge and eye for the big picture never ceases to astound. At Berkeley, David Bates, Thomas Laqueur, Hanna Pitkin, Hans Sluga, and Jan de Vries, among others, shaped my thinking in important ways. In addition, a tremendous cohort of fellow students made my time in Berkeley intellectually stimulating and more than enjoyable. Thanks especially to Arianne Chernock, Nick Daum, Aaron Freundschuh, Peter Gordon, Benjamin Lazier, Samuel Moyn, Manuel Rota, and Priya Satia. Finally, Berkeley's extraordinary library system made it possible to begin research on a serious note.

The experience of research and writing in Paris has been consistently wonderful, and again it is a pleasure to thank the institutions and individuals that made my trips there so rich. The École des Hautes Études en Sciences Sociales and Sciences Po were institutional homes while I was still a graduate student. The Bibliothèque Nationale, the Archives Nationales, the Bibliothèque Historique de la Ville de Paris, the Archives des Affaires Étrangères, and the Archives de l'Institut National offered magnificent research collections. Patrice Gueniffey welcomed me into his seminar, Pierre Serna shared his thoughts on the Directory, and Anne Verjus shared her notes on Pierre-Louis Roederer. Charly Coleman, Benjamin Kafka, Emmanuel Saadia, Dana Simmons, and Anoush Terjanian made a fantastic discussion group, providing penetrating feedback on ideas and chapters—and great food and wine—that thankfully did not end when we all left Paris.

The Department of History at Queen's University has provided a collegial and stimulating environment for completing this project. The library system and interlibrary loan office made it possible to finish.

A number of scholars have generously provided comments and suggestions over the years. Parts or all of the manuscript were read at various stages by Howard Brown, Dan Edelstein, Steven Englund, Patrice Gueniffey, Dick Howard, Samuel Moyn, Helena Rosenblatt, Pierre Serna, and K. Steven Vincent. Thomas Kaiser talked through questions of foreign policy while we were both working in the Archives des Affaires Étrangères and James Livesey offered encouragement at an important stage. I owe a special thanks to David Bell and Kent Wright for their extremely helpful and insightful, initially anonymous, reviews of the manuscript for Cornell University Press.

I have presented some of the ideas from the book in progress at the Western Society for French History (twice), the Liberalism's Return conference at Columbia University, the Society for French Historical Studies, the Toronto Area French History Group, the Queen's University History Department, and the Workshop on Pluralism in French History in Durham (U.K.). I thank the audiences and fellow panel participants for valuable feedback. An earlier version of chapter 1 was published in *French Historical Studies,* and I am grateful for permission to use the material here.

Research and writing during the various stages have been generously supported by a number of institutions I am grateful for the opportunity to thank: the University of California Predoctoral Humanities Fellowship, the Berkeley History Department's Sidney Hellman Ehrman and Peder Sather Fellowships, the Berkeley Graduate Division Humanities Research Grant, the Andrew W. Mellon Foundation Dissertation Prospectus Fellowship, the Georges Lurcy Foundation Fellowship, the Institut Français de Washington's Gilbert Chinard Research Fellowship, the Cultural Services of the French Government's Chateaubriand Fellowship, the Société des Professeurs Français et Francophones d'Amérique's Jeanne Marandon Fellowship, the Society for French Historical Studies' John B. and Theta H. Wolf Award, and Queen's University's Research Initiation Grant and Advisory Research Committee Grant. Without this material support, this book would not have been written.

At Cornell University Press, a heartfelt thanks to John Ackerman, who has been an enthusiastic editor from the beginning, and to Jamie Fuller and Candace Akins.

Andrew Janiak has been an irreplaceable friend and inspiration for as long as I can remember. Nicolas Constantinesco has been a similarly exceptional friend, interlocutor, and *compagnon de route.*

I am grateful to my parents, sisters, and brothers for far too much to articulate here.

Finally, I thank Rebecca Manley. Her love, friendship, support, and intellect have marked every word of this book and every moment of the life I lived—from Berkeley to Paris to Kingston—while writing it. Our life together has since been enriched immeasurably by our wonderful daughter, Anna. This book is dedicated to Rebecca and Anna.

Note on Translations and Abbreviations

All translations are my own unless indicated otherwise.

AI, SMP	Archives de l'Institut, Académie des Sciences Morales et Politiques
AN	Archives Nationales de France
BN	Bibliothèque Nationale de France
CP	Correspondance Politique
MAE	Archives du Ministère des Affaires Etrangères
MD	Mémoires et Documents
Moniteur	The original edition of *Le Moniteur universel,* which I have used for citations to the *Moniteur* dated from the beginning of the Year 4 in the revolutionary calendar (from 23 September 1795). Citations are by date and page.
Nouv. Acqu. Fr.	Nouvelles Acquisitions Françaises

RM — *Réimpression de l'ancien Moniteur,* 32 vols. (Paris, 1847–50). This is the standard nineteenth-century reprint of *Le Moniteur universel,* which I have used for citations to the *Moniteur* dated until the end of the Year 3 in the revolutionary calendar (22 September 1795); after this date the reprint is highly abridged and no longer useful. Citations are by volume and page.

Reimagining Politics after the Terror

Introduction

> The field of politics is and has been, in a significant and radical sense, a created one. The designation of certain activities and arrangements as political, the characteristic way that we think about them, and the concepts we employ to communicate our observations and reactions—none of these are written into the nature of things but are the legacy accruing from the historical activity of political philosophers.
>
> Sheldon Wolin, *Politics and Vision: Continuity and Innovation in Western Political Thought*

> There was a republic, I believe, only during the Directory. Before, it was anarchy and confusion. After, only the despotism of a single man, under the name of First Consul.
>
> Louis-Marie de La Révellière-Lépeaux, *Mémoires de Larevellière-Lépeaux*

On 27 July 1794 a group of disaffected politicians acted to end the reign of Robespierre and with it the Terror. The coup against Robespierre, Saint-Just, and the radical Jacobins, immortalized in the annals of French history as "9 Thermidor," its date in the revolutionary calendar, marked a new beginning in the French Revolution. The nation's political and intellectual elites emerged from the furies of the Terror, took a collective deep breath, and set out to refound the Republic. They did so informed by the extraordinary experiences of the preceding five years. These experiences cast politics in a new light and prompted a fresh engagement with the fundamental questions of political philosophy. Over the next ten years—until

1804, when Napoleon Bonaparte crowned himself Napoleon I, Emperor of the French—these questions were repeatedly discussed and debated, making for a moment of intense, and fertile, reflection on politics.

This book is a study of this moment. At its center stands a loose-knit group of politicians and intellectuals who were at or near the hub of power throughout Thermidor, the Directory, and the beginnings of the Consulate, the three brief regimes spanning the years 1794 to 1804.[1] Certain figures in this "republican center" then went on to form the backbone of the liberal opposition to Napoleon Bonaparte as his rule turned authoritarian, while others "collaborated" with the First Consul (and then Emperor).[2] The post-Terror republican center included some of the most famous political actors and theorists of the French Revolution, such as Benjamin Constant, Pierre-Claude-François Daunou, Louis-Marie de La Révellière-Lépeaux, Pierre-Louis Roederer, Emmanuel-Joseph Sieyès, and Germaine de Staël. Predominantly revolutionary veterans, the majority occupied key positions in government, many were members of the National Institute (France's official learned academy), and most wrote for or edited the leading journals of the day. Several penned extended theoretical treatises on politics and the nature of the republic. They frequented the same salons and often corresponded when out of Paris. These figures self-identified as politicians and as savants, dominating political and intellectual life in post-Terror France, so much so that the historian R. R. Palmer has remarked of these years that a "takeover of the Revolution by the intellectuals had occurred."[3]

The republican center materialized after 9 Thermidor, united in the mission of refounding the Republic in the wake of the Terror. Its goal was to preserve the Republic and consolidate the gains of the Revolution by staving off both a monarchical counterrevolution and the potential recrudescence of Jacobinism. Like any political class, however, the republican center was not a perfectly united or coherent group. Individuals moved in and out of positions of power, internal divisions existed, alliances shifted.

1. Thermidor (1794–95), the Directory (1795–1799), and the Consulate (1799–1804) are the names accorded to the successive political regimes of these ten years.

2. "Collaborate" is Isser Woloch's term in *Napoleon and His Collaborators: The Making of a Dictatorship* (New York, 2001).

3. R. R. Palmer, *The Improvement of Humanity: Education and the French Revolution* (Princeton, 1985), 236.

The republican center then split, for all intents and purposes, during the Consulate. While a substantial majority supported the coup of Brumaire that brought Napoleon Bonaparte to power, they subsequently differed in their response to his increasingly dictatorial propensities. Some, most importantly Roederer and Cambacérès, collaborated with Bonaparte until his eventual fall in 1814–15. Others, however, dissented and formed a liberal, if fragmentary and largely ineffectual, opposition. The continuity in personnel from Thermidor to the moment of liberal dissent under the Consulate is tellingly suggested by the Napoleonic police, who in 1801 labeled the emergent liberal opposition "the Thermidorians."[4] While the coherence of the republican center should not be overstated, it was nonetheless an identifiable cohort that stood at or near the heart of power from 1794 to 1804. What follows is a study of the political imagination, "the presuppositions that underpinned . . . politics,"[5] of the post-Terror republican center, and of how its political imagination, in turn, shaped political practice. More specifically, this book examines the political culture of Thermidor, the Directory, and the Consulate, and the origins of French Liberalism within that political culture.

Analysis of "political imagination" or "political culture" entails examination of political language and what might be called the conceptual foundations of politics. The term "political language" is broadly inclusive, perhaps excessively so, but its capaciousness is precisely its strength: the study of political language allows the historian to bring together a range of otherwise discrete utterances in order to investigate patterns of usage, justification, and, ultimately, meaning.[6] Political questions are asked and answered in historically specific ways that reflect underlying conceptual frameworks and categories of analysis. The political imagination of a historical moment is revealed, however obliquely, through the very concerns

4. Alphonse Aulard, ed., *Paris sous le Consulat: Recueil de documents pour l'histoire de l'esprit public à Paris,* 4 vols. (Paris, 1903–9), 2:188, 192.

5. The phrase is John Brewer's in *Party Ideology and Popular Politics at the Accession of George III* (Cambridge, 1976), 267.

6. On the study of political language, see Keith Michael Baker, *Inventing the French Revolution: Essays on French Political Culture in the Eighteenth Century* (Cambridge, 1990); and J. G. A. Pocock, *Virtue, Commerce, and History: Essays on Political Thought and History, Chiefly in the Eighteenth Century* (Cambridge, 1985). On "conceptual history," see Ian Hacking, *Historical Ontology* (Cambridge, Mass., 2004); and Pierre Rosanvallon, *Pour une histoire conceptuelle du politique* (Paris, 2003).

that arose, the problems diagnosed, the questions posed, and the answers offered or the solutions attempted; through the claims made and the arguments that ensued. All point, even if only in glimpses, to the concepts that framed the political imagination of a given historical moment, to the multifaceted meanings those concepts held and how they became constituted, and to the changes taking place within that conceptual space. While the study of language and concepts is clearly more transparent when a single thinker or a handful of actors are analyzed, it is the intention of this book to attempt such an analysis for a group or, even more speculatively, for a "moment."[7]

In addition to analyzing political language and conceptual categories, I aim to elucidate the interplay between words and concepts on the one hand and practices and institutions on the other. To this end, I study "political culture" in a wide-ranging sense. I examine the mechanics of politics during the post-Terror years and the institutional implications of the concepts in play. Specifically, the chapters below investigate a number of sites in which political concepts structured political practice and were themselves transformed as a result of such practices. These include the redaction of constitutions in 1795 and 1799, the fashioning of education policy, and the elaboration of foreign policy. I thus aim to cast interpretive light on post-Terror political culture in the broadest sense of the term.

The starting point for understanding the post-Terror political imagination is the fact that France was a republic. In the late eighteenth century there were thought to be a handful of basic political forms, each with its own rules and dynamics. The crucial distinction, given renewed analytic point in Montesquieu's *The Spirit of the Laws*[8]—which in so many ways established the political lexicon of the second half of the eighteenth century—was between monarchy and republic. The political language of a republic differed significantly from that of a monarchy.[9] Different anxieties, problems, solutions, claims, and, ultimately, practices arose. Republics

7. Outstanding examples of such an analysis of a "moment" are Pierre Rosanvallon, *Le moment Guizot* (Paris, 1985); Baker, *Inventing the French Revolution,* pt. 3.

8. See Michael Sonenscher, *Before the Deluge: Public Debt, Inequality, and the Intellectual Origins of the French Revolution* (Princeton, 2007), esp. 149–50.

9. As Claude Lefort writes of Machiavelli's Florence, "The Republic speaks a language that distinguishes it at this time from other states." *Le travail de l'oeuvre Machiavel* (Paris, 1972), 765.

encountered specifically republican quandaries that demanded specifically republican answers. The term "republic," however, was notoriously imprecise. John Adams famously wrote that "the name republic is given to things in their nature as different and contradictory as light and darkness, truth and falsehood, virtue and vice, happiness and misery."[10] Montesquieu considered the republic one of three distinct "types of government," along with monarchy and despotism, and defined "republican government" as "that in which the people as a body, or only a part of the people, have sovereign power.... When, in a republic, the people as a body have sovereign power, it is a *democracy.* When the sovereign power is in the hands of a part of the people, it is called an *aristocracy.*"[11] Montesquieu's rather expansive definition was replicated nearly word for word in Diderot and d'Alembert's *Encyclopédie,* while the *Dictionnaire de l'Académie française* defined a republic as a "state governed by several."[12] Rousseau, the century's greatest republican political philosopher, stuck closely to the literal, etymological meaning of the word and defined a republic as any state governed for the public good:[13] "I call Republic any state ruled by laws... because then the public interest alone governs and the public good counts for something."[14] As these different attempts at a definition make clear, the term "republic" did not signal a precise constitution or political arrangement. It did, however, carry a number of powerful resonances and connotations. First, and most important, the term was inseparable from its historical legacy, specifically its classical legacy. While there were a variety of "modern" republicanisms on offer in the late eighteenth century, the dominant understanding of the republic grew out of the early modern Atlantic classical-republican tradition.

10. John Adams, *A Defence of the Constitutions of Government of the United States of America,* 3 vols. (Philadelphia, 1787), 1:87.

11. Charles-Louis de Secondat, baron de Montesquieu, *De l'esprit des lois* [1748], in *Oeuvres complètes,* ed. Roger Caillois, 2 vols. (Paris, 1949–51), 2:239.

12. Denis Diderot and Jean Le Rond d'Alembert, eds., *Encyclopédie, ou Dictionnaire raisonné des sciences, des arts et des métiers,* 35 vols. (Paris, 1751–72), s.v. "République" (article by M. le Chevalier de Jaucourt); *Dictionnaire de l'Académie française,* 1st ed. (1694), 4th ed. (1762), and 5th ed. (1798), s.v. "République" (online at http://humanities.uchicago.edu/orgs/ARTFL/).

13. *République* in French and "republic" in English are derived from the Latin *rēspublica,* a compound of *rēs* (thing, affair) and *publicus* (public).

14. Rousseau, *Du contrat social* [1762], in *Oeuvres complètes,* 5 vols. (Paris, 1959–95), 3:379–80.

Classical Republicanism

The political language of classical republicanism, which has received much scholarly attention in recent decades, was not a perfectly uniform political language in the early modern European and Atlantic world. It assumed different incarnations at different historical junctures and in response to specific political, cultural, and social circumstances. Despite its diversity of incarnation, however, classical republicanism was in the main defined by the problem it posed: it imagined the republic as radically contingent, subject to vicissitude, always precarious. To quote J. G. A. Pocock, "the republic was seen as confronting its own temporal finitude, as attempting to remain morally and politically stable in a stream of irrational events conceived as essentially destructive of all systems of secular stability."[15] As a result, classical republicanism was more often than not a diagnostic political language, defined as much by its anxieties as by its prescriptions.[16] The republic's instability could be combated, and the republic stabilized, it was thought, only through the civic virtue and active engagement of a citizenry completely identified with the public good. Classical republicanism thus placed great emphasis on politics, or "the political," as the lifeblood of the republic—not divine right, customary law, dynastic legitimacy, or any of the other essentially prepolitical foundations typically invoked in early modern Europe. In tying the health of the republic to the civic virtue of its active citizens, classical republicanism could define the citizenry in both popular and elitist forms—it was not a priori democratic or aristocratic. For the most part, though, it was an elitist doctrine defining the virtuous citizenry in exclusive and, moreover, exceedingly masculine terms. The republic was to be ruled by "the best," by a limited group of men only. On the constitutional level, classical republicanism did not require a specific idea of sovereignty. Rather, it held, in Polybian terms, that a constitution must balance the three forms of government—monarchy, aristocracy, and democracy—each of which on its own would degenerate into its corrupt form—tyranny, oligarchy, and anarchy.

15. J. G. A. Pocock, *The Machiavellian Moment: Florentine Political Thought and the Atlantic Republican Tradition* (Princeton, 1975), viii.

16. Keith Michael Baker, "Transformations of Classical Republicanism in Eighteenth-Century France," *Journal of Modern History* 73 (2001): 35–36.

Attention to the political language of classical republicanism in eighteenth-century and revolutionary France has been largely absent from the historical literature.[17] However, it has long been noted that the revolutionaries were fascinated by and even revered classical antiquity, specifically republican antiquity.[18] Over two hundred years ago, the famously perceptive critics of the Revolution Edmund Burke and François-René de Chateaubriand both attributed France's republican ferment to readings in classical sources. Burke, in his *Letters on a Regicide Peace* of 1797, noted with evident disgust that eighteenth-century republicans "had continually in their hands the *Observations* of Machiavel on Livy. They had Montesquieu's *Grandeur et Décadence des Romains* [*The Greatness of the Romans and Their Decline*] as a manual; and they compared, with mortification, the systematic proceedings of a Roman senate with the fluctuations of a monarchy."[19] Likewise, Chateaubriand remarked in his *Essay on Revolutions,* also in 1797, that "our revolution was generated by men, more residents of Rome and Athens than their own country, who sought to revive

17. A handful of historians, most importantly Keith Baker, have begun to investigate the role played by classical republicanism in eighteenth-century France and the Revolution, but in 2001 Baker could still remark that "its usefulness in mapping French political discourse in the late eighteenth century has barely been assayed." Ibid., 34. See also Baker, *Inventing the French Revolution,* esp. chaps. 4 and 6; Johnson Kent Wright, *A Classical Republican in Eighteenth-Century France: The Political Thought of Mably* (Stanford, 1997); Wright, "The Idea of a Republican Constitution in Old Régime France," in *Republicanism: A Shared European Heritage,* ed. Martin Van Gelderen and Quentin Skinner (Cambridge, 2002), 1:289–306; Michael Sonenscher, "Republicanism, State Finances and the Emergence of Commercial Society in Eighteenth-Century France—or from Royal to Ancient Republicanism and Back," in ibid., 2:275–92; Jean-Fabien Spitz, *La liberté politique: Essai de généalogie conceptuelle* (Paris, 1995); Marisa Linton, *The Politics of Virtue in Enlightenment France* (Basingstoke, U.K., 2001); Catherine Larrère, "Libéralisme et républicanisme: Y a-t-il une exception française?" *Libéralisme et républicanisme: Cahiers de philosophie de l'université de Caen* 34 (2000): 127–46; Rachel Hammersley, *French Revolutionaries and English Republicans: The Cordeliers Club, 1790–1794* (Rochester, N.Y., 2005); Raymonde Monnier, *Républicanisme, patriotisme et Révolution française* (Paris, 2005).

18. Harold Parker, *The Cult of Antiquity and the French Revolutionaries: A Study in the Development of the Revolutionary Spirit* (Chicago, 1937); Jacques Bouineau, *Les toges du pouvoir, ou la révolution de droit antique (1789–1799)* (Toulouse, 1986); Claude Mossé, *L'antiquité dans la Révolution française* (Paris, 1989); Catherine Volpilhac-Auger, *Tacite en France de Montesquieu à Chateaubriand,* Studies on Voltaire and the Eighteenth Century 313 (Oxford, 1993); François Hartog, "La Révolution française et l'Antiquité," in *Situations de la démocratie,* ed. Marcel Gauchet, Pierre Manent, and Pierre Rosanvallon (Paris, 1993).

19. Quoted in Sonenscher, "Republicanism, State Finances and the Emergence of Commercial Society in Eighteenth-Century France," 277.

classical morals and manners [*moeurs*] in Europe."[20] Some twenty years later, the liberal political philosopher Benjamin Constant similarly blamed the Terror on "the modern imitators of the republics of antiquity" who wanted to "give the liberty of the ancients to the moderns."[21] Throughout the Revolution, the revolutionaries employed classical symbols, cited canonical figures from the classical-republican corpus, and related their experiences to classical models. Classical antiquity, specifically the version relayed by early modern political philosophers and historians such as Machiavelli, Montesquieu, and Rollin, was the foundational political experience of late-eighteenth-century republicanism. Republican Rome was the most important example, but references to classical Athens, Sparta, and Rome were mixed and matched and the differences between them frequently elided. In short, the lessons of republican antiquity collectively served as a fount of republican political wisdom and profoundly shaped the revolutionaries' political imagination. As Burke, Chateaubriand, and Constant all suggested, the revolutionaries' veneration of republican antiquity was not idle chatter.

The post-Terror period was no different. The republican center remained enthralled by republican antiquity, the self-sacrifice of its heroes, the patriotism of its citizens, the civic virtue of its republican moeurs. And it likewise remained wary of republican antiquity's pitfalls and took those lessons to heart. In October of 1794 Pierre-Louis Ginguené, a prominent intellectual and politician then sitting on the Commission on Public Instruction, eulogized the republican heroes Brutus and Cato while reviewing a recent translation of Thomas Gordon's *Discourses* on Tacitus and Sallust. Ginguené extolled the power of "books made for inspiring love of country, love of liberty, grandeur of spirit, disinterestedness, all of the virtues.... Do you want to make republicans? May your young read Titus-Livy, Sallust, Tacitus, Plutarch, etc." "We hope," he wrote, "that in our new education the language of great men, of Cicero, of Brutus, will not be neglected."[22] Similarly, Baudin des Ardennes, a fixture of the post-Terror

20. Quoted in Hartog, "La Révolution française et l'Antiquité," 30.

21. Benjamin Constant, *De l'esprit de conquête et de l'usurpation dans leurs rapports avec la civilisation européenne* [1814], in *Écrits politiques,* ed. Marcel Gauchet, 2d ed. (Paris, 1997), 211–22.

22. Ginguené also praised Machiavelli and Thomas Gordon as great modern republicans. [Ginguené], review of *Discours historiques, critiques et politiques de Thomas Gordon, sur Tacite et sur Salluste, La Décade philosophique, littéraire et politique,* 20 Vendémiaire, Year 3 (11 October 1794), 104.

republican center, in the spring of 1795 equated "republican liberty" with "great models" such as Cicero and Cato.[23] Intellectuals at the National Institute researched, wrote about, presented to each other, and drew lessons from classical antiquity on a seemingly constant basis.[24] A number of histories were published during these years narrating in strikingly classical-republican terms the fortunes of classical Athens, Sparta, and the Roman Republic, sometimes adding to the story modern-day Holland, Geneva, and the French Republic up to 1795. Among these were a four-volume pocket-sized *Histoire abrégée des républiques anciennes et modernes, où l'on voit leur origine et leur établissement, et les causes de leur décadence et de leur ruine (Short History of the Ancient and Modern Republics in Which One Sees Their Origin, Their Establishment, and the Causes of Their Decline and Ruin)* by Bulard, the author of several revolutionary catechisms intended for the instruction of youth during the Directory, and a nearly four hundred-page compendium of excerpts from the English republican Montagu that ended with the warning: "The fate of the classical republics should alarm us about our destiny, unless, educated by their misfortunes, we prevent our own ruin by avoiding their mistakes."[25] A final, ironic, example is provided by Napoleon Bonaparte, who as general of the Army of Italy voiced one of classical republicanism's central tropes in writing to the Executive Directory that he feared the growing status of the military in the Republic. In response, the Directory praised Bonaparte's attention to the threat of praetorianism and, invoking Cicero's words, responded, "Nothing is healthier for the maintenance of republics than the maxim *cedant arma togae* [let arms yield to the toga]. It is not one of the least glorious features in the life of a general placed at the head of a triumphant army to express such concern about so important a point."[26]

23. Pierre-Louis-Charles Baudin des Ardennes, *Anecdotes et réflexions générales sur la constitution* (Paris, 1795), 4.

24. In the Class of Moral and Political Sciences during the Year 7 (1798–99) alone, Bouchard presented *Les édits des Dictatures, des Consuls, et autres Magistrats Romains;* Mercier gave his *Fragmens historiques sur la vie de Caton le censeur;* De Sales presented *Du gouvernement fédératif dans les anciennes Républiques* by Sainte Croix; and Levesque read a mémoire titled *Sur la Législation de Lycurgue.* "Registre des Procès-verbaux et rapports de la Classe des Sciences morales et politiques," AI, SMP, A2.

25. Bulard, *Histoire abrégée des républiques anciennes et modernes, où l'on voit leur origine et leur établissement, et les causes de leur décadence et de leur ruine,* 4 vols. (Paris, 1796); C. Turpin, *Histoire du gouvernement des anciennes républiques, où l'on découvre les causes de leur élévation et de leur dépérissement, nouvelle édition* (Paris, 1796), 398.

26. Directory to Bonaparte, 30 Vendémiaire, Year 6 (21 October 1797), AN, AF III 473, p. 13. The letter did not mention Cicero, but the quote is from *On Duties,* 1.77.

As these examples, which could be multiplied many times over, all suggest, France's post-Terror political culture was powerfully influenced by classical models. Such references were not mere rhetoric. They were a constitutive feature of the republican center's political imagination and point to the revolutionaries' "mental toolkit,"[27] the categories, preconceptions, and experiences, however distant in the past, by which they understood republican political life. Simply put, the conceptual matrix through which the post-Terror republican center understood politics was essentially classical republican in nature. In this regard, the French revolutionaries inhabited a wider early modern Atlantic cultural-intellectual world. While there were of course fundamentally important differences within this world, such as the French tradition of absolutist sovereignty or the Americans' inheritance of the English tradition of rights, the similarities should not be underestimated. Books and ideas circulated, classical history was a cross-cultural lingua franca, and the early modern political-philosophical canon largely transcended national borders. And throughout this Atlantic intellectual world the republic as a political form was understood in light of the classical tradition as rendered in early modern history and political philosophy. The political language of classical republicanism furnished key terms in the moment's political lexicon and many of its essential political principles. As a result, the institutions developed in post-Terror France reflected the concerns and precepts of the early modern classical-republican tradition. Post-Terror political culture was tuned to a classical-republican key.

The influence of classical republicanism was, in fact, more important during the post-Terror period than at any other point in the French Revolution. Moreover, it was only after the Terror that the political culture of the Revolution can be said to have fallen within the mainstream of the early modern European classical-republican tradition. In this regard, my argument differs from that of Keith Baker, who views classical republicanism as reaching its apogee in the political discourse of the Terror.[28] The role of classical-republican tropes in the political discourse of radical Jacobinism and the Terror was, in my view, overshadowed by more powerful currents external to the early modern classical-republican tradition—namely,

27. To use Lucien Febvre's phrase in *The Problem of Unbelief in the Sixteenth Century, the Religion of Rabelais,* trans. Beatrice Gottlieb (Cambridge, Mass., 1982).

28. Baker, "Transformations of Classical Republicanism."

a chiliastic sense of time and voluntarist democratic sovereignty. The chiliastic sense of time exhibited in the political discourse of the Terror was wholly foreign to the classical-republican tradition, in which political time was imagined to be historical, cyclical, and degenerating. The language of sovereign will was also foreign to the classical-republican tradition, stemming from a very different lineage. Schematically, it had roots in medieval theology, received its canonical articulation in Jean Bodin's epoch-making *Six Books of the Republic* and Thomas Hobbes's *Leviathan,* and was fused, perhaps unstably, with a range of classical-republican themes in Rousseau's *The Social Contract.* The presence of classical-republican tropes in the discourse of the Terror is probably best understood in the way that Mona Ozouf describes the role of classical forms in the revolutionary festivals—as an essentially negative "purging" move that would clear a conceptual space for a radically new politics.[29] France fully participated in the early modern Atlantic "Machiavellian Moment," to use Pocock's terminology, only after the Terror.

Liberalism

Although classical republicanism was the dominant political language of post-Terror France, it was not the only political language on offer. There were also self-styled modern republicans in and around the republican center.[30] One of the principal arguments of this book is that the years 1794 to 1804 were a watershed in the transition from classical to modern republicanism. Contingently, almost haphazardly, a modern language of liberalism began to emerge at this time in response to the political crises of the Directory and, especially, the experience of Napoleonic despotism under the Consulate. Crucially, this liberal language was decisively shaped by a host of classical-republican concerns and themes stemming from post-Terror political culture and, as a result, is best described as "liberal republicanism." Liberal republicanism began with a commitment to liberal principles

29. Mona Ozouf, *Festivals and the French Revolution,* trans. Alan Sheridan (Cambridge, Mass., 1988), 271–76. I thank David Bell for suggesting this analogy.

30. James Livesey's *Making Democracy in the French Revolution* (Cambridge, Mass., 2001) emphasizes the importance of modern republicanism in the post-Terror period.

but held that such principles could be realized, and preserved, only in a republic with an active commitment to politics itself, or "the political." Without a robust political life, it was thought, liberty would be lost. Liberal republicanism was an emergent minority current during Thermidor and the Directory, began to coalesce under the Consulate as the basis for opposition to Bonaparte, and eventually constituted the central kernel of nineteenth-century French Liberalism as articulated by Benjamin Constant and Alexis de Tocqueville.[31]

Liberal republicanism was, in the first place, a political language centered on "modern liberty." The latter received its canonical definition from Benjamin Constant, who famously claimed in 1819 that the "aim of the moderns is security in the enjoyment of private pleasures; and they call liberty the guarantees accorded by institutions to these pleasures."[32] In its emphasis on modern liberty, liberal republicanism was, at its core, liberal in orientation. Liberalism's political-philosophical starting point is a first-order commitment to "the liberty of the moderns" such that the foremost priority of politics becomes the legal protection of the individual pursuit of happiness—what contemporary moral philosophy refers to as "the right" over "the good."[33] However, no full-blown political program flowed from this source along a set course. As a first principle, modern liberty could be the wellspring for a number of tributaries.

Perhaps the most important result of assigning priority to modern liberty was the conviction that "the social" took precedence over "the political." "Society," "commerce," "public opinion," or some other such figuration of the social would come first, and thus politics would reflect, rather than shape, a prior social reality.[34] The political theorist Sheldon Wolin traces this cardinal feature of liberal political philosophy—"the emergence of society as a self-subsistent entity" that would be "the support of the political

31. I use "French Liberalism" as a term of art to refer to the liberalism of Constant and Tocqueville and not the rationalist liberalism of François Guizot and the Doctrinaires. See the epilogue.

32. Constant, "De la liberté des anciens comparée à celle des modernes" [1819], in *Écrits politiques,* 603.

33. John Rawls, *A Theory of Justice* (Cambridge, Mass., 1971).

34. David Bell describes society, commerce, and public opinion as three of several secular foundational concepts for ordering human existence that emerged in the eighteenth century. *The Cult of the Nation in France: Inventing Nationalism, 1680–1800* (Cambridge, Mass., 2001), esp. 24–27. See as well the works Bell cites on 230, nn. 15, 16, 18.

order rather than the reverse"—to John Locke.[35] In their reflections on the French Revolution, liberal-minded thinkers criticized Jacobinism for believing that politics could remake a prior social reality, for assigning priority to the political rather than the social. Pierre Rosanvallon has usefully described this problem as one of political embodiment. As he puts it, in the Revolution there was a crisis of politically embodying the social, of "being able to integrate the full diversity of the social into the unity of the political body."[36] Liberals objected to the Jacobin impulse to force the plurality of the social order to conform to a single political One.

Another important consequence of assigning priority to modern liberty was the view that representative government was superior to democracy. According to liberals, the representative institution would allow people to disentangle their lives from the burdens of citizenship and pursue their individual ends—what Constant called "private pleasures." Liberals, in other words, rejected the Aristotelian notion that humans are political animals. Rather, they averred, many, if not most, people would prefer an apolitical life. Liberals thus held representative government to be more than a substitute for democracy. It was a replacement of democracy that freed modern individuals rather than, as Rousseau had famously claimed, disempowered them. Bernard Manin describes the difference, as expressed by Madison and Sieyès, arguably the two most paradigmatically modern thinkers of the age of revolutions: representative government was not seen "as an approximation of government by the people made technically necessary by the physical impossibility of gathering together the citizens of large states.... [It] was not one kind of democracy; it was an essentially different and furthermore preferable form of government."[37] In his private notes, Sieyès insisted on the superiority of representative government over democracy in precisely these terms: "The representative regime is not required solely by the size of the territory. In all cases there is everything

35. Sheldon Wolin, *Politics and Vision: Continuity and Innovation in Western Political Thought* (Boston, 1960), 312, 308.

36. Pierre Rosanvallon, *Le peuple introuvable: Histoire de la représentation démocratique en France* (Paris, 1998), 41. See also Marcel Gauchet's essay on Ernst Kantorowicz's *The King's Two Bodies,* "Des deux corps du roi au pouvoir sans corps: Christianisme et politique I et II," *Le Débat* 14, 15 (1981): 133–57, 147–68.

37. Bernard Manin, *The Principles of Representative Government* (Cambridge, 1997), 2–3. See also Hanna Fenichel Pitkin, *The Concept of Representation* (Berkeley, 1967); and Pierre Rosanvallon, *La démocratie inachevée: Histoire de la souveraineté du peuple en France* (Paris, 2000), esp. 12.

to gain for the people by putting into representation all the powers which form the public establishment."[38] As a result of such thinking, liberals tended to argue that more direct forms of democracy were an outmoded form of politics and thus advocated displacing the affairs of government to representative elites who would govern while the population at large pursued their individual ends.

The political-philosophical commitments underpinning liberalism could lead to the abandonment of politics itself. In fact, liberalism in its purest form is indifferent to politics and more often than not rejects politics as such.[39] In the post-Terror period, the most important such strand of political thought was "liberal authoritarianism."[40] Liberal authoritarianism held that liberal political principles could be realized only in an apolitical polity, a stable order secure from the tumult of political life. It saw modern liberty and politics as essentially antithetical. Liberal authoritarianism was championed by the most paradigmatically modern thinkers of the post-Terror period, Sieyès and Roederer, was institutionalized in 1799 with the Constitution of the Year VIII, and then shaped the political culture of the Consulate.

Unlike liberal authoritarianism, liberal republicanism remained committed to a robust and vigilant political life. In the 1819 lecture in which Constant defined modern liberty, he also warned that abandoning ancient liberty, which he defined as "the sharing of social power among the citizens of the same *patrie,*" would lead to the extinction of liberty in all of its forms. "Individual liberty, I repeat, is the true modern liberty. Political liberty is its guarantee; political liberty is consequently indispensable." He thus urged that, "far from renouncing either of the two types of liberty,... we must... learn to combine the one with the other."[41] In this regard, liberal republicanism was powerfully influenced by the emphasis on politics in the early modern classical-republican tradition and, more specifically, by the post-Terror political cultural context in which it emerged. The political thought of Constant and Tocqueville, to cite the

38. Sieyès, *Des Manuscrits de Sieyès, 1773–1799,* ed. Christine Fauré, Jacques Guilhaumou, and Jacques Valier (Paris, 1999), 519–20.

39. Wolin, *Politics and Vision,* esp. ch. 9; Pierre Rosanvallon, *Le capitalisme utopique: Histoire de l'idée de marché,* 3d ed. (Paris, 1999).

40. I take the term "liberal authoritarianism" from Howard G. Brown, *Ending the French Revolution: Violence, Justice, and Repression from the Terror to Napoleon* (Charlottesville, Va., 2006).

41. "De la liberté des anciens comparée à celle des modernes," 603, 612, 618.

two most famous exponents of French Liberalism, bore lasting traces of the classical-republican tradition. While neither figure could be described as a classical republican proper, both articulated a liberalism marked by classical-republican themes. The influence of classical republicanism helps to explain much of what made French Liberalism distinctive, notably its ongoing concern with political liberty and the moral and political personality of the citizenry. French Liberalism cannot be properly understood without an appreciation of the persistence of classical-republican concerns and themes.

Scholars have for too long treated classical republicanism and liberalism as purely discrete political languages. In the scholarly literature on the early United States, for example, it is assumed that there was a transition from republicanism to liberalism involving something like a gestalt switch; the ensuing historiographical debates have focused on precisely when such a switch occurred.[42] Similarly, political and legal theorists argue over the relative merits of republicanism and liberalism, treating the two traditions as hermetically sealed off from one another.[43] While the two political languages may be antithetical in rigorously formal terms, in historical practice they mutually influenced each other in important ways. There was frequent slippage across the theoretical boundary. The two ideal-types stand up in the historical record nowhere less than in France. French Liberalism is best understood as liberal republicanism, a polymorphous synthesis of classical republican and liberal political languages that first began to emerge between 1794 and 1804.

The arguments presented here aim to revise current interpretation of both the origins and character of French Liberalism, a topic that has generated a rich body of scholarship in recent years.[44] This explosion in interest

42. The disagreement between Gordon Wood and J. G. A. Pocock on whether the passage of the federal constitution in 1787 signaled a sea change from "classical politics" to a modern "American science of politics" established the contours of debate. Wood, *The Creation of the American Republic, 1776–1787* (Chapel Hill, N.C., 1969), esp. chap. 15; Pocock, *The Machiavellian Moment,* chap. 15.

43. See Laura Kalman's excellent overview in *The Strange Career of Legal Liberalism* (New Haven, 1996).

44. E.g., Marcel Gauchet, "Benjamin Constant: L'illusion lucide du libéralisme," which is the introduction to *De la liberté chez les modernes: Écrits politiques,* by Benjamin Constant, ed. Gauchet (Paris, 1980) (a modified version was reprinted in 1997 at the head of Constant, *Écrits politiques;* citations here are to the later edition); Gauchet, "Tocqueville, l'Amérique et nous: Sur la genèse de la démocratie," *Libre* 7 (1980): 42–120; Stephen Holmes, *Benjamin Constant and The Making of Modern Liberalism* (New Haven, Conn., 1984); Pierre Manent, *Tocqueville et la nature de la démocratie* (Paris, 1982); Manent, *Histoire intellectuelle du libéralisme: Dix leçons* (Paris, 1987); Cheryl Welch,

can be traced to a very specific historical context, the French "antitotalitarian" moment of the 1970s and 1980s, which has decisively shaped the scholarship on French Liberalism. As French intellectuals, notably those grouped around François Furet, rejected the allegedly "totalitarian" impulses of the traditional French left, many turned to liberal political-philosophical alternatives.[45] And most prominent among these alternatives were the great French liberals of the early nineteenth century, especially Constant, Guizot, and Tocqueville. The revival of these figures led to a flurry of frequently brilliant scholarship, which, however, was often overdetermined by the broader antitotalitarian agenda.[46]

Furet and his disciples, notably Marcel Gauchet, located early-nineteenth-century French Liberalism's generative moment in Thermidor and, specifically, in a rejection of Rousseau's notion of the general will and its supposed culmination in high Jacobinism and the Terror. Analytically, the leap from a politics of "social interests," as Furet described Thermidor (discussed below), to a liberal political language was a natural step. Furthermore, the Thermidorians' postrevolutionary mentality was said to have fostered the turn to liberalism.[47] To my mind, this line of analysis begins with a mischaracterization of post-Terror politics. Moreover, the

---

Liberty and Utility: The French Idéologues and the Transformation of Liberalism (New York, 1984); Biancamaria Fontana, *Benjamin Constant and the Post-Revolutionary Mind* (New Haven, 1991); Lucien Jaume, *L'individu effacé ou le paradoxe du libéralisme français* (Paris, 1997).

45. See Andrew Jainchill and Samuel Moyn, "French Democracy between Totalitarianism and Solidarity: Pierre Rosanvallon and Revisionist Historiography," *Journal of Modern History* 76 (2004): 107–54; Helena Rosenblatt, "Why Constant? A Critical Overview of the Constant Revival," *Modern Intellectual History* 1 (2004): 439–53; Serge Audier, *Tocqueville retrouvé: Genèse et enjeux du renouveau tocquevillien français* (Paris, 2004); and, on France's antitotalitarian moment, Michael Scott Christofferson, *French Intellectuals Against the Left: The Antitotalitarian Moment of the 1970's* (New York, 2004).

46. Gauchet, for example, published essays on Constant and Tocqueville in 1980 (cited in n. 44, above) that read the two political philosophers almost obsessively against the backdrop of totalitarianism and its alleged origins in the modern democratic project. In a 1997 reprint of the Constant essay, Gauchet conceded "the slight anachronism of my argument" but did not change his basic interpretation: Constant's genius lay in his "diagnosis" of Rousseauian democracy, a "diagnosis . . . remarkable for its continuing validity for almost all of the totalitarian derailments that followed." "Benjamin Constant," 11, 54–55.

47. Gauchet in particular seems to feel a deep personal connection with the Thermidorians' postrevolutionary mentality. In a recent interview, he compared "the return of liberalism" in recent French intellectual life, and his part in that return, with "the circumstances of 1794 or 1815." Gauchet, *La condition historique: Entretiens avec Francois Azouvi et Sylvain Piron* (Paris, 2003), 266–67; see also Gauchet, "Benjamin Constant," 27.

central ideas of French Liberalism were as much a response to the republican center's experience under Bonaparte as they were an immediate reaction against Jacobinism. While much of French Liberalism was later elaborated in rhetorical antagonism to Jacobinism, and much of its distrust of popular democracy materialized in revulsion to Jacobinism, the actual emergence of the liberal-republican position that constituted the central kernel of French Liberalism owed more to the experience with Bonaparte's authoritarianism. Finally, current accounts of French Liberalism have neglected its crucial classical-republican sources. This book thus seeks to revise contemporary understanding of both the origins and the character of French Liberalism.

Post-Terror Politics

The political discourse of the republican center between 1794 and 1804 differed markedly from that of the heady early years of the Revolution. A disabused, anxiety-ridden politics of closure supplanted both the optimism of 1789–92 and the combustible mix of messianic, paranoid, and democratic discourses marking the crisis years 1792–94. The most repeated phrase of the post-Terror period was that it was time, at long last, to end the Revolution. The passage of the Constitution of the Year III in the summer of 1795 closed with a "Discussion on the means of ending the revolution" and the official proclamation upon the promulgation of the Constitution of the Year VIII declared that "the Revolution is established on the principles that began it: It is finished."[48] The revolutionary veterans of the republican center sought a stable, constitutional republic.[49]

48. *RM,* 25:534; "Procès verbal de la séance des Consuls," 24 Frimaire, Year 8 (15 December 1799), AN, AF IV 911.

49. Outside the republican center there existed other political programs. Babeuf's Society of Equals and then the "neo-Jacobin" movement that culminated in 1798–99 both championed a radical democratic politics, while the counterrevolutionary movement was newly emboldened in the wake of the Terror. On Babeuf, see the bibliography compiled by Jean-René Suratteau in Georges Lefebvre, *La France sous le Directoire, 1795–1799,* 2d ed. (Paris, 1984). On the neo-Jacobin movement, see Isser Woloch, *Jacobin Legacy: The Democratic Movement Under the Directory* (Princeton, 1970); and Bernard Gainot, *1799, un nouveau Jacobinisme? La démocratie représentative, une alternative à brumaire* (Paris, 2001). For an analysis of conservative political discourse, see Marcus Lowell Ackroyd, "Constitution and Revolution: Political Debate in France, 1795–1800" (PhD diss.,

The most important immediate result of their quest for an orderly republic was a rejection of Jacobinism and its two principal buzzwords: "democracy" and "equality." In the eyes of the post-Terror republican center, democratic politics were inherently disorderly, even anarchic, and equality was little more than a "chimera."[50] The rejection of Jacobinism, though, did not entail a turn to counterrevolution or monarchy. The republican center was ideologically committed to the Republic, but only a republic governed by a virtuous few who would ensure that the people did not drag the nation down into anarchy and terror. Indicative of this shift was the elision of the words "the people" from the Constitution of the Year III's description of its locus of sovereignty. While the Constitution of 1793 had declared under the heading "On the sovereignty of the people" that "the sovereign people is the universality of French citizens," that of 1795 stated that "the universality of French citizens is the sovereign" with "citizens" meaning only those accorded the franchise.[51] Similarly, the important journal *Le Conservateur*—established by the republican center stalwarts Chénier, Daunou, and Garat in the summer of 1797 during the lead-up to the coup of 18 Fructidor (and the recipient of government subsidies after the coup)—described its political position as dedicated to the constitution and the Republic but made no mention of the people or popular sovereignty.[52] A paradigmatic articulation of the republican center's views regarding democracy is provided by Louis-Marie de La Révellière-Lépeaux in his personal jottings:

> When you allow the exercise of political rights to a crowd of men who have nothing and value nothing, you place in the hands of the ambitious numerous instruments of trouble and of revolutions, you introduce a horrible

---

Oxford University, 1995), chap. 2; and Darrin M. McMahon, *Enemies of the Enlightenment: The French Counter-Enlightenment and the Making of Modernity* (Oxford, 2001), chap. 3.

50. François-Antoine Boissy d'Anglas, *Projet de constitution pour la République française et discours préliminaire prononcé... au nom de la Commission des onze* (Paris, 1795), 27.

51. Jacques Godechot, ed., *Les constitutions de la France depuis 1789* (Paris, 1979), 83, 103. See Sergio Luzzatto, *L'automne de la Révolution: Luttes et culture politique dans la France thermidorienne,* trans. S. Messina (Paris, 2001), 242, 265; Michel Troper, "La mutation du concept de citoyen en l'An III," in *La Constitution de l'an III, ou l'ordre républicain,* ed. Jean Bart et al. (Dijon, 1998), esp. 90, 94.

52. "Prospectus," *Le Conservateur, journal politique, philosophique et littéraire; par les Citoyens Garat, Daunou, Chénier* (n.d.).

> corruption among both the rich, who find men to buy, and among the poor, who find men to buy them.... The result of all of this is a source of unrest, disorder, and profound corruption which leads to the loss of political liberty for all.... But when, to the contrary, you confine political rights only to those who have some interest in the preservation of the republic, the choices are better and the deliberations wiser, corruption is introduced less.

As a result, La Révellière-Lépeaux stipulated, political rights could be denied to some as long as "the separation is founded uniquely on fortune and not on the odious privilege of birth, and, at the same time, it is placed neither too high nor too low."[53] In a word, the post-Terror republican center did not trust "the people" to play an active role in France's political life.[54] The political and intellectual elites of the day wanted active sovereignty restricted to those deemed worthy of citizenship, those who possessed the independence and virtue needed to sustain the republic. This outlook resulted in a range of antidemocratic practices, such as limiting suffrage in the Constitution of the Year III, decreeing that two-thirds of the outgoing National Convention take up seats in the legislative chambers of the Directory, the establishment of educational programs that abandoned the goal of reaching the entire population, and even annulling electoral results in a series of coups from 1797 to 1799.

The republican center rejected strong notions of democracy and championed a form of republicanism that would restrict democratic practice. Within the scope of nondemocratic republicanism, post-Terror French intellectual and political life was marked by a creative tension, almost a dialectic, between classical and modern visions of the republic. In effect, the republican center spoke two distinct, although sometimes intermingled, political languages: classical republicanism and liberalism. During Thermidor and the Directory, classical republicanism predominated. By 1799 and the coup of Brumaire, a more liberal, or modern, view triumphed. The liberal republicanism of the opposition to Bonaparte was an amalgamation, although not a sublation, of the two. It blended elements of both political languages without necessarily reconciling their constitutive

53. "Fragments," n.d., Louis-Marie de La Révellière-Lèpeaux Papers, Beinecke Rare Book and Manuscript Library, Yale University, box 3, folder 68.

54. For a classic statement of the issue, see Alphonse Aulard, "L'exercice de la souveraineté nationale sous le Directoire," *La Révolution française* 40 (1901): 5–29.

differences. This liberal republicanism formed the genealogical kernel of French Liberalism.

My analysis of post-Terror political culture revises prevailing interpretations of the period. The post-Terror years, it should be noted, have traditionally been neglected by scholars of the French Revolution, who have predominantly focused their research on the extraordinary events and drama of 1789 to 1794. As a result, the political culture of Thermidor, the Directory, and the Consulate remains, to a surprising extent, terra incognita.[55] The principal reason for this neglect is the considerable shadow cast by Napoleon Bonaparte. Historians have tended to teleologically reduce the politics of these years to a sequence of precursors to Bonaparte's rise to power. Consequently, attention has focused on the series of coups d'état, and the republican center has been judged a collection of cynical and opportunistic "mediocrities."[56] This line of interpretation, however, loses the richness of the historical moment, specifically the depth of the efforts undertaken to anchor the republic in stable ground and the subsequent experimentation in republicanism. The republican center fought for a version of the republic that would reflect its members' sincerely republican political-philosophical commitments. After Brumaire, moreover, many of its members came to resist Bonaparte in the name of a liberal republic. Understanding post-Terror France requires taking seriously the politics and political thought of the republican center. Furthermore, a historically sensitive understanding of French Liberalism requires careful study of the political cultural context from which it emerged.

Scholarly consensus on the post-Terror period was for many years dominated by the "classic" interpretation of the Revolution handed down by

55. Pierre Serna has issued a summons to serious study of the post-Terror period in "Le Directoire... Un non lieu de mémoire à revisiter," in *La République directoriale,* ed. Philippe Bourdin and Bernard Gainot, 2 vols. (Clermont-Ferrand, 1998); and more recently in *La République des girouettes: 1789–1815... et au-delà: Une anomalie politique, la France de l'extrême centre* (Paris, 2005), chaps. 8–9. The era received the greatest scholarly attention a century ago at the hands of Aulard (see Serna's essay) and his students and followers, e.g., Albert Mathiez, *La Théophilanthropie et le culte décadaire: Essai sur l'histoire religieuse de la Révolution* (Paris, 1903); Raymond Guyot, *Le Directoire et la paix de l'Europe: Des traités de Bâle à la deuxième coalition (1795–1799)* (Paris, 1911); Albert Meynier, *Les coups d'état du Directoire,* 3 vols. (Paris, 1927–28).

56. "Mediocrities" is Meynier's term in *Le dix-huit Brumaire an VIII (9 Novembre 1799) et la fin de la République,* vol. 3 of *Les coups d'état du Directoire,* 159.

the great "official" historians of the French Revolution at the Sorbonne, notably Alphonse Aulard, Georges Lefebvre, and Albert Soboul. In their collective view, the years after 9 Thermidor were defined by "bourgeois reaction" against the democratic ideals of 1792–94 and thus marked the end of the democratic revolution.[57] This assessment was so pervasive that the word "Thermidor" has come to be a synonym for "reaction." François Furet's "revisionist" reading of the Revolution then overturned the classic account in describing Thermidor as an end of a quite different type, as "not the end of *the* Revolution, but that of its purest form.... [Thermidor] did not simply involve substituting one power for another—as in a *coup d'état* or in a change of majority—but substituting one *type* of power for another. In that sense, but in that sense alone, Thermidor was the end of the Revolution." In Furet's eyes, Thermidor marked the return of a politics of "social interest." The rightful independence of "society" from "ideology" was "restored" such that "social interests" could assume center stage in the nation's political life.[58] Because Furet attributed the politics of 1789–94 to the ideology of democracy, his interpretation in many ways did not in fact break with the classic argument that Thermidor marked the end of the democratic revolution. Analytically, the "social interests" Furet championed are remarkably similar to the "bourgeois reaction" Aulard and Lefebvre bemoaned, only they take on a positive valence in Furet's reading. Thus, in an important sense, both the classic and the revisionist interpretations describe the post-Terror period as defined by a politics of interest, whether that is to be lamented or celebrated.

More recently, a "postrevisionist" tack has emerged, one that emphasizes continuities in the Revolution's political culture across the Thermidorian divide—what Ozouf described as the Thermidorians' being caught between the simultaneous necessity and impossibility of breaking with

57. Aulard, *Histoire politique de la Révolution française: Origines et développement de la démocratie et de la République (1789–1804)* (Paris, 1901), 549; Lefebvre, *La France sous le Directoire, 1795–1799;* Soboul, *La 1ère république* (Paris, 1968). See also Jacques Godechot, *La vie quotidienne en France sous le Directoire* (Paris, 1977); and Denis Woronoff, *La République bourgeoise de Thermidor à Brumaire, 1794–1799* (Paris, 1972).

58. Furet, *Interpreting the French Revolution,* trans. Elborg Forster (Cambridge, 1981), 71–75. Patrice Gueniffey has reaffirmed the contours of Furet's interpretation with the claim that Thermidor marked "the dissolution of illusions about politics, allowing the recovery of the world of real politics." *La politique de la Terreur: Essai sur la violence révolutionnaire, 1789–1794* (Paris, 2000), 344–45.

the immediate past.[59] Bronislaw Baczko's extraordinarily rich *Ending the Terror: The French Revolution after Robespierre* built on Furet's analysis of political discourse during the Terror but tacitly challenged Furet's diagnosis of a change in "type of power" on 9 Thermidor. In Baczko's analysis, the Terror was quashed in the name of a similarly monistic political culture and the Thermidorian "counterimaginary" was likewise marked by an antipluralist conception of politics. Rather than radicalize the Revolution, though, the Thermidorians sought to end it.[60] Gauchet, taking a broader view than Baczko, has written that the entire Thermidorian and Directorial political experience was determined by congenital Jacobinism, by the revolutionaries' inability to break with "the thinking about power that established itself in 1789."[61] These accounts regret the failure of post-Terror France to sever itself from "the revolutionary logic"; Gauchet even comments that there was something "pathetic" about all of this.[62]

My argument that post-Terror political culture was a "republican moment" fundamentally defined by a classical-republican language of politics revises the accounts of these scholars as well as the most recent work on the post-Terror period, that of James Livesey, Bernard Gainot, Pierre Serna, and Howard Brown.[63] There is a sense in which my analysis is closest to

59. Ozouf, "Thermidor ou le travail de l'oubli," in *L'ecole de la France: Essais sur la Révolution, l'utopie et l'enseignement* (Paris, 1984).

60. Baczko, *Ending the Terror: The French Revolution after Robespierre,* trans. Michel Petheram (Cambridge, 1994), esp. 254.

61. Marcel Gauchet, *La Révolution des droits de l'homme* (Paris, 1989), 266.

62. Ibid; and Gauchet, *La condition historique,* 281. See also Gauchet, *La Révolution des pouvoirs: La souveraineté, le peuple, et la représentation, 1789–1799* (Paris, 1995). The argument that the Directory failed because of an inability to recognize political pluralism, in the form of party politics, has also been made by Lynn Hunt, David Lansky, and Paul Hanson, "The Failure of the Liberal Republic in France, 1795–1799: The Road to Brumaire," *Journal of Modern History* 51 (1979): 734–59.

63. Livesey argues that the Directory was the period of the Revolution in which "a democratic culture was created, that the norm of democracy found a content." *Making Democracy in the French Revolution,* 13. In my view, Livesey overstates the democratic character of the political center, but his important research stands as a reminder that significant aspects of the Revolution's democratic aspirations persisted after 9 Thermidor. Gainot focuses on the neo-Jacobinism of 1799, thus highlighting a more specific if highly significant aspect of the post-Terror years. *1799, un nouveau Jacobinisme?.* Serna's book provocatively argues that a new "political type" dominated these years, the "turncoat" that occupied the "extreme center," which would then go on to play an important role in nineteenth- and twentieth-century French politics. *La République des girouettes.* Brown, for his part, advances a very different, far bleaker vision of the post-Terror scene: the defining features of these years, he claims, were "chronic violence, ambivalent forms of justice, and

the classic view that post-Terror political life was characterized by a turn away from democracy. However, I find the term "bourgeois" lacking in interpretive specificity and, in many ways, misleading. Thus, beyond the very general observation that the political culture of the years 1794 to 1804 was marked by an abandonment of strongly democratic ideals, this book is more than a friendly amendment to the work of Aulard and those who traveled in his steps. My argument breaks with the revisionist and post-revisionist lines in that my emphasis on the importance of classical republicanism proposes a different interpretation than a politics of "social interest" on the one hand or congenital Jacobinism on the other. Finally, my argument that a liberal-authoritarian political order was established with Bonaparte's rise to power is indebted to Brown for the concept and term, although my analysis of such an order and my description of when it came about differ from his—where he sees a liberal-authoritarian regime established through military-juridical practices beginning in 1797, I see the establishment of a liberal-authoritarian constitution after the coup of Brumaire in November of 1799 as the more fundamental rupture.[64]

* * *

To explain these developments, this book adopts a chronological structure with thematically based chapters. The story begins with the republican center's attempt to refound the Republic in the wake of the Terror. Chapters 1 and 2 highlight the importance of classical-republican concerns and precepts in the effort to anchor the republic in stable ground. Chapter 1 undertakes an in-depth study of the redaction of the Constitution of the Year III during the summer of 1795, which established the political architecture of the Directory. Chapter 2 then turns to post-Terror attempts to reform and republicanize the moeurs of France's population during the Directory. The chapter focuses on (1) educational reform; (2) attempts to

---

repeated recourse to heavy-handed repression" such that a liberal-authoritarian "security state" emerged. *Ending the French Revolution,* 1, 16.

64. My work agrees with that of Brown in one other important regard: periodization. Brown presents a spirited argument for viewing the years 1795 to 1802 as a single bloc. While I propose the chronology 1794 to 1804, I endorse wholeheartedly Brown's iconoclastic move across the standard Brumairian divide. In addition to *Ending the Revolution,* see *Taking Liberties: Problems of a New Order from the French Revolution to Napoleon,* ed. Brown and Judith A. Miller (Manchester, U.K., 2002).

establish a civic religion in France, especially the *théophilanthropie* movement; and (3) an essay contest held at the National Institute that asked, "What are the most effective institutions to establish the morality of a people?" and the response penned by Jean-Baptiste Say, *Olbie, or an Essay on the Means of Reforming the Moeurs of a Nation.* Together, these different case studies show the decisive role played by the political language of classical republicanism in the establishment of the post-Terror political order. Chapters 1 and 2 thus detail, through analysis of debates and institutions, the extent to which Thermidorian and Directorial political culture was informed by classical-republican concerns and anxieties.

In chapter 3 the narrative turns to two modern voices during the Directory, those of the important but relatively unknown thinker Charles-Guillaume Théremin and of Germaine de Staël. I argue that Théremin's writings on commercial civilization and the political status of women in republics comprised a significant early voice for modern, or liberal, republicanism, one articulated in a Kantian lexicon, while Staël advanced an aristocratic version of liberal republicanism. Although Théremin and Staël were minority voices within the predominantly classical-republican post-Terror republican center, their writings constituted early articulations of the liberal republicanism that would later form the genealogical kernel of French Liberalism.

Chapter 4 traces the interplay between classical-republican and modern ideas in the domain of foreign policy through an examination of debate about expansion, natural frontiers, and the establishment of "sister republics" in Europe. Post-Terror debate on foreign policy and the policies adopted were largely structured by classical-republican anxieties about expansion. However, there was also an identifiable modern position that simultaneously pushed the Republic's foreign policy toward more aggressively expansionist programs and helped to lay the conceptual foundation of the Napoleonic Empire. Foreign policy, so often treated as separate from domestic politics, is shown in this chapter to refract the wider post-Terror dialectic between classical-republican and modern political languages.

Chapter 5 takes up the coup of Brumaire, which brought Napoleon Bonaparte to power in late 1799, and the subsequent drafting of a new constitution. As disillusionment with the political tumult of the Directory grew, a substantial majority within the republican center supported the coup and the redaction of the new constitution. I argue that this constitution was the culmination of the rationalist liberal political-philosophical programs of Roederer and, especially, Sieyès. The Constitution of the Year VIII signaled the triumph of liberal authoritarianism in the Revolution, and thus the displacement of classical-republican ideas, and thereby laid the groundwork for the political culture of the Consulate and the Empire.

Chapter 6 examines the emergence of dissent among Bonaparte's erstwhile supporters as his rule turned dictatorial. The chapter focuses on a debate in the Tribunate over whether to establish extralegal military tribunals, an essay contest held at the National Institute asking respondents to discuss "the influence of Luther's Reformation on the political situation of the different European states and on the progress of Enlightenment," and Benjamin Constant's *On the Possibility of a Republican Constitution in a Large Country.* I argue in this chapter that a liberal-republican position combining both classical-republican and liberal principles emerged in these different contexts as a response to Bonaparte's growing authoritarianism. The principal themes of this liberal republicanism—limned beforehand by Théremin and Staël but receiving its fullest expression in Constant's *Republican Constitution*—constituted the central kernel of French Liberalism.

Finally, an epilogue discusses the fate of French liberal republicanism in the first half of the nineteenth century, focusing on Restoration Liberalism, Benjamin Constant's "The Liberty of the Ancients Compared with that of the Moderns," and Alexis de Tocqueville's *Democracy in America.*

1

The Constitution of the Year III

It was, in a way, the Revolution that explained [Rousseau's] *Social Contract* to us.

Joseph Lakanal, *Rapport sur J. J. Rousseau, fait au nom de Comité d'instruction publique*

In the summer of 1795, six years after the staggering events of 1789 and one year removed from the end of the Terror, the representatives of the French nation met and debated a proposed new constitution for France, the third of the Revolution. The newly emergent republican center sought to end the Revolution and establish the Republic on a lasting basis, to replace the "revolutionary state" with "a constitutional order."[1] In their efforts to end the Revolution, the members of the National Convention addressed a vast array of constitutional issues and revisited many of the fundamental questions posed during the first five years of the Revolution. In effect, they set out to form, in the words of the journalist Adrien Lezay, a new "social contract."[2] In so doing, the republican center understood the problems facing the French Republic in classical-republican terms and articulated solutions drawn from the classical-republican repertoire. The result was

1. Pierre-Louis-Charles Baudin des Ardennes, *RM,* 25:532.
2. Adrien Lezay, *Qu'est-ce que la constitution de 95?* (Paris, 1795), 14.

a constitution, passed on 22 August 1795, that reflected the early modern classical-republican tradition, both its anxieties and its prescriptions. The Constitution of the Year III, and the classical republicanism it embodied, heralded a break in the political culture of the Revolution, codifying developments in motion since the coup against Robespierre on 9 Thermidor of the Year II (27 July 1794). The redaction of the Constitution of the Year III institutionalized an elitist republicanism and signaled the secularization of political time in the Revolution, both of which constituted profound ruptures with the radical-democratic and chiliastic political language of Jacobinism.

The completion of the Constitution of the Year III marked the culmination of the Thermidorian moment, a transitional period defined first and foremost by the two-pronged aspiration to break forever with the Terror and radical Jacobinism on the one hand and to anchor the republic in stable ground on the other. From the overthrow of Robespierre until the passage of the new constitution, seemingly every project undertaken, every proposal put forward, and every speech in the National Convention manifested a deep-seated desire to bury forever the "tyranny" and "anarchism" of the reign of Robespierre. In this regard, the Thermidorian moment was indelibly marked by what Bronislaw Baczko has called "the political, cultural and existential experience of the Terror."[3] The Thermidorians closed the Paris Jacobin Club, rehabilitated the proscribed members of the Gironde, and put prominent figures on trial, most famously Carrier, the so-called Butcher of Nantes.[4] Beyond this set of largely negative maneuvers, the Thermidorians also faced the task of offering a positive program that could stand as an alternative to Jacobinism and provide a foundation for the post-Terror Republic. Even their positive efforts, however, were suffused with the negative project of breaking with Jacobinism. One of the most revealing of the Thermidorians' often groping efforts on this front was the attempt to reappropriate the ideas of Jean-Jacques Rousseau from

3. Bronislaw Baczko, "La Constitution de l'an III et la promotion culturelle du citoyen," in *L'institution de la raison: La Révolution culturelle des Idéologues,* ed. François Azouvi (Paris, 1992), 22. On the Thermidorian moment more broadly, see Baczko, *Ending the Terror: The French Revolution after Robespierre,* trans. Michel Petheram (Cambridge, 1994); and Sergio Luzzatto, *L'automne de la Révolution: Luttes et culture politique dans la France thermidorienne,* trans. Simone Carpentari Messina (Paris, 2001).

4. On the rehabilitation of the Girondins, see Baczko, "Les Girondins en Thermidor," in *La Gironde et les Girondins,* ed. François Furet and Mona Ozouf (Paris, 1991); on Carrier's trial, see Baczko, *Ending the Terror,* chap. 3; and Luzzatto, *L'automne de la Révolution,* 23–31.

the legacy of Robespierre. The Committee on Public Instruction purchased unpublished manuscripts from Rousseau's widow,[5] and Rousseau's ashes were placed in the Pantheon on 12 October 1794 in a dramatic ceremony that Baczko calls "the first truly Thermidorian festival."[6] Jacobins were officially excluded from the event, Robespierre was roundly criticized for never having placed Rousseau in the Pantheon, and the message of Rousseau's teachings was pitted against the Terror.[7] A pamphlet "recording" a fictional dispute among Rousseau, Voltaire, and Marat over who truly belonged in the Pantheon captured the spirit of the event: as Marat criticized Rousseau's moderatism, Rousseau in turn ordered Marat to leave the Pantheon, calling him a "Preacher of death" and telling him "Do not disturb my ashes with your odious maxims."[8] The post-Terror Rousseau would have nothing to do with Robespierre, Marat, or their ilk and would stand as a political moderate. The Thermidorians' most important step toward anchoring the Republic in stable ground, however, was the creation of a new constitution, the Constitution of the Year III.

Robespierre had been overthrown in the summer of 1794, but the revolutionary government remained legally in effect and the nation continued to be governed by the Committee of Public Safety. The Constitution of 1793 lingered in suspense, neither dissolved nor formally reinstated. The question of the constitution's status was raised at various junctures during the winter of 1794–95 and then came to the fore in the wake of the Germinal and Prairial uprisings in Paris in the spring of 1795. On 1 April and then again on 20–21 May, following a winter of severe shortages and rising prices, Parisian radicals stormed the National Convention demanding "bread and the Constitution of 1793," as the latter had instituted universal male suffrage, guaranteed the right to subsistence, and proclaimed the right to insurrection as "the most sacred of rights and the most indispensable of duties."[9] The rioting revived fears of urban radicalism and

5. *Archives parlementaires de 1787 à 1860, recueil complet des débats législatifs et politiques des chambres françaises. Première série (1787 à 1799),* ed. M. J. Mavidal et al., 100 vols. at present (Paris, 1867–), 98:77–79, 94.

6. Bronislaw Baczko, "Rousseau au Panthéon," in *Job, mon ami: Promesses du bonheur et fatalité du mal* (Paris, 1997), 240.

7. *RM,* 22:223–24.

8. [Dubrail], *Grande dispute au Panthéon, entre Marat et Jean-Jacques Rousseau* ([Paris], [1794]), 14.

9. Jacques Godechot, ed., *Les constitutions de la France depuis 1789* (Paris, 1979), 83.

prompted a purge from the Convention of sixty-one deputies deemed to have been too closely associated with Robespierre.[10] The insurgents' invocation of the democratic Constitution of 1793 also rendered it, as it stood, all but unviable in the eyes of the Thermidorians.

As a result, on 3 April, after the first of the two uprisings, a "Commission of Seven" was established with the official mandate to "prepare the organic laws" of the suspended constitution.[11] To "prepare" in this case meant to establish provisions that would neutralize the constitution's untoward features. On 18 April the committee was enlarged to a "Commission of Eleven" and charged with "preparing the laws necessary to activate the Constitution" of 1793.[12] The commission then decided on its own, without a formal vote of the Convention, to draft an entirely new constitution.[13] Following "the example of the Greek legislators," contributions from the citizenry were solicited and the commission received almost nine hundred letters and political tracts.[14] The commission first met on 6 May, completed its work within one and a half months, and presented a draft constitution to the Convention on 23 June. Debate opened on 4 July and lasted until 17 August. The Constitution of the Year III was passed by the Convention on 22 August and ratified by popular referendum less than one month later.

10. Françoise Brunel, "L'épuration de la Convention nationale en l'an III," in *Le tournant de l'an III: Réaction et Terreur blanche dans la France révolutionnaire,* ed. M. Vovelle (Paris, 1997), 17.

11. The seven members were Jean-Jacques Régis de Cambacérès, Jacques-Antoine Creuzé-Latouche, Denis-Toussaint Lesage d'Eure-et-Loir, Jean-Baptiste-Charles Mathieu, Phillipe-Antoine Merlin de Douai, Emmanuel-Joseph Sieyès, and Antoine-Claire Thibaudeau. *RM,* 24:142.

12. *RM,* 24:248. The new commission, named on 23 April, included the seven men listed above, minus Mathieu, plus the new members Théophile Berlier, François-Antoine Boissy d'Anglas, Pierre-Claude-François Daunou, Louis-Marie La Révellière-Lépeaux, and Jean-Baptiste Louvet. Then, on 4 May, the Convention decreed that no one could sit on both the Commission of Eleven and either the Committee of Public Safety or the Committee of General Security, and Cambacérès, Merlin de Douai, and Sieyès renounced their seats on the Commission of Eleven and were replaced by Baudin des Ardennes, Pierre-Toussaint Durand de Maillane, and Jean-Denis Lanjuinais.

13. Louis-Marie La Révellière-Lépeaux, *Mémoires de Larevellière-Lépeaux publiés par son fils sur le manuscrit autographe de l'auteur et suivis des pièces justificatives et de correspondances inédites,* 3 vols. (Paris, 1895), 1:229; Antoine-Claire Thibaudeau, *Mémoires sur la Convention et le Directoire,* 2 vols. (Paris, 1824), 1:179–80.

14. Jean-Jacques Régis de Cambacérès, *Rapport sur le mode de préparer les lois organiques de la constitution, et sur les moyens de la mettre partiellement et successivement en activité* (Paris, 1795), 12. On the contributions received, see Françoise Brunel, "Aux origines d'un parti de l'ordre: Les propositions de constitution de l'an III," in *Mouvements populaires et conscience social, XVI–XIX siècles,* ed. Jean Nicolas (Paris, 1985); and Luzzatto, *L'automne de la Révolution,* chap. 5.

The Constitution of the Year III stood until the coup of Brumaire in November 1799, longer than any previous constitution of the Revolution.

In creating the new constitution, the Thermidorian elites drew on the political language and lessons of the early modern classical-republican tradition. They related their political experiences to classical models, employed classical symbols, and referred to canonical figures from the classical-republican corpus. More significantly, the Thermidorian republican center repeatedly exhibited anxieties about the contingency of the republic and, as a solution, drew on staples of the classical-republican tradition such as balancing constitutional powers, stressing the independent and virtuous political personality of the active citizenry, promulgating citizens' duties that aimed to orient the citizens' moral disposition toward the public good, and emphasizing the patriarchal family.[15] They displayed a marked preference for the lessons of historical experience over the postulates of theory and deployed historicist and contextual modes of understanding in advancing their arguments. Finally, they rejected recourse to natural law or any other prepolitical framework, and defined rights as postpolitical or social—Pierre-Claude-François Daunou, the principal architect of the constitution, declared plainly in a manuscript born of discussion in the Commission of Eleven and entitled "Observations on the Way to Draft a Declaration of Rights" that "I would not want to establish any system on the state of nature."[16] The influence of classical models on the proposed constitution was widely noted. Richard de Serizy's *L'Accusateur publique,* while praising the new constitution, poked fun at its reliance on constitutional mechanisms borrowed from the classical republics.[17] Similarly, Frédéric-François-Venceslas Jacquemont criticized the Commission of Eleven for relying too heavily on ancient examples.[18] And Joseph Eschassériaux

15. On this last point, see Suzanne Desan, *The Family on Trial in Revolutionary France* (Berkeley, 2004), chap. 7.

16. Pierre-Claude-François Daunou, "Observations sur la manière de rediger une déclaration des droits," [1795], BN, Nouv. Acqu. Fr. 21891, f. 3. Near the beginning of the manuscript, Daunou wrote, "I will collect...the reflections suggested to me by the discussion in the commission." Ibid.

17. Luzzatto, *L'automne de la Révolution,* 266.

18. Jacquemont, *Lettres critiques sur le projet de constitution* (Paris, 1795); cited in Marcel Gauchet, *La Révolution des pouvoirs: La souveraineté, le peuple, et la représentation, 1789–1799* (Paris, 1995), 181, n. 3.

(the elder) worried during the constitutional debate in the Convention that the commission had followed the classical models too closely.[19]

The classical-republican tenor of that summer's constitutional debates and the Constitution of the Year III signaled an important shift in French political life: classical republicanism supplanted the democratic ideals of the Year II (1793–94). Thermidorian classical republicanism sought to establish an elite-based republic, restricting the franchise and looking to the virtuous legislator rather than the people as the foundation of the nation's political order. Pierre-Antoine Antonelle, one of the most important critics of the Constitution of the Year III, expressed the matter succinctly: "I look for the people in this constitutional project; I find it nowhere."[20] Moreover, Thermidorian classical republicanism broke with the messianic, antihistorical rhetoric of Jacobinism, which had been decisively marked by the temporal horizon of "the Enlightenment conception of revolution," as Keith Baker describes it,[21] and by the absolutist monarchy's discourse of an eternal sovereign will. Jacobinism had been rife with tropes of political transcendence—France would leap two thousand years into the future, Robespierre famously proclaimed.[22] By the summer of 1795, however, the Thermidorians were weary from having "consummated six centuries in six years," as François-Antoine Boissy d'Anglas put it while introducing the proposed new constitution to the Convention.[23] Disabused of the Jacobins' messianic belief that an ever-vigilant republic could eventually explode the bounds of history, the Thermidorians imagined the body politic as rooted in and subject to the vicissitudes of history, thus signaling a "secularization" of political time in the revolutionary

19. *RM,* 25:270.

20. [Antonelle], *Observations sur le droit de cité, et sur quelques parties du travail de la commission des onze* (Paris, 1795), 25. On Antonelle, see Pierre Serna, *Antonelle: Aristocrate révolutionnaire, 1747–1817* (Paris, 1997).

21. Keith Baker, "Transformations of Classical Republicanism in Eighteenth-Century France," *Journal of Modern History* 73 (2001): 45.

22. Quoted in ibid., 51. On the early revolutionaries' attempts to transcend history, see Mona Ozouf, "La formation de l'homme nouveau," in *L'homme régénéré* (Paris, 1989); Lynn Hunt, *Politics, Culture, and Class in the French Revolution* (Berkeley, 1984); and, for an important assessment of this scholarship, Joseph Zizek, "The Politics and Poetics of History in the French Revolution, 1787–1794" (PhD diss., University of California, Berkeley, 1995).

23. Boissy d'Anglas, *Projet de constitution pour la République française et discours préliminaire prononcé... au nom de la Commission des onze* (Paris, 1795), 7.

political imagination.[24] Thermidorian classical republicanism was decisively shaped by the fact that it was engaged, like two paradigmatic earlier versions of Machiavellism, in the attempt to found a republic in the wake of a failed chiliastic revolution.[25] It developed after the Republic had signally failed to adopt the quasi-divine character of the king's abiding will and was forced to confront its own finitude in time. This refusal of transcendence through politics marked a "secularizing" break with the political imagination of the eighteenth-century monarchy and a decisive moment in the long-term development of French republicanism. "In the final analysis," Claude Nicolet has suggested, "the Republic reposes on the conscious refusal of all forms of transcendence."[26] That is, the republic is imagined to exist in human time and puts human beings and human action, in word as well as fact, at the center of political life. Informed by the vertiginous experiences of the previous five years and drawing on the classical-republican tradition in France and elsewhere, Thermidorian politics was rooted in exactly such a refusal of political transcendence, signaling the beginning of the end of the absolutist political temporality and a decisive break in the revolutionary political imagination.

History and Experience

On 23 June 1795 Boissy d'Anglas presented the Commission of Eleven's proposed new constitution to the National Convention. The proposal seems to have quickly become the talk of Paris. One police inspector reported that throughout the city "the project of the new constitution constituted the subject of the citizens' conversations," while another related that "in the cafés . . . people spoke of the new constitution in the most satisfied manner, which promises us, they were saying, a very happy future."[27] Even if France's immediate future did not turn out quite as rosily as forecast in

24. The term "secularization" of political time taken is taken from J. G. A. Pocock, *The Machiavellian Moment: Florentine Political Thought and the Atlantic Republican Tradition* (Princeton, 1975).

25. "English Machiavellism appeared—as Machiavelli's own thinking had done—in the defeat of a chiliastic revolution." Ibid., 360.

26. Claude Nicolet, *L'idée républicaine en France (1789–1924): Essai d'histoire critique,* 2d ed. (Paris, 1995), 484.

27. Alphonse Aulard, ed., *Paris pendant la réaction thermidorienne et sous le Directoire, recueil de documents pour l'histoire de l'esprit public à Paris,* 5 vols. (Paris, 1898–1902), 2:36–37.

Paris's cafés, Boissy d'Anglas's speech nonetheless signaled an important change in the nation's political culture. It was time to end the messianic revolution. France had arrived at the moment when, he told his colleagues, "ceasing to be gladiators for liberty, we can be its true founders."[28]

Boissy d'Anglas began his speech by paying homage to the history of the Revolution and the experiences acquired thereby. "Make sure," he admonished his audience, "that such a costly experience will not be lost on you." Boissy d'Anglas then proceeded to outline the history of those six years and told a story of plots and intrigue, of accidents, near-accidents, and virtuous actions. The people scored a magnificent victory on 14 July 1789, and soon after a plot was discovered in the court, a plot that was heroically defeated. The nation triumphantly asserted itself, but the weakness of the Constituent Assembly in failing to proclaim France a republic then caused "the explosion of a new revolution that violently took down a throne which needed no more than to be left to collapse." France was meanwhile threatened from both the right and the left as "the priests preached the counterrevolution" and the Jacobins established "the empire of death, terror and crime." Finally, the Republic was saved on 9 Thermidor. "The day of 9 Thermidor," he declared, "was not a victory of one party; it was the dawn of a great and salutary revolution." Boissy d'Anglas's message was adamant: do not, he exhorted the Convention, "shroud in the shadow of forgetting those days in which innocence was so often slain."[29]

The lesson to be drawn from his account was that France's history would have been different if not for the virtuous action of those who defeated the aristocracy and the monarch, saved France from counterrevolution, and, finally, overthrew Robespierre and his cohort. In Boissy d'Anglas's vision it was human action that had saved the Republic. The French Republic was not a political order maintained by the grace of God, nor would it be sustained by construction according to the proper a priori rational principles. Rather, it demanded active, vigilant preservation against its enemies, both internal and external. It was a republic that existed in human history and secular time, a domain characterized first and foremost by contingency and instability. It could thus be perpetuated only through the virtuous action of its active citizenry and its political leadership.

28. Boissy d'Anglas, *Projet de constitution,* 4.
29. Ibid., 7–15.

Boissy d'Anglas's historically grounded constitutional presentation differed markedly from the representations of the body politic articulated during the Revolution's earlier phases. The revolutionaries of 1789 had declared themselves to be throwing off history and creating a new polity based on abstract reason alone. The men who declared the National Assembly, ended feudalism, and announced the rights of man and citizen imagined themselves to be creating a political system that would explode the bounds of history and endure through time. As Antoine de Baecque has written, "In 1789 the body drastically transformed by politics is straightaway established as a two-sided variety: the 'before' and the 'after' "; the latter, the *homo novus* after its regeneration, is a "utopian tendency, designing a future described as a space of perfection," and "speaks and acts for eternity."[30] Experience from a corrupt "before" was thus inapposite and innovation the order of the day. In 1793, Saint-Just went so far as to proclaim that "everything that is not new in a time of innovation is pernicious."[31] As the revolutionary process accelerated, its leaders became increasingly convinced of the Revolution's messianic, world-historical mission, and the drive to transcend history intensified. Just as the sovereignty of the absolutist monarchy informed the way the revolutionaries conceived of the sovereignty of the people, the temporality of the monarchy's eternal body shaped the way in which the political temporality of the Republic was imagined. The body politic envisaged by Robespierre, Saint-Just, and radical Jacobinism, while perceived to be constantly threatened by its enemies, was weighted with world-historical significance and projected into a regenerated, utopian future.

The body politic envisaged by Boissy d'Anglas, by contrast, was neither "before" nor "after," but "during." The Republic, shorn of its messianic dimension, was imagined as a particular in the flow of historical time. The disabused politicians of the Year III sounded classical-republican notes in emphasizing history as a repository of experience from which they could draw lessons to aid in the navigation of republican political life.[32] As a result, references to history and experience abounded in political discourse.

30. Antoine de Baecque, *The Body Politic: Corporeal Metaphor in Revolutionary France, 1770–1800,* trans. Charlotte Mandell (Stanford, 1997), 137, 140.

31. Quoted in Lucien Jaume, *Échec au libéralisme: Les Jacobins et l'état* (Paris, 1990), 7.

32. As Blair Worden explains, "History to republicans was the beginning of political wisdom." "English Republicanism," in *The Cambridge History of Political Thought, 1450–1700,* ed. J. H. Burns (Cambridge, 1991), 446.

Cambacérès advised his fellow *conventionnels* that "experience alone can dispel the illusions of theory; we must use its lessons," and Eschassériaux insisted during the constitutional debates that "it is in the experience of our mistakes and our misfortunes...that we should find our constitution."[33] Boissy d'Anglas, while presenting the proposed constitution to the Convention, pointed not only to the revolutionaries' own experience but to that of the nascent United States of America, "our elder on the path of liberty."[34] This sea change in consciousness is captured in two remarks by the abbé Grégoire, the first from 1789 and the second from 1795. In the heady days of 1789 Grégoire declaimed against using history as a guide because "the history that is too often invoked," with its inconveniently messy array of counterexamples, only confuses the issues. "Instead of supporting a principle," claimed Grégoire, "the multiplicity of facts often demonstrates the violation of principles."[35] In 1795, however, weary of the travails of a revolution that eschewed historical referent, Grégoire proclaimed the need for a "new history" to help navigate the rocks and shoals of republican politics.[36] After Thermidor, in the words of Bronislaw Baczko, "the Revolution lost in transparency what it gained in historicity.... It arrived at a moment where it no longer commanded time; it is time that affirmed itself as its [the Revolution's] master."[37]

The Balance of Powers

In response to the perceived contingency of the republic, the Commission of Eleven invoked a staple feature of the early modern classical-republican tradition: mixed or balanced government. The commission, ever mindful of the experience of the Terror, feared concentrating power in one institution, especially in a unicameral legislature. There cannot be a "stable

33. Cambacérès, *Rapport sur le mode de préparer les lois organiques de la constitution,* 16; Eschassériaux at *RM,* 25:270.

34. Boissy d'Anglas, *Projet de constitution,* 39.

35. Grégoire, quoted in Keith Michael Baker, *Inventing the French Revolution: Essays on French Political Culture in the Eighteenth Century* (Cambridge, 1990), 278–79.

36. Grégoire, quoted in Carla Hesse, *Publishing and Cultural Politics in Revolutionary Paris, 1789–1810* (Berkeley, 1991), 150.

37. Baczko, "Le tournant culturel de l'an III," in *1795: Pour une République sans Révolution,* ed. Roger Dupuy and Marcel Morabito (Rennes, 1996), 21–22.

constitution," proclaimed Boissy d'Anglas while introducing the proposed constitution to the Convention, "where there exists in the legislative body only one sole and unique assembly." Where powers become "collected in the same hands," he explained, or "they find themselves brought together, everywhere where they are merged, there exists no more liberty; there is no more than despotism." Boissy d'Anglas then quoted John Adams's *A Defence of the Constitutions of Government of the United States* that there could be "no good government, no stable constitution... without the balance of the three powers," adding that "it is this principle that we propose to put into practice."[38]

The three powers Boissy d'Anglas outlined were an executive power and two separate legislative councils, three powers that corresponded in functional but not social terms to the classical triad of monarchy, aristocracy, and democracy, or the one, the few, and the many.[39] The proposed executive power would be a five-person Executive Directory (*Directoire exécutif*) charged with executing the laws and the direction of foreign affairs and the military, among other functions. The two legislative councils would be a Council of Five Hundred (*Conseil des 500*) and a Council of Elders (*Conseil des Anciens*), with laws proposed by the former and approved by the latter. The division of the legislative power along these lines marked a rupture of sorts in the Revolution, as the establishment of a second legislative assembly had previously been rejected for fear that it would serve the aristocracy along the lines of the English House of Lords. The three powers

38. Boissy d'Anglas, *Projet de constitution,* 38, 45, 46. Adams, whom Boissy d'Anglas mistakenly referred to as Samuel Adams, was in fact the only authority Boissy d'Anglas cited. Adams's *Defence* has been firmly set in the classical-republican tradition by Gordon Wood, *The Creation of the American Republic, 1776–1787* (Chapel Hill, N.C., 1969), chap. 14; and Pocock, *The Machiavellian Moment,* 526–31.

39. The judiciary was not included in Boissy d'Anglas's description of the balance of powers. Although the constitution established a judicial power, he made it clear in his speech that the three powers to be balanced were the two legislative councils and the executive. He did refer to the importance of a well-constructed judiciary, but for "civil liberty" rather than for "political liberty." Ibid., 46, 55. Here the commission was faithful to the republican tradition of mixed or balanced government rather than the more modern concept of the tripartite separation of executive, legislative, and judicial powers. On the differences between the two conceptions, see M. J. C. Vile, *Constitutionalism and the Separation of Powers,* 2d ed. (Indianapolis, 1998), 36–43; and Bernard Manin, "Checks, Balances and Boundaries: The Separation of Powers in the Constitutional Debate of 1787," in *The Invention of the Modern Republic,* ed. Biancamaria Fontana (Cambridge, 1994), 30–31. The lack of a judicial power in the Constitution of 1795 is taken up by Gauchet in *La Révolution des pouvoirs,* 125–86.

thus had clearly defined, and separate, functions: laws would be proposed by the Council of Five Hundred, approved or rejected by the Council of Elders, and carried out by the Executive Directory. The Council of Elders could not propose a law, and the Executive Directory was not assigned any role in the legislative process, such as a veto. Boissy d'Anglas took great pains to avoid the politically charged historical associations this constitutional design might provoke and assured his audience that the Council of Elders would not institute an aristocracy and the Executive Directory would not be a "throne." Rather, he explained, all three powers "emanate from the people."[40] Nonetheless, the qualities that the institutions were meant to embody revealed the underlying categories from which they were devised. This is most telling in the case of the Council of Elders, which in an early draft of the constitution was given the more aristocratic title of "Senate."[41] It was to be the Republic's "wisdom" and "reason," and its members would be at least forty—past "the age of passions," Boissy d'Anglas told the Convention during the debates[42]—married or widowed, and resident in France for at least the last fifteen years. The Council of Elders would serve as a counterweight to the potential "impetuosity" of the Council of Five Hundred, which, in turn, was to be "the thought" and "the imagination" of the Republic, its members aged at least thirty (twenty-five until the Year VIII), and resident for at least ten years.[43] As Daunou explained, "The Council of Elders, composed of experienced men, wiser, will know how to temper the excessive fervor of the other [council]." The imagined character of the Council of Elders is perhaps nowhere more clear than in a description given by Eschassériaux. "I see," he told the Convention, "one of those ancient senates whose knowledge, austerity of moeurs and of virtues, are still the model for posterity. I see a multitude of virtuous men animated by the desire for good, continuously watching over the destiny of the republic."[44]

40. Boissy d'Anglas, *Projet de constitution,* 45–46.

41. "Travail de la commission," [1795], AN, C 232, d. 183, p. 65. See also, Thibaudeau, *Mémoires,* 1:182.

42. *RM,* 25:287.

43. Boissy d'Anglas, *Projet de constitution,* 41.

44. *RM,* 25:282, 269. Eschassériaux in fact argued that France should not adopt such a classical model and that the Council of Elders should have less power. "If I look at the same council from another angle," he continued, "I see men and passions" (269).

While it is impossible to locate the precise provenance of this constitutional architecture in the commission's thinking, the intellectual genealogy of putting the three classical forms in a state of balance or equilibrium runs through the canonical figures of the classical-republican tradition—from Cicero and Polybius through to Machiavelli, Harrington, Mably, and John Adams. More specifically, the idea of a bicameral legislature in which one body proposes the laws and the other approves them had been advocated by Harrington in his famous metaphor of having one person cut the cake and the other choose which half, and, explicitly following Harrington, by John Adams in his *A Defence of the Constitutions of Government of the United States of America*—liberally translated into French in 1792 as *Défense des constitutions américaines, ou De la nécessité d'une balance dans les pouvoirs d'un gouvernement libre (A Defense of the American Constitutions, or On the Necessity of a Balance in the Powers of a Free Government).* As Adams's French translator rendered it, if the division and the choice are made in one assembly, "It will eat all the cake, pastry, and jam."[45] Adams's text, firmly in the classical-republican tradition with three volumes detailing the histories of republics and long sections discussing and extensively quoting the canonical thinkers of the classical-republican tradition, was undoubtedly known to the members of the commission. Adams, vice president of the United States in 1795, had spent much of the 1780s in Paris and even befriended Mably. Moreover, not only did Boissy d'Anglas quote Adams (the sole authority he cited in his speech) on the need for the balance of powers, but the commission had printed under its aegis a pamphlet titled *L'Equiponderateur, ou Une seule manière d'organiser un gouvernement libre (The Equibalancer, or A Single Way to Organize a Free Government)* sent to them by a certain Lamare, of the Executive Commission on Public Instruction, who was an avowed disciple of Adams and the translator of Adams's *Defence* into French.[46]

45. "Elle mangera tout le gateau, pâte et confitures." John Adams, *Défense des constitutions américaines, ou De la nécessité d'une balance dans les pouvoirs d'un gouvernement libre,* 2 vols. (Paris, 1792), 1:240. The original English reads, "If all authority is to be collected into one central assembly, ... it will soon have possession of all the cake, loaves, and fishes." Adams, *A Defence of the Constitutions of Government of the United States of America,* 3 vols. (Philadelphia, 1787), 1:135).

46. Lamare, *L'Equiponderateur, ou Une seule manière d'organiser un gouvernement libre, par Lamare, de la Commission de l'instruction publique; Imprimé par ordre de la Commission des onze* (Paris, 1795). Lamare acknowledged, referring to Adams's *Defence,* "having drawn on some ideas in a work that I was the first to make known in France and of which I am the translator" (6, n. 1).

Lamare's text, which was presented to the commission just three days after its first meeting, argued in unmistakably classical-republican language that the "only" and "unique" manner of organizing a "free government" is "the equilibrium or balance of powers." Building his case with reference to Adams and a host of figures from the classical-republican pantheon—Cicero, Polybius, Machiavelli, Harrington, and Sidney—Lamare established the classical triad in Polybian terms and warned, citing Machiavelli's *Discourses,* that without balance any one form would usurp power and become despotic. "There are only . . . three basic types of government," he explained, "*monarchy* or government of one, *aristocracy* or government of the best, *democracy* or government of the entire people. . . . Monarchy degenerates easily into tyranny, aristocracy into oligarchy, and democracy into anarchy. Whoever, in forming a new state, attaches himself to one of the first three, can be assured that the government will not be of a long duration because there is no precaution that can prevent the transition from the one to the other."[47] In arguing for balancing the classical triad, though, Lamare was careful to explain that in modern France the three powers are to be understood in purely functional, and not social or historical, terms. In modern France, monarchy means "the executive magistracy" and aristocracy "wisdom and virtue."[48] Democracy was to be embodied in a five hundred-person *Conseil des Ephores,* aristocracy in an eighty-five-member *Sénat,* and "monarchy" in a *Consul*—a "title at once impressive, striking and republican"—of two people serving nonrenewable four-year terms. The Consul was openly modeled on that of republican Rome, and the five-person Executive Directory established by the Commission of Eleven clearly paralleled it. Lamare proposed functionally dividing the three powers in exactly the same manner as the constitution put forward by the Commission of Eleven: "One power that *proposes,* another that *decides,* a third that *executes.*"[49] Citing the seven-year term in England and echoing

47. Ibid., 1–2, 4–5. Lamare, like Adams, was adamant that a judiciary was not one of the three powers to be balanced (7, n. 1). On Adams's constitutional construction, see Wood, *Creation of the American Republic,* 577, esp. n. 15.

48. Lamare, *L'Equiponderateur,* 4. Virtually the same argument was made in the anonymous pamphlet, F. P. B***, *De l'Equilibre des trois pouvoirs politiques, ou Lettres au représentant du peuple Lanjuinais, Sur son opinion de diviser le Corps législatif en deux sections* (Paris, 1795), 46–49.

49. Lamare, *L'Equiponderateur,* 26–53, 37. In fact, Lamare proposed that the executive be allowed to return legislation to the two legislative bodies for "further discussion," which the latter bodies would then be able to ratify anyway with majorities of two-thirds. Lamare insisted that this

Bolingbroke's attacks against the Septennial Act, Lamare proposed that terms of two years be used in his Conseil des Ephores in order to prevent officials from becoming entrenched and corrupt.[50] The commission followed his thinking on this issue and proposed that half of the members of each council be replaced every two years—Creuzé-Latouche warned during debate that not replacing would lead to the formation of a nobility, while the deputy Antoine-François Hardy cited Mably on the dangers of reelection—and the final version of the constitution stipulated that one-third of the members of each council would be rotated out of office annually.[51] *L'Equiponderateur,* with the imprimatur of the Commission of Eleven on its first page, adhered more literally to the classical-republican model than the constitution proposed by the commission but outlined in political-philosophical terms the constitutional logic undergirding the latter.

When the constitution was proposed to the Convention by the Commission of Eleven, there was little debate over the principle of balance underpinning it. This turn to the rhetoric of balance signaled a shift in the Revolution, a consensus, as François Furet put it, "to limit sovereignty by dividing it."[52] Only the deputy Alexandre Deleyre defended unicameral government, charging that the Council of Elders would harbor an aristocracy, but his speech was countered by Cambacérès, who called the division of the legislative body "the *palladium* of liberty," and discussion promptly moved forward.[53] The proposed constitutional architecture was, however, dealt a serious challenge on 20 July by Sieyès, the Revolution's most modern thinker and preeminent constitutional theorist.[54] Sieyès had sat on the original Commission of Seven but then divorced himself from the drafting of the constitution and shunned a series of overtures made to him by the Commission of Eleven.[55] Making his first appearance of the summer's constitutional debates, Sieyès agreed with the commission's

---

procedure, openly taken from the American example, was not a veto—which he called "incompatible with republican liberty"—but "a simple right of representation" (51, 55–56).

50. Ibid., 42.

51. *RM,* 25:278; Godechot, *Les constitutions de la France,* 109. On rotation, see Bernard Manin, *The Principles of Representative Government* (Cambridge, 1997), 31–32, 55–56, 68–70.

52. François Furet, *Revolutionary France, 1770–1880,* trans. Antonia Nevill (Oxford, 1992), 165.

53. *RM,* 25:275–77.

54. On Sieyès, see chapter 5.

55. La Révellière-Lépeaux, *Mémoires,* 1:230.

decision to fracture sovereignty but attacked the manner in which it chose to do so. He mocked the principle of balance as an inherently inefficient redundancy of function, alleging that "assigning two or three representatives to exercise the same public function" could only lead to constitutional gridlock. Instead, he proposed a constitution centered on a "constitutional jury" that would stand above day-to-day governance, adjudicate constitutional dispute, and ensure that the entire system functioned smoothly and efficiently. More broadly, Sieyès's proposal was based on a division of labor in which the different organs of government would specialize in the different facets of lawmaking and governance and thereby achieve greater efficiency; he termed this scheme, alternately, "division with unity," "organized unity," and "*unity of action.*"[56] Sieyès's intervention amounted to a modern challenge to the classical-republican conception of balance and was supported by modern-minded figures outside the Convention, most notably Pierre-Louis Roederer.[57]

The Convention unanimously rejected Sieyès's proposal, opting for the principle of balance over that of unity.[58] In fact, however, the Constitution of the Year III separated powers more than it balanced them, as it established three bodies carrying out three different functions—proposition, approval, and execution—with almost no countervailing prerogatives. The only true "balancing" function was the Council of Elders' ability to reject

56. *RM,* 25:291–97, 442–45, 449–52. On Sieyès's scheme, see Gauchet, *La Révolution des pouvoirs,* 159–78.

57. Roederer supported Sieyès's proposal in print and in testimony before the Commission of Eleven. Roederer, "Opinion de Sieyès" (1795) and "De l'opinion de Sieyès" (1795), in the *Journal de Paris,* reprinted in Pierre-Louis Roederer, *Œuvres du comte P.-L. Roederer,* ed. Antoine-Marie Roederer, 8 vols. (Paris, 1853–1959), 6:104–5; and Roederer to Sieyès, [1795], AN, 284 AP 9–5. In addition, Dupont de Nemours and François de Neufchâteau both wrote to Sieyès expressing their support. 21 Thermidor, Year 3 (8 August 1795) and 18 Messidor, Year 3 (6 July 1795), AN, 284 AP 9–5.

58. *RM,* 25:495. Ironically, one person who converted to Sieyès's ideas was Lamare, despite the fact that Lamare's *L'Equiponderateur* argued for exactly the constitutional structure Sieyès mocked in his speech, and that Lamare, writing to Sieyès, described himself as "irrevocably attached" to "the balance of three powers" and resolutely against "*the unity of a chamber or of action.*" Lamare to Sieyès, 6 Germinal, Year 3 (26 March 1795), AN, 284 AP 9–5. Lamare wrote four letters to Sieyès in the spring and summer of 1795, first asking Sieyès to read his pamphlet and then later pronouncing his conversion: "I have just read with indescribable pleasure, citizen, the piece of writing you sent me, even though you lay into the poor partisans of *balance.*... I am ready to renounce my *balance,* and to line up first in support of *your* organized unity." Lamare to Sieyès, 7 Thermidor, Year 3 (25 July 1795), AN, 284 AP 9–5.

legislation proposed by the Council of Five Hundred. Crucially, the Executive Directory could only execute the law and did not possess a veto or any other countervailing or balancing power in the legislative process.[59] The decision to establish such a weak executive stemmed in all likelihood from the combination of the experience of the Terror, when the Committee of Public Safety wielded virtually unchecked power, and the deep-seated early modern classical-republican distrust of executive power as inherently tyrannical. As Thibaudeau put it during the debates, "the history of all peoples teaches us that executive power... tends to increase its power" and that "it is almost always by its usurpations that liberty perishes."[60] This distrust was amplified to the point that it undermined the principle of balance. The result was an incongruity between the language of balance and the proposed constitutional mechanics, one noted by a handful of commentators. Louis-Philippe de Ségur, for example, chided the commission and the Convention in the summer of 1795 for this discrepancy between words and facts: "While adopting the principle of the balance of powers, you have not followed it in your plan.... It is impossible with these combinations.... There is no balance if the powers cannot reciprocally stop each other." Citing Mably and Lamare, Ségur called for a Senate with the right to propose laws and an executive that possessed a veto. "You speak constantly about the Romans," he exclaimed, yet "you do not copy them in their best institutions."[61] As Ségur's commentary suggests, the framers of the Constitution of the Year III, in their search for stability, divided powers along functional lines while articulating their relationship in the classical-republican language of balance.[62]

59. Within the commission, Daunou and Lanjuinais supported giving the Executive Directory a veto but were outvoted. La Révellière-Lépeaux, *Mémoires,* 1:238.

60. *RM,* 25:325. The classical-republican distrust of executive power is emphasized by Raymonde Monnier in "Républicanisme, libéralisme et Révolution française," in *Les libéralismes au regard de l'histoire, Actuel Marx* 32 (Paris, 2002), 108.

61. [Ségur], *Réflexions sur le plan de constitution présenté par la Commission des onze, par l'auteur des "Réflexions sur les bases d'une constitution"* (Paris, 1795), 18, 27, 29, 12, 21. In a previous pamphlet, Ségur had pointed to the constitutions of Rome, Sparta, England, and the nascent United Sates as examples of balance among the three powers. *Réflexions sur les bases d'une Constitution, par le Cit. ***, et présentées par Bresson, Député à la Convention nationale* (Paris, 1795), 11–12.

62. Modern commentators have noted the same contradiction. See Michel Troper, *La séparation des pouvoirs et l'histoire constitutionnelle française* (Paris, 1980), 188–200; Gauchet, *La Révolution des pouvoirs,* 154.

Grounding the Political Personality

The constitution proposed by the Commission of Eleven deployed not only classical-republican ideas about balance but also the typical classical-republican emphasis on the virtuous legislator and on the independent political personality of the citizenry. At the end of his speech, Boissy d'Anglas told the Convention that even the most perfect constitution would be for naught if "legislators without talent and without virtue" were elected. If this were to happen, "all is lost:... liberty is ruined, the republic overthrown, virtue has no more for her than despair and death, and there remains nothing more for you than to choose between the scaffold of Sidney, the hemlock of Socrates, or the sword of Cato!" To avoid such a fate and ensure that the country would be governed only by virtuous legislators, the commission attempted to ground the independence and virtue of the citizenry in a two-pronged foundation of property and education. That is, they instituted a material and a moral requirement for active citizenship, or "the rights of the city." As Boissy d'Anglas explained while outlining the proposed constitution's suffrage requirements,

> We should be governed by the best; the best are the best educated and the most interested in the maintenance of the laws: apart from a few exceptions, you will not find such men except among those who, possessing property, are attached to the land that contains it, to the laws that protect it, to the tranquility that preserves it, and who owe to this property and the ease that it brings the education which has made them able to discuss, wisely and accurately, the advantages and inconveniences of the laws that determine the fate of their country. The man without property, on the contrary, needs a constant effort of virtue to feel an interest in an order that maintains nothing for him, and to oppose movements that give him some hope. One has to suppose such a man's ideas to be fully worked out and quite profound for him to prefer the real good to the apparent good, the interest of the future to that of the present.... A country governed by property holders is in the social order; that in which the non-property holders govern is in the state of nature.[63]

While the importance the commission assigned to property and education was not unique to classical republicanism in eighteenth-century and

63. Boissy d'Anglas, *Projet de constitution,* 78, 27–28.

revolutionary France, Boissy d'Anglas's description of "the best" as those who possess the foundation to ensure their independence, to distinguish the real from the illusory, and to appreciate what constitutes the public good signals the role of classical-republican precepts underpinning the material and moral requirements of the citizen.

The Constitution of the Year III in fact established two different sets of "the rights of the city." Like the Constitution of 1791, it set up a two-tiered voting system of primary assemblies and electoral assemblies with specific requirements to be eligible to vote at each level. To be a citizen and thus eligible to vote in the primary assemblies, a man—and only a man—must be born in France, aged twenty-one (down from twenty-five in the original proposal), inscribed in the civic register of his canton, have remained in the territory of the Republic for at least a year, and have paid direct personal or property taxes (article 8). Those who did not meet the tax requirements could pay a sum equal to three days' wages. In keeping with the revolutionary valorization of citizen soldiers and strongly echoing the classical-republican idea that those who defend the city make up its citizenry, "veterans of one or more campaigns for the establishment of the Republic" were declared "citizens, without any condition of contribution" (article 9). The Convention also instituted a requirement of literacy and the exercise of a profession, which, however, would not take effect until the Year XII (article 16).[64] While there is no precise figure for just how many adult French men this enfranchised, Patrice Gueniffey estimates the number at 5.5 million out of a possible 8 million.[65] In addition, to sit in the electoral assemblies that directly elected the members of the two councils, the new constitution required that one be at least twenty-five years old and own or rent property equal to one hundred to two hundred days of work in value, depending on the region (article 35).[66] Again, the exact figure for how many men this left eligible to be second-degree electors is not known, but Gueniffey estimates the figure as six hundred thousand, with thirty thousand electors actually sitting and choosing the nation's representatives.[67] Finally, it was originally proposed that a man must own "some kind

64. Godechot, *Les constitutions de la France,* 104–5.

65. Gueniffey, *Le nombre et la raison: La Révolution française et les élections* (Paris, 1993), 101.

66. Godechot, *Les constitutions de la France,* 107.

67. Gueniffey, *Le nombre et la raison,* 101. Malcolm Crook gives the less precise but more generous number of "less than one million." *Elections in the French Revolution: An Apprenticeship in Democracy, 1789–1799* (Cambridge, 1996), 119.

of landed property" to hold a seat in one of the councils, but this condition was dropped following the establishment of such restrictive requirements to sit in the electoral assemblies.[68]

Not surprisingly, these requirements prompted commentary from a number of quarters. One particularly telling criticism, launched from outside the Convention, came from Pierre-Louis Roederer and Amaury Duval, writing, respectively, in the *Journal de Paris* and *La Décade philosophique*. The two journalists denounced the proposed constitution for what they considered its outdated notion of property as land. Roederer argued that owners of transferable and industrial property should also hold the rights of the city, and he went so far as to argue that, in fact, such types of property conferred a deeper interest in a modern, commercial nation like France than did land. Duval, writing under the pseudonym "Polyscope," applauded the commission's desire to limit suffrage to a smaller percentage of the population than had the Constitution of 1793, but, citing Roederer, he called for a more expansive definition of property ownership, one not limited to land. The criticisms advanced by Roederer and Duval are revealing in that they charged the commission with employing an essentially precommercial definition of property and thus an archaic notion of interest, a frequent criticism of classical-republican precepts in the early modern Atlantic world.[69]

Within the Convention, the prospective requirements encountered only scant resistance. The most forceful objection was put forward by Thomas Paine, who argued on 7 July that the citizenship requirements spelled out in the constitution did not reflect an interest in the common good but only in the good of particular interests; that rather than guarantee equality, they instituted inequality; and that, instead of protecting people's liberty, they violated it. The heart of Paine's criticism, however, was that the property requirements would vitiate the popular enthusiasm that had been the wellspring of the Revolution. Paine warned, "If you turn the base of the Revolution from principles to property, you will extinguish all the enthusiasm that until now has supported the Revolution." For Paine, the maintenance of the political order was rooted not in property but in popular enthusiasm. Paine's criticism of the commission and his alternative vision

68. Boissy d'Anglas, *Projet de constitution,* 28–29; and Daunou's explanation at *RM,* 25:288.

69. Roederer, "Constitution" (1795), reprinted in *Œuvres du comte P.-L. Roederer,* 6:95; [Duval], *La Décade philosophique, littéraire et politique,* 10 Messidor, Year 3 (28 June 1795), 21–22.

of the foundation of the body politic were received coldly, and debate over the property requirements was tabled for two days.[70]

The issue was taken up again on 9 July when Merlin de Douai, a member of the original Commission of Seven and a staunch ally of the Eleven, took the floor to counter Paine's speech. He objected to Paine's accusation that under the proposed constitution only those with property would be able to participate in the political process and pointed out that nonpropertied wage earners who pay sufficient taxes "would be able to exercise equally the rights of the citizen." He then argued that, as for "mendicants, . . . you will not want to entrust the fate of the state to a man who has nothing and who produces nothing." Lanjuinais, a member of the Commission of Eleven, followed Merlin and warned against giving political rights to people who "have nothing" because their needs "put them at the mercy of the first who pays them." The danger of poverty, in Lanjuinais's eyes, was that the political personality is rendered dependent and is therefore unstable and open to suasion. Echoing Merlin and Lanjuinais, Creuzé-Latouche, another member of the Eleven, reminded his colleagues on 11 July that it was only after waiving mandatory contributions that "Athens lost her liberty" and "Rome ceased to exist." The Thermidorian elites plainly feared that if those who did not possess the independence and virtue guaranteed by property were to participate in the political process, the Republic would decay.[71]

The issue of property requirements resurfaced on 21 July in a debate over the conditions for eligibility to sit in the electoral assemblies. Grégoire argued that while the Convention had guarded against "abandoning the elections to corruptible men," it should also guard against "the corrupters." Likewise, Pierre-Marie Guyomar reasoned that if the Convention

70. *RM,* 25:171–72. Paine's objections were supported in the Convention only by Jean-Joseph-Victor Génissieu and Edmond Dubois-Crancé. Ibid., 196–97 and 214–16. Important tracts published against the property requirements included François Lanthenas (who had translated Paine's work into French), *Droit de cité, exercice de la souveraineté du peuple français, et garantie de la liberté publique contre les abus de l'égalité en droits* (Paris, 1795); Julien Souhait, *Opinion sur le droit de suffrage dans les assemblées primaires et électorales* (Paris, 1795); and [Antonelle], *Observations sur le droit de cité.* See Yannick Bosc, "Arrêter la révolution, conserver la Révolution: Le débat sur les institutions de l'an III," in Vovelle, *Le tournant de l'an III.*

71. *RM,* 25:195–96, 215–16. My interpretation of the role of property here parallels Suzanne Desan's argument that the Thermidorian discourse of property was focused on sustaining order rather than protecting individual property rights. See *Family on Trial,* chap. 7.

"demands a guarantee against men susceptible to being corrupted, I want a guarantee against the corrupters; I demand that any citizen who has more than 30,000 *livres* of rent cannot be an elector." An unidentified conventionnel supported Guyomar's proposal, arguing that such a measure would be "a genuine guarantee against corruption." This line of argument is noteworthy because it agreed with the Commission of Eleven's anxiety regarding the corruption of electors and the threat thereby posed to the health of the Republic, and likewise insisted on the independence of those who participated in the electoral process, if in rather different terms. In the end, however, the commission's proposals were ratified and the new constitution required that second-tier electors must own or rent property equal in value to one hundred to two hundred days of work (depending on the region).[72]

In addition to requiring that the active citizenry possess a material foundation, the Commission of Eleven also sought to institute a moral foundation. They thus established delayed literacy requirements for voting in order to help ensure the voter's independence. In his presentation of the proposed constitution, Boissy d'Anglas argued that literacy was requisite for independence and should thus be a requirement for citizenship. "A man is only truly independent when he does not need anyone to enlighten him about his duties and to convey his ideas. Since the use of printing, the faculty of knowing how to read should be regarded as a sixth sense, the development of which can alone make us truly men and thus citizens."[73] Furthermore, the commission and the Thermidorian elites held that a widespread program of public instruction and cultural didacticism, including the establishment of a National Institute, civic festivals, and a program of government-subsidized cultural production, was necessary to promote civic virtue among the population and thus ensure the stability of the Republic.[74] An entire section of the constitution was devoted to public

72. *RM,* 25:307. On Guyomar's interventions in the summer's debates, see Bernard Gainot, "Pierre Guyomar et la revendication démocratique dans les débats autour de la constitution de l'an III," in Dupuy and Morabito, *1795: Pour une République sans Révolution,* 262–66.

73. Boissy d'Anglas, *Projet de constitution,* 30–31. See also Daunou's speech on 12 July, *RM,* 25:227.

74. See chapter 2; Baczko has emphasized the Thermidorians' cultural didacticism in a number of essays: "La Constitution de l'an III et la promotion culturelle du citoyen"; "Le tournant culturel de l'an III"; and "Instruction publique," in *Dictionnaire critique de la Révolution française: Institutions et créations,* ed. François Furet et Mona Ozouf (Paris, 1992).

instruction, an early draft of which had stipulated that primary schools would teach children "republican morality" while "national festivals" would maintain "all of the republican virtues."[75] Virtue, for the Thermidorians, was seen as acquired, the product of laws and institutions. It was not assumed to be intrinsic to human nature and thus had to be formed through public instruction—an important break with Robespierre's discourse of virtue and recuperation of the pre-Jacobin classical-republican idea of virtue as a learned quality.[76] Classical republicanism stressed, as J. B. Schneewind puts it, "the human as a political animal shaped by the community" and therefore the "social or political arrangements" that mold the citizen's character.[77] In the Thermidorian regime, in the words of Daunou, the nation's moeurs would be "modified" and "coordinated" by the constitution to fit "the republican system." The Commission of Eleven, he told the Convention, had therefore "occupied itself with the means to assure the French people the level of instruction necessary to maintain its liberty."[78] If the people could not be "forced to be free," in the infamous words of Rousseau, they could be educated to be virtuous.

Boissy d'Anglas spelled out the role public instruction would play in the new regime when he introduced the proposed constitution to the Convention. He emphasized the importance of state-centered didacticism for republican government and outlined a series of measures designed to encourage the development of civic consciousness so that the revolution would "end under the influence of reason and virtue." "The true education of peoples," he told the Convention, "is in their laws, and, even more, in their institutions; it is by them that peoples' moeurs purify, that their soul rises up, that their character grows." The new government would therefore establish a National Institute, sponsor the arts and promote good taste,

75. M. J. Guillaume, ed., *Procès-verbaux du Comité d'instruction publique de la Convention nationale,* 7 vols. (Paris, 1891–1907), 6:946.

76. As Keith Baker makes clear, Robespierre's discourse of virtue, by assigning virtue to human nature, broke with the classical-republican tradition: "Even as the Incorruptible adopted classical-republican language in speaking of virtue, this language underwent an important transformation. The virtue to which he referred was not simply a political effect of good laws that restrained human passions by identifying individual interest with the public good. It was innate in human nature." "Transformations of Classical Republicanism," 49–50.

77. Schneewind, "Classical Republicanism and the History of Ethics," *Utilitas* 5 (1993): 190, 186.

78. *RM,* 25:244.

"reward the simple and private virtues," and encourage public morality through festivals designed "to support brotherhood among citizens and to attach them to the constitution, to the patrie, and to the laws." "That is how," he told his audience, "you raise men to the stature of your laws; that is how you render them worthy of the sacred name of republican." Boissy d'Anglas even criticized the Revolution's early leaders for not having been didactic enough, for having effected a purely negative program of clearing out the old without establishing new values on which to base the new, republican political order. They had failed to grasp the importance of "instruction, without which there cannot be liberty."[79]

The Thermidorian elites held that the population needed instruction not only to realize its common political interest, but, in a sense, to realize its full humanity. In this process, in Paul Bénichou's words, "the legislator, the man of letters, and the educator are admirable in the same way: it is they who bring humanity into being."[80] This comes into sharp focus in Bronislaw Baczko's brilliant account of Thermidorian representations of the "vandal" and the "vandal plot" wherein the image of the vandal served to point out the Revolution's "*other,* opposed to civilization and the Enlightenment," and thus legitimated, even demanded, a vigilant program of "protective and educational action, which implied benevolent supervision by revolutionary authority, by its enlightened elites."[81] In this, the didactic programs of the new regime, in addition to forming a virtuous citizenry, buttressed the classical-republican emphasis on rule by the virtuous few, the sentiment that France, as Boissy d'Anglas put it, should be governed by "the best."

The Rights of Man and Citizen

The constitution proposed by the Commission of Eleven began, like the Revolution's earlier constitutions, with a "Declaration of the Rights of Man and Citizen." Debate on the proposed declaration began on 4 July and

79. Boissy d'Anglas, *Projet de constitution,* 70–74.

80. Paul Bénichou, *Le sacre de l'écrivain, 1750–1830: Essai sur l'avènement d'un pouvoir spirituel laïque dans la France moderne* (Paris, 1973), 48.

81. Baczko, *Ending the Terror,* 200, 210.

was the first feature of the new constitution discussed by the Convention. Daunou took the floor and explained that the commission did not want to "write a new declaration of rights, but to remove from the first [that of 1789] that which it retained of royalism, and from the last [that of 1793] that which it had of anarchism, in order to compose an ensemble as perfect as possible. A declaration of rights," he continued, "should be the rallying point of republicans, and not an arsenal for insurgents."[82] Immediately, a number of deputies sought the podium. At stake in the discussions that followed was a range of pressing political problems, from the definition of the common good to the freedom of the press. Undergirding the diversity of specific issues, however, were two fundamental problems: just how much political pluralism the French body politic would admit in 1795 and whether rights are fundamentally natural or social. In taking up the former question, the deputies' fear of popular insurrection led them to conceive of political pluralism as factionalism—one of the great bugbears of the early modern classical-republican tradition. In regard to the latter question, they defined rights as postpolitical rather than natural and thus employed a classical-republican conception of rights.

The Thermidorians' fear of popular insurrection and factionalism was plainly expressed from the opening moments of the discussion. Debate opened with article 1, which read, "The goal of society is the common good. The government is instituted to guarantee man the enjoyment of his rights." Immediately, Pierre Boissier demanded that the "common good" be defined, to which Lanjuinais retorted that over the last two thousand years "288 kinds of good" had been counted, and that the Convention was not going to resolve this age-old philosophical dilemma that day. Rather, he argued, the common good could not be defined; moreover, its presence in the declaration would only offer a potential means "to oppose to justice a false general interest." Lanjuinais feared that the idea of the common good might be invoked in the name of insurrection and recommended that the first article be discarded altogether, which provoked a series of responses and alternative proposals. In the end, the issue was tabled and debate moved on. At stake in this disagreement, however, more than the definition of the common good itself, were the possible political uses in

82. *RM,* 25:148.

whose name the concept might be wielded. The irony is telling: the very idea of an ostensibly unitary common good was feared for its potentially antimonistic applications.[83]

The fear of insurrection again assumed center stage when the Convention took up debate on article 2, which declared, "The rights of man in society are liberty, equality, safety, and property." The delegate Jean-Antoine Debry promptly objected that the article omitted an essential right, the right to work for subsistence. Debry's motion tacitly recalled the declaration of 1793 and prompted a chorus of protests. The deputy Anne-Alexandre Thibault agreed with Debry that such a right ought to exist but suggested that it would be better put in the body of the constitution and not in the declaration. If placed in the latter, he warned, "we will have furnished malevolence with new weapons. Tomorrow they will come demand bread from us again.... The *décemvirs* will organize anarchy once again." Lanjuinais added that it was not clear that work should even be considered a right, and, he warned, it would be dangerous to put in the declaration because it could be misinterpreted and become "a terrible weapon in the hands of factions."[84]

The twin-headed specter of political factions and popular insurrection resurfaced during discussion of article 6, which began with the claim that "the law is the expression of the general will." The deputy Jean-Baptiste Mailhe promptly objected to this statement. Such a claim, he explained, would be an accurate description of the constitution itself because the constitution was to be ratified by the people in a popular referendum before its implementation. It would not be true, however, in regard to laws passed by the people's representatives during the normal course of governing. A society of 27 million, he reasoned, could express its will only through representative government, and never directly. The law could thus never be an expression of the general will. To state that it was would be to inscribe a potentially seditious contradiction into the constitution and the nation's political life. "Factionals," Mailhe warned, will take advantage of this

83. Ibid., 150–51. The Convention's fear of popular unrest was clearly manifested in articles 360 through 364 of the constitution, which collectively outlawed all "corporations" and "associations" deemed "contrary to public order" and explicitly forbade popular societies from engaging in any political activities, and article 355, which allowed for the suspension of the freedom of the press. Godechot, *Les constitutions de la France,* 139–40.

84. *RM,* 25:151.

discrepancy and tell the people that "the declaration of your rights is being violated," that the law is not expressing the general will. The declaration, Mailhe argued, should state that "the law is the general will *expressed* by the universality of citizens that it governs, or by their representatives freely and constitutionally elected." The Convention followed his proposal, and the final version of the declaration passed at the end of the summer read, "The law is the general will, expressed by the majority either of the citizens or of their representatives."[85]

The terms by which the language of the original proposal was rejected merit examination. While the original proposition was rebuffed because of the fear of factions, there was another fundamental issue in question as well, one that had surfaced numerous times during the Revolution: reconciling the general will with representative government. In 1795, Mailhe and his colleagues rejected the Rousseauian formulation of the general will while guarding the phrase and guaranteeing its ultimate unity and representability. Instead of finding a problem with the substitution of the representative's will for the people's, they assigned a privileged role to the legislator. The representative body would decide the nation's will, not the other way around. That the general will could be thus expressed implied that the representatives could speak in the name of the people's will over and above the people itself. In this conception, the legislative body assumed a position akin to the great legislator of the classical-republican tradition, licensed to instruct the people in the name of their true, if unknown, interest.

By and large, the remaining articles passed with little fanfare until the always-explosive issue of equality came to the fore. Boissy d'Anglas had launched an initial salvo in his preliminary discourse by declaring absolute equality to be a "chimera." Civil equality, he had maintained, is all that anyone can reasonably demand.[86] The issue then remained largely sidelined until the deputy Jacques Defermon pointed to what he perceived to be a lacuna in the declaration. "I don't see," he said, "an article that was in the other declarations: 'All men are born and remain free and equal in rights.'" Daunou responded in the name of the commission that the claim was implicit in the other articles and did not need to be spelled out

85. Ibid., 25:155–56; Godechot, *Les constitutions de la France,* 101.

86. Boissy d'Anglas, *Projet de constitution,* 27.

on its own. Lanjuinais in turn argued that such an article was unnecessary because the nobility, against whom it had originally been intended, no longer claimed hereditary privileges. He had been the author of the original article in 1789, he explained, and had put the language in the original declaration only to serve as a counterweight against the nobility. In addition, Lanjuinais argued that to speak of whether men are really born and remain free and equal would be to open an eternal discussion in which the Convention would have to define "what is before society, what is equal during society, and what is after society." Defermon retorted that the declaration needed recourse to "man before society," that is, to natural rights theories. Mailhe then interjected that this would open yet another debate regarding the relationship between nature and society, a discussion the Convention should not broach. After subsequent interventions by Guyomar and Jean-Philippe Garran in support of natural rights, Defermon's proposition was adopted and remitted to the Commission of Eleven to be formally drafted.[87]

The proposition did not, however, survive the second round of debate on the declaration that took place on 13 August. Daunou again presented the constitution to the Convention, and again the declaration did not mention natural equality. When it became clear that Defermon's amendment was not in the declaration, objections began to be voiced. In response, Mailhe again took the floor and charged that men do not in fact remain equal in rights, even if they are born that way. This is, he said, implicit in the many conditions and laws imposed on the citizenry by the constitution. Mailhe called for a practical approach to the problem and, just as he had in speaking against the article invoking the general will, warned against planting seeds of dissent in the declaration. He then moved to undercut the stream of objections that would surely follow with reference to the one unassailable authority of French political culture at the time, Rousseau. Significantly, however, he referred to Rousseau's *Poland,* with its concern for concrete institution building, and not the more abstract *Social Contract.*

> We have frequently cited J. J. Rousseau in these halls; well, I will cite him myself on this occasion, and I will set him against those who, unintentionally, would plant a germ of anarchy in the constitution that would overturn

87. *RM,* 25:157–58.

> it sooner or later. Look at J. J. Rousseau set down principles; how great and sublime he is! He is the genius who encompasses the universe in his thought. But look at him draw his consequences, it is no longer the same thing; how prudent and reserved he is! Read his work on the government of Poland, and you will see that he proposed only things that could be executed easily and assuredly.

After a few more rounds of discussion, Lanjuinais, as he had earlier in the summer, weighed in against the amendment, arguing that there are inequalities in society and that it is enough to outline people's rights in society without recourse to hypothetical natural rights. In the end, Defermon's amendment was rejected, and the declaration was stripped of any reference to natural rights.[88]

As a result, article 1 of the declaration detailed "the rights of man *in society*."[89] It did not, as had the declarations of rights of 1789 and 1793, invoke natural rights. The language of social rights thus displaced that of natural rights, and a contextual, relational mode of reasoning displaced that of ahistorical, abstract reason, a turn that parallels both the shift to historical, experientially based argument and the didactic stress on context and environment for shaping the citizen's character discussed above. Social rights take context and the subject's relationship to others as their starting point. They are relational and emphasize heteronomy over individual autonomy. As Marcel Gauchet explains, the point of departure is not the hypothetical, autarkic individual found in the state of nature but "the individual immediately exposed to an other."[90] Natural rights, in contrast, are transhistorical and claim validity regardless of time, place, or whoever the other might be. The rhetoric of Lanjuinais's argument is noteworthy in this respect. Rather than point to the universal qualities of humanity, he invoked highly particular, contextualized scenarios and described rights defined in relation to their time and place. "The man born in Isphahan," he averred, "cannot lay claim to exercising the rights that

88. Ibid., 497–99.

89. Godechot, *Les constitutions de la France,* 101 (emphasis added). See Yannick Bosc, "Le droit naturel: Enjeux d'une référence dans le débat sur la déclaration de l'an III," in *Langages de la Révolution (1770–1815)* (Paris, 1995); Marcel Gauchet, *La Révolution des droits de l'homme* (Paris, 1989), 276–83.

90. Gauchet, *La Révolution des droits de l'homme,* 280–81.

the Constitution of the United States guarantees to Americans." Daunou, at a different point during the debates, described the "rights of the city" as "so little in nature that one only acquires them by convention, that is, after being put in society."[91] And, as mentioned above, he wrote in his notes born of discussion in the Commission of Eleven that "I would not want to establish any system on the state of nature." This Thermidorian "refusal of transcendence," in Claude Nicolet's apt phrase,[92] was rooted in a classical-republican conception of rights. In classical republicanism, rights, when they are postulated, are not the transcendental prepolitical rights of the natural rights tradition. Rather, they take their character and legitimacy from the specific, historically situated social and political arrangements from which they issue.[93] They are thus particular, historical, and social or postpolitical.

The Duties of Man and Citizen

Perhaps the single most noteworthy feature of the Constitution of the Year III is that it is preceded by a declaration of duties as well as of rights. Unlike its predecessors in 1789 and 1793, the Constitution of 1795 specifically spelled out the population's obligations toward society and the body politic. Article 1 plainly stated that the "Declaration of Rights contains the obligations of legislators. The maintenance of society demands that those who compose it know and fulfill equally their *duties*."[94] The declaration of duties was to serve as a counterweight to the individual liberties established by the declaration of rights, as "a sort of commentary or antidote," in the later words of Thibaudeau.[95] At its heart, the declaration of duties posited the interdependence of private and public virtues and thus sought to orient the population's moral disposition toward the public good so that individual passions and interests would not tear the Republic apart. The declaration of duties instantiated both the classical-republican emphasis

91. *RM,* 25:498–99, 219.

92. Nicolet, *L'idée républicaine en France,* 129.

93. See the discussion of Renaissance humanist ideas of rights in Richard Tuck, *Natural Rights Theories: Their Origin and Development* (Cambridge, 1979), esp. 33–34, 40, 42.

94. Godechot, *Les constitutions de la France,* 102.

95. Thibaudeau, *Mémoires,* 1:180.

on instructing the population and the classical-republican impulse to create a fully reconciled, integral "man and citizen."

The idea of a declaration of duties, while first institutionalized in 1795, had nevertheless enjoyed political currency for quite some time. To give but a few examples, a declaration of duties had been championed by Mably in *Des droits et des devoirs du citoyen* (penned in 1758 but published only in 1789), considered by the National Assembly in 1789 and again by the National Convention in 1793 (the same year one was passed in Geneva), and had been championed before the Convention in several proposals during the spring of 1795.[96] The impulse behind decreeing duties received fresh momentum after 9 Thermidor when, in the wake of the Terror, there was a widely perceived need for a new set of secular moral principles in which to ground the political order. Emblematic of this was the establishment by the Thermidorian Convention of a Class of Moral and Political Sciences in the newly formed National Institute, which a few years later would sponsor a prize contest asking, "What are the most effective institutions to establish the morality of a people?"[97] The declaration of duties was the Convention's proleptic answer to that question.

The declaration of rights first proposed by the Commission of Eleven on 4 July made no mention of duties. The campaign for duties began immediately, though, when Mailhe, the first deputy to speak, pointed to what he perceived to be the dangers inherent in a declaration of rights not supplemented by duties and demanded that reference to duties be added in order to curtail people from recklessly pursuing their passions. What, he asked, is the object in drawing up a declaration of rights of man and citizen? Is the declaration to be "obligatory" or "only to present a brilliant series of philosophical abstractions?" What is meant to be signaled, he demanded, by principles that one can "invoke, follow and in turn infringe according to one's momentary passions or interests?" Rather than give the nation a set of hollow principles that would only lead to "the slavery of anarchy," the Convention, he urged, ought to bolster the proposed rights by joining them to duties. Only duties could guarantee true liberty, that found in society. Mailhe

96. Baker, *Inventing the French Revolution,* 264–67; Gauchet, *La Révolution des droits de l'homme,* 241–56; *RM,* 25:38, 111, 122, 129; Lanthenas, *Nouvelle déclaration de la morale républicaine, ou des devoirs de l'homme et du citoyen* (Paris, 1795).

97. Discussed in chapter 2.

distinguished between "the rights and the duties of the man and of the citizen: one is a man in the state of nature; one is *man and citizen* in the social state." In nature, he continued, "man is independent, but his independence causes his unhappiness because...everyone becomes, by turns, tyrant and victim." Implicit in Mailhe's soliloquy was the squarely classical-republican claim that the heteronomous citizen in society is actually more free than the autonomous man in nature. His proposal was supported by several members of the Convention but not enough to begin a real debate over whether to add duties to the declaration. The motion was tabled but then gained enough support during the following month that when the Convention took up the issue of the declaration again on 13 August, the revised version contained a "Declaration of Rights and Duties of Man and Citizen."[98]

The only article that sparked serious debate was the third, which read, "Probity is composed of the public and the private virtues." This brought an immediate challenge from the deputy Jean-François Ehrmann, who objected to the word "probity" and proposed that the article read "Republican virtue is made up of the public and the private virtues." The deputy Jean-Baptiste Quirot then protested that "probity" should be removed because "we do not want to make here a moral treatise, but a declaration of man's duties toward his patrie." In a sharp retort that encapsulated the larger movement for legislating duties, Creuzé-Latouche of the Commission of Eleven responded with a powerful proclamation of the need to combine private and public morality. "You agree," he said to them,

> that the safety of society rests on the virtues of its citizens; well, those virtues need to be made an obligation.... [Spelling them out] is necessary because every day we see men who in private fulfill all their duties toward their families, but who in society are traitors or rogues; we see others, on the other hand, who are irreproachable in their political career, but who, foolishly thinking that the austerity of public virtues excludes the private virtues, are bad husbands and bad fathers. This error must be destroyed; all of the virtues must be reunited and demanded of citizens: that is why we proposed to declare that the good citizen should practice all the virtues.

Ultimately, the proposed language was dropped and an alternative was adopted that read, "The obligations of each toward society consist in

98. *RM,* 25:148–49, 499.

defending it, serving it, living under its laws, and respecting those who are its organs." This was followed by an article declaring, "No one is a good citizen if he is not a good son, good father, good brother, good friend, and good husband."[99] The new article repeated almost exactly Rousseau's declaration in *Emile* that it is "the good son, the good husband, the good father who makes the good citizen,"[100] and was deemed sufficient to make clear that the private and public virtues are mutually dependent and that the citizens' moral disposition was to be oriented toward the public good.

Ending the Revolution

At the end of the Convention's session on 17 August, after its president had declared that the second reading of the constitution had ended, Daunou addressed his fellow deputies and requested that the next day a member of the Commission of Eleven be permitted to offer a "report on the means of ending the revolution."[101] The following day, Baudin des Ardennes, a political veteran since the days of the Legislative Assembly and a future member of the National Institute's Class of Moral and Political Sciences, delivered a speech on the potentially explosive topic. At stake in his speech was whether sovereignty lay in the people or in the Convention.

Baudin began his speech, as Boissy d'Anglas had almost two months before, with reference to the tumultuous history of the Revolution and the experience gained thereby. In his historically grounded discussion, he remarked upon the differences between the constitutional discussions of 1789 and 1795, on how "the questions which in 1789 we treated expansively and with solemnity, because they were new," were in the summer of 1795 dealt with quickly because "they are today familiar." The deputies had benefited from the experience of the last six years and were finally in a position to end the Revolution. The enemies of liberty could be identified, and internal peace thus attained. Experience had taught the deputies to stand vigilant in the face of those who plotted against the nation, both the

99. *RM,* 25:501.

100. Rousseau, *Emile, ou, De l'éducation* [1762], in *Oeuvres complètes,* 5 vols. (Paris, 1959–95), 4:700.

101. *RM,* 25:522.

Robespierrists and the Royalists. In dramatic fashion, Baudin proclaimed that "for a long time we have posted fraternity on the doors of our homes, but it was only that of Cain and Abel."[102]

To prevent these enemies from ascending to power, Baudin proposed that two-thirds of the current members of the National Convention should carry over into the new legislative body. The new constitution already stipulated that one-third of the legislative body would be replaced each year, but this would only apply after the constitution had been ratified. As there were 750 deputies in the current Convention, and there would be exactly that many in the two chambers combined under the new constitution, the numbers worked. More controversially, Baudin proposed that the two-thirds who were to remain would be selected by a specially appointed jury. In this way, he argued, a possible Royalist or Robespierrist conspiracy would be prevented from developing. The National Convention could thus "conquer the passions" and ensure a smooth transition from "a revolutionary state to a constitutional order." As had been learned from the withdrawal of the Constituent Assembly, an "untried constitution" should not have a new legislature usher it in; this is "an infallible means of overturning it [the constitution]." At stake, he urged, was the success of the Revolution itself.[103]

The Convention immediately began a "Discussion on the means of ending the revolution," as it was officially titled, but which was really a debate over the two-thirds decree and the jury proposed by Baudin to oversee its implementation. While only one deputy, Georges Desgraves, opposed the two-thirds decree itself, deputies from diverse political backgrounds took the floor to speak out against the proposed jury. The first was Jacques-Charles Delahaye, who took exception to Baudin's and the commission's proposal to assign to a jury a matter as important as who would remain in the new legislature and whose seats would be open to election. He supported the proposal to "preserve a large majority of the legislature" but urged that such a decision be made by the people, not "a mysterious, inquisitorial, [and] arbitrary committee." Likewise, Eschassériaux maintained that the people should decide which two-thirds would be returned. The deputy Thomas-François Jouenne, in a play on Robespierre's famous statement that "virtue will always be in the minority," also argued for

102. Ibid., 526–33.
103. Ibid.

electoral assemblies to decide who would continue, pleading that "virtue is not in the minority" and that the people could and should choose who would represent them. More fundamentally, he explained, there was a contradiction in the commission's proposal. The Convention claimed to represent the people's will yet seemed to believe that counterrevolutionary sentiment was rife among the people.[104]

On 21 August, after further debate, the Convention voted to keep the two-thirds decree in order to ensure a smooth transition to the new constitutional order but to do away with the proposed jury. In its place, they substituted electoral assemblies so that the process of deciding which deputies would remain and which would be replaced would be more democratic. Yet, even in its more democratic form, the two-thirds decree did not allow the people to elect whomever they chose and flatly contradicted the Convention's proclamations that sovereignty inhered in the people. As the deputy Jouenne pointed out, the deputies professed to represent the people yet distrusted the choices they might make. Simply put, the Thermidorian Convention did not have faith in the French people. Although they claimed to represent the people and to derive their sovereignty from the people, the Thermidorian political leaders held that the survival of the body politic depended upon their own virtue and their own ability to shape the nation's general will. In the end, the Thermidorian Convention decided to end the Revolution by sustaining itself and established the property-holding, educated, and virtuous lawmaker at the pinnacle of France's political order.

The republican center, in its efforts to end the Revolution, imagined the body politic in terms and categories rooted in the early modern political language of classical republicanism. Marked by the experience of the Terror, the Thermidorian elites were preoccupied with the twin threats of "anarchy" and "despotism." In response, they sought to ground the body politic not in the sovereign people but in the virtuous few who would act for the people. The Thermidorian lawmaker, on whose skill and virtue the Republic's existence was thought to depend, was akin to the great legislator of the classical-republican tradition and charged with directing, watching over, and instructing the French people. While the Thermidorian elites acknowledged the idea of democratic sovereignty—in this, they reiterated

104. Ibid., 534–38, 553–54, 557–58.

a discourse that was unavoidable in France by 1795—the Constitution of the Year III in fact established the republican center, as the critic Antonelle put it, as "a new caste."[105] In addition, Thermidorian classical republicanism signaled the "secularization" of political time in the French Revolution, the refusal of revolutionary chiliasm and of political transcendence more generally. These profound changes in the revolutionary political imagination in turn fundamentally shaped the political culture of the Directory and the genealogical development of French Liberalism.

105. [Antonelle], *Observations sur le droit de cité,* 17, 18.

2

The Post-Terror Discourse of Moeurs

It is moeurs that most strongly attach men to the patrie, that immortalize, so to speak, the existence of political principles.

Minister of the Interior Benézech, *Instruction sur la célébration des fêtes nationales, adressées par le Ministre de l'Intérieur aux Commissaires du Pouvoir exécutif près des Administrations départementales & municipales*

On 24 September 1794, just two months after the overthrow of Robespierre, Jean-Antoine-Joseph Debry delivered a speech to the National Convention on "the foundations of public morality." Debry began his speech by explaining that the legislator's task is to "direct the human passions to the public benefit." To do this, he explained, the Convention must reform France's moeurs by creating a new "empire of habits" among the population, habits that would fully attach people to the public good, fully integrate the private and the public. "It is by habits that a people becomes good or depraved; it is when there is no longer any difference between the customs of a people and what the laws prescribe that the government runs effortlessly and individuals work by inclination, and not by obligation, for the common good." To illustrate his point, Debry chose examples from Athens and Rome showing that "their education, their habits, their moeurs were republican." These republics collapsed, he explained, only when their habits and moeurs became corrupted by self-interest. Debry insisted on the overriding importance of habits and moeurs, admonishing his colleagues in the National Convention to follow the example of "three of the greatest legislators of antiquity, Moses, Lycurgus and Numa, [who] felt the truth of this principle so strongly that... all of their attention was focused on customs, which formed, in a way, the foundation of their political system."[1]

How were such habits to be inculcated? The method Debry proposed was education. In eighteenth-century and revolutionary France "education" had a much wider scope than the teaching of reading, writing, arithmetic, and so forth, which was considered "instruction." Education signaled the broader process of forming a personality and inculcating civic values. In the *Encyclopédie,* "education" was introduced as an "abstract and metaphysical term," while the *Dictionnaire de l'Académie française* of 1798 defined it as "the care that one takes for the instruction of children, whether concerning exercises of the spirit or of the body, and, principally, concerning moeurs."[2] The power of education was widely extolled in eighteenth-century and revolutionary France. As the philosopher Helvétius famously exclaimed, "education can do anything."[3] Eloquent testimony to the power of education was given just two weeks before Debry's speech by Joseph Lakanal, who located the causes of the Revolution in the eighteenth century's greatest treatise on education. According to Lakanal, the book "that led us to the Revolution, raised us up, instructed us, shaped us for it... is [Rousseau's] *Emile,* the only educational code sanctioned by nature.... It brought about an immense revolution in our institutions and in our moeurs."[4] When Debry and his compatriots in post-Terror France spoke of education, they spoke of the complete formation of the individual and, in turn, the citizen.

This vision of education was based on a particular understanding of both human nature and republican government. According to Debry, human nature is thoroughly indeterminate. "The soul of man is a fertile

1. Debry, *Discours sur les fondements de la morale publique* (Paris, 1794), 2, 5, 9, 8, 12.

2. Denis Diderot and Jean Le Rond d'Alembert, eds., *Encyclopédie, ou Dictionnaire raisonné des sciences, des arts et des métiers,* 35 vols. (Paris, 1751–72), s.v. "éducation"; *Dictionnaire de l'Académie française* (Paris, 1798), s.v. "éducation."

3. Quoted in R. R. Palmer, *The Improvement of Humanity: Education and the French Revolution* (Princeton, 1985), 3.

4. Lakanal, *Rapport sur J. J. Rousseau, fait au nom du Comité d'instruction publique* (Paris, 1794), 6.

field, fit to produce bad as well as good; everything depends on the seed." Republics, in turn, are uniquely suited to undertake the education of the population. Whereas "tyrants" could only punish and deploy coercive measures, "a free government...has in its hands more certain methods of implementation. It makes wanted that which it recommends; it makes anticipated that which it ordains." Thus for Debry, perhaps paradoxically, a "free government" was especially capable of molding its population. And this was imperative, he told his audience, "if you want your laws to be stable and for the revolution to make of the people a great body so well bound that the shock of individual interests and passions cannot weaken it or divide it." He announced to the Convention that this task was already under way, but that there was still work to be done. "The largest parts are prepared, but there remains more to do; our chains are broken, but the scars are still bloody: habits are not changed, wiser moeurs do not yet reduce the work of the laws." As a result, Debry dramatically declared, "the moment is propitious: change habits, found a race of new men."[5]

To accomplish this vast and ambitious program, Debry proposed three principal mechanisms: changes in parenting, the establishment of public censors, and a robust program of public festivals. First, he discussed the need to reform parenting, especially fatherhood, a proposal very much in step with the general post-Terror emphasis on paternal authority and the interdependence of private and public morality. Specifically, Debry proposed that mothers be honored for breast-feeding their infants (he did not seem to imagine any other role for mothers) and that fathers supervise their children's moral education. Most notable among the father's tasks was the requirement to make known the constitution, "accounts of heroic and virtuous actions, and songs of triumph: it will be shameful and punishable to leave them unknown." In this vein, Debry spoke repeatedly of the inseparable ties between private and republican virtue, mustering examples from the great republicans of classical antiquity such as Epaminondas. Public morality, Debry made clear, begins in the home. He sought to license the state to enter the private sphere in order to guarantee that parents raise their children in a properly republican fashion, that the republic's future citizens were being properly formed. Passing from "this

5. Debry, *Discours sur les fondements de la morale publique,* 10, 5, 11, 3, 18.

first education" to "the general education that all ages can receive," Debry advocated the establishment of public censors, as in classical Rome, and public festivals. How can the legislator, he asked, influence the habits of the population past the age of schooling? How to "change moeurs and replace the habits that took root in a depraved civilization with just and honest ones? By a simple institution...*censors.*" Debry quoted at length Rousseau's recommendations for a censor in *The Social Contract* and proposed that "the Convention add to the public authorities the moral power of the censor," which would "monitor the conformity of moeurs with the spirit of the law." In addition, Debry urged the formation of festivals and honorific awards, which, he argued, "perpetuate in our hearts all the reasons to love the laws and liberty" and have been proven effective both in the classical republics and in the modern church. Using festivals, he explained, in "the classical polities... the legislator steered men toward the purpose of society." Only through such a far-reaching program, argued Debry, would the republic be able to fashion a truly republican population. His proposals, announced amid a flurry of calls in the press for a government-led program of moral reform, were taken seriously enough that the Convention remitted them to the Committees of Public Safety, Public Security, Public Instruction, and Legislation.[6]

Debry's speech stands as a foundational statement for the post-Terror republican center. The Thermidorian and Directorial elites were convinced that the very health of the Republic depended on educating the population to become fully and resolutely republican. Their calls for reform, and the various programs and initiatives that resulted, centered on the idea of "moeurs."[7] The term was constantly invoked in post-Terror

6. Ibid., 6, 21, 8, 21, 35, 25–26; *Archives parlementaires de 1787 à 1860, recueil complet des débats législatifs et politiques des chambres françaises. Première série (1787 à 1799),* ed. M. J. Mavidal et al., 100 vols. at present (Paris, 1867–), 97:390.

7. Moeurs is difficult to translate, with no adequate English equivalent. In the eighteenth century, "manners" was the closest cognate, but the modern meaning of "manners" no longer works. "Mores" derives from the same Latin root as moeurs but is inadequate. "Manners and morals" captures the breadth of the term, while "culture" may be the best approximation in contemporary English. The term's scope of application is suggested by the 1798 version of the *Dictionnaire de l'Académie française,* which defined moeurs as "natural or acquired habits, for good or for bad, in everything that concerns the conduct of life.... Also taken for the way of living, inclinations, customs, *façons de faire,* and the particular laws of each nation." *Dictionnaire de l'Académie française,* s.v. "moeürs." I have chosen to leave the French term *moeurs* untranslated.

intellectual and political discourse. The republican center repeated time and again the anxiety that France's moeurs were corrupt. As Henry-Larivière, speaking for the Committees of Public Safety, Public Security, and Legislation, put it to the National Convention on 6 August 1795, "Public morality is corrupted. Public morality is corrupted! . . . Representatives of the people, it is your responsibility to fix public opinion and turn it back to its true direction" so that France will not become "lost" like "the republics of Athens, Sparta, Lacedaemonia and Rome."[8] Similarly, a pamphlet published in 1798 by the author Henri Lemaire warned that "Rome lost its liberty when it lost its moeurs. Without virtue, no republic!"[9] And in 1799, former minister of the interior Dominique Garat delivered a speech to the Council of Elders urging that the government promote republican enthusiasm among the population to counteract the encroaching corruption of the nation's moeurs. He had, he told his colleagues, "consulted the history of the ancient and the modern republics; I examined the reasons why their liberty was everywhere ruined and lost. . . . If Sparta, Athens and ancient Rome could arise from their tombs, they would tell us: . . . it is the corruption of moeurs that prepared the ruin of our liberty."[10] As the statements by Henry-Larivière, Lemaire, and Garat all suggest, the threat posed by the corruption of France's moeurs was widely understood through the lens of classical, especially Roman, decline and fall.[11] It was standard wisdom that, as the preface to a 1796 translation of Christophe Meiners's *History of the Decline of Moeurs among the Romans and their Effects on the Final Years of the Republic* put it, "the corruption of moeurs is, and in the final analysis always will be, the principal cause and the first stage of the decline of states, large and small."[12] Likewise, a new edition of

8. P.-F.-J. Henry-Larivière, *Rapport et projet de décret présentés à la Convention Nationale . . . au nom des trois comités réunis de salut public, de sûreté générale et de législation* (Paris, 1795), 2, 5, 6.

9. Lemaire, *Du Gouvernement républicain et de la constitution française de l'an III* (Paris, 1798), 15.

10. Garat, *Discours prononcé par Garat, en présentant l'hommage des Tableaux historiques des campagnes et révolutions d'Italie pendant les ans 4, 5, 6 et 7 de l'ère républicaine* (Paris, 1799), 3–6.

11. On the history of the historiogaphy of Roman decline and fall and for the different early modern versions of the story, see J. G. A. Pocock, *Barbarism and Religion,* vol. 3, *The First Decline and Fall* (Cambridge, 2003).

12. René Binet, translator's preface to *Histoire de la décadence des moeurs chez les Romains et ses effets dans les derniers tems de la République,* by Christopher Meiners, trans. Binet (Paris, 1796), vii–viii.

Montesquieu's complete works published in 1795 emphasized his analysis of Rome, which "established that when virtue . . . cedes place to corruption, the state is lost."[13] Corrupt moeurs, it was thought, would inexorably lead to the death of the Republic.

The corruption of the nation's moeurs was generally held to spring from two different sources. First was the problem of the nation's lingering monarchical moeurs, a concern that had been pronounced during the Revolution's early years and would linger for some time to come. As Benjamin Constant put it in September of 1797, "monarchical education, monarchical customs, monarchical memories, monarchical castes besiege us from all sides. Fourteen hundred years of monarchy. . . ."[14] After 9 Thermidor and the overthrow of Robespierre, the problem of moeurs took on a second valence: the possibility that France's moeurs had been corrupted by Robespierre, Saint-Just, and the radical Jacobins.[15] Both points of view—that the nation's moeurs were still monarchical or, alternatively, that they had been perverted during the Terror—pointed to the same conclusion: France's moeurs were corrupt, and, to counter the potentially deadly consequences, an activist, didactic state was needed to reform the nation's moeurs and buttress the Republic.

Such concern with the state of France's moeurs led the post-Terror republican center to undertake some of the most aggressive state-sponsored didactic projects of the entire Revolution, an ongoing intensive effort to establish a new cultural infrastructure for the nation. France's political and intellectual elites believed that the civic virtue needed to sustain the Republic was not innate among the population and could only be acquired. As a result, reforming France's moeurs became a virtual obsession of the republican center. This was especially true during moments of political crisis, most notably in the wake of the coup of 18 Fructidor, Year 5 (4 September 1797) carried out by La Révellière-Lépeaux, Reubell, and Barras of the Executive Directory against the recently elected royalist members

13. "Avertissement sur cette nouvelle édition," in Montesquieu, *Oeuvres de Montesquieu. Nouvelle édition,* 5 vols. (Paris, 1795), 1:xxxvi–xxxvii.

14. Benjamin Constant, *Discours prononcé au cercle constitutionnel, pour la plantation de l'arbre de la Liberté* (Paris, 1797), 6–7. Constant's speech was reprinted with a subvention provided by the Executive Directory's Bureau politique, AN, AF III 45, d. 162, f. 103.

15. See Bronislaw Baczko, *Ending the Terror: The French Revolution after Robespierre,* trans. Michel Petheram (Cambridge, 1994), esp. chap. 4.

of the two councils and the two other members of the Directory (Carnot and Barthélemy).[16] The coup was a resounding victory for the republican center, and in its aftermath the centrist republicans emerged newly empowered and emboldened to enact far-reaching programs aimed at deepening the Republic's roots. For example, a Commission on Republican Institutions was created the day after the coup and the government set about trying to enforce the revolutionary calendar and the *fête décadaire* (a civic festival celebrated every tenth day).[17] The widespread zeal for republicanizing the nation's moeurs is captured in a dispatch sent by the minister of the interior to the departmental and municipal administrations in April of 1798: "It is imperative to work towards the reform of public moeurs. You will have earned the recognition of the patrie if you secure the reform of moeurs.... Republics are consolidated by moeurs, and moeurs by institutions."[18] The range of programs undertaken to "secure the reform of moeurs" in the post-Terror period had to confront two distinct, although indissolubly connected, problems: shaping the moeurs of France's next generation and reforming those of its adult population. The various didactic programs thus addressed the problem of moeurs in two different temporal registers. Some, such as public instruction, were future-oriented, seeking to republicanize the young and thus future generations. Others—notably festivals, censors, and civic religion—would promote republican values among the population much more immediately and thereby reform the nation's extant moeurs.

The notion that moeurs could be actively, didactically shaped had a distinguished eighteenth-century genealogy.[19] The *Encyclopédie,* for example,

16. See esp. Albert Meynier, *Les coups d'état du Directoire,* vol. 1, *Le dix-huit Fructidor an V (4 Septembre 1797)* (Paris, 1927); and, on the "Fructidorian Terror" that followed, Howard G. Brown, *Ending the French Revolution: Violence, Justice, and Repression from the Terror to Napoleon* (Charlottesville, Va., 2006), chap. 6.

17. Isser Woloch, "'Republican Institutions,' 1797–1799," in *The French Revolution and the Creation of Modern Political Culture,* vol. 2, *The Political Culture of the French Revolution,* ed. Colin Lucas (Oxford, 1988).

18. François-Sébastien Letourneux, *Copie de lettre du ministre de l'Intérieur aux administrations centrales des départements et aux administrations municipales de toute la République* (Toulouse, 1797), 3.

19. Here I distinguish the didactic genealogy from the broader, more common eighteenth-century use of moeurs (or manners, its eighteenth-century English cognate) as a master category of analysis for philosophical, social, and historical reflection in works such as Montesquieu's *The Spirit of the Laws,* Voltaire's *Essai sur les moeurs,* the great histories of Ferguson and Hume, or the

defined moeurs with a strong accent on the idea that they could be directed: "the free actions of men, natural or acquired, good or bad, *susceptible to rules and direction.*"[20] Republican writers at the end of the old regime had obsessed over the question of how to make France's moeurs republican and often proposed vigorously didactic solutions.[21] The most important forerunner was Jean-Jacques Rousseau, who had spilled much ink outlining the programs a state ought to undertake to instill republican moeurs in a population, especially in his *Considerations on the Government of Poland and on Its Projected Reformation.* "There will only ever be a good and solid constitution where the law rules the citizens' hearts," Rousseau wrote. Pointing to the historical examples of Moses, Lycurgus, and Numa, he praised their efforts to "attach the citizens to the patrie and to each other" through institutions such as religious ceremonies, public spectacles, and the teaching of history. "It is national institutions which form the genius, the character, the tastes, and the moeurs of a people.... It is education that must give souls the national strength and direct their opinions and tastes so that they will be patriotic by inclination, passion, necessity."[22] Rousseau's *Poland* focused on the role of political "institutions" that were "practicable" and was thus, according to a new edition of Rousseau printed in 1796, the perfect post-Terror text.[23] Rousseau stressed the role of politics in forming a people's moeurs, especially that of the great legislator and of education in the broad, eighteenth-century sense of the term. Post-Terror didacticism followed Rousseau in ascribing primacy to the political—"it is laws that make moeurs," as Creuzé-Latouche, president of the Council of Elders told his colleagues on 23 January 1796.[24] This sentiment was later given a paradigmatic articulation by the historian and economist

---

numerous writings on foreign cultures during the eighteenth century such as Volney's *Voyage en Égypte et en Syrie* of 1787.

20. *Encyclopédie,* s.v. "moeurs" (emphasis added).

21. See David Bell, *The Cult of the Nation in France: Inventing Nationalism, 1680–1800* (Cambridge, Mass., 2001), chap. 5.

22. Rousseau, *Considérations sur le gouvernement de Pologne et sur sa réformation projetée* [1772], in *Oeuvres complètes,* 5 vols. (Paris, 1959–95), 3:955–60, 966.

23. "Avertissement des éditeurs," in Jean-Jacques Rousseau, *Oeuvres complètes de J. J. Rousseau; nouvelle édition conforme à celle de Geneve, 1782, et augmentée de quelques nouvelles pièces,* 33 vols. (Lyon, 1796), 1: vi–vii.

24. Quoted in Albert Mathiez, *La Théophilanthropie et le culte décadaire: Essai sur l'histoire religieuse de la Révolution* (Paris, 1903), 115.

Sismondi in his *Histoire des républiques italiennes du moyen âge* (*History of the Italian Republics of the Middle Ages*) of 1807. Sismondi opined that "one of the most important conclusions that one can draw from the study of history is that government is the most successful cause of the character of peoples. The virtues or vices of nations, their energy or their laxness, their talents, their enlightenment or their ignorance . . . are the work of the laws."[25] Exactly such an emphasis on the legislator and the law stood at the heart of the post-Terror discourse of moeurs.

The political and intellectual discourse of moeurs was a foundational discourse of the Thermidorian and Directorial regimes. It took shape in scholarly treatises as well as parliamentary speeches and administrative directives, reflecting the broader intensive interconnection between intellectual and political life in post-Terror France. Its lexicon was that of public morality, which placed it squarely in line with the general intellectual climate of the moment. "After Thermidor," as Carla Hesse explains, "moral duty became the order of the day, and moral philosophy the *lingua franca* of thermidorian cultural life."[26] The post-Terror discourse of moeurs was further defined by a sharp anti-Catholicism. As Alphonse Aulard and Alexis de Tocqueville before him observed long ago, the rejection of Catholicism came to be a unifying, even defining, feature of the post-Terror republican center.[27] Another pronounced feature of this discourse was a strong emphasis on ostensibly masculine qualities and the patriarchal family as the anchor of moral and thus political order.[28] Women were regularly blamed for the corruption of the nation's moeurs, and in turn their exclusion from public life was frequently demanded. Reflecting the discourse of moeurs, the Republic's leading intellectuals and politicians called for a

25. Jean-Charles-Leonard Simonde de Sismondi, *Histoire des républiques italiennes du moyen âge,* 8 vols. (Zurich, 1807–9), 1:1.

26. Carla Hesse, *The Other Enlightenment: How French Women Became Modern* (Princeton, 2001), 105.

27. Tocqueville, *Oeuvres complètes,* ed. J.-P. Mayer, vol. 2, pt. 2, *L'Ancien Régime et la Révolution: Fragments et notes inédites sur la Révolution* (Paris, 1953), 239–40; Aulard, *Histoire politique de la Révolution française: Origines et développement de la démocratie et de la République (1789–1804)* (Paris, 1901).

28. Suzanne Desan, *The Family on Trial in Revolutionary France* (Berkeley, 2004), chap. 7; Jennifer Ngaire Heuer, *The Family and the Nation: Gender and Citizenship in Revolutionary France, 1789–1830* (Ithaca, 2005), pt. 2; Lynn Hunt, *The Family Romance of the French Revolution* (Berkeley, 1993), chap. 6; Mathiez, *La Théophilanthropie et le culte décadaire,* 38.

host of specific initiatives to inculcate republican moeurs such as censorship, the use of public instruction, civic festivals, and, for some, even the establishment of a civil religion.

The key features of the post-Terror discourse of moeurs highlight the extent to which it was inscribed within the political language of classical republicanism. The very diagnosis of the threat posed to the republic by the corruption of moeurs, and the subsequent need to stave off such corruption through the inculcation of virtue among the population, mimed the central trope of early modern classical republicanism. Also squarely in the classical-republican vein were the privileged status accorded the role of the legislator and politics more generally; the collapsing of public and private morality into one integrated sphere and the resultant focus on public morality and the political personality of the citizenry; and the misogynistic view of the place of women in public life. The post-Terror discourse of moeurs was deeply, determinately, shaped by concerns and themes stemming from the early modern classical-republican tradition. Furthermore, this discourse casts important interpretive light on the historical genesis of French Liberalism and the long-term historical relationship between classical republicanism and liberalism in France. Specifically, it highlights the origins of the tendencies in French Liberalism to emphasize politics and the political personality of the citizenry and to distrust democracy from below, sensibilities deeply tied to the classical-republican tradition.

The Power of Ideas

One of the most notable features of the republican center's efforts to republicanize France's moeurs was the great weight accorded to the power of ideas. The post-Terror political and intellectual elites believed wholeheartedly that the circulation of republican ideas would work toward inculcating properly republican values among the population. As a result, the government subsidized certain books, censored others, and, especially, promoted public instruction. The republican center's faith in the political potency of ideas was given eloquent testimony by Pierre-Louis Ginguené in October of 1794, just three months after the overthrow of Robespierre, in the influential journal *La Décade philosophique, litteraire et politique.*

The principal cause of the Revolution, wrote Ginguené, was the "bizarre contradiction of our education under the Old Regime. We had put in our hands, while we were still infants, books made for inspiring love of country, love of liberty, grandeur of spirit, disinterestedness, all of the virtues. Our young hearts palpitated at the heroic traits of Aristides, Epaminondas, Cato, etc. . . . Do you want to make republicans? May your young read Titus-Livy, Sallust, Tacitus, Plutarch, etc." "We hope," he wrote, "that in our new education the language of great men, of Cicero, of Brutus, will not be neglected."[29] Ginguené's confidence in the power of ideas was widely echoed throughout the post-Terror years in official and learned discourse as well as policy.

One of the first and most important steps undertaken in the post-Terror effort to promote the circulation of republican ideas was a massive subsidization of books and journals between 1794 and 1796—what Hesse has dubbed the Revolution's "cultural Thermidor."[30] This concerted attempt to structure what the public would read began in essence with Grégoire's report on the patronage of the arts to the National Convention on 5 October 1794 and then gained steam with the ascension of Pierre-Louis Ginguené to the chair of the Commission on Public Instruction. Government spending to subsidize book production dropped off after 1796, but the Directorial regime nonetheless continued to monitor and reward intellectual production through the *Bureau consultatif pour l'encouragement des lettres* of the Ministry of the Interior, directed by Ginguené. In addition, in the wake of the coup of 18 Fructidor, the Directory established a *Bureau politique* to launch a progovernment media campaign of publishing unattributed pamphlets and planting articles in the press.[31] Emblematic of the government's efforts was a *Republican Manual* printed by the Ministry of the Interior in June of 1799, the animating idea of which was to make a "library for those citizens with little wealth" and the price of

29. [Ginguené], review of *Discours historiques, critiques et politiques de Thomas Gordon, sur Tacite et sur Salluste, La Décade philosophique, littéraire et politique,* 20 Vendémiaire, Year 3 (11 October 1794), 104. See quote at text accompanying note 22 in the introduction.

30. Carla Hesse, *Publishing and Cultural Politics in Revolutionary Paris, 1789–1810* (Berkeley, 1991), 136–56.

31. On the Bureau politique, see Laurence Walter Stoll, "The *Bureau Politique* and the Management of the Popular Press: A Study of the Second Directory's Attempt to Develop a Directorial Ideology and Manipulate the Newspapers" (PhD diss., University of Wisconsin, 1975); and Albert Mathiez, "Le Bureau politique du Directoire," *Revue historique,* no. 81 (1903): 52–76.

which would not exceed "the means of the simplest worker." Volume 1, over two hundred pages long, included a range of useful documents such as the constitution and a "vocabulary of republican measures," while a second volume, already in press, was "an excellent Handbook of the celebrated Mably's *Observations on the History of France*. . . . The history of the monarchy is essential to know; it is the most appropriate way to make one love the Republic." The third volume in the *Manual* would contain medical information, while the fourth and fifth would be "anthologies of moral philosophy accessible to everyone."[32] The ministry's *Republican Manual* testifies not only to the efficacy ascribed to books but, more specifically, to the great political importance that history and moral philosophy were imagined to possess. It is also worth noting that Mably's *Observations* was one of the great classical republican texts of eighteenth-century France.[33] Books, the republican center believed, not only caused revolutions but could end them.

Just as the post-Terror regime was to subsidize certain books and journals, it would censor others. While there had been a general freeing of the presses in the immediate aftermath of 9 Thermidor, this freedom quickly gave way to censorship, a development due in large part to the explosion of right-wing, royalist journals in 1794–95 and that would only intensify over the next five years.[34] For example, in May of 1795 the Convention passed legislation presented by Marie-Joseph Chénier in the name of the committees of Public Safety, General Security, and Legislation that exiled for life "individuals who, by their writings or their seditious speech, prompt either the degradation of the national representative body or the return

32. Announced in *La Décade philosophique,* 20 Prairial, Year 7 (8 June 1799), 493–95. Only the first two volumes were printed: *Le Manuel républicain. Première partie, contenant la Constitution de la République française, suivie d'Instructions sur les nouveaux Poids et Mesures, sur l'usage de ces Mesures relativement aux terrains, sur les Monnoies républicaines, sur l'Annuaire républicain; d'un Vocabulaire des Mesures républicains, et de Tables des matières sous la forme de questions* (Paris, 1799); *Abrégé des révolutions de l'ancien gouvernement français. Ouvrage élémentaire, extrait de l'abbé Dubos et de l'abbé Mably, par Thouret, membre de l'assemblée constituante; pour l'instruction de son fils* (Paris, 1800).

33. See Johnson Kent Wright, *A Classical Republican in Eighteenth-Century France: The Political Thought of Mably* (Stanford, 1997); Keith Michael Baker, *Inventing the French Revolution: Essays on French Political Culture in the Eighteenth Century* (Cambridge, 1990), chap. 4.

34. See Hugh Gough, *The Newspaper Press in the French Revolution* (London, 1988), chaps. 4 and 5.

of the monarchy."[35] On 16 April 1796 the Directory announced the death penalty for anyone who publicly called for the return of the Constitution of 1791 or the Constitution of 1793.[36] This trend reached its apex in September of 1797, after the coup of 18 Fructidor, when a severe and wide-ranging crackdown on the press resulted in the closure of seventy-four journals. Yet there was simultaneously an influential current of thought that linked the very existence of the Republic to the free circulation of ideas and considered freedom of expression all but nonnegotiable. In addition, a good number of centrist republicans feared that stifling the free expression of ideas might impinge upon the ability of public opinion to act as a source of moral regulation. Daunou acknowledged these dilemmas while proposing a press code to the Council of Five Hundred in November of 1796 in the name of a special commission convened to review the situation. Despite his concerns, however, Daunou argued for a fairly strict code and warned against envisioning "the press as an abstract being, as some type of moral person" endowed with full rights. "I know well that virtue is the conserving principle of republican states," he concluded, "but that does not merit saying that in order to give virtue a fuller exercise, it is necessary to allow greater leeway to all sorts of licentiousness and crime."[37] Overall, the history of press regulation during the Directory was marked by a tension between anxiety about the potential corruption of the Republic's moeurs on the one hand and the desire to allow the relatively free expression of ideas on the other; but it was a tension that more often than not resolved in the state's careful oversight of public expression.

The most important site in which the post-Terror republican center promoted the inculcation of republican moeurs, however, was public instruction. The post-Terror period was of course not the first in the Revolution to witness a turn to public instruction as a means to reform—in the spring of 1796, the editors of *La Décade philosophique* remarked that "for five or six years we in France have spoken of public instruction

35. *RM,* 24:362. However, Hugh Gough argues, juries were usually reticent to convict in the face of such extreme penalties. *The Newspaper Press in the French Revolution,* 124.

36. Isser Woloch, *Jacobin Legacy: The Democratic Movement Under the Directory* (Princeton, 1970), 25.

37. P.-C.-F. Daunou, *Rapport fait par Daunou, au nom d'une Commission spéciale, sur la répression des délits de la presse* (Paris, 1796), 4, 12.

more than anyone in Europe since the Renaissance."[38] Yet the intensity with which they pursued reform through pedagogy, especially during the first eighteen months after the overthrow of Robespierre, was unmatched throughout the Revolution, paralleling the "cultural Thermidor" in publishing.[39] The post-Terror expansion of public instruction began in essence in the winter of 1794–95 with the recall of the Girondins, the ascension to power of figures such as Daunou and Chénier, and the attendant rise of Garat and Ginguené in the Executive Commission on Public Instruction and Lakanal in the Convention's parallel Committee on Public Instruction. The initial upsurge was tied to the widespread discourse linking the causes of the Terror to ignorance and vandalism.[40] Public instruction was championed as the only force that could counteract such "barbarism" and form a properly republican population. The prevalent mood was captured by Lakanal in a speech to the Convention in the fall of 1794 in which he called for students to read "the authors of antiquity" because they "breathe the sacred love of patrie, the enthusiasm of liberty, and that virtuous hatred that all sensitive beings owe to the oppressors of humanity."[41] Public instruction remained a central component of the government's efforts to shore up the republic throughout the Directory, to reform the nation's moeurs and orient the population toward the public good.

Public instruction during the Directory was structured by the "Daunou law," as it is known, which was passed on 24 October 1795, shortly after the ratification of the Constitution of the Year III. The most ambitious overhaul of the nation's educational system passed during the Revolution, the Daunou law ranged from primary schools up to a newly founded National Institute and a program of national festivals. The Daunou law was conceived in tandem with the new constitution, with members of the relevant committees working together during the summer of 1795, and stands as a foundational document of the Thermidorian-Directorial moment, one that helps reveal the educational and political priorities of the

38. "Instruction Publique," *La Décade philosophique,* 10 Germinal, Year 4 (30 March 1796), 15.

39. Baczko, "Le tournant culturel de l'an III," in *1795: Pour une République sans Révolution,* ed. Roger Dupuy and Marcel Morabito (Rennes, 1996).

40. Baczko, *Ending the Terror,* chap. 4.

41. Lakanal, "Rapport sur les Ecoles centrales," in *Une éducation pour la démocratie: Textes et projets de l'époque révolutionnaire,* ed. Bronislaw Baczko, 2d ed. (Geneva, 2000), 494.

republican center. Daunou, speaking in the name of both the Commission of Eleven that drafted the recently passed constitution and the Committee on Public Instruction, told the Convention, "Do not allow your memorable session to finish without having finally organized this moral institution that will complement the other institutions you established." Republican government and public instruction, Daunou explained, have a symbiotic relationship such that one cannot exist without the other. "In a word, a system of public instruction can establish itself only next to a republican constitution. The former needs the latter, but today it is the latter that in turn requires the support of the former, a support for which no other could be substituted.... It is up to Letters to finish the Revolution that they began."[42]

The Daunou law exemplified the wider priorities of the post-Terror discourse of moeurs. It simultaneously stressed the importance of inculcating republican moeurs in the population and concentrated its resources at the level of elites. The new law established "republican morality" alongside reading, writing, and arithmetic as the principal focus of primary-school instruction while simultaneously forsaking the commitment to free and universal primary instruction endorsed earlier in the Revolution.[43] The fact that the law was written by the same men who wrote the Constitution of the Year III, which made literacy requisite for voting within ten years of the constitution's adoption, reveals much about the priorities of the republican center. As R. R. Palmer observes, "These decisionmakers of 1795, in requiring that male citizens beginning in 1804 should know how to read and write and yet providing neither free nor compulsory primary education, were not eager to enlarge the electorate."[44] In its second section, the law established a central school in each department, but total enrollment in the central schools never exceeded ten thousand students.[45]

42. P.-C.-F. Daunou, "Rapport sur l'instruction publique," in Baczko, *Une éducation pour la démocratie,* 504, 508, 513. Other relevant documents and speeches related to the passage of the law can be found in M. J. Guillaume, ed., *Procès-verbaux du Comité d'instruction publique de la Convention nationale,* 7 vols. (Paris, 1891–1907), 6:786–800 and 869–73; and *RM,* 26:255ff. and 323–26.

43. "Décret sur l'organisation de l'instruction publique," in Baczko, *Une éducation pour la démocratie,* 514. On the primary schools, see Isser Woloch, *The New Regime: Transformations of the French Civic Order, 1789–1820s* (New York, 1994), chaps. 6 and 7.

44. Palmer, *The Improvement of Humanity,* 231. An important contextual factor was that the French state was virtually bankrupt.

45. The figure of ten thousand is reached by Palmer, ibid., 248–49.

The central schools, far from an attempt to educate the entire population, were intended to "build an elite" and embodied the Daunou law's emphasis on "constructing an educational system from above."[46] No standard curriculum was established for the central schools, and the courses' content varied wildly from department to department. This situation was eventually deemed unsustainable, and, beginning in 1797, the Ministry of the Interior moved to homogenize the curriculum.[47] Perhaps to make up for this absence of lower-level instruction, and seemingly subscribing to a "trickle-down" plan for public instruction, the Daunou law devoted resources to the encouragement of elite-level intellectual and cultural production—namely, the establishment of the National Institute (title IV) and the paying of subsidies, rewards, and public honors (title V).

The capstone of the law was undoubtedly the National Institute. While some form of such an institute had been proposed on several occasions during the Revolution's early years, with different sorts of missions, that of 1795 was intended to create an official intellectual elite who would then embark on reforming the nation's moeurs.[48] From the beginning, the Institute was conceived as a politically engaged institution that would establish something like an official state philosophy, or at least an official set of questions, given the frequently intense disagreement among its members. In addition, the Institute was closely tied to the nation's political leadership, with its members frequenting the same salons and clubs as those in power. Moreover, many of its members *were* those in power. From the Class of Moral and Political Sciences alone, ten members served in the Council of Elders and twelve in the Council of Five Hundred.[49] Daunou was the first president of the Council of Five Hundred, La Révellière Lépeaux the president of the Executive Directory, and Garat the minister of the interior. The work performed in the National Institute often carried blatantly political overtones, and the various sections' prize contests—their principal

46. Claude Désirat and Tristan Hordé, "La Fabrique aux élites: Théories et pratiques de la grammaire générale dans les écoles centrales," *Annales historiques de la Révolution française* 243 (1981): 85.

47. See below, p. 80–84.

48. On the National Institute, see François Azouvi, "L'Institut national: une 'encyclopédie vivante'?" in *L'Institution de la raison: La Révolution culturelle des Idéologues,* ed. Azouvi (Paris, 1992); Martin Staum, *Minerva's Message: Stabilizing the French Revolution* (Montreal, 1996).

49. Martin Staum, "The Class of Moral and Political Sciences, 1795–1803," *French Historical Studies* 11 (1980): 371–97.

method of engaging with France's larger intellectual community—were frequently dedicated to overtly political subjects. Several of the contests' subjects also testified to the widespread interest in the political stakes of cultural infrastructure. The Class of Literature and Fine Arts announced a prize contest in 1796 asking respondents to "examine what has been, and what could again be, the influence of painting on the moeurs and the government of a free people."[50] The Class of Moral and Political Sciences sponsored prize contests asking, "By what causes has the spirit of liberty developed in France from François I to 1789?" and "What are the most effective institutions to establish the morality of a people?"[51]

Taken as a whole, the Daunou law blended an extreme emphasis on republican pedagogy with an explicit de-democratization of public instruction. It thus illustrates clearly the simultaneous didacticism and elitism of the post-Terror political scene. However, the shortcomings of the Daunou law should not occlude the importance assigned by Directorial elites to public instruction. The government's intellectual mouthpieces, centrist journals such as *La Décade philosophique* and *Le Conservateur,* all contained sections devoted to public instruction. Indeed the "central aim" of *La Décade philosophique,* as one historian recently described it, was "to foster republican virtues and make them habitual."[52] In addition, key figures such as Destutt de Tracy wrote extended treatises on the subject.[53] As the *Décade philosophique* put it, "the government that devotes itself entirely to the health and the prosperity of the Republic... will favor with all its power the propagation of public instruction."[54] Or, as Daunou proclaimed in enthusiastic prose in the pages of *Le Conservateur,* "restore to public instruction not its shackles but its fertile activity, and you will have guaranteed the fruits of many victories over anarchy and monarchy."[55]

50. Announced in *La Décade philosophique,* 30 Messidor, Year 4 (18 July 1796), 160.

51. This last contest is discussed below.

52. Richard Whatmore, *Republicanism and the French Revolution: An Intellectual History of Jean-Baptiste Say's Political Economy* (Oxford, 2000), 115. See also Joanna Kitchin, *Un Journal 'philosophique': La Décade (1794–1807)* (Paris, 1965); and Marc Régaldo, *Un milieu intellectuel: "La Décade philosophique," 1794–1807,* 5 vols. (Lille, 1976).

53. Antoine-Louis-Claude Destutt de Tracy, *Observations sur le systême actuel d'instruction publique* (Paris, 1801).

54. "Instruction Publique," *La Décade philosophique,* 10 Messidor, Year 4 (28 June 1796), 21.

55. *Le Conservateur, journal politique, philosophique et littéraire; par les Citoyens Garat, Daunou, Chénier,* 1 Vendémiaire, Year 6 (22 September 1797), 174.

One aspect of the effort to enlist public instruction in the service of shoring up the Republic was the government's attempt to procure new educational literature, especially "revolutionary catechisms." While Saint-Lambert's *Principes des moeurs* was a best-seller and Lachabeausièrre's *Catéchisme républicain*—which had the reader articulate his identity as "a free and thinking man, by choice a republican"—was the staple catechism of the schools and was reprinted each year during the Directory,[56] the government spent large sums of money on contests for new republican catechisms for use in the primary and central schools. For example, in one such contest announced in May of 1799 the government gave out 225,500 francs in prize money.[57] The importance accorded to such schoolbooks was evident even in the Republic's foreign policy, which can be seen in an incident in the Directory's relations with one of its "sister republics," the Cisalpine Republic. In October of 1797 the Executive Directory of the Cisapline Republic asked the Directory of the French Republic for aid in overcoming a shortage of books needed for public instruction. The French Directory, in turn, asked its Bureau consultatif pour l'encouragement des lettres of the Ministry of the Interior to study the request. In its report, the bureau, which was directed by Ginguené, noted the importance of "the propagation of Enlightenment" and urged the Directory to fulfill the request, offering both books printed by the government for public instruction and books from a sort of emergency "literary depot" in the bureau.[58] The president of the Executive Directory then wrote to the Cisalpine Executive Directory offering the books and underlining the importance of the matter at hand.

> Public instruction will become the principal object of the Directory's concerns and of the encouragements it dispenses. . . . The Directory believes that there is no communication that better assures the liberty of peoples, and the goodness of their government, than that which relates to the propagation of

56. Lachabeausièrre's text was also translated into Dutch and Italian for use in the "sister republics." Palmer, *The Improvement of Humanity,* 239, n. 23.

57. *La Décade philosophique,* 20 Floréal, Year 7 (9 May 1799), 319.

58. "Rapport au Directoire exécutif par le Ministre de l'Intérieur, 5e Division, Bureau consultatif pour l'encouragement des lettres," 5 Brumaire, Year 6 (26 October 1797), BN, Nouv. Acq. Fr. 9192, f. 91–92.

> Enlightenment. It is very pleased to form the first relations of this kind with the Directory of the Cisalpine Republic.[59]

The second great moment concerning public instruction in post-Terror France was in the wake of the coup of 18 Fructidor in September 1797, when the government increased its surveillance of the schools and stepped up its efforts to ensure that public instruction was sufficiently republican and anticlerical. The minister of the interior, François de Neufchateau, sent out a questionnaire to all the central schools asking for information about the content of their courses so that he could "paint for the Directory a general picture of the progress of enlightenment, the state of knowledge, and of social moeurs."[60] While the goal of the questionnaire was ostensibly to gather information, there can be little doubt, as Claude Désirat and Tristan Hordé point out, that the ministry wanted to "make sure that the professors were developing theoretical and moral principles that conformed to the objectives of the regime" and were appropriate for "molding the future cadres of the nation, the intellectual elite."[61] As one teacher wrote back, "You want to know if the professors warrant the confidence of the government, [if]...all work with the Executive Directory to mold the French youth to republican moeurs."[62] The ministry's intentions on this front are all the more evident in a second round of letters sent out to remind tardy schoolteachers to fill out the questionnaires but that also served to remind them of what, exactly, they should be teaching. In its letter on "the course of morals and legislation," the ministry explained in forthright terms that the purpose of the course was "to give to the young sound principles of private and public morality,...to make them virtuous citizens, enlightened

59. "Le Président du Directoire exécutif de la République française au Directoire du Directoire exécutif de la République cisalpine," Brumaire, Year 6 (October–November 1797), BN, Nouv. Acq. Fr. 9192, f. 93.

60. Quoted in E. Kennedy and M. L. Netter, "Les écoles primaires sous le Directoire," *Annales historiques de la Révolution française* 243 (1981): 3–4. The survey and the responses received have been studied by several historians. See Désirat and Hordé, "La Fabrique aux élites"; Marcel Guy, "L'enseignement de l'histoire dans les écoles centrales (an IV–an XII)," *Annales historiques de la Révolution française* 243 (1981): 89–122; Palmer, *The Improvement of Humanity,* chap. 5, esp. 242–57; Martin Staum, "Human, Not Secular Sciences: Ideology in the Central Schools," *Historical Reflections/Réflexions historiques* 12 (1985): 49–76; James Livesey, *Making Democracy in the French Revolution* (Cambridge, Mass., 2001), 182–97.

61. Désirat and Hordé, "La Fabrique aux élites," 68, 81.

62. Quoted in ibid., 69.

about their interests and those of their country."[63] This information gathering culminated in the formation of a special Council on Public Instruction charged with conducting an examination of the state of the central schools.[64] The eight-member council, which sat from late 1798 to October 1800, included a number of prominent figures, notably Ginguené, Garat, and Destutt de Tracy (Daunou was originally selected but declined to serve).[65]

The Council on Public Instruction completed a final report in early 1800, although by the time it issued the report Bonaparte had already come to power (he then dissolved the central schools in 1802 and replaced them with the Napoleonic lycées). The report reveals both the educational priorities of the centrist republicans and what they imagined the purposes of public instruction to be. The report reproduced the Daunou law's elitism in continuing to charge school fees. However, it proposed a major modification of the law in calling for the standardization of the curricula of the central schools. The full and effective reform of France's moeurs, it was felt, could not be accomplished if students were learning different material in each department. The council's report also called for adding an additional chair of ancient languages to each central school in the Republic, the only subject for which it proposed adding instructors. In this vein, the council also sought to increase the role of classical languages in the curriculum, stipulating that students in the central schools study Latin for six years and Greek for four.[66] Instruction in ancient languages meant, beyond learning Latin and Greek, the teaching of the great classical authors such as Cicero and Tacitus and, frequently, ancient history. In 1798, Félix Bonnaire, delivering a report to the Council of Five Hundred in the joint name of the Commission on Public Instruction and the Commission on Republican Institutions, lamented that students would never be able to

63. "Le Ministre de l'intérieur au Professeur[s] de législation de l'école centrale du département[s]," reprinted in Destutt de Tracy, *Élemens de l'Idéologie; troisième partie, tome deuxième: De la logique* (Paris, 1825), 270.

64. In addition, there was a drawn-out legislative debate throughout the Year 7 (1798–99). See Palmer, *The Improvement of Humanity,* 257–68.

65. François de Neufchateau to Daunou, 13 Vendémiaire, Year 7 (4 October 1798), BN, Nouv. Acqu. Fr. 21882, f. 493.

66. "Conseil d'Instruction publique. Extrait du Procès verbal de la séance du 16 Pluviose, an 8 de la République française, composée des citoyens Lagrange, Garat, Palissot, Ginguené, Domergue, Darcet, Lebreton, Jacquemont, Tracy," BN, Nouv. Acqu. Fr. 9193, f. 178–84.

read Tacitus if a second chair in ancient languages were not added.[67] The priority accorded to Latin and Greek indicates not only the continued importance assigned to classical education but that the report's authors were more interested in educating elites than in reaching a wide audience.[68] The report also reveals that the council assigned great importance to the course on morals and legislation. Almost repeating the questionnaire quoted above, it argued that the course of morals and legislation should "teach the principles of private and public morality...that are necessary for citizens to know their rights and duties, and the interests of their patrie." Furthermore, it strongly recommended that the state establish *Ecoles spéciales pour les sciences morales et politiques* to train future teachers of the course on morals and legislation. The commission wrote that "it is essential to form men capable of teaching the moral and political sciences; it is to be desired that soon no one will reach an important position in the Republic without having undertaken a detailed study of them."[69] The course on moral and political sciences would begin with grammar and culminate with history, the subject that was to tie the entire course together.[70]

The council's placement of history at the apex of the moral and political sciences followed from the important political role assigned to the subject of history throughout the post-Terror period—recall the ministry of the interior's handbook of Mably's *Observations on the History of France* in its *Republican Manual,* discussed above. History was conceived as a vital foundation of republican virtue, an emphasis squarely within

67. Bonnaire, *Rapport...au nom des Commissions d'instruction publique et des institutions républicains réunies, sur les écoles centrales* (Paris, 1799), 5–6. The report was given on 13 November 1798 but was not published until 1799.

68. Palmer, *The Improvement of Humanity,* 276. On the eighteenth-century debate about how much weight to accord to Latin, see Dominique Julia, *Les trois couleurs du tableau noir: la Révolution* (Paris, 1981), 250–57.

69. "Conseil d'Instruction publique," f. 185–87.

70. It should be pointed out that in 1799, according to R. R. Palmer's calculations, only 462 students enrolled in the course of morals and legislation and 826 in history. *The Improvement of Humanity,* 249. Livesey, however, overstates the case when he writes that "very few students would actually be exposed to the history and jurisprudence courses; the majority would receive a literary education," by which he means the course of belles lettres *Making Democracy in the French Revolution,* 194. Again according to Palmer's numbers, only 707 students took the belles lettres course. Moreover, Livesey's assertion that the belles lettres curriculum, composed of distinctly "modern" authors, signaled the displacement of classical authors is called into question by the fact that most classical authors were still read in the ancient languages course, which counted an enrollment of 2,154 students, the second largest of any subject (behind only drawing).

the classical-republican tradition.[71] As a subject of instruction, history furthermore carried special political symbolism because, before the mid-eighteenth century, the teaching of history in France had been for the education of princes and kings (although ancient history was taught with classical languages and literature).[72] But in the second half of the eighteenth century, as history became the lingua franca of eighteenth-century political debate, there was an upsurge in calls for educational curricula to include history as an elementary subject. By the time of the Directory, the study of history had come to be seen as the anchor of a republican education, a development very much in step with the wider post-Terror increase in historical consciousness: whereas the Jacobins had been antihistorical and rejected the lessons of historical experience, the post-Terror republican center tended to venerate experience against abstract theory. Emblematic of history's role, and particularly of its inversion from politics for kings to politics for republicans, was an edition of Condillac's *Cours d'études pour l'instruction du prince de Parme,* an educational program for Ferdinand de Bourbon-Parma that was republished in 1794–95 and intended to be "placed in the hands of republican youth."[73] Condillac's book went on to become the most widely used history text in the nation's central schools.[74] Also widely used were Millot, Mably, and Rollin, whose history of Rome has been credited with helping shape a classical vision of the republic in the American colonies.[75] As one study of the central schools concludes, the history courses "often had a strong republican tone.... There was nearly universal acceptance of history as a 'school of morals and politics,' a favored quotation from Mably's *De l'étude de l'histoire.*"[76] This attitude toward historical knowledge was widely shared. Bonnaire, in the report issued jointly by the Commission

71. See the discussion in chapter 1.

72. Guy, "L'enseignement de l'histoire dans les écoles centrales," 89–92.

73. As related in Sergio Luzzatto, *L'automne de la Révolution: Luttes et culture politique dans la France thermidorienne,* trans. Simone Carpentari Messina (Paris, 2001), 154 (citation to *RM,* 22:532).

74. "Conseil d'Instruction publique," f. 182.

75. William Gribbin, "Rollin's Histories and American Republicanism," *William and Mary Quarterly* 29 (1972): 611–22. On Rollin's role in shaping the reception of classical history in France, see Jacques Bouineau, *Les toges du pouvoir, ou la révolution de droit antique (1789–1799)* (Toulouse, 1986), 15–16.

76. Staum, "Human, Not Secular Sciences," 68–69.

on Public Instruction and the Commission on Republican Institutions, argued for the importance of classical history, rhetorically asking, "Is it not in the history of ancient republics... that students should be able to draw their lessons? Do they not then have under their eyes examples of virtue, courage, [and] patriotism... that engrave themselves into the students' spirit and begin for them a course of morality and politics?"[77] And, in similar terms, Daunou praised a work of history titled *Abrégé de l'histoire de la Grèce* to the Council of Five Hundred on 9 March 1799, explaining that in these two volumes one can find "brilliant examples of almost all the domestic and civic virtues that should give honor to republicans." "If we want our children to remain free, it is necessary to offer them the lessons that prompted us to become free."[78]

In sum, the Thermidorian and Directorial regimes placed great emphasis on the power of ideas, and especially public instruction, in their efforts to reform France's moeurs, but it was an effort marked by the wider elitism of the post-Terror moment. While France's republican center sought to instill republican moeurs in the population, they limited their focus to high-level programs rather than the education and democratic empowerment of the entire population.

Civil Religion: Théophilanthropie

Public instruction promised to republicanize France's next generation but did not address the pressing question of how to inculcate republican moeurs among the population more immediately. One option considered for this latter problem, notably in the wake of the coup of 18 Fructidor, was a civil religion. While the Constitution of the Year III formally separated the state from any particular religion and guaranteed the free practice of religious belief in France, there were nonetheless a number of endeavors during Thermidor and the Directory to establish an at least quasi-official civil religion. Notable among these were the system of public festivals,

77. Bonnaire, *Rapport,* 6–7.

78. P.-C.-F. Daunou, *Discours prononcé par Daunou sur un ouvrage qui a pour titre:* Abrégé de l'histoire de la Grèce (Paris, 1799), 2.

the *culte décadaire,* and the *théophilanthropie* movement that exploded onto the Parisian scene in 1797 before declining precipitously in 1799.

Théophilanthropie was a deistic religion emphasizing "the moral law," the virtues of simplicity, and the interdependence of domestic and public life that emerged in September of 1796 with the anonymous publication of an obscure pamphlet titled the *Manuel des théoanthropophiles.*[79] Its "general object," according to its Committee of Moral Direction, was to "search man's heart in the silence of his private life, in the interior of his family, to make of him a virtuous and benevolent being, to trace for him his social duties, to make him a good citizen."[80] The goal was, "above all, the love of the patrie."[81] In organizational terms, it explicitly rejected the idea of a clergy and was instead presided over by a Committee of Moral Direction made up of a "small number of fathers" who decided which moral treatises would be read during services. Its liturgy, recounted Amaury Duval in the *Décade philosophique,* consisted of "hymns and speeches of moral philosophy" and the reading of "maxims taken from the best ancient and modern philosophers." In its services, wrote Duval, "one does not fear saying the words patrie and republic," while the young received instruction in not only morality but patriotic courage and virtue.[82] Germaine de Staël reproached théophilanthropie's boosters for sometimes carrying its civic mission too far, for treating it "as a political method and not as a true faith."[83] Théophilanthropie was, in short, a moral doctrine in religious

79. [Jean-Baptiste Chemin-Dupontès], *Manuel des théoanthropophiles ou adorateurs de Dieu et amis des hommes, contenant l'exposition de leurs dogmes, de leur morale et de leurs pratiques religieuses, avec une instruction sur l'organisation et la célébration du culte, rédigé par C**** (Paris, 1796). Subsequent editions of Chemin-Dupontès's *Manuel* used the spelling "théophilanthropes" rather than "théoanthropophiles." The best treatment of théophilanthropie remains Mathiez, *La Théophilanthropie et le culte décadaire.* For a recent account of théophilanthropie that differs from my own, see Livesey, *Making Democracy in the French Revolution,* 206–8.

80. "Exposé sommaire du plan arrêté par le comité de Direction de la morale théophilantropique," 18 Prairial, Year 6 (6 June 1798), Louis-Marie de La Révellière-Lépeaux Papers, Beinecke Rare Book and Manuscript Library, Yale University, box 5, folder 157.

81. "La Théophilantropie considerée dans ses raports essentials avec le Gouvernement Républicain," n.d., Louis-Marie de La Révellière-Lépeaux Papers, Beinecke Rare Book and Manuscript Library, Yale University, box 5, folder 159.

82. [Duval], "Morale. Lettre de Polyscope sur une Réligion nouvelle," *La Décade philosophique,* 30 Floréal, Year 5 (19 May 1797), 344–45.

83. Germaine de Staël, *Des circonstances actuelles qui peuvent terminer la révolution et des principes qui doivent fonder la république en France,* ed. Lucia Omacini (Geneva, 1979), 234.

trappings directed toward political ends. As such, it followed nearly to the letter its genesis as explained by its Committee of Moral Direction:

> The Committee felt that it was necessary...to form a totality that could serve from now on as a manual for all men joined together in society and living under republican laws. In the middle of the storms that preceded, accompanied, and even followed the operations of a Revolution that philosophy had long prepared in France, the members of the Committee heard those energetic voices that rang out in the sanctuary of the laws and said to the legislators: 'The stability of a good government depends on the stability of moeurs, which must have for their base morality. To obtain this happy result it is necessary to see born an entirely integrated religious and moral system founded on respect for religious opinions and on the truth.'[84]

Within a year of the publication of the *Manuel des théoanthropophiles* théophilanthropie had swept through elite circles, enjoyed evident official favor, and even received covert government funding. By June of 1798, a police report testified that "the Théophilanthropes, whose pure morals should one day replace the superstitions of Catholicism," were holding services in all but two of Paris's churches and recommended continued subsidization from the minister's "secret funds." And by the fall of 1798 the police reported that théophilanthropie was using all of Paris's churches.[85] Théophilanthropie was championed by a number of important figures in the republican center, notably Daunou, Dupont de Nemours, Chénier, David, Amaury Duval, Creuzé-Latouche, Leclerc, and especially La Révellière-Lépeaux. Although théophilanthropie never did become an official civil religion, it is remarkable that so many key members of the republican center devoted time, energy, and resources to promoting it.[86] Their support for théophilanthropie directly echoed a long line of republican authors, most prominently Machiavelli and Rousseau, who had championed a civil religion that would instill civic virtue and love of the patrie along the lines

84. "Exposé sommaire du plan arrêté par le comité de Direction de la morale théophilantropique."

85. Alphonse Aulard, ed., *Paris pendant la réaction thermidorienne et sous le Directoire: Recueil de documents pour l'histoire de l'esprit public à Paris,* 5 vols. (Paris, 1898–1902), 4:732; 5:108.

86. As Isser Woloch writes of the *fête décadaire,* "To an extent that ought to astonish us, the Directory made the republican calendar a touchstone of its political ideology and administrative practice." "'Republican Institutions,' 1797–1799," 383.

of the Roman model.[87] It was commonly held among early modern republicans that, as Ginguené put it in an essay on Montesquieu published in *La Décade philosophique* in 1797, "the policy of the Romans in religion was one of the causes of their greatness, and the relaxation of this policy one of the causes of their decline."[88] Support for théophilanthropie within the republican center was driven by exactly such sentiments, by the concern that France's moeurs were corrupt and that a civil religion was needed to instill republican morality among the population.

Théophilanthropie, it should be emphasized, was not the first or only moment of interest in creating a civil religion during the Revolution. The establishment of a civil religion had been championed within the *Cercle Social* and by Volney in his famous *Catéchisme du citoyen* of 1793.[89] Later, in 1798–99, the political philosopher Germaine de Staël and the historian Jean de Sales both argued that the republic, as a form of government, needed a civil religion.[90] Moreover, the attempt to establish a constitutional church in the Revolution's early years was, in a sense, an attempt at establishing a civil religion, as was the more infamous cult of reason and the cult of the Supreme Being. More broadly, the institution of revolutionary festivals constituted a form of civil religion as well—as Mona Ozouf has so brilliantly argued.[91]

Festivals were an omnipresent feature of the post-Terror political and cultural scene and were repeatedly extolled by the Thermidorian and Directorial elites for their ability to promote public virtue and social

87. Rousseau is normally credited with coining the term "civil religion" in *The Social Contract* (chap. 8, bk. 4), but the institution had been supported by a number of early modern republicans. For a recent concise overview of early modern interest in civil religion, see Jeffrey R. Collins, *The Allegiance of Thomas Hobbes* (Oxford, 2005), 36–57.

88. Ginguené referred to Montesquieu's "Dissertation sur la politique des Romains dans la religion" in a review of the newly published *Oeuvres posthumes de Montesquieu* (Paris, 1797), in *La Décade philosophique,* 10 Nivôse, Year 6 (30 December 1797), 30.

89. Gary Kates, *The Cercle Social, the Girondins and the French Revolution* (Princeton, 1985), 100ff.

90. Germaine de Staël, *Des circonstances actuelles,* 222–38; Jean-Baptiste-Claude Delisle de Sales, *J. de Sales, membre de l'Institut national, au Gouvernement provisoire chargé de préparer la liberté de la France et la paix de l'Europe* (Paris, 1799).

91. Ozouf, *Festivals and the French Revolution,* trans. Alan Sheridan (Cambridge, Mass., 1988). The French title of Ozouf's classic study is *La fête révolutionnaire,* which highlights her argument more directly.

cohesion.[92] In the words of the Constitution of the Year III, they would "attach citizens to the Constitution, to the patrie, and to the laws."[93] Chénier went so far as to criticize Robespierre for neglecting the importance of festivals.[94] There was a cycle of ten official festivals per year during the Directory, celebrating such themes as agriculture, youth, old age, the foundation of the Republic, and the execution of Louis XVI, and composed of "patriotic songs," "discourses on the morality of the citizen," banquets, games, and the dispensation of awards.[95] In addition, there were festivals every *décade* (the tenth day of the republican calendar).[96] Festivals were deeply political events, as Minister of the Interior Benézech made abundantly clear in a notice sent throughout the federal administration in March of 1797 reminding its agents of the "importance the government attaches to festivals." Festivals play a vital role in the republican order, he explained while quoting the constitution, because they "promote fraternity among citizens and attach them to the patrie and to the laws." Benézech concluded his notice with the exclamation, "We will never forget the influence of political institutions on the moeurs and the spirit of peoples. It is moeurs that most strongly attach men to the patrie, that immortalize, so to speak, the existence of political principles."[97] Festivals were thus to reform the population's moeurs and deepen the republic's foundations. The institution of revolutionary festivals was both a version of a civil religion and a template for the théophilanthropie movement.

The fullest—and most idiosyncratic—of the théophilanthropie movement's predecessors was perhaps the program sketched in several works by François Lanthenas, an associate of Thomas Paine and a deputy to the National Convention and then the Council of Five Hundred. Lanthenas

92. E.g., J. M. Coupé, *Des Fêtes en politique et en morale, par J. M. Coupé (de l'Oise), membre du Conseil des Cinq-Cents* (Paris, n.d.); and [C. A. de Moy], *Des fêtes, ou quelques idées d'un Cen Français, relativement aux fêtes publiques et à un culte national* (Paris, 1799).

93. Jacques Godechot, ed., *Les constitutions de la France depuis 1789* (Paris, 1979), 133–34.

94. *Archives parlementaires,* 98:112.

95. Daunou, "Rapport sur l'instruction publique," 511.

96. While the *fête décadaire* had been established earlier, it was largely unenforced until after the coup of 18 Fructidor in September 1797. See Woloch, "'Republican Institutions,' 1797–1799"; and Mathiez, *La Théophilanthropie et le culte décadaire.*

97. Benézech, *Instruction sur la célébration des fêtes nationales, adressées par le Ministre de l'Intérieur aux Commissaires du Pouvoir exécutif près des Administrations départmentales et municipales* (Toulouse, 1797), 8. Quoted in part in epigraph to chapter.

argued throughout the Revolution that the government should legislate public morality and to accomplish this goal should establish a civil religion. He claimed that only a "purely civic declaration of faith" that prescribed "public morality and duties" could restrain people's "vices and passions," "ensure harmony in the Republic," and guarantee that there would be no conflict between public and private.[98] Lanthenas buttressed his argument with citations from Rousseau and claimed to have distilled a republican essence from a range of religious and philosophical systems, which, in turn, he advocated turning into an official republican morality and civil religion. Lanthenas's proposals, made to the National Convention in 1795 and discussed (in a later version) in the Class of Moral and Political Sciences at the National Institute in 1797, can be viewed as something of a precursor to the théophilanthropie movement that took off in 1797.[99]

Théophilanthropie was transformed from a minor, somewhat bizarre movement into a politically charged, somewhat bizarre potential civil religion when La Révellière-Lépeaux, the president of the Executive Directory and a member of the National Institute's Class of Moral and Political Sciences, delivered a speech to the class on 1 May 1797 titled *Reflections on Religion, Civil Ceremonies, and National Festivals.* La Révellière-Lépeaux did not openly mention théophilanthropie, but his address was unmistakably about the new religion.[100] Within the Executive Directory, he had advocated the Republic's adopting a civil religion on several occasions and in fact had proposed to the Executive Directory just days before his speech that they support the théophilanthropie movement.[101] The central

98. F. Lanthenas, *Nouvelle déclaration de la morale républicaine, ou des devoirs de l'homme et du citoyen; objet constitutionnel; et projet de loi pour la promulger & lier par elle les opinions réligieuses & les cultes au soutien de la République* (Paris, 1795), 4, 7–8, 36–37.

99. His "On civil religion in a representative government" was discussed on 12 Brumaire, Year 6 (2 November 1797), before publication as *Religion civile proposée aux républiques pour lien des gouvernemens répresentatifs* (Paris, 1798). AI, SMP, A1.

100. La Révellière-Lépeaux later claimed that the théophilanthropists adopted the ideas he spelled out in this piece. *Mémoires de Larevellière-Lépeaux, publiés par son fils,* 3 vols. (Paris, 1895), 2:166–67. However, Georgia Robison points out, many of the ideas he put forward appeared in the *Manuel des théoanthropophiles* of September 1796. *Revelliere-Lepeaux, Citizen Director, 1753–1824* (New York, 1938), 169–70.

101. Mathiez, *La Théophilanthropie et le culte décadaire,* 137; Georges Lefebvre, *La France sous le Directoire, 1795–1799,* 2d ed. (Paris, 1984), 553–54. Barras later claimed that on 21 April La Révellière-Lépeaux stated to the Directory that he was the founder of théophilanthropie and "asked us to take part in his creative work." *Memoirs of Barras, Member of the Directorate,* trans.

idea of La Révellière-Lépeaux's *Reflections* was that "institutions are the surest support of constitutions and should be perfectly coordinated with them." He pointed to three institutions in particular—"religious practice, civil ceremonies, and national festivals"—all of which needed to be mobilized and carefully coordinated so that "all advance toward a common goal, the preservation of moeurs and the maintenance of the republic." La Révellière-Lépeaux devoted the most time to "religious practice," which he claimed to be necessary to ensure public morality in a republic. He advanced his argument in thoroughly elitist terms, which merit an extended citation:

> You cannot inculcate moral principles in the people, in their ideas or in their practice, without some form of dogma and some form of external rite.... A man who has received a carefully thought-out education, who has grown accustomed to reflection, who has drawn from his studies and from his life experience certain ideas of propriety and a well-reasoned love of order, can practice all the social virtues without religion. But that is not true of a people.... The multitude cannot elevate itself to these ideas of order and propriety.... It is necessary to give a people support, a dogma or two to serve as the basis of its morality, and rites to direct its application or at least serve as a reminder.[102]

La Révellière-Lépeaux continued in this same vein and addressed the second two institutions in the title of his speech, civil ceremonies and national festivals. Civil ceremonies, he argued, should be marked by the state because "is it not in the domestic affections that the germ of benevolence forms and develops? And the ties that unite the different members of the family, are these not the model and the spirit of those that bind society?" In other words, La Révellière-Lépeaux argued for the importance of intermingling the private and public virtues in order to cultivate the latter. Finally, he spoke of festivals, to which he assigned a thoroughly political purpose. "The goal of festivals should be to show man in his

---

Charles E. Roche, 4 vols. (London, 1895–96), 2:494. La Révellière-Lépeaux, however, claimed that he did not propose support for théophilanthropie to the Directory until after his address. *Mémoires,* 2:166–67.

102. La Révellière-Lépeaux, *Réflexions sur le culte, sur les cérémonies civiles et sur les fêtes nationales* (Paris, 1797), 3–5.

connection with the patrie, seen in its entirety, and, so to speak, in an abstract manner." While La Révellière-Lépeaux was careful to respect the constitutional interdiction against an official state religion established in the Constitution of the Year III (which he had helped draft), he suggestively pointed to Calvinism as a positive example of the type of regime he had in mind. "You will find in the Calvinist countries happier households, women who are more chaste and frugal, husbands who are more tender and harder-working, children who are more beloved and more respectful,... much more public spirit and a genuine love of the patrie."[103] The reference to Calvinism is especially significant. Chemin-Dupontès had pointed to the similarities between théophilanthropie and the "sects of the Reformation," which he considered the second stage of Christian history—with théophilanthropie the third.[104] If La Révellière-Lépeaux's France was not to be Calvin's Geneva, it would nonetheless be a state with a strong civil religion—namely, théophilanthropie—vigorously inculcating a virtuous republican morality.

La Révellière-Lépeaux's proselytizing for théophilanthropie coincided with a legislative campaign to establish a civil religion undertaken by his childhood friend and the future president of the Council of Five Hundred, Jean-Baptiste Leclerc. On 26 August 1797, Leclerc proposed in the Council that the government establish a civil religion.[105] Describing civil religion as "the inalterable basis of public morality," he argued that one needed to be established in coordination with public instruction as well as the more general "political and moral organization of civil institutions."[106] The historian Jean-René Suratteau argues that Leclerc's speech "paraphrased the *Manuel des théophilanthropes,*"[107] a judgment also reached by several deputies who took his motion to be a covert attempt to establish théophilanthropie as the official state religion. Indeed, LeClerc and La Révellière-Lépeaux seemed to be working in tandem. Shortly after, in January of 1798, the

103. Ibid., 22–25, 33, 13–14, 10.

104. Chemin-Dupontès, *Qu'est-ce que la théophilanthropie?* (Paris, 1801), 26–27, 31, 36–37. See also, Mathiez, *La Théophilanthropie et le culte décadaire,* 84.

105. Jean-Baptiste Leclerc, *Motion d'ordre, par J. B. Leclerc (de Maine-&-Loire) sur l'existence & l'utilité d'une religion civile en France* (Paris, 1797), reprinted with a fictional dialogue at the front and back as Leclerc, *Discours sur l'existence et l'utilité d'une religion civile en France* (Paris, 1797).

106. Leclerc, *Discours sur l'existence et l'utilité d'une religion civile en France,* 13, 24.

107. Jean-René Suratteau, "Le Directoire avait-il une politique religieuse?" *Annales historiques de la Révolution française* 283 (1991): 89–90.

publisher Henri Jansen published a volume titled *Moral Opuscules of L. M. Révellière-Lépeaux and J. B. Leclerc* containing their most important tracts and speeches preceded by an epigraph that read, "The same principles, same views, [and] same sentiments have united them from their youth by bonds of friendship that only death will be able to break."[108] La Révellière-Lépeaux's and Leclerc's campaign to establish a civil religion was driven by a shared anxiety about the corruption of France's moeurs—that, as La Révellière-Lépeaux would later put it, "public and private morality no longer rested on any foundation"[109]—and about the inherent fragility of republican forms of government. The decline of the republic, they felt, could be staved off only by a republican civil religion.

Théophilanthropie assumed a markedly greater role in French political and cultural life following the coup of 18 Fructidor on 4 September 1797, carried out by the Executive Directory and led by La Révellière-Lépeaux. While théophilanthropie's star was already on the ascent, the coup provided a decisive opportunity for both implementation and radicalization amid a wide range of forceful government actions. As mentioned earlier, a Commission on Republican Institutions was created the day after the coup and seventy-four royalist journals were closed. It was decreed that new deputies to the two councils would be required to "swear an oath of hatred of royalty and of anarchy, and of loyalty to the Republic and the Constitution of the Year III."[110] The Catholic Church was especially targeted, and priests who refused to take a newly decreed oath of "hatred of royalty and of anarchy" were exiled. The Directory's actions were celebrated by republicans of all stripes, with republican journals in the center and on the left praising its decisive action. Moreover, reports Isser Woloch, the Executive Directory received hundreds of letters and petitions celebrating its accomplishment.[111] The coup of 18 Fructidor

108. La Révellière-Lépeaux and Leclerc, *Opuscules moraux de L. M. Révellière-Lépeaux et de J. B. Leclerc* (Paris, 1798). Jansen, who seems to have enjoyed official favor, had published in 1797 both Leclerc's *Discours sur l'existence et l'utilité d'une religion civile en France* and La Révellière-Lépeaux's *Réflexions sur le culte, sur les cérémonies civiles et sur les fêtes nationales.* On Jansen, see Hesse, *Publishing and Cultural Politics,* 192.

109. *Mémoires,* 2:158.

110. "Loi du 19 fructidor contenant différentes mesures de sûreté publique," in *Les procès-verbaux du Directoire exécutif, an V–an VIII,* vol. 2, *11 prairial–5e complémentaire an V [30 mai–21 septembre 1797],* ed. Pierre-Dominique Cheynet (Paris, 2001), 215–17.

111. Woloch, *Jacobin Legacy,* 77.

reconfigured the political playing field and opened the door to a revitalized republican center, which, more than ever, saw its task as remaking France's moeurs. It was in just this context that, according to Mathiez, "the théophilanthropists were openly protected, received subventions, and had their books appear in the program of the state schools."[112]

The republican center's renewed drive to reform France's moeurs stemmed from a widely felt sense that the royalists' electoral success was due to the population's lingering prerevolutionary, and hence royalist, moeurs. A number of commentators and politicians called for heightened didactic programs as immunization against a possible recurrence. Benjamin Constant, in the above-quoted speech to the *Cercle constitutionnel* that was reprinted with a government subvention, proclaimed the coup a great victory for "principles and patriotism" against the counterrevolution and offered a highly cultural analysis of the problems facing the republic while demanding an unforgiving response. "Two nations share French soil, that of free men and that of slaves." As a result, he argued, France needed a strong central government that would wield the sword of justice. "We should not confuse impartiality with justice. Justice is a duty of the government, impartiality is only madness and a crime. To make liberty advance, it is necessary to be biased toward liberty." Constant called for a robust cultural program to reverse "1400 years of monarchy" and counter the influence of the aristocracy, to prevent the aristocracy from "mixing with our austere and male ways the dangerous softness of feminine ways and corrupting refinements." As an antidote, and sounding one of the Revolution's most tried-and-true themes, he recommended programs such as "republican festivals" to reinforce the "austere duties" of the citizen.[113] The important centrist journal *Le Conservateur,* edited by Garat, Daunou, and Chénier, praised Constant's speech and repeated many of the same themes, also pointing to the problem of moeurs and similarly calling for an activist didactic program. "Almost everywhere ideas, manners, and moeurs were royalist," warned the pages of *Le Conservateur.* "A great act of strength and a victory are not enough to render moeurs,

112. Mathiez, *La Théophilanthropie et le culte décadaire,* 196. Covert support and subsidies had actually commenced before the coup. See La Révellière-Lépeaux, *Mémoires,* 2:166–67.

113. Constant, *Discours prononcé au cercle constitutionnel,* 6–7, 10–13, 16.

manners, and ideas republican."[114] Moreover, and most important, the official pronouncement of the Executive Directory, dated a few days before Constant's speech and signed by La Révellière-Lépeaux, itself echoed exactly such themes. Its official statement referred to the pernicious effects of lingering royalist moeurs and the importance of inculcating virtue in a republic.

> Remember the principles that your immortal Montesquieu assigns to the three governments.... The basis of republics, their essence, is virtue.
>
> People of France, see by this word what your constitution, your government, your patrie requires of you today. Do not make others say, and do not say yourself, that you are not republican because virtue is the basis of republics.... People of France, be virtuous, love your constitution, your government, your patrie; and you will be republican and nothing will equal your glory and your happiness.[115]

It was exactly this heightened clamor for cultural solutions to France's political problems that provided the context for théophilanthropie's ascent to quasi-official status under La Révellière-Lépeaux's aegis. In the wake of the coup, La Révellière-Lépeaux delivered a flurry of speeches calling for the reform of the nation's moeurs, all of which strongly echoed the principal themes of théophilanthropie—so much so that he was given the epithet "the pope of the republic."[116] For La Révellière-Lépeaux the only

114. "Nouvelles Intérieures," *Le Conservateur,* 1er and 2eme jour complémentaire, Year 5 (17 and 18 September 1797), 141 (the pagination in the journal repeats from 17 to 18 September; the relevant citations are on p. 141 for both dates). There is good reason to believe that *Le Conservateur* was a quasi-official journal. Its first issue appeared just days before the coup, suggesting that its founding may have been related to the preparation of the coup, and a letter from Laran of the Bureau politique to Merlin de Douai of the Executive Directory praised the journal for its role in consolidating the coup. Laran to Merlin, 26 Ventôse, Year 6 (16 March 1798), AN, AF III 45, d. 162, p. 101. More generally, the journal hewed closely to the official line of the Directory and was directly subsidized by the Bureau politique (subvention records can be found in ibid., p. 98 and 99). In addition, Laurence Stoll has discovered that the journal published fourteen articles planted by the Bureau politique in the winter of 1797–98. "The *Bureau Politique* and the Management of the Popular Press," 79.

115. La Révellière-Lépeaux, *Extrait des registres des délibérations du Directoire exécutif du 23 Fructidor, an 5* (Paris, 1797), 7–8. The use of the word *patrie,* rather than *nation,* in this pronouncement is significant as *patrie* carried the resonance of the classical republics. See Bell, *The Cult of the Nation in France,* 40–42, 47.

116. See La Révellière-Lépeaux, *Mémoires,* 2:165–66; and Robison, *Revelliere-Lepeaux,* 162.

way to save the Republic was to embark on what might be called a "cultural Fructidor."[117] As he put it in an essay on festivals, "it is of the utmost importance to put to use all that can change, so to speak, the substance of man so as to identify him with the form of government and to make the love of liberty his dominant passion."[118] Or, as he explained in another treatise, "A good administration is not enough to attach someone exclusively to republican government: it is necessary to form a public spirit, to put citizens in harmony with the laws. Thus the need to swiftly create institutions that seize man in all periods, ... in all moments, of his public and his private life."[119] The result of such a program, in La Révellière-Lépeaux's eyes, would be a nation in which the private, domestic virtues were encouraged so that they would reinforce the public ones. "Public virtues," he wrote elsewhere, "have no more solid base than domestic moeurs."[120] Only then would the people be good republicans, attached to the patrie.

To accomplish this goal, La Révellière-Lépeaux proposed that the government use a program of emotive stimuli to play on peoples' affective sentiments. He highlighted especially the construction of a Pantheon in the woods outside Paris, a national theater, and a program of "dramatic institutions whose style and scope serve to maintain the principles of morality and of republicanism."[121] The "dramatic institutions" were to be plays with squarely republican morals and civic festivals. The festivals in particular would seamlessly blend the population and the patrie in a religiously constituted civic experience in which those who attended were to take part, becoming participants and not just spectators. La Révellière-Lépeaux's ideas here were deeply indebted to théophilanthropie and received further stimulation from the great success of General Hoche's public funeral on 1 October 1797.[122] After Hoche's funeral, Mathiez reports, La Révellière-Lépeaux was inspired to develop a "republican liturgy" and soon penned

117. I here duplicate Hesse's idea of a "cultural Thermidor," discussed above.

118. La Révellière-Lépeaux, *Essai sur les moyens de faire participer l'universalité des spectateurs à tout ce qui se pratique dans les fêtes nationales* (Paris, 1797), 5–6.

119. La Révellière-Lépeaux, *Du Panthéon et d'un Théatre national* (Paris, 1797), 5.

120. "Fragments," n.d., Louis-Marie de La Révellière-Lépeaux Papers, Beinecke Rare Book and Manuscript Library, Yale University, box 3, folder 168.

121. La Révellière-Lépeaux, *Du Panthéon et d'un Théatre national,* 12.

122. La Révellière-Lépeaux, *Discours prononcé à la cérémonie funèbre exécutée en mémoire du général Hoche* (Paris, 1797).

his essay on spectator participation in festivals.[123] The latter text, as Mona Ozouf argues, put forward an essentially Rousseauian, and indeed almost Robespierrist, idea of the civic festival.[124] The extent to which this was informed by the blending of the religious and the civic is symbolized in the (literal) centerpiece of La Révellière-Lépeaux's festival: an "altar of the patrie" around which the festivals would physically revolve. "I strongly insist on the name altar of the patrie," he wrote. "This word bears an idea at once religious and civic that should, in my opinion, characterize these sorts of institutions if one wants them to produce effects as extensive as they are salutary."[125] La Révellière-Lépeaux's "altar of the patrie" embodied the thorough amalgamation of the religious and the civic that underpinned not only his festivals but the entire théophilanthropie movement.

The short history of théophilanthropie, especially after the coup of 18 Fructidor, shows just how seriously certain figures in the republican center flirted with the idea of establishing a civil religion. La Révellière-Lépeaux was the central figure in this endeavor, but he was not alone. While théophilanthropie waned quickly and even at its zenith never really spread beyond Paris, where it was limited to rather small, elite-based circles, the fact that leading members of the republican center backed it so fervently highlights the depth of their engagement with the problem of reforming France's moeurs. Théophilanthropie amounted to an attempt to stave off the corruption of the republic by instilling republican moeurs.

"The Most Effective Institutions to Establish the Morality of a People"

The effort to reform the nation's moeurs embodied in ventures such as reforming public instruction and establishing a civil religion was vigorously theorized by France's intellectual elites throughout Thermidor and the Directory. The Class of Moral and Political Sciences at the National Institute, for example, regularly read papers and heard reports about the

123. Mathiez, *La Théophilanthropie et le culte décadaire,* 192.

124. Ozouf, *Festivals and the French Revolution,* 123.

125. La Révellière-Lépeaux, *Essai sur les moyens de faire participer l'universalité des spectateurs,* 23, n. 1.

problem of moeurs. One of the most interesting examples of this ongoing intellectual enterprise was a prize contest the class launched in the summer of 1797 asking respondents to answer the question, "What are the most effective institutions to establish the morality of a people?" after initially considering the more specific, "After political revolutions, what are the most appropriate means to restore a people to the principles of ethics?"[126] Then, in June of 1798, the class decided to reopen the contest with the rather different wording, "What are the most suitable institutions to give man in society habits capable of making him happy? Discuss the nature of habit."[127] Despite the change in wording, the class clearly still envisioned the question as addressing the problem of how to establish morality among the population.[128] "The idea of morality and the idea of happiness," Ginguené explained in his final report on the contest, "are interconnected in a well-ordered society."[129] The question, in both its permutations, was clearly packed with political meaning. The historian Martyn Lyons has even interpreted the contest as a maneuver in the wider "quest for a Republican civil religion" during the Directory.[130] The members of the class who analyzed the responses included some of the leading figures in the republican center. At various junctures, Creuzé-Latouche, Roederer, Baudin des Ardennes, Grégoire, Dupont, Daunou, and Ginguené all participated.[131] As discussed above, the National Institute was a highly political institution. Its prize contests were meant both to promote public debate on fundamental issues and to collect

126. 7 Messidor, Year 5 (25 June 1797), AI, SMP, A1. Because of a transcription error of some kind, the contest was actually announced as "What are the most effective means to establish the morality of a people?" and then quickly changed back to "most effective institutions." *La Décade philosophique,* 20 Messidor, Year 5 (8 July 1797), 106; and 30 Frimaire, Year 6 (20 December 1797), 534–37. Ginguené, "Rapport fait à la classe des Sciences morales et politiques de l'Institut national, sur les mémoires envoyés au concours pour le prix de morale, qui devait être distribué dans la séance publique du 15 Nivôse, an 8," AI, SMP, B4. Ginguené's report was delivered on 7 Nivôse, Year 8 (28 December 1799). AI, SMP, A2.

127. 27 Prairial, Year 6 (15 June 1798), AI, SMP, A1.

128. The leading historian of the prize contests, Martin Staum, treats the two questions as forming a seamless whole in "The Enlightenment Transformed: The Institute Prize Contests," *Eighteenth-Century Studies* 19 (1985–86): 153–79, esp. 156–63.

129. Ginguené, "Rapport."

130. Martyn Lyons, *France Under the Directory* (Cambridge, 1975), 110–11.

131. 22 Germinal, Year 6 (April 11 1798) and 7 Fructidor, Year 6 (24 August 1798), AI, SMP, A1; 17 Vendémiaire, Year 8 (9 October 1799), AI, SMP, A2.

concrete suggestions for the formulation of policy. The question on "the most effective institutions to establish the morality of a people" asked, in essence, what was the best way to republicanize the moeurs of France's population.

The class launched the contest in the hope that it would receive both "general principles" and "positive and practical suggestions." Toward this end, an official explication of the question published by Roederer in *La Décade philosophique* explained that contestants should focus on "moral institutions," specifically "public instruction," "monuments and national ceremonies," and "domestic institutions." Roederer dwelled longest on the category of domestic institutions, observing that "perhaps a nation survives as much by domestic habits as by its laws and magistrates." He repeated a familiar trope in citing "the ancient legislators," specifically Lycurgus, Moses, and Confucius, who all "subjected all the details of private life to the law,... moeurs and manners were all regulated, ordered."[132] Institutions that promoted private virtues, in other words, would stand as key pillars of public morality. Contestants were thus invited to prescribe a far-reaching set of "moral institutions" that could even reach into the domestic sphere. The effort to reform France's moeurs, it was clear, should leave no stone unturned. Indeed, in his report to the class on the first round of the contest, Roederer criticized an essay he deemed one of the three best submitted for not reaching far enough in its didactic prescriptions, for "stating that if there is a good government, any institution specially consecrated to morality is superfluous. This conclusion appears too absolute." Rather, Roederer argued, "moral institutions... are extremely useful for establishing the morality of [even] a well-governed people. If they only served to facilitate the work of the government, that would be an important enough service. And if it were true that a good constitution suffices to eventually establish perfect moeurs, it is no less true that a constitution might have need of good moeurs to establish itself."[133] The Class of Moral and Political Sciences clearly believed that the state needed to legislate public morality

132. Pierre-Louis Roederer, "Précis des Observations sur la Question proposé par l'Institut national pour le sujet du premier prix de la Classe des Sciences Morales et Politiques," *La Décade philosophique,* 30 Frimaire, Year 6 (20 December 1797), 535.

133. Roederer, report to the Class of Moral and Political Sciences, n.d., AN, 29 AP 111, f. 261–63.

and adopt an aggressive set of didactic programs to accomplish this program. In fact, the broad scope Roederer encouraged was later criticized for not being capacious enough. Ginguené, in his final report to the class on the contest, lamented that Roederer had neglected the importance of specifically political institutions, notably the constitution itself. He explained that "there can be good civil and, especially, domestic and moral institutions only when the larger framework in which they are placed is itself a good institution. This amounts to saying that the best moral institutions presuppose the best political constitution, or that the best of political constitutions is that in which the best moral institutions fit most perfectly and develop the most fruitfully.... The political institution most favorable to sound morality is a republican constitution."[134]

The different phases of the contest attracted a total of twenty-four respondents, offering a wide range of proposals.[135] Two-thirds of the essays submitted recommended festivals of some kind and one-half called for boards of public censors. "Most contestants," reports Martin Staum, "chose as 'moralizing' institutions the now familiar ritual of public festivals and an unprecedented system of boards of censors to help monitor and control behavior.... Imbued with images of Roman virtue, many authors concluded that censors would enable republican France to achieve the moral grandeur of republican Rome."[136] Perhaps not surprisingly for a contest on public morality, seemingly all sounded such classical-republican notes. One of three singled out for distinction stressed the importance of "the study of Latin," and of education more generally, for forming the citizenry. Latin, the author noted, was "one of the great means to propagate republican spirit.... The study of Cicero, Titus Livy, Tacitus, Seneca, etc., introduced among us the spirit of liberty." Another deemed worthy of distinction stipulated that "without virtue there is no liberty, only a change in master.... Vices are for arbitrary power, virtue alone for the Republic." A third submission captured perfectly the two temporal registers of the

134. Ginguené, "Rapport."

135. The essays can be found in the archives of the National Institute: "Concours–Manuscrits et Rapports des sciences morales et politiques: Institutions propres à fonder la morale d'un peuple," AI, SMP, B4. Detailed summaries prepared by Roederer at the end of the first round can be found in Roederer's papers at the French National Archives, AN, 29 AP 111, f. 265–369. Quotations in this paragraph are from Roederer's summaries.

136. Staum, "The Enlightenment Transformed," 159–60.

Directorial didactic projects in stating, "The French Republic needs republican morality, morality must mirror the state of the government.... Two institutions suffice: censors and education. The first takes responsibility for men today, the second for men tomorrow."[137] Of the twenty-four respondents, the two most prominent by far were Antoine-Louis-Claude Destutt de Tracy and Jean-Baptiste Say. Destutt de Tracy's submission was a somewhat rambling essay titled simply *What Are the Means to Establish the Morality of a People?* that in the eyes of the class did not even merit a special mention.[138] Say's submission, which went on to become his first substantial published work, earned the contest's Second Honorable Mention.

Submitted in 1799 and then published in 1800 with a new preface after Bonaparte had come to power, Say's *Olbie, or an Essay on the Means of Reforming the Moeurs of a Nation,* is a highly idiosyncratic fictional account of a "land named Olbios, or Olbie in French," and its purported inhabitants, "the Olbiens."[139] Written in the style of the great utopias, such as More's *Utopia* or, closer to home, his contemporary Louis-Sébastien Mercier's *The Year 2440: A Dream If There Ever Was One,* Say's treatise presented a template for a thoroughgoing reform of France's moeurs. The equation of Olbie and revolutionary France was unmistakable. Olbie was "a society that established its political liberty on the ruins of an absolute monarchy" through a great political revolution.[140] The transparent allegory with France suggests another model, Harrington's *Oceana,* a text that similarly straddled the genres of utopia and political philosophy and had been translated into French in 1795.[141] Moreover, like Harington's *Oceana,* Say's *Olbie* was structured by classical-republican concerns and themes.

137. Roederer, summaries of *mémoires* 6, 9, and 13, n.d., AN, 29 AP 111, f. 293–95, 317, 351–53.

138. [Antoine-Louis-Claude Destutt de Tracy], *Quels sont les moyens de fonder la morale chez un peuple? par le Cit. D. T**** (Paris, 1798). The heart of Destutt de Tracy's argument was that "legislators and government are the true tutors [*précepteurs*] of the mass of humanity, the only ones whose lessons will be effective. Moral instruction above all, one cannot repeat it too often, lies entirely in legislative and administrative action" (22).

139. Jean-Baptiste Say, *Olbie, ou essai sur les moyens de réformer les moeurs d'une nation* (Paris, 1800). The manuscript submitted can be found in AI, SMP, B4, mémoire 7.

140. Say, *Olbie,* 20.

141. I thank Dan Edelstein for pointing out the parallel between the two texts. James Harrington, *Oeuvres politiques, contenant la République d'Océania, les Aphorismes et les autres traités du même auteur,* 3 vols. (Paris, Year 3); Harrington, *Aphorismes politiques de Harrington* (Paris, Year 3).

In fact, *Olbie* is best read as a classical republican utopia that encapsulates the wider post-Terror discourse of moeurs.[142]

The central problem of *Olbie* is how a people's moeurs can be shaped by its government. Say defined moeurs as "the constant habits of a person or of a nation in the conduct of its life," and left no doubt that he took the reform of France's moeurs to be an issue of the utmost importance.[143] He praised the contest's question as "one of the best that any learned society has ever proposed," although in the manuscript version of the text he lamented the class's decision to encourage the analysis of strictly moral institutions at the expense of political institutions.[144] Indeed, his commitment to mobilizing the broadest possible range of institutions in the service of moral reform was such that he decided to answer "the spirit rather than the letter of the program" and discussed at length "political institutions."[145] Say insisted on the practical nature of his 140-page pamphlet, stating that "my principal aim in writing this work is to make myself useful," and declared his hope that "the leaders of the nation, on whom its institutions depend, have a firm will to regenerate the moeurs of their fellow citizens."[146]

The history of the land of Olbie as told by Say proves the importance of moeurs for republican government. Olbie underwent a political revolution that remained incomplete until followed by a comparable cultural revolution—Olbie "arrived at consolidating its edifice of liberty only by completely changing its moeurs, or, if you like, its habits." In fact, wrote Say, "the greatest revolutions are not political revolutions.... A revolution in political institutions has never been consolidated unless there has been at the same time a revolution in moral habits." The problem Olbie had faced was the persistence of prerevolutionary, monarchical moeurs, which were antithetical to the newly acquired political liberty. The fate of the French Revolution, Say was clearly saying, depended on an equally complete

142. Compare with Michael Sonenscher's recent reading of *Olbie,* which emphasizes the theory of political economy outlined in the text, *Before the Deluge: Public Debt, Inequality, and the Intellectual Origins of the French Revolution* (Princeton, 2007), 334–39; and Whatmore, *Republicanism and the French Revolution,* 126–29.

143. *Olbie,* 1.

144. Ibid., v–vi; Say, untitled manuscript of *Olbie,* n.d., AI, SMP, B4, mémoire 7.

145. Say, untitled manuscript of *Olbie,* n.d., AI, SMP, B4, mémoire 7.

146. *Olbie,* ix, 21.

reform of France's moeurs. "We must hurry to reform those aspects of our customs that tend to corrupt our moeurs. It is a question for us of surviving or perishing because a republic without republican moeurs will not survive." Crucially, though, Say argued not only that republics depend on republican moeurs but that a republic is the best type of government for promoting virtue among the population. "To reform the moral behavior of a people, there is no better institution than a Republic. . . . The establishment of a republican government is favorable to the purity of moeurs." For Say, in other words, the issue at hand was not only the importance of reforming moeurs for the health of the republic but the converse as well: the moral virtue of the population depended on the successful establishment of republican government.[147]

The fundamental dynamic in Say's narrative of Olbie's quest to republicanize its moeurs is the conflict between virtue and corruption. Throughout *Olbie,* the specter of corruption threatens to undermine the republic's moeurs and therefore the republic itself. In this regard, Say's *Olbie* can be read as squarely within the classical-republican idiom, or at least as reproducing perhaps the central anxiety of classical republicanism's long history—the threat posed to republics by corruption.[148] As a remedy, and also sounding classical-republican themes, Say urged vigorous legislative action to inculcate virtue in the population and placed great emphasis on the figure of the founding legislator. "Virtue or corruption," he stated simply, "springs from the summit of power."[149] In the epigraph used for the manuscript submitted (but not the printed version), Say chose a quote from Montesquieu's *The Greatness of the Romans and Their Decline* that similarly emphasized the role of the founding legislator and the profound importance of the institutions created: "When societies are born, it is the leaders of republics that create the institutions; afterward, it is the institutions that make the leaders of republics."[150]

147. Ibid., 20, 97, 22, 127, 22, 98.

148. Say had pointed to the dangers corruption posed to republics in his articles in *La Décade philosophique* throughout the Directory. Whatmore, *Republicanism and the French Revolution,* 118.

149. Say, *Olbie,* 6.

150. Say, untitled manuscript of *Olbie,* n.d., AI, SMP, B4, mémoire 7. The quote from Montesquieu's *Romans* can be found in Charles-Louis de Secondat, baron de Montesquieu, *Considérations sur les causes de la grandeur des Romains et de leur décadence* [1734], in *Oeuvres complètes,* ed. Roger Caillois, 2 vols. (Paris, 1949–51), 2:70.

Say drew on the historical example of Lycurgus, whom he credited with shaping Sparta's moeurs. In one passage, after praising the courage of Spartan soldiers in battle, he exclaimed, quoting Rousseau's *Considerations on the Government of Poland,* "Let us do for virtue what Lycurgus did for courage and, in the words of J. J. Rousseau, 'it can open all the doors that fortune enjoys closing.'"[151] Say's image of virtue counteracting the effects of fortune is also, it bears emphasizing, highly classical republican. Further echoing the principal concerns of eighteenth-century classical republicanism, he highlighted three principal sources of corruption against which legislative initiatives should be directed: unchecked commerce, idleness, and the influence of women.

Olbie is marked by anxiety concerning the corrupting effects of commerce on a nation's moeurs, which, Say thought, would vitiate the republic's vigor and thereby jeopardize its liberty. "Among certain peoples or even the inhabitants of certain cities too addicted to commerce, any idea except getting rich is regarded as foolish, and any sacrifice of money, time, or abilities is seen as a trap.... Nations of this kind are, often quite soon, subjected, dominated, and finally overthrown by those who follow different principles." Say pointed to the new state of America, which he described as populated with hard-working and virtuous "people whose moeurs, in general, have provided the nations of Europe, even during the storms of revolution, with examples of virtue unknown to the Europeans," but he cautioned that America stood in danger of becoming corrupted by its commercial wealth. To illustrate his point, Say pointed to the demise of great commercial states such as Phoenicia, Carthage, Venice, and Holland and warned, "United States of America, guard against the general tendency of *esprits* in your beautiful republic. If what is said of you is true, you will become rich but you will not remain virtuous, and you will not long be independent and free." In a note to this warning, Say explained that "when the influence of money becomes great in a nation, and when the need to obtain it is the first of all needs, the politics of this nation become narrow, exclusive, and even barbarous and perfidious."[152] Say, however, did not believe all commerce to be evil. In the modern

151. Say, *Olbie,* 18. The quote from Rousseau can be found in *Considérations sur le gouvernement de Pologne et sur sa réformation projetée,* 3:1029.

152. Say, *Olbie,* 29–30, 19, 31, 106.

world, he thought, commerce was necessary but had to be carefully monitored and checked so that it would not pervert the republic's moeurs. Indeed, *olbios* is a Greek word "meaning the happiness that comes from a proper enjoyment of wealth."[153]

A further threat posed by commerce, in Say's eyes, was that it could lead to the excessive accumulation of wealth, which, in turn, would spawn decadence and luxury and their corrupting effects, especially idleness. Again, this smacks of classical republicanism, specifically of Harrington's idea that only a relatively equal distribution of property can undergird republican moeurs.[154] In this Harringtonian vein, Say warned about the corruption caused by poverty and also cautioned that "great wealth is no less damaging to good moral behavior." As a result, the Olbiens had passed laws prohibiting the excessive accumulation of wealth and "reducing excessive inequality of fortunes." To guard against "the evils of idleness," the Olbiens required that everyone both account for their wealth and show that they were productive with their time; if someone was too idle, he would be publicly exposed and "his name was never again recalled without the qualification *useless man.*" With his anxiety about idleness, Say entered the great eighteenth-century debate on luxury and came down squarely against it. "The leading Olbiens expressed a great contempt for luxurious display.... In Olbie, simplicity of tastes and of manners were the basis for preference and an object of respect." With "luxury attacked in its basis,... happiness increased at the same time as moeurs were reformed." Yet, as in his discussion of commerce, Say was not atavistic. "In criticizing luxury," he explained in a note, "I do not have the crazy pretension of returning man to a savage state." Say strove for a happy medium of productive work and thrift, a nation without decadence and idleness. Because it would be disastrous if commerce and wealth were to expand unchecked, "a good system of political economy" was indispensable.[155]

The steps Say prescribed to prevent idleness extended to seemingly minute details such as his recommendation that a system of hedges be used

153. Jean-Baptiste Say, *An Economist in Troubled Times: Writings selected and translated by R. R. Palmer* (Princeton, 1997), 33.

154. On Harrington, see in particular J. G. A Pocock, *The Machiavellian Moment: Florentine Political Thought and the Atlantic Republican Tradition* (Princeton, 1975).

155. Say, *Olbie,* 25, 23, 27–29, 42, 43, 123, 10.

when animals grazed so that no one would have to accompany the animals and thereby idly watch them. Say warned in particular about the idleness caused by a nation's having a standing army. He felt that a standing army was in all likelihood necessary in the modern world but was fearful of its effects on the Republic's virtue. "As long as the current political system demands a permanent standing army, even in times of peace, it is necessary to avoid the corruption that is born of the idleness of soldiers in the garrisons. The best method would be to imitate the Romans, who filled their soldiers' spare time by having them construct those useful roadways that extended to the ends of the empire, those bridges, amphitheaters, and porticos that still arouse our admiration."[156] For Say, it was imperative that every member of society engage in productive work.

The third major threat to moeurs specified by Say was women who were not properly "chaste and gentle." As Say had it, women were the fount of a nation's morality. "The Olbiens would have been poor moralists if they had not understood the great influence of women on moeurs.... [Women's] destiny is to rule us by the empire of benefits and pleasures. Where they are not virtuous it is in vain that we would want to become so. It is by the education of women that the education of men must begin." While men and women were encouraged to mix in Olbie—Say was highly critical of Plato's idea of separating the sexes in the *Republic*—there were a number of jobs and other domains not open to women. Furthermore, chastity was, for Say, the most important virtue for a woman. "A woman who is not chaste is nothing." A man who was not chaste, however, "could be an honest businessman, solid friend, good son, good brother, and, finally, a useful citizen." Because of the extreme danger posed to society by unchaste women, in Olbie there are state-run homes for single women to ensure their chastity, which women leave only when they are ready to marry. Say devoted several pages to describing such homes and left no doubt as to just how seriously he took the effects of women on a nation's moeurs.[157] Once again, Say's anxieties regarding the influence of women on the republic's moeurs and his prescriptions to control them clearly echoed the early modern classical-republican tradition.

156. Ibid., 105–6.
157. Ibid., 44, 49.

In addition to legislation aimed at countering the specific corrupting influences of unchecked commerce, idleness, and the influence of women, Say prescribed a series of more general measures designed to promote virtuous moeurs. He was adamant that this system be rigorously secular, arguing that in all of human history no religion had ever improved a people's moeurs. To achieve his goal, Say theorized two general types of institutions that paralleled exactly the two temporal registers of the post-Terror discourse of moeurs: "those that give good moeurs to people to come" and those "that can reform men who are formed." The former category fell under "education," the power of which could be learned, Say advised the reader, by studying the history of Sparta. The second category, institutions that "reform men who are formed," occupies the majority of *Olbie.* In outlining the various means employed by the government of Olbie to encourage virtuous moeurs, Say included many of the favorite institutions of the Directorial discourse of moeurs, such as didactic theater and a system of national festivals. He also called for hundreds of didactic monuments to be built throughout the country and described an institution called "relaxation societies, where all the citizens inscribed in the civic register often go in the evenings, mainly on rest days, and can even bring their families." These relaxation societies were designed to help citizens of the same canton get to know one another so that they could then make informed choices in elections. Finally, Say described a board of public censors titled the Guardians of Moeurs. Charged with judging people's behavior, the censors rendered verdicts that were public and would be preserved in two books, one titled the *Book of Merit* and the other the *Book of Condemnation.* The institution, Say explained, was modeled on homologous boards of censors in Sparta and the Roman Republic that Say credited, respectively, with "preserving the purity of Spartan moeurs" and with helping the Roman Republic to survive for three hundred years.[158] Say clearly insisted here that the contemporary world had much to gain by imitating the peoples of antiquity. Indeed, his ideal republic would closely resemble the great classical republics on a variety of fronts. Say called for a republic in which the government would actively ward off corruption by promoting virtuous moeurs among the population. The inculcation of such republican morality

158. Ibid., 3, 8, 38, 58.

was to be accomplished through the regulation of practically all aspects of life, the virtual collapsing of the private and public realms into one politicized sphere. And it was political institutions that would accomplish this project. Say believed, as he would write to Sismondi in 1807, that "It is the nature of governments that makes nations what they are."[159] Say's *Olbie,* a text strikingly indebted to the early modern classical-republican tradition, both reflected and illustrated the wider post-Terror discourse of moeurs.

* * *

The discourse of moeurs, and especially its didactic version, was a foundational language of politics and political philosophy in post-Terror France. In the eyes of men such as Daunou, La Révellière-Lépeaux, Say, and even Benjamin Constant, France was not a nation in which politics would "reflect" society and its moeurs but one in which politics and institutions would "make" the nation and reform its moeurs. These figures, and many others in the republican center, sought to end the Revolution through vigorous didactic programs designed to instill republican virtue and morality in the population.

The post-Terror discourse of moeurs was, in its essence, rooted in the early modern political language of classical republicanism. The political and intellectual elites of the republican center believed that republican morality and, specifically, republican virtue, had to be inculcated among the French population. Otherwise, they feared, the republic would become corrupt and rot from within. In addition, the discourse of moeurs echoed the elitist tendencies of classical republicanism and reinforced the broader post-Terror consolidation of political power in the hands of a circumscribed few—"the best." Both of these features of the post-Terror discourse of moeurs, and of post-Terror political culture more broadly, importantly influenced the liberal-republican political ideas so central to the genealogy of French Liberalism. The next chapter turns to two early articulations of liberal republicanism, the writings of Charles-Guillaume Théremin and Germaine de Staël.

159. Say to Sismondi, 8 February 1807; quoted in Whatmore, *Republicanism and the French Revolution,* 203, n. 54. Say would later deemphasize the imortance of government. See ibid., 200–201.

3

Liberal Republicanism during the Directory

Post-Terror France witnessed a veritable explosion of tracts, treatises, and essays reflecting on the nature of the republic as a political form. From obscure pamphlet writers such as Louis-François Cherhal Mont-Rèal to towering figures such as Jacques Necker, the proper organization of the polity was widely, fervently, discussed.[1] Pamphlets, journals, and books streamed off the presses, unpublished manuscripts were circulated, and speeches echoed through the halls of the National Institute. The Constitution of the Year III had established a new political order for the French Republic, and a host of didactic programs aimed to anchor the republic in virtuous moeurs, but the continued instability of the post-Terror years—the constitutional conflict between the Executive Directory and the two councils, ongoing international war, and the persistent threat of counterrevolution—kept

1. Louis-François Cherhal Mont-Rèal, *Gouvernement des hommes libres, ou Constitution républicaine* (Paris, 1795); Mont-Rèal, *Éloge philosophique et politique de Guillaume-Thomas Raynal* (Paris, 1796); Jacques Necker, *De la révolution française,* 2 vols. (Paris, 1797).

first-order political principles on the table. The result was a virtual torrent of political argument during the Directory. While the political language of classical republicanism predominated within the republican center, there were multiple minority currents advancing a range of political claims, from neo-Jacobin to monarchist. Among these various sets of claims, on the margins of the republican center, was an explicitly modern liberal republicanism put forward by Charles-Guillaume Théremin and Germaine de Staël. Théremin and Staël each articulated a distinctive version of liberal republicanism that called into question the foundational principles of the day's classical republicanism and sketched, however roughly, the core ideas that would later define French Liberalism in its mature form during the first half of the nineteenth century. Even as they challenged the classical-republican mainstream, however, Théremin's and Staël's respective writings were crucially inflected by the classical-republican concerns and themes that so marked the post-Terror political imagination.

Modern republicanism in the late eighteenth century could take a variety of forms and call on a host of different predecessors and sources. In its essence, however, modern republicanism was a political language centered around the deceptively simple proposition that the modern age demanded a modern version of the republic to match. The model provided by the ancients, however awe-inspiring their histories might be, was simply unsuitable to the modern world. Modern people and their politics were qualitatively different from those of classical antiquity. Modern republicans challenged in particular the notion that modern French citizens would sacrifice their private wants and desires in the name of a higher public virtue. The modern republic would have to take "modern liberty" as its first principle, and the purpose of politics would be the juridical protection of individual liberties, of civil liberty. Benjamin Constant was to give this principle its canonical expression in 1819 when he compared the liberty of the ancients to that of the moderns, but he was not the first to do so. Théremin and Staël, as well as a handful of eighteenth-century writers, had suggested essentially the same construct.[2] Post-Terror modern republicanism derived from this distinction.

2. J. G. A. Pocock suggests that the construct was first developed by Baron John Hervey's *Ancient and Modern Liberty Stated and Compared* (London, 1734). *Barbarism and Religion,* vol. 3, *The First Decline and Fall* (Cambridge, 2003), 309, n. 5.

Modern republicanism, it should be emphasized, frequently involved an act of rhetorical positioning in addition to advancing a set of political-philosophical claims. Proponents of modern liberal republicanism fashioned themselves an up-to-date alternative to antiquated ancient principles, which they linked to Jacobinism and especially to the austere republicanism of Rousseau. Modern republicans blamed the Terror on the ancient doctrines of Jacobinism and their ostensible roots in *The Social Contract,* on what they described as the attempt to impose superannuated political values on a modern nation. For example, in 1795 the journalist Adrien Lezay, a close associate of Pierre-Louis Roederer, expressed incredulity that from 1793 to 1794 "we were constantly referred back to" Rome and Athens and that "France was subjected to the regime of a Swiss canton."[3] While the disparaging label "ancient" was a rhetorical move to smear certain ideas as outdated and polluted by their association with Jacobinism, it points to the self-consciously modern stance assumed by proponents of liberal republicanism. Modern republicanism was both a political-philosophical program and an act of rhetorical positioning, even of self-fashioning.

The liberal republicanism of Théremin, Staël, and, later, Constant was but one variety of modern republicanism on offer during the late eighteenth century. The most important antecedent of post-Terror liberal republicanism was the modern republicanism of the Girondins articulated during the Revolution's early years most notably by Condorcet, Jacques-Pierre Brissot, and Jean-Marie Roland. The Girondins had advocated a "republicanism of the moderns" that, in Keith Baker's words, "was couched in the language of rights, reason, and representation; it deployed the rationalist discourse of modernity and social progress, the individualist discourse of civil society."[4] Like the Girondins before them, post-Terror liberal republicans looked to individual rights, representative government, and commercial society as the foundations of a distinctively modern republic. However, the liberal republicanism that began to take shape in the post-Terror years broke with that of the Girondins in two crucial respects.

3. Adrien Lezay, *Qu'est-ce que la constitution de 95?* (Paris, 1795), ix–x, vi.

4. Keith Michael Baker, "Transformations of Classical Republicanism in Eighteenth-Century France," *Journal of Modern History* 73 (2001): 32. See as well Gary Kates, *The Cercle Social, the Girondins, and the French Revolution* (Princeton, 1985); James Livesey, *Making Democracy in the French Revolution* (Cambridge, Mass. 2001), chaps. 1–2; Philippe Raynaud, "Y a-t-il une philosophie girondine?" in *La Gironde et les Girondins,* ed. François Furet and Mona Ozouf (Paris, 1991).

First, in comparison with the Girondins, the post-Terror liberal republicans were not as sanguine about the effects of commerce on the modern world, nor did they take commercial developments to be as fully autonomous. The nature of commercial modernity was one of the great topics of eighteenth-century writing, with authors such as Jean-François Melon celebrating the capacity of *doux commerce* to civilize Europe and bring an end to the vestiges of feudal barbarism.[5] At its most inflated, the idea of doux commerce claimed that the advent of commercial society signaled the emergence of an entirely new civilization in which the increasingly complex human interactions stemming from commerce and trade would supplant older forms of life and, ultimately, warfare. Although a heterogeneous group, the Girondins for the most part celebrated commercial modernity and advocated a version of economic liberalism that would allow commerce to develop according to its own internal dynamics.[6] While Théremin, Staël, and Constant all thought the astonishing commercial developments of the eighteenth century were both irreversible and on the whole beneficial, they took a more skeptical view of the complete package, so to speak, than did the Girondins and their eighteenth-century predecessors. Most important, the liberal republicans feared the proclivity of international trade to promote war—what Hume labeled "the jealousy of trade."[7] While Hume and others in the eighteenth century believed commerce to be inherently based on a "logic of reciprocity," Istvan Hont explains, they also feared that commercial competition might produce "a pathological conjunction between politics and the economy" that threatened to transform

5. Jean-François Melon, *Essai politique sur le commerce* (n.p., 1734). On eighteenth-century debate over commerce, see Albert O. Hirschman's classic *The Passions and the Interests: Political Arguments for Capitalism before Its Triumph* (Princeton, 1977); Catherine Larrère, *L'Invention de l'économie au XVIIIe siècle: Du droit naturel à la physiocratie* (Paris, 1992); Paul Burton Cheney, *Revolutionary Commerce: Colonial Expansion and the French Monarchy* (Cambridge, Mass., forthcoming); Istvan Hont, *Jealousy of Trade: International Competition and the Nation-State in Historical Perspective* (Cambridge, Mass., 2005); Anoush Terjanian, "*Doux commerce* and Its Discontents: Slavery, Piracy and Monopoly in Eighteenth-Century France" (PhD diss., Johns Hopkins University, 2006); John Shovlin, *The Political Economy of Virtue: Luxury, Patriotism, and the Origins of the French Revolution* (Ithaca, 2006); and Michael Sonenscher, *Before the Deluge: Public Debt, Inequality, and the Intellectual Origins of the French Revolution* (Princeton, 2007).

6. As emphasized in Shovlin, *Political Economy of Virtue,* 199–204.

7. David Hume, "Of the Jealousy of Trade" [1758], in *Hume: Political Essays,* ed. Knud Haakonssen (Cambridge, 1994). See Hont, *Jealousy of Trade,* esp. 1–37.

"the globe into a theater of perpetual commercial war."[8] Therémin and Constant shared this concern and tended to view commerce as a form of international competition rather than as a civilizing force that would weave nations closer and closer together. As Constant would put it in 1814, writing of "the age of commerce," "War and commerce are only two different means to achieve the same goal: possessing what one desires."[9] Théremin, Staël, and Constant were thus not as optimistic about the ameliorating effects of commercial modernity as their Girondin forerunners. They feared the warfare and corruption commerce might promote.

Second, and more important, Théremin, Staël, and, later, Constant, placed considerably greater emphasis on the liberty of the ancients than had the Girondins. The post-Terror liberal republicans all held that an active political life was necessary to prevent the growth of despotic central power and therefore to safeguard the liberty of the moderns. Modern liberty, they believed, could not survive without a healthy dose of ancient liberty promoted by the state. The Girondins, for their part, had been more content to let society run its natural course, with politics in a largely secondary role. While both thought the state should promote the regeneration of the nation's moeurs, the Girondin version looked, on balance, more to society and less to politics than did post-Terror liberal republicanism. To an extent, the difference on this front stemmed from an important divergence in analytic approach. The Girondins adhered to the emergent tradition of social science (indeed, Condorcet was social science's principal progenitor in France), which took social forces to have their own logic that could be understood in scientifically rational and systematic terms.[10] The point of politics, in turn, was to reflect properly analyzed social forces. Liberal republicanism, to the contrary, adhered to a less rationalist approach to political analysis and did not share the same faith that society could be understood in scientific terms. As a result, the liberal republicans were less content to treat society as a self-regulating entity and looked more to politics and institutions to promote the liberty of the ancients in order to preserve modern liberty.

8. Hont, *Jealousy of Trade,* 6.

9. Benjamin Constant, *De l'esprit de conquête et de l'usurpation dans leurs rapports avec la civilisation européenne* [1814], in *Écrits politiques,* ed. Marcel Gauchet, 2d ed. (Paris, 1997), 130.

10. See esp. Keith Michael Baker, *Condorcet: From Natural Philosophy to Social Mathematics* (Chicago, 1975).

Liberal republicans' aspiration to preserve modern liberty without abandoning "the liberty of the ancients" is precisely what made liberal republicanism a unique strand of modern republicanism and of modern liberalism more broadly. While it entailed an unambiguously modern political-philosophical stance, liberal republicanism was not willing to forgo political liberty. It was a blend of classical and modern republicanism, of a discourse of political participation and one of individual rights. In 1796, the same year Constant began to use the term "liberal" to define his political views,[11] he also emphasized the importance of public political life in his pamphlet *De la force du gouvernement actuel de la France et de la nécessité de s'y rallier (On the Strength of the Current Government and the Need to Rally around It)*. Constant applauded the energy and public-spiritedness of republican political life, which he contrasted to the torpor that resulted from excessive concern with "narrow and private" interests under monarchies, and praised "republican forms" for preserving "a sort of tradition of liberty."[12] This attempted hybrid of the two forms of liberty would not receive systematic and explicit articulation by Constant until the early nineteenth century, but the conceptual kernel was limned during the post-Terror period, largely in response to the political crises of these years, by Théremin and Staël during Thermidor and the Directory and then in Constant's *On the Possibility of a Republican Constitution in a Large Country* during the Consulate.[13] Théremin published an array of pamphlets and articles that collectively advanced a distinctively Kantian liberal republicanism grounded in commercial civilization and moral universalism. Staël, in her unpublished *Des circonstances actuelles qui peuvent terminer la Révolution et des principes que doivent fonder la République en France (On the Current Circumstances That Could End the Revolution and the Principles That Should Found the Republic in France),* spelled out the lineaments of an aristocratic liberal-republican political order. While Théremin's and Staël's respective political-philosophical programs differed on a number

11. See K. Steven Vincent, "Benjamin Constant, the French Revolution, and the Origins of French Romantic Liberalism," *French Historical Studies* 23 (2000): 607–637, esp. 622.

12. Constant, *De la force du gouvernement actuel de la France et de la nécessité de s'y rallier* [1796], in *De la force du gouvernement actuel de la France et de la nécessité de s'y rallier; Des réactions politiques; Des effets de la Terreur,* ed. Phillipe Raynaud (Paris, 1988), 71–74.

13. Constant's *Republican Constitution* is discussed in chapter 6.

of issues, the intermixture of classical-republican and liberal themes that characterized both of their writings highlights the importance of classical republicanism in the genesis of French Liberalism.[14]

A Kantian Variation: The Modern Republicanism of Charles-Guillaume Théremin

One of the most distinctive versions of modern liberal republicanism articulated during the post-Terror years was that of Charles-Guillaume Théremin. Théremin articulated a Kantian variation of liberal republicanism, which he advanced in five pamphlets and short books as well as a number of articles in the influential journal *La Décade philosophique.* His theoretical reflections covered a range of topics, from the economic foundations of the modern republic to foreign relations to the situation of women in republics. He struck his most characteristically modern notes in *De l'incompatibilité du système démagogique avec le système d'économie politique des peuples modernes (On the Incompatibility of the Demagogical System with the Political Economy of Modern Peoples),* published in 1799, which ascribed the Terror to the Jacobins' attempts to impose an outdated political vision on France's modern population—an argument that clearly foreshadowed Constant's famous analysis in his 1819 lecture "The Liberty of the Ancients Compared with That of the Moderns."[15] Théremin's political-philosophical project, however, should not be reduced to an embryonic forerunner of Benjamin Constant's mature writings. Théremin articulated a distinctive vision of the liberty of the moderns using a Kantian lexicon. His Kantian version of modern republicanism was somewhat unique in post-Terror France but constituted an important, and underappreciated,

14. It is worth noting that Théremin, Staël, and Constant were all outsiders of a sort in post-Terror France. All were Protestant, and Théremin was born in Prussia, Constant in Switzerland, and Staël in France to the Swiss-born Jacques Necker. Perhaps in part because of their status as outsiders, they all looked to political-philosophical traditions outside France's mainstream.

15. For this reason, Théremin, when he has attracted scholarly attention, is usually mentioned only parenthetically as having advanced an early version of Constant's idea of the liberty of the moderns. E.g., Pierre Rosanvallon, *La démocratie inachevée: Histoire de la souveraineté du peuple en France* (Paris, 2000), 87–88; Marcel Gauchet, *La révolution des pouvoirs: La souveraineté, le peuple, et la représentation, 1789–1799* (Paris, 1995), 181–82, n. 3.

undercurrent of French Liberalism.[16] Théremin's modern republicanism revolved around two basic propositions. First, he argued that the modern republic is fundamentally different from the classical version because of underlying changes in the economy and in people's wants and needs. Second, he advocated that women be accorded full "political existence," as he called it, in the modern republic (which was not itself a Kantian consideration but was one for which Théremin mobilized Kantian arguments). Both of these positions crucially differentiated him from the classical-republican tradition that so deeply informed post-Terror political discourse. While his political philosophy was often marked by tensions between classical-republican and liberal themes, on the whole Théremin was resolutely and explicitly a modern republican.

Théremin was born in Prussia, where he lived before coming to France in 1795 after spells in Madrid and London as a member of Prussia's diplomatic corps.[17] His ancestors were Huguenots who had fled France following the revocation of the Edict of Nantes in 1685, an identity he announced in a letter to Sieyès in the summer of 1795: "I descend from refugees from the time of the revocation of the Edict of Nantes."[18] Upon his arrival in Paris, he renounced his title at the Prussian court and, taking advantage of the revolutionary laws extending French citizenship to the descendants of Frenchmen who had emigrated for religious reasons, became a French citizen. Théremin found employment in the foreign relations section of the Committee of Public Safety and then in the Directory's Ministry of Foreign Affairs. He became a close associate of Sieyès, to whom he sent his assorted writings.[19] At one point, he even helped put Sieyès in touch

16. To my knowledge, the only references to Théremin as a Kantian are the brief comments in Alain Ruiz, "Aux origines de la légende jacobine de Kant en France: Le traité vers la paix perpétuelle traduit et commenté dans la presse parisienne en 1796," *Cahiers d'histoire littéraire comparée* 8/9 (1985): 205–15; and Ruiz, "A l'aube du Kantisme en France: Sieyès, Karl Friedrich Reinhard et le traité *Vers la paix perpétuelle* (1795–1796), avec le texte inédit de l'adaptation française du traité par Reinhard," *Cahiers d'études germaniques* 4 (1980): 147–93, and 5 (1981): 119–53. Overall, the reception of Kant's philosophy during the Revolution was rather limited. See esp. the document collection with commentary, François Azouvi and Dominique Bourel, *De Königsberg à Paris: La réception de Kant en France (1788–1804)* (Paris, 1991).

17. Alain Ruiz, "Une famille huguenote du Brandebourg au XVIIIe siècle: Les Thérémin," *Revue d'Allemagne* 14 (1982): 225–26.

18. Théremin to Sieyès, 12 Fructidor, Year 3 (29 August 1795), AN, 284 AP 17–8/10.

19. Sieyès's papers contain nearly twenty letters from Théremin written between the summer of 1795 and the winter of 1800 to 1801. In addition, the letters suggest that they saw each other on a

with Kant through his brother, a Kantian philosopher in Memel (a short distance from Kant's home in Königsberg).[20] During these years he was also actively involved with *La Décade philosophique* and published a series of political pamphlets that articulated his Kantian vision of the modern republic.

Théremin's Kantian vision centered on the promotion of the liberty of the moderns under a republican form of government and was underpinned by a faith in progress and attendant moral universalism that echoed Kant's key political writings, notably *Idea for a Universal History with a Cosmopolitan Purpose, On the Common Saying: "This May Be True in Theory, but It Does Not Apply in Practice,"* and *Perpetual Peace: A Philosophical Sketch.* While Théremin often diagnosed threats to the republic in terms redolent of classical republicanism, he took the modern world to be not only different from the ancient but superior to it. He claimed that Europe "has reached a certain stage of perfection" and witnessed such a marked progress in morality and moeurs over the centuries that "nothing proves that they [the nations of Europe] could not advance even further on the path of perfection."[21] Elsewhere, he optimistically remarked—in Kantian vocabulary—that "we are seeing universal history... unfold before our eyes."[22] Moreover, he regularly invoked the possibility of Europe's achieving an "eternal peace" that plainly paralleled Kant's vision in *Perpetual*

---

regular basis. AN, 284 AP 17–8. See also Marcelle Adler-Bresse, *Sieyès et le monde allemand,* 2 vols. (PhD diss., Université de Paris I, 1976; reproduced by Université de Lille III, 1977).

20. A philosophical correspondence between the two luminaries was proposed as Kant was informed that Sieyès considered "the study of Kant's philosophy... a complement to the Revolution." Charles-Guillaume Théremin to Antoine-Ludwig Théremin, 2 January 1796, and Antoine-Ludwig Théremin to Kant, 6 February 1796, in *Gesammelte Schriften, herausgegeben von der Königlich Preussichen Akademie der Wissenschaften,* vol. 12, *Kants Briefwechsel (1795–1803)* (Berlin, 1922), 58–60. The correspondence, however, never got off the ground in part because the potential association with one of Europe's most famous revolutionaries seems to have caused Kant trouble at home in Königsberg. In a letter Kant wrote to Antoine-Ludwig Théremin dated 9 March 1796 that Charles Théremin then translated and sent to Sieyès, Kant refers to "the rumors that have been spread... as though this correspondence should have a political subject" and, more specifically, to "the disadvantage that I would find upon entering into correspondence, in the present circumstances, with this famous man who plays one of the primary roles in the politics of the French Revolution." AN, 284 AP 17–8/8.

21. Théremin, *De la Situation intérieure de la République* (Paris, 1797), 55–56; Théremin, review of *Olbie, ou essai sur les moyens de réformer les moeurs d'une nation,* by Jean-Baptiste Say, *La Décade philosophique, littéraire et politique,* 20 Ventôse, Year 8 (11 March 1800), 477.

22. Théremin, *De la condition des femmes dans les Républiques* (Paris, 1799), 12.

Peace.[23] In more practical terms, it led him, for example, to endorse a plan to end the slave trade and establish a European colony on the African coast that would, "instead of buying them and selling them," "civilize the Africans" by teaching them "the cultivation of the earth and the principal mechanical arts."[24] Théremin's belief in human progress and moral universalism fundamentally informed all of his political-philosophical writings, crucially differentiating his thought from the classical-republican tradition.

The progress of humanity, Théremin thought, involved the establishment of the modern republic. There was no question in his mind that a republic was the best form of government.[25] Monarchy was little more than an antiquated remnant of a prior age, simply unsuitable for the modern world. As he watched the Directory lurch from one crisis to the next, Théremin devoted great intellectual energy to pondering the nature of the modern republic. In *De la Situation intérieure de la République* (*On the Republic's Domestic Situation*) he informed his readers that he was at work on a more ambitious analysis, which, however, he never completed.[26] Nonetheless, Théremin made it perfectly clear in his assorted published writings that the most important issue in his eyes was that "a modern republic" should be "adapted to our moeurs, our needs, above all our system of industry."[27] While the exact relationship between the "system of industry" and moeurs is not always precisely defined in Théremin's writings—in

23. One of the most important pieces in which Théremin elaborated his thoughts on the topic, *Des intérêts des puissances continentales relativement à l'Angleterre* (Paris, 1795), was published on 12 Thermidor, Year 3 (30 July 1795), two weeks before the original edition of Kant's *Perpetual Peace* was sent to his publisher (13 August 1795). However, many of the key ideas in Kant's *Perpetual Peace* were spelled out in his *Idea for a Universal History with a Cosmopolitan Purpose* of 1784 and, to a lesser extent, his *On the Common Saying: "This May Be True in Theory, but It Does Not Apply in Practice"* of 1793. Of course, both Kant and Théremin were in dialogue with an almost century-old idea in Europe, espoused most famously by the abbé de Saint-Pierre in his *Projet pour rendre la paix perpétuelle en Europe* of 1713 and then commented on by, among others, Montesquieu, Voltaire, Mably, and Rousseau. Théremin's formula for an "eternal peace" is discussed in detail in chapter 4.

24. Théremin, review of *Essai sur la transportation comme récompense, et la déportation comme peine,* by Charles Montlinot, *La Décade philosophique,* 10 Messidor, Year 5 (28 June 1797), 26–27.

25. E.g., Théremin, *De la Situation intérieure de la République,* 49; Théremin, *De l'incompatibilité du système démagogique avec le système d'économie politique des peuples modernes* (Paris, 1799), 11.

26. The new work was to be titled *De la Garantie de la République.* Théremin, *De la Situation intérieure de la République,* 87.

27. Théremin, *De l'incompatibilité du système démagogique,* 8–9, 15.

at least one place, he describes moeurs as almost derivative of a people's "means of subsistence"—both are nonetheless markers of "the progress of civilization toward the perfection of the species."[28] The contemporary world, with its modern economy, should have modern republics to match. A people's "means of subsistence" and its "manner of being governed," he explained, "are two different things, but there is a necessary harmony between them." France should respect this harmony and not try to imitate the classical republics, whose economies were based on slavery. He blamed the excesses of the Revolution on the radical Jacobins' attempts to impose an outdated political form on a modern economy, on "the disparity between ideas and things produced by this eruption of antiquity among us." As Théremin explained it,

> When one wants to give a new form of government to a people, it is necessary to leave untouched their way of subsisting, that is, their system of political economy. One must establish the new form of government on this system, or at least put the two in the greatest possible harmony.... The political system, as it was conceived during the Terror, was transmitted to us by different hands than was our system of political economy. In other words, the republican system, as it is generally known, comes to us from people who did not have our system of industry, that is, from the Greeks and the Romans.[29]

The reason that classical republics were not appropriate in the modern world, on Théremin's account, was that modern economic conditions had brought about fundamental changes in people's wants and needs. Older political forms, he argued, could never satisfy the desires of the modern individual. While many claimed that "it is with Roman virtue that we keep the Republic alive," Théremin responded that modern peoples do not seek "the virtues and habits of an austere and savage republic founded on poverty and a system of abnegation."[30] More specifically, moderns demanded civil liberty rather than political liberty. France's "system of industry" requires "the greatest degree of civil liberty possible" and "political liberty" only secondarily. Whereas the ancient republics had slavery so that citizens

28. Théremin, *De la condition des femmes dans les Républiques,* 34–35.
29. Théremin, *De l'incompatibilité du système démagogique,* 4, 10, 5.
30. Théremin, *De la condition des femmes dans les Républiques,* 47.

could devote themselves to public affairs, in the more civilized modern world people spent their days working and thus desired the liberty to enjoy the fruits of their labors. As a result, an entirely new calculus developed, and, as he put it, misery rather than slavery is "the great enemy of modern peoples." According to Théremin, "The ancient republics were founded against slavery and for liberty. Modern states have as their goal avoiding poverty and obtaining affluence. For people today, liberty is less a moral need than a means and an instrument for satisfying physical needs. This is not brilliant, nor is it romantic, but it is the truth and it is natural."[31] While Théremin sounded almost wistful, he was nonetheless adamant that the modern republic should reflect this sea change in people's wants and needs—that political liberty should be deemphasized in favor of private concerns arising from modern, commercial civilization. As a result, he insisted, the modern republic had to employ the representative system so that people would be unencumbered from the burdens of political life.[32]

Théremin's analysis, however, did not lead him to advance the doux commerce thesis. While he thought modern politics had to reflect the stunning transformations effected by modern commerce—and thought the arrival of commercial civilization was, on the whole, a positive development—he never celebrated commerce in an uncritical fashion. Théremin remained wary of commerce's potentially corrosive effects, especially in regard to foreign relations and the international order. Specifically, he worried about the potential inequities of commercial exchange and about the proclivity of the international commercial system to promote war. Théremin outlined these views in a polemical piece he penned on English commerce and foreign policy that claimed commercial exchange was normally peaceful but also had a latent dangerous side, especially as practiced by England. "Commerce, viewed on a large scale, has a generous character and nothing is less hostile by its nature. To prosper, it asks that everyone prospers, buyers and sellers alike, because then the one will have greater means to buy and the other more commodities to sell. But monopolistic commerce, which is

31. Théremin, *De l'incompatibilité du système démagogique,* 19–20, 14–15.

32. E.g., Théremin, "Discours sur la question: Est-il de l'interêt de la République Française de reculer ses limites jusqu'aux bords du Rhin," in *La Rive gauche du Rhin, limite de la République française, ou Recueil de plusieurs dissertations jugées dignes des prix proposés par un négociant de la rive gauche du Rhin,* ed. Georges-Guillaume Boehmer (Paris, 1795), 15, 6.

what England practices, is by its nature hostile toward all its objects and an enemy of equality. Far from a contract between equals, it is a contract between master and slave whereby the former wins everything he can and the latter loses all that can be lost. It is a commerce that deserves the name robbery." England thus practiced a monopolistic form of commerce that turned exchange into a zero-sum competition. Théremin contrasted England's monopolistic monarchical commerce with open republican commerce, writing "the commercial world is a republic" but England "makes it a monarchy." In addition, Théremin wrote, commerce as the English practiced it triggered international conflict. England "nourishes its commerce with war, and war with its commerce." He charged England with fomenting war on the European continent in order to preserve its "commercial monarchy" in Europe, which he compared to its colonial "monarchy" in the West Indies.[33] Moreover, commerce, along with "artificial" paper money, was a corrupting influence that undermined the freedom and strength of a state. Such corrupting commerce he again linked specifically to England and its national culture, in which "everything is for sale."[34] Finally, commercial strength was not real strength but illusory. England's power, he wrote, was entirely artificial. The English monarchy was weak and corrupt, slave to the country's financial interests, and promoted tyranny abroad.[35] In his most scathing moments, Théremin called England a "universal monarchy" comparable only to imperial Rome and the papacy.[36] Yet England's universal monarchy, founded on commerce, promoting war, and corrupting England and other states, lacked the greatness of Rome. Whereas a "Roman citizen" could say with pride that Rome had defeated kings, an "English bourgeois" could say only that "he can pay them."[37] Théremin's depiction here was a reversal of Voltaire's praise for commerce

33. Théremin, *Des intérêts des puissances continentales,* 18, 86, 19, 5.

34. Ibid., 39, 65, 109, 6–7. See also Théremin, "Remarques sur le Traité de commerce entre la France et l'Angleterre de l'an 1786," Floréal, Year 5 (April–May 1797), MAE, MD Angleterre 46, f. 287–97.

35. Théremin, *Des intérêts des puissances continentales,* 19, 49; Théremin, "Discours sur la question," 20.

36. Théremin, *Des intérêts des puissances continentales,* 119. Later, in 1816, Théremin would contrast the "universal monarchies" of ancient Rome, the Catholic Church, and modern England with a "European political republic" made up of representative governments. *De l'État présent de l'Europe et de l'accord entre la légitimité et le système représentatif* (Paris, 1816), chaps. 11–12.

37. *Des intérêts des puissances continentales,* 21.

in the tenth of his *Philosophical Letters,* titled "On Commerce," in which Voltaire compared England's commercial prowess to Roman conquest and stated that an English merchant could take "just pride" in having paid Prince Eugene to defeat Louis XIV at Turin and "dare compare himself, not without reason, to a Roman citizen."[38] Théremin effectively inverted Voltaire's famous tribute to English commerce and painted England as a warmongering, corrupt nation that had been utterly debased by its commercial system.

Théremin's diatribe against English commerce was undoubtedly fueled by the continuing hostilities between France and England and most likely by Théremin's desire to establish himself in France (the tract was published in summer 1795, shortly after his arrival in Paris from London).[39] Nonetheless, it reveals Théremin's deep-seated suspicions about the potential dangers of modern commerce. England's malicious commercial practices are presented as a perversion of commerce that is latent within commerce itself, not as a mutation of commerce's true nature. Théremin's misgivings about the potentially pernicious effects of commerce and credit thus echoed a range of eighteenth-century writers, from David Hume and his jealousy of trade to a host of classical republicans who claimed that the modern commercial system was breeding widespread corruption among the states of Europe. While Théremin certainly never advocated a return to Spartan autarky, he did view commerce and trade as potentially corrupting and therefore to be carefully circumscribed so that they remained republican in character rather than becoming monarchical or despotic.[40] In this regard, his modern vision was importantly tempered by concerns and anxieties about the newfound dangers commercial modernity might produce.

Just as Théremin did not think commerce a purely positive force in the modern world, he also did not want modern polities to focus on civil liberty to the complete exclusion of public political life. His political-philosophical vision, for all his emphasis on civil liberty as what moderns needed, simultaneously bore the marks of classical-republican concerns in his insistence

38. François-Marie Arouet de Voltaire, *Lettres philosophiqes* (Amsterdam [Rouen], 1734), 89. Voltaire's comparison is discussed in Sonenscher, *Before the Deluge,* 101–2.

39. Théremin's criticisms of English commerce mirrored a wider French and European discourse (which included Kant himself). See Marc Belissa, *Repenser l'ordre européen (1795–1802): De la société des rois aux droits des nations* (Paris, 2006), 253–65.

40. Théremin, *Des intérêts des puissances continentales,* 86–87, 118–19.

that public spirit and a shared public life should be cultivated.[41] Rather than endorse an "antipolitics" along the lines of Physiocracy or liberal authoritarianism, Théremin lamented the decline of public spirit in the French Republic. In *De la Situation intérieure de la République,* he even argued that political division in a republic is essential for the preservation of liberty (for which he was roundly criticized by Amaury Duval in the pages of *La Décade philosophique*).[42] The rise of the absolutist monarchy, in his narrative, was enabled by the repression of political division. In one of the strongest attacks in his entire oeuvre, he blamed the ultimate consolidation of absolutism and the rise of the Ultramontanes on Richelieu's corruption of the public spirit of France's nobles through the encouragement of the frivolous luxuries of court life. Linking the decline of public-spiritedness to the rise of Ultramontanism, and thus to the revocation of the Edict of Nantes, was nothing less than the sharpest of censures coming from a descendant of Huguenot refugees, in a tract in which Théremin identified himself on the title page as the descendant "of a Protestant who left France for religious reasons."[43] Théremin was unyielding in his conviction that a healthy dose of public-spiritedness and concern for the public good was essential if the republic were to survive and prosper.

In this vein, and strongly echoing Kantian themes and Kantian vocabulary, Théremin praised the roles of publicity and public reason in republican political life. As he put it in praise of the institution of public prize contests, "it would be desirable to submit all important political subjects to public reason in this way. This device, in addition to providing those who govern with a great amount of enlightenment and a large number of ideas, among which they would have to choose, would offer the further advantage of being a highly republican institution since public affairs essentially concern the public and do not belong to anyone else."[44] Prize contests, in other words, would both gather an array of potentially fruitful

41. Martin Nadeau has emphasized the classical-republican dimensions of Théremin's use of *esprit public.* See Nadeau, "De l'Esprit public," introduction to *Esprit Public,* vol. 9 of La Décade philosophique *comme système,* ed. Josiane Boulad-Ayoub and Nadeau (Rennes, 2003).

42. In an otherwise favorable review, Duval took issue with Théremin's endorsement of "political division." *La Décade philosophique,* 20 Germinal, Year 5 (9 April 1797), 67.

43. Théremin, *De la Situation intérieure de la République,* esp. 6–8.

44. Théremin, "Discours sur la question: Est-il de l'interêt de la République Française de reculer ses limites jusqu'aux bords du Rhin," 1.

ideas about a topic and make certain that the public remained aware of the major political issues of the day. More specifically, he advocated entrusting the public good to "men of letters," whom he described as uniquely qualified for the role. "Because they teach general knowledge and their continual occupation is to work for others rather than themselves, they are particularly qualified for the affairs of the Nation. Whether one calls them *lettrés, philosophes, politiques,* or whatever other name one wants, it is they who, ever since we have emerged from barbarism, and above all since the invention of the printing press, govern the affairs of the world."[45] Théremin's modern republic, dedicated to enabling the fulfillment of the full range of modern individuals' wants and needs, was to be governed by the free and critical use of public reason.

Théremin's liberal-republican political philosophy took one of its most original, and radical, turns when he argued for the extension of what he termed "political existence" to women. In a treatise entitled *De la condition des femmes dans les Républiques (On the Condition of Women in Republics),* Théremin observed that "women have always been considered to have no existence by themselves in political society."[46] As he rendered it, women have historically been denied the full use of their moral faculties, have not been permitted to live as morally free and independent beings. As a result, they have been forced to live for the ends of men rather than for themselves. Théremin called for an end to this situation and for according political existence to women. This call was advanced in fundamentally Kantian terms. That is, it was articulated using the categories and lexicon of Kant's universalist ethics.[47] That Théremin viewed ethical questions in Kantian universalist terms can be seen in a review he wrote of Benjamin Constant's *Des Réactions politiques.* In an otherwise complimentary piece, Théremin criticized Constant for the position he took in the now-famous dispute between Constant and Kant over "the right to lie."[48] Théremin

45. Théremin, *De la Situation intérieure de la République,* 53–54.

46. Théremin, *De la condition des femmes dans les Républiques,* 5.

47. Kant himself did not fully apply these to women. There is an immense literature on both Kant's ethics and their implications for women. On the former, see in particular Allen Wood, *Kant's Ethical Thought* (Cambridge, 1999); on the latter, see Robin May Schott, ed., *Feminist Interpretations of Immanuel Kant* (University Park, Pa., 1997).

48. On the dispute, see Benjamin Constant and Emmanuel Kant, *Le droit de mentir,* ed. Jules Barni (Paris, 2003).

described Constant's line of reasoning as amounting to the claim that "one is obliged to tell the truth only to he who possesses the right to know" and argued that Constant's stance would undermine the absolute moral law that formed the unconditional basis of political order and human progress.

> *One is obliged to tell the truth only to he who possesses the right to know.* Following this, each man becomes the judge of another's right to know the truth, of the cases in which it is suitable to tell him the truth, that is, of the truth itself. In our opinion, we believe that if this maxim were accepted, men would truthfully have a common measure and a solid foundation for the exchange of monetary commodities, but they would have no such foundation for the exchange of thoughts, which is the truth, that is, the absolute truth, to which every man has a right.[49]

Théremin's argument for the extension of "political existence" to women was undergirded by exactly this Kantian universalism.

Théremin's analytic starting point was the claim that a woman is "a being endowed with her own morality." A woman, he argued, possesses the same capacity for moral reasoning as a man. For Théremin, as for Kant, the ability to make critical use of one's reason, and especially the ability to engage in moral reasoning, was the sine qua non of autonomy or self-legislation and thus of personhood itself.[50] As Kant wrote in the *Groundwork of the Metaphysics of Morals* of 1785, "*Autonomy* is ... the ground of the dignity of human nature and of every rational creature."[51] Théremin argued that women are autonomous beings since, like men, they are endowed with a "moral being." Echoing Kant's fundamental antinomy between freedom and nature in the *Critique of Pure Reason* (the third antinomy), as well as his positing of the a priori existence of both freedom and the soul, Théremin argued that women and men are composed of two "beings," a moral being and a physical being. Crucially, Théremin then asserted that the moral being of a woman is no different from that of a man.

49. Théremin, *La Décade philosophique* 20 Prairial, Year 5 (8 June 1797), 460.

50. See Wood, *Kant's Ethical Thought,* 156. On the prehistory of Kant's idea of self-legislation, see J. B. Schneewind, *The Invention of Autonomy: A History of Modern Moral Philosophy* (Cambridge, 1998).

51. Kant, *Groundwork,* quoted in Wood, *Kant's Ethical Thought,* 159.

> There are two beings in a woman, as there are in a man: the first is a moral being made up of the same elements as that of men, free in essence and knowing no laws except those of its own morality; this being has no sex, there is only individual superiority or inferiority; in terms of this moral being, a woman is as much a man as a woman; the soul, prior to the body if it is immortal, does not lose its essence, its responsibility, its equality with that of man as a result of inhabiting a female body.[52]

Théremin's description of a woman's moral being in this passage is articulated in strikingly Kantian terms. "Free in essence and knowing no laws except those of its own morality" is, for all intents and purposes, a Kantian description of autonomy. In the *Groundwork*, Kant wrote that "freedom must be presupposed as a property of the will of all rational beings" and argued that the autonomous will must be able to legislate to itself its own laws.[53] Théremin wielded Kant's framework to claim that women, because they possess a full moral being, should enjoy the same "political existence" as men. Théremin's argument that the difference in physical being between women and men did not produce an ensuing difference in moral being constituted a tacit rejection of the long-standing philosophical tradition denying women political existence based on their physical differences from men.[54]

The extent to which Théremin's analysis was undergirded by a Kantian framework can be seen further in his discussion of the effects of the historical failure to recognize women as free and independent beings. The result, explained Théremin, had been the exclusion of women from the full use of their faculties and thus from both individual happiness and the public, more collective pursuit of perfection. Whereas "the happiness and perfection of humanity consists... in the most absolute and unlimited use of its faculties,... men have confined women's activity to a narrow sphere. Women, however, have received from nature the same type of faculties as men and have an equal right to the exercise of these faculties since they are intelligent

52. Théremin, *De la condition des femmes dans les Républiques,* 20–21. This argument was adopted by Constance Pipelet in her *Rapport sur un ouvrage de C^{en} Théremin, intitulé:* De la condition des Femmes dans une République (Paris, 1800).

53. *Groundwork,* quoted in Wood, *Kant's Ethical Thought,* 175.

54. On this wider discourse in revolutionary France, see in particular, Geneviève Fraisse, *Muse de la raison: La démocratie exclusive et la différence des sexes* (Aix-en-Provence, 1989); and Carla Hesse, *The Other Enlightenment: How French Women Became Modern* (Princeton, 2001), 130–36.

beings, endowed with morality and a conscience. They do not live for us [men] but for themselves." This restriction on the political status of women had hindered not only the development of countless individual women, but, argued Théremin in Kantian terms, had impeded the overall perfection of "the moral law" and thus of humanity itself, which is the purpose of all human beings. "The fulfillment of the supreme moral law is the ultimate end of the existence of any intelligent being, no matter the sex its body has assumed."[55]

According to Théremin, the political status of women had not always been so restricted. Replicating his above-discussed comparison of the different forms of liberty in ancient and modern republics, he explained that "whoever reads attentively the history of ancient peoples, especially that of the Romans and the Spartans, will find [that]... women in the ancient polities enjoyed more political liberty and less domestic liberty. In our polities they enjoy a great domestic liberty, but do not have a political existence." Women, Théremin proposed, should enjoy both types of liberties. In the modern republic, after the progress of civilization, women should be accorded both "political liberty" and "domestic liberty." Théremin asked, "Should the fate of women not improve in proportion to the civilization of the human species, which is not made up of men alone? The Republic being unquestionably an improvement over the monarchy, should their fate not be better in the Republic than under the monarchy?"[56] Here we can clearly see how Théremin's faith in progress informed his belief that women should be accorded political rights as well as his more general insistence on the importance of political liberty.

The practical proposals Théremin advocated were, however, somewhat more limited than his rhetorical flourishes augured. Specifically, he stopped short of calling for women's suffrage. While he insisted that a woman "is a citizen before a wife" and "has greater need of good laws than of a good husband," he nonetheless argued that a married couple constitutes "one political person" and therefore should possess only one vote, to be cast by the husband. The vote of the wife, Théremin contended, "is included virtually in that of the husband." He explained that "women cannot vote in political assemblies in a state where men fill the public functions, and name those who do so, for

55. Théremin, *De la condition des femmes dans les Républiques,* 18–19.
56. Ibid., 5–6, 10, 11.

the same reason that men would not vote in political assemblies in a state where women filled the public functions, and named those who do so; that is, because of the simple reason that one does not want the same vote cast twice."[57] Théremin did not pause to consider the political status of unmarried women or widows, however, and thus seemed to envision women's political existence as taking shape only through their representation in families or households, rather than as individuals.[58] As a result, his call for women's political liberty fell short of establishing full and equal citizenship.

The principal way in which Théremin did envision fulfilling women's political existence was by according women what he called "rights like those of men." These included the right to own property, to receive an education, and what he vaguely labeled "political rights" but never spelled out in any detail. Essentially, Théremin advocated civil equality for women. The extension of full property-owning rights to women as well as complete access to education, it should be emphasized, represented a fairly radical departure from Directorial policy. While women were allowed to own property at this point, there were nonetheless significant gender-specific restrictions. Directorial education policy, moreover, did not provide schooling for women beyond the age of primary school. Théremin's argument for according property rights to women is noteworthy because it was made in terms that can almost be described as carrying classical-republican anxieties about women and corruption to their fullest logical extension, to a reductio ad absurdum that turned such classical-republican anxieties on their head. The corruption of women, he explained, poses a grave danger to republics because "women alone are the conservators" of "the moeurs by which republics survive or become corrupted." Allowing women full and unfettered ownership of property, he reasoned, would make them less susceptible to corruption because of the independence that property confers. Thus, on his account, women's property ownership would help to stave off the corruption of the republic itself. "No one has calculated," he wrote, "how much the absence of property among women... rapidly leads a state towards its ruin" due to "the vices" and "the corruption" that ensued.[59] His thinking on this matter, however, did more than invert classical-republican anxieties about women. It reoriented

57. Ibid., 29, 59–60.

58. See Anne Verjus, *Le cens de la famille: Les femmes et le vote, 1789–1848* (Paris, 2002).

59. Théremin, *De la condition des femmes dans les Républiques,* 51–53, 56–58.

them so that the very conceptual starting point shifted. Whereas classical-republican anxieties about women led to the misogynistic policing of women, Théremin proffered a more optimistic view that would assign women full civil equality while still in the name of staving off corruption.

Théremin's argument that France should abandon its post-primary school single-sex education policy and establish schools for women was also couched in practical terms. Pointing to the fundamental role played by public instruction in forming republicans, he asked, "To maintain itself, why would the Republic not do what the Christian religion, which had almost as many foundations for women as for men, ceaselessly did to maintain and propagate itself? Why, having central schools for men in every department,... would it not have institutions that favor women? Are we therefore a Republic of men only? Should we have in France only *républicains* and no *républicaines?*"[60] In other words, France was passing up the opportunity to form cadres of republican women who would be devoted to the Republic. Théremin made the same point in much more general terms in a letter to Sieyès, then president of the Executive Directory, when he sent him a copy of *De la condition des femmes dans les Républiques* in 1799: "I believe... that it [the extension of political rights to women] is an abundant source of public spirit.... It will be truly in vain for anyone to attempt to overthrow the representative system, or to slow down its progress, once we have found the means to interest women in an order of things that until now has seemed to be made for men only."[61] In the text, Théremin also posited a further practical, if less immediately political, benefit to educating women: the Republic would be able to make use of "all possible aspects of all the moral faculties spread across the nation so as to make them work together for the common prosperity."[62] In other words, the Republic would be able to marshal the full array of women's specific talents and abilities and direct them to the public good and the continued movement toward human perfection. Théremin's treatment of women's political status demonstrates, once again, the extent to which Théremin's work was inscribed in Kantian categories—even if Théremin used Kant's concepts and lexicon to advance an argument Kant himself did not make.

60. Ibid., 53–54.

61. Théremin to Sieyès, 27 Messidor, Year 7 (15 July 1799), AN, 284 AP 17–8/11.

62. Théremin, *De la condition des femmes dans les Républiques,* 71.

Charles-Guillaume Théremin's post-Terror writings amounted to an original liberal republican program for the French Republic, one articulated in a Kantian lexicon. His argument that the modern republic should reflect modern economic conditions and his attendant emphasis on representative government as the only form appropriate to modern polities paralleled contemporaneous modern political philosophies, while his concerns about the potentially corrosive effects of commerce on the body politic and about the desiccation of public political life both spoke to a more classical-republican style of thinking about politics. Théremin thus combined a first-order emphasis on the liberty of the moderns with a number of political anxieties redolent of the early modern classical-republican tradition. Théremin's liberal republicanism was distinctive on the post-Terror scene in its grounding in a universalist ethics and its resultant serious engagement with the issue of the political status of women. Overall, Théremin's Kantian liberal republicanism constituted a unique political-philosophical voice in post-Terror France. While Théremin's influence is impossible to gauge with any precision, his writings would certainly have been known to a broad swath of learned society, not least through his connection with *La Décade philosophique,* which both published and reviewed his writings, and his association with Sieyès. In the review of *De la Situation intérieure de la République* published in the *Décade,* Théremin was singled out along with Benjamin Constant as a foreigner "who consecrates his pen to the glory of France."[63] Théremin's political-philosophical writings, largely unstudied, contributed an important modern voice to political-philosophical debate during the post-Terror years and advanced one of the most significant early articulations of French liberal republicanism.

Germaine de Staël's Aristocratic Liberal Republicanism

A rather different liberal republicanism, more conservative in nature, was developed at around the same time by Germaine de Staël in her never-completed manuscript *On the Current Circumstances That Could End the Revolution and the Principles That Should Found the Republic in France.*

63. [Duval], review of *De la Situation intérieure de la République,* by Charles Théremin, *La Décade philosophique* 10 Floréal, Year 5 (29 April 1797), 208.

Staël composed the manuscript primarily in 1798 and 1799, in the wake of the coup of 18 Fructidor, preoccupied with the Directory's recurrent instability. The text was, however, never completed and remained unpublished until 1906.[64] As a result, it is somewhat unwieldy and at points inconsistent. Although unpublished at the time of its composition, however, it did not go unread. Benjamin Constant, for example, read and annotated the entire manuscript, and there is no question that it influenced his thinking in important ways. Moreover, Staël was exceedingly active within the republican center—"at the heart of political *Tout-Paris,*" in the words of François Furet.[65] She was later labeled by Thibaudeau as one of the prime intriguers behind the coup of 18 Fructidor (4 September 1797).[66] Moreover, she hosted a famous salon and corresponded extensively with Pierre-Louis Roederer.[67] The fundaments of Staël's liberal-republican program would have been known to a range of figures within the republican center, whether through direct circulation of the manuscript or through Staël's famed conversation. As Furet writes of Staël's text, "One thing is certain, and that is that a whole group of liberal Republicans found their best spokesperson in her."[68]

On the Current Circumstances That Could End the Revolution and the Principles That Should Found the Republic in France offers, as the title suggests, a prescriptive program both for ending the French Revolution and for establishing the republic on a lasting basis. Marked by currents springing from both the classical-republican and the liberal traditions, Staël's text is first and foremost a resolute defense of the Revolution and of republicanism

64. On its composition and publication, see the introduction to the critical edition prepared by Lucia Omacini. Germaine de Staël, *Des circonstances actuelles qui peuvent terminer la révolution et des principes qui doivent fonder la république en France,* ed. Omacini (Geneva, 1979).

65. François Furet, *Revolutionary France, 1770–1880,* trans. Antonia Nevill (Oxford, 1992), 203. See also Louis Marie de La Révellière de Lépeaux, *Mémoires de Larevellière-Lépeaux, publiés par son fils,* 3 vols. (Paris, 1895), 1:215–17.

66. Antoine-Claire Thibaudeau, *Mémoires sur la Convention et le Directoire* 2 vols. (Paris, 1824), 2:244. On the coup, described briefly in chapter 2, see esp. Albert Meynier, *Les coups d'état du Directoire,* vol. 1, *Le dix-huit Fructidor an V (4 Septembre 1797)* (Paris, 1927).

67. Roederer's personal papers at the French National Archives contain thirty-one letters between Staël and Roederer dated from 21 Prairial, Year 3 (9 June 1795) to 19 Nivôse, Year 8 (9 January 1800); all but one are from Staël to Roederer (Roederer's letters to Staël have, to my knowledge, been lost). AN, 29 AP 12, f. 225–53. Many are reprinted in Staël, *Correspondance générale,* ed. Louis de Narbonne and Béatrice W. Jasinkski (Paris, 1960–93), vol. 3, pt. 2, and vol. 4, pt. 1.

68. Furet, *Revolutionary France, 1770–1880,* 204.

as a form of government, both of which she took great pains to divorce from the legacy of the Terror. Staël considered the republic the only form of government suitable to the modern world, and her text was peppered with references, asides, and notes addressing the long history of republics, classical and modern. Staël's text worked on both a theoretical level, considering the republic as a form of government, and a more concrete one, specifying constitutional changes for the post-Terror French Republic. In abstract terms, Staël argued, the modern republic should be established on a two-pronged basis. The first foundation, she wrote, should be "political equality," or "the right of each man possessing the conditions required to be a citizen to participate in the formation of the laws that govern him"—in other words, political participation among the citizenry, with the latter restricted to those who met certain criteria (unspecified in the text). In the modern world, "political equality" had displaced hereditary privilege as the foundation of the political order. The second foundation Staël proposed was the liberty of the moderns, for which she provided a definition some twenty years before Constant's famous lecture: "The liberty of today's world is all that guarantees the independence of citizens against the power of the government. The liberty of the ancient world is all that assures citizens the greatest part in the exercise of power."[69] While her text called for both ancient and modern liberty, for both political participation in the formation of the laws and civil liberty, the overall balance of Staël's program fell on the liberty of the moderns. Despite her declaration that the republic's starting point should be the right "to participate in the formation of the laws," Staël's vision of the post-Terror republic was in fact animated first and foremost by the liberty of the moderns.

Staël advanced both moral and practical arguments for grounding the republic in the liberty of the moderns. The principal moral reason was the "opportunity to exist in isolation from public affairs." This opportunity, Staël wrote, "is, I believe, a great good for the majority of men.... This rest [from politics], unknown to the ancients,... is a chance for more happiness given to the diversity of individuals." Staël, like Théremin, viewed modern liberty as superior because it allowed people to pursue their own individually chosen ends. Thus, in modern France, with "private life easily

69. Staël, *Des circonstances actuelles,* 13, 111–12.

providing so many pleasures,...civil liberty and individual liberty should be extremely respected." Ancient liberty, to the contrary, forced people to participate in public affairs regardless of their individual wants and desires and dragged them away from private goods. At one point, in her notes to the text, Staël even described "activity in politics" as "useless" in the face of modern "private happiness," which she juxtaposed to the situation "among the ancients," in which there was a "great influence of public affairs on the fate of each individual." Ancient liberty, Staël believed, was simply obsolete in the modern world. As a result, she denied the relevance of classical examples for modern France and caustically dismissed her contemporaries' seemingly reflexive invocations of Spartan and Roman austerity: "France will be lost due to a few features of Roman history that people cite because they are so surprised to know them. The poverty of a few famous Greek and Roman republicans is not applicable to our social order and...our association of 30 million men." Modern polities, and modern France in particular, had to be built on private desires. Staël's treatise, in short, put forward one of the most resolute moral defenses of the liberty of the moderns of the entire revolutionary period.[70]

On a practical level, Staël considered the liberty of the moderns crucial to securing a sense of loyalty to the Republic among the population. She rejected as outmoded and unrealistic the classical notion that the republic could be anchored in the citizenry's primordial identification with the common good. Whereas in the Roman republic "the interest of Rome encompassed all the interests of the Roman citizens," in modern France "it is respect for individual existence, for private fortune, that alone can make the Republic loved." Staël believed that the modern republic would be anchored in stable ground only if it reflected people's interests, their "private existences." Modern people would not put the public good above their own interest, but they would serve the public good if that *was* their interest. Employing a rhetorical trope she used throughout the text, Staël posed the objection she expected: "'What,' someone will say to me, 'we

70. Ibid., 109–11, 363–64, 167. Lucien Jaume argues that Staël's version of the liberty of the moderns in the text was not based on individual rights and the autonomy of the individual. According to Jaume, Staël "formulates the theory of the liberty of the moderns...more as an alternative vision vis-à-vis methods of terror than as a consequence of the primacy of individual rights." *L'individu effacé ou le paradoxe du libéralisme français* (Paris, 1997), 51. In my view, Jaume underestimates the strictly moral component of Staël's argument.

cannot count on the courage of virtue?'" Her response was that "we should never make mass calculations except on the basis of personal interest."[71] Her argument here was typical of the liberal tradition and constitutes an important example of the liberal penchant to assign priority to the social over the political.

At the same time, however, Staël also devoted great attention in the manuscript to arguing for the importance of republican moeurs among the population. No republic, she thought, classical or modern, would survive if the "national character" and the "principle of government" were not in accord with one another. The need for harmony between the population's moeurs and the form of government constituted one of the foremost themes of Staël's manuscript, and her discussions were frequently in line with the Directorial discourse of moeurs and early modern classical republicanism more broadly. In republics, as opposed to monarchies, she wrote, a widespread "morality" was essential: "If the power of morality is not, so to speak, the constituent power of a republic, the republic does not exist." In arguing for the importance of moeurs, Staël furthermore pointed to the models of classical antiquity. "The ancients assigned much greater importance to laws concerning moeurs than to strictly constitutional arrangements. How correct they were!" Her preoccupation with the question of moeurs led her, in turn, to argue for the importance of religion in a republic. She perceived religion and republican morality to be indissolubly tied and even claimed that "republics cannot succeed monarchies except by a change of religion." Her logic was that republican moeurs differed so dramatically from monarchical moeurs that only a new religion could foster the moral sea change necessary to sustain the republic. In the case of France, she thought it necessary that the nation become Protestant.[72] The weight Staël assigned to moeurs was, to an important extent, in tension with her conviction that the republic should reflect people's interests since she prescribed a certain degree of homogeneity among the population and even the didactic reorientation of people's interests, at least in the short term. Staël never resolved this tension in the manuscript, perhaps because it remained incomplete, but it was clear that her ideal republic would be

71. Staël, *Des circonstances actuelles,* 109–11, 165.
72. Ibid., 373, 38–39, 373–76, 227, 229–35.

based on the liberty of the moderns but be made up of a population that simultaneously possessed uniformly republican moeurs.

As Staël surveyed the contemporary French political scene, she concluded that the single greatest concrete problem facing France was that the nation's moeurs were not yet republican. As a result, in her eyes, the people were not yet ready to exercise sovereignty. This was a running theme in her text, and she concluded that democratic practices had to be restricted until the population had become sufficiently republican in its moeurs: "You can democratize the constitution to the extent that public spirit makes progress," she wrote. In time the people would be able to exercise sovereignty through full and regular elections but not until republican public education had sufficiently republicanized the population. Until then, elections would be nothing more than a recurrent hazard because the royalists had learned how to manipulate the democratic process. Before republican education had done its job, France would have to be governed by representatives licensed to act independently of the people's opinions. "Public spirit has not yet acquired in France the firm direction that a long apprenticeship in liberty alone can give.... It is necessary, in France, until the moment when public instruction will have trained a new generation in liberty, to extend several portions of the conserving power among the hands of republicans." The pace of France's "apprenticeship of liberty," it seemed, would be quite slow.[73]

The "conserving power" Staël referred to in this passage was an integral feature of her liberal-republican vision and the constitutional revisions she believed necessary to save the French Republic. A "conserving power," she wrote, "is an essential feature...of representative government." Staël proposed that the Council of Elders in the Constitution of the Year III be turned into a "Conserving Body" whose members would serve lifetime appointments and be provided "a significant income" by the state that would "assure them not only the independence, but the respect, attached to wealth." When first established, the Conserving Body's 250 seats would be filled with a selection of members drawn from France's existing representative bodies, intellectuals, and a few distinguished members of the military. In the future, the Conserving Body would itself select

73. Ibid., 160–64.

new members from the Council of Five Hundred. Staël's strategy for the Conserving Body's autoregeneration, combined with the fact that its members would serve lifetime appointments, constituted a fervent rejection of the Constitution of the Year III's highly classical-republican emphasis on the regular replacement of the members of the two legislative councils. In Staël's opinion, rotation was a recipe for chaos rather than conservation:

> There is nothing at once more adverse to the liberty of the people and more favorable to demagogues who want to cause trouble than this law that prohibits reelection.... The most distinguished men in a nation, those most experienced, are never so numerous that we can, at any time, go without those who have earned the public trust.... Put men in a situation that promises them, for their entire life, independence, wealth and a certain degree of power, and you will be assured that they will defend, at the risk of their own life, the order that will ensure all of this life.... But if you give men three years of an existence so weak that nothing guarantees it, and whose renewal is highly uncertain, they will, for the most part, yield to all the opportunities for change; and, above all, they will not expose themselves to any danger in order to avoid such change.[74]

Staël's inspiration for the Conserving Body was the constitutional jury Sieyès had proposed during the constitutional debates of the summer of 1795. In particular, Staël admired Sieyès's seemingly clairvoyant scheme to create a body that would check conflict between the different branches of government: "Sieyès predicted the problems with the constitution so clearly that he wanted to prevent the probable struggle between the two powers with a Constitutional Jury." What France needed, Staël wrote with Sieyès's scheme in mind, was the "union" of properly separated powers rather than an ill-conceived "division of powers that forces them to become enemies with each other."[75] Staël's version of Sieyès's constitutional jury, however, would play a more active day to day role in the nation's political life than Sieyès's would have. Staël's Conserving Body was, essentially, a fusion of Sieyès's constitutional jury and the Council of Elders. Whereas the primary responsibility of Sieyès's constitutional jury was the adjudication of constitutional dispute, Staël's Conserving Body would also possess the full

74. Ibid., 172, 166, 187, 165.
75. Ibid., 162–63, 179.

complement of powers held by the Council of Elders and participate in the passage of legislation and other more commonplace affairs of government. Staël's Conserving Body, like Sieyès's constitutional jury, broke with the classical-republican notion of constitutional balance as it would possess markedly greater power than any other branch of government. In Staël's opinion, the solution to the Directory's continuous coups d'état was to establish a Conserving Body that stood above the fray of politics.

Staël anticipated that some would object that "this is an aristocratic institution. Here is my response," she wrote. "Yes, it is an aristocratic institution, one composed of the destroyers and the irreconcilable enemies of the true aristocracy." In Staël's view, only an aristocratic institution could save the republic from the inherent vagaries of democratic elections and, specifically, from the royalists' manipulations of the Directory's elections. "The inverse of this system [of democracy] should be the guide for republicans. To establish popular institutions on a solid basis, we must adopt a few ideas from the aristocracy. Democrats know how to conquer, aristocrats know how to conserve. Democrats, after their victory, should study aristocratic methods carefully in order to adopt those that are not prejudiced but calculated." In fact, Staël hoped that the Conserving Body would produce a "natural aristocracy" in France. In a representative democracy, she wrote, "the natural aristocracy, in opposition to the artificial aristocracy," should come to the political forefront. "This should be the government of the best."[76] Such preference for a "natural aristocracy" was a common theme among early modern republicans, from James Harrington to Thomas Jefferson. Only a natural aristocracy, above democratic accountability, it was thought, could lead a polity through the swamps and thickets of republican political life.

Staël's Conserving Body would install an unelected "natural aristocracy" at the pinnacle of France's political order. However, Staël did not want the Conserving Body to completely dwarf the elected Council of Five Hundred. She considered the election of the council by the people and the enshrinement of representative democracy in the constitution one of the foundational principles that made France a republic.[77] As discussed earlier,

76. Ibid., 163–64, 170; see also 11–12. Staël had made a similar argument in *De l'influence des passions* in 1796, calling for government by an "aristocracy of the best" (quoted in Jaume, *L'individu effacé,* 62).

77. Staël, *Des circonstances actuelles,* 157–58.

a cardinal feature of liberal republicanism, and liberalism more generally, was a marked preference for representative government over more vigorously democratic forms of government. Within the scope of liberals' inclination for the representative system, however, there was significant disagreement over just how far representative government should depart from more direct forms of democracy. Should the representative system create a republic that tended toward democracy or toward aristocracy?[78] Staël considered this one of the great questions facing the establishment of the modern republic and gave a somewhat inconsistent answer. On the one hand, she described representative democracy as a "technical" solution to the practical impossibility of the political community's coming together and making a collective decision.[79] "The only democracy is in the public square in Athens.... But since political reasons have brought about associations too large to assemble all of a country's inhabitants in a public square, it was necessary to compensate for this situation with representative government." In other words, the classical model of the citizenry assembling in the agora was spatially unsuited to modern France and, essentially, to all polities save the classical Athenian city-state. In the face of this physical challenge, the purpose of the representative system, even if only a heuristic purpose, was to replicate the collective will that would be expressed if the nation actually were able to come together and collectively deliberate. Representative democracy was to emulate direct democracy as closely as possible. "The object of the representative system is that the will of the people, in other words the interests of the nation, are all defended and protected as if the nation itself were able to do so by gathering together in the public square."[80]

On the other hand, Staël was more than prepared to concede this ideal in the face of France's political situation. She thought the French people

78. See Bernard Manin, *The Principles of Representative Government* (Cambridge, 1997); and Giovanni Lobrano, "Republique et démocratie anciennes avant et pendant la Révolution," in *Révolution et République: L'exception française,* ed. Michel Vovelle (Paris, 1994).

79. "Technical" is Bernard Manin's term in *The Principles of Representative Government*, 2–3.

80. Staël, *Des circonstances actuelles,* 159, 14, 171; see also 19. Staël's vision in this passage, it is worth noting, is more Burkean than Madisonian, as she thought there was a single national interest that enlightened elites, "unattached" from their more particular interests, could represent ("unattached" is Hanna Fenichel Pitkin's term to describe Burke's position in *The Concept of Representation* [Berkeley, 1967], chap. 8).

not yet ready to exercise sovereignty until they had finished their "apprenticeship of liberty," however long that might take. For representative government to function, the modern republic had to ask "in what proportion should these rights [political liberty] be sacrificed? ... This sacrifice is like that of taxes: make it too great, and the people are oppressed; make it too weak, [and] the government will not be able to maintain public security." The answer, she wrote, was not prescribed by theory but could be based only on the specific situation, on "the calm, the happiness, and the liberty of the country" in question. The extent to which representative democracy would extend the franchise thus had a temporal dimension as well—it would parallel the progress of the country's apprenticeship of liberty. While Staël never provided concrete numbers in answer to this question, she declared at one point that for representative democracy "to come close to the results of its model, pure democracy, it must move away from pure democracy in its forms." In the case of post-Terror France, Staël, despite her paean to "pure democracy," clearly held that representative democracy was to produce a government substantially distanced from the population. It was to produce government by "the best," by those who possessed "virtue, enlightenment, education, and even property."[81] On the post-Terror political cultural scene, Staël's outlook and the specific vocabulary used to describe those who should be elected were in line with the classical-republican emphasis on rule by the best that predominated within the republican center. More broadly, this position constituted one of the principal points of convergence between classical republicanism and the nascent liberalism in post-Terror France.

In addition to turning the Council of Elders into a conserving body and keeping the Council of Five Hundred, Staël proposed revamping the Executive Directory so that it would become a powerful, highly independent executive. Staël's advocacy of a strong executive power within the constitution signaled a rejection of the classical-republican mindset that had predominated during the drafting of the Constitution of the Year III. A cardinal feature of the classical-republican tradition in France and elsewhere was distrust of the executive as naturally prone to tyranny.[82] Those

81. Staël, *Des circonstances actuelles,* 14–15, 24, 11.

82. This point is emphasized by Raymonde Monnier in "Républicanisme, libéralisme et Révolution française," in *Les libéralismes au regard de l'histoire, Actuel Marx* 32 (Paris, 2002), 108.

whose political thought fell within the early modern classical-republican tradition took great pains to ensure that the executive, while in a state of balance vis-à-vis the other constitutional powers, would never be able to act independently of the legislature. Against this tradition, and against the Constitution of the Year III, Staël argued that "an executive power must never be able to be forced to execute a law that it disapproves. This would be an executing power, so to speak, a government without force and without moral respect.... A Directory will consider itself, and should consider itself, as a representative of the nation and not as the Legislative Body's delegate."[83] In the summer of 1795, at the time of the constitution's drafting, Staël had similarly written to Roederer that "an executive power that has no connection with the fabrication of the laws is naturally the enemy of those who impose on it decrees that go against its views.... An executive power that has no share in the laws that it makes obeyed is much closer to being an executing power." Yet in 1795 she did not advocate an executive veto, which she described to Roederer as too great an "influence" to give "a republican executive power."[84] By the time she wrote the manuscript of 1798–99, however, Staël had decided that the Executive Directory should possess a suspensive veto and be able to dissolve the Council of Five Hundred, and that its members should be inviolable. The intervening years of constitutional conflict, it seems, led her to favor an even more powerful executive than she had in 1795. As with her ideas about the "aristocratic" Conserving Body, Staël expected her proposals regarding the executive to provoke strident objections from her contemporaries. "What power, someone will say, what power you will give to the Executive Directory!" Her response was that this power was "much less than it [the Executive Directory] has at this moment, since it must [now] govern illegally just to maintain itself and make the government work."[85]

Although never completed, Staël's *On the Current Circumstances That Could End the Revolution and the Principles That Should Found the Republic in France* was perhaps the most important articulation of liberal-republican

83. Staël, *Des circonstances actuelles,* 180–81.

84. Staël to Roederer, 21 Prairial, Year 3 (9 June 1795), AN, 29 AP 12, f. 225, reprinted in Staël, *Lettres d'une nouvelle républicaine, 17 mai 1795–novembre 1796,* vol. 3, pt. 2, of her *Correspondance générale,* 15–17.

85. Staël, *Des circonstances actuelles,* 180–86, 182.

political ideas, and arguably the most important overall reflection on politics and the republic, composed during Thermidor and the Directory. The text reflected aspects of both the classical-republican and the liberal traditions but taken as a whole was unambiguously modern in orientation. While Staël invoked political liberty as one of the republic's two first principles, the weight she accorded the liberty of the moderns trumped that allotted to citizen "participation in the formation of the laws." The result was a rather conservative vision. On the liberal-republican political-philosophical spectrum, Staël's text clearly stood toward the aristocratic end. Her version of the modern republic would establish a powerful unelected "natural aristocracy" and a highly independent executive, thereby largely sapping her wider republican vision of any robust political content. While it did not veer to the antipolitical extreme that liberalism sometimes did, as in the case of liberal authoritarianism, Staël's *On the Current Circumstances That Could End the Revolution and the Principles That Should Found the Republic in France* amounted to a highly aristocratic liberal-republican text.

* * *

The political-philosophical writings of Charles-Guillaume Théremin and Germaine de Staël stand out as two of the era's most systematic attempts to articulate a liberal-republican political philosophical program. Théremin's vision would have established a quasi-Kantian modern republic built upon commercial civilization in which women would hold what Théremin referred to as political rights. Staël's version of the modern republic, for its part, would be grounded in modern liberty while assigning final political authority to an unelected natural aristocracy serving lifetime appointments. Both visions made the liberty of the moderns the republic's axial point, yet both were also marked by a host of classical-republican themes and anxieties. Théremin and Staël, in the course of engaging with the day's major political issues, each articulated in embryonic form certain key ideas that would later lie at the heart of French Liberalism. While this chapter and the preceding two have looked at political debate in regard to domestic political concerns, the next chapter will turn to the interplay between classical-republican and modern ideas in a different setting, debate about foreign policy and the international order.

4

A Republican Empire?

Debate on Expansion, 1794–99

Our government should always have before its eyes this axiom of public law: the tranquility of republics diminishes as they grow.

Anonymous petitioner, "Apperçu des Relations politiques et commerciales de la République française avec les diverses puissances d'Italie"

Thus far this book has focused on debate about domestic political questions. The republican center, however, grappled just as fully with matters of foreign policy. From 1794 to 1799 questions relating to foreign policy and the international order were never far from the forefront of political discussion, reflecting the ongoing war and international crisis that marked the era. It was widely felt, not surprisingly, that the republic could be anchored in stable ground only when peace was achieved and the international situation settled. Indeed, in the summer of 1795 La Révellière-Lépeaux labeled "achieving peace in Europe" one of three keys "to solidly founding the Republic."[1] Yet, at the same time, the Republic was emerging as continental Europe's hegemonic power. From 1794 to 1798 French armies won a string of decisive victories in the Austrian Netherlands (modern-day Belgium), Holland, the German states, and across the Italian

1. Louis Marie de La Révellière-Lépeaux, *Discours sur les rélations extérieures* (Paris, 1795), 1–2.

peninsula, establishing a wide zone of French predominance and laying the foundations of the Napoleonic Empire. These exploits led to the question of what the Republic should do with the territories it controlled and, more broadly, the hegemonic position it occupied on the European stage. The result was a lively and serious debate about republican expansion and the nature of the international order.

From a historical perspective, France's political leaders found themselves in a novel situation, of which they were all too aware: while monarchies had conquered and annexed one another's territories for centuries, no European *republic* had acquired a land-based empire on this scale since Rome. And the Roman Republic, as anyone educated in the eighteenth century knew, perished as Rome became an empire. Should the French Republic annex new territories, thus expanding its territorial limits, and risk becoming an empire? Should it use these territories as bargaining chips at the peace table (as was standard practice in eighteenth-century diplomacy)?[2] Or should it explore other options and establish satellite republics, called "sister republics" during the Revolution, in the conquered territories?

The question of what to do with the conquered territories—and, more generally, of the nature of the international order—emerged as one of the day's most pressing issues. Crucially, these questions were apprehended in light of the fact that France was a republic. In terms of diplomacy, the French Republic would not follow the old conventions but would play by new, republican rules.[3] More important still, foreign policy would be assessed according to its effect on the republic's domestic health. Thus, debate on foreign policy was shaped by the day's conceptual presuppositions regarding the nature of the republic as a political form. Those more classical in their republicanism feared the potentially corrosive effects of expansion,

2. On the balance-of-power notions that governed eighteenth-century diplomatic practice, see Paul Schroeder, *The Transformation of European Politics, 1763–1848* (Oxford, 1994), 5–11; and Jeremy Black, *The Rise of the European Powers, 1679–1793* (London, 1990), chap. 4.

3. E.g., Joseph Eschassériaux, *De la Diplomatie, des droits des peuples, des principes qui doivent diriger un peuple républicain dans ses relations étrangères* (Paris, 1794); Flassan, "Considérations sur la nature de nos relations futures avec l'Espange," Year 3 (1794–95), MAE, MD Espagne 50, f. 250–56. More broadly, see Linda Frey and Marsha Frey, "'The Reign of the Charlatans Is Over': The French Revolutionary Attack on Diplomatic Practice," *Journal of Modern History* 65 (December 1993): 706–44; Marc Belissa, *Repenser l'ordre européen (1795–1802): De la société des rois aux droits des nations* (Paris, 2006), 183–95.

while those with a more modern orientation held that new political forms, notably representative government, enabled France to expand without endangering the body politic. If discussion turned on the differences between classical and modern visions of the republic as a political form, however, classical-republican anxieties fixed the terms of debate. Those opposed to expansion invoked such concerns while those in favor explicitly aimed to refute them. No one could ignore them. Debate on foreign policy was thus structured along the same lines as domestic political debate, further highlighting both the persistence of classical-republican presuppositions about politics into the post-Terror period and the significance of the moment as a watershed in the transition from classical to modern republicanism.

Debate on foreign policy and the international order also reprised a number of specific themes from domestic debate. Perhaps most prominently, the Republic's political elite worried whether the Belgians, Germans, and Italians possessed the virtuous moeurs necessary for life in a republic, be it an expanded French Republic or an autonomous sister republic. Their concerns on this front plainly paralleled those regarding the moeurs of the French. While in domestic policy such unease led to the range of didactic programs discussed in chapter 2, in foreign policy it led France's decision makers to ask repeatedly if the various peoples of Europe were "ready for liberty."[4] Such considerations, in keeping with the dominant ethos of post-Terror France, were a central component of decision making about foreign policy.

Domestic and foreign policy were thus intertwined at the most foundational of levels. Virtually the same questions, issues, and forms of justification organized debate in both realms. This should come as no surprise, given that most members of the republican center were actively involved in both domestic and foreign policy. Sieyès, for example, negotiated the Treaty of the Hague in 1795 and was then France's ambassador to Prussia in 1798–99, while Daunou served as France's commissioner in Rome and drafted both the Cisalpine Republic's second constitution and the Batavian Constitution in 1798. In addition, authors such as Toussaint Guiraudet, Louis-Pierre Anquetil, and Théremin were employed by the Ministry of

4. In the Caribbean, it helped lead the republican commissioners to impose a harsh transitional regime from slavery to freedom. See Laurent Dubois, *A Colony of Citizens: Revolution and Slave Emancipation in the French Caribbean* (Chapel Hill, N.C., 2004), pt. 2.

Foreign Affairs as analysts and agents. Guiraudet was Foreign Minister Delacroix's general secretary, apparently translating Machiavelli's complete works during his leisure time.[5] Théremin was the ministry's leading authority on German affairs, at one point singled out by Prussia's ambassador to France as "the great expert who is consulted."[6] Current scholarship has largely overlooked the vital interrelations between domestic and foreign policy, but questions of the international order were of integral importance to the republican center's political thinking, just as its political thinking was of integral importance to Europe's emerging international order.[7]

It should be noted that consideration of both the Republic's existing overseas possessions and further overseas expansion was largely absent from the debate on foreign policy and the international order. This was in part because sea-based empire was generally viewed in different terms from land-based empire in early modern political thought, provoking different sets of questions and concerns.[8] Moreover, article 6 of the Constitution of the Year III stipulated that "the French colonies are integral parts of the Republic and are subjected to the same constitutional law."[9] In other words, the French constitution was to be applied identically in the colonies and in the metropole. The colonies were departments with representation in proportion to their populations, including the emancipated slaves.[10] While the Constitution of the Year III was not in fact promulgated outside Saint-Domingue and Guyana, France's overseas territories were nonetheless considered at this point simply part of the republic and

5. Niccolò Machiavelli, *Oeuvres de Machiavel; traduction nouvelle par T. Guiraudet,* 9 vols. (Paris, 1799).

6. Sandoz-Rollin, letter of 2 August 1796, in Paul Bailleu, ed., *Preussen und Frankreich von 1795 bis 1807. Diplomatische correspondenzen,* 2 vols. (Leipzig, 1881–87), 1:84. Sydney Biro, citing this letter, calls Théremin "the Directory's consultant in such matters." *The German Policy of Revolutionary France: A Study in French Diplomacy during the War of the First Coalition, 1792–1797,* 2 vols. (Cambridge, Mass., 1957), 2:624.

7. On foreign policy more broadly during the Directory, see above all Raymond Guyot, *Le Directoire et la paix de l'Europe: Des traités de Bâle à la deuxième coalition (1795–1799)* (Paris, 1911); and Belissa, *Repenser l'ordre européen.*

8. David Armitage, *The Ideological Origins of the British Empire* (Cambridge, 2000), chaps. 5–6; Anthony Pagden, *Lords of All the World: Ideologies of Empire in Spain, Britain and France, c.1500–c.1850* (New Haven, 1995).

9. Jacques Godechot, ed., *Les constitutions de la France depuis 1789* (Paris, 1979), 104.

10. E.g., *Liste formée en exécution de l'article II du décret de la Convention nationale, du 13 Fructidor de l'an troisième, des Membres de la Convention qui y sont en activité* (Paris, 1795).

did not occupy the same conceptual space as foreign policy. Further overseas expansion was not widely discussed in no small part because, with the important exception of Santo Domingo (acquired from Spain in 1795) and a few smaller Caribbean islands briefly occupied in 1798, France did not occupy new overseas possessions during the Revolution and in fact lost Martinique for eight years at this time (1794–1802).[11] More speculatively, potential expansion into the Americas did not provoke the same anxieties and concerns as expansion into Europe, in large measure because the Americas seem to have been envisioned, on a certain level, as "empty lands" without native peoples, which could be settled by Europeans (and African slaves prior to the emancipation decree of 1794). For example, a petition sent to the Ministry of Foreign Affairs in the summer of 1797 advocated the acquisition of an American colony "in a temperate climate where Europeans can cultivate the earth" without any consideration of native peoples.[12] And Sieyès mused in his personal notes in the fall of 1795 that in the future France might need colonies for its excess population, noting that the Greek republics followed this "system"—and again not seeming to consider the presence of native peoples.[13] As a result of these different factors and despite the occasional discussion, post-Terror debate on expansion generally did not include sustained consideration of overseas colonies.

The major geographic region in which the Republic did entertain overseas annexationist ambitions was the eastern Mediterranean, where it annexed the islands of Corfu and Cephalonia and launched Napoleon Bonaparte's infamous invasion of Egypt. Expansion into the region had been discussed in France since the middle of the century, but there was

11. In the case of Santo Domingo (the present-day Dominican Republic), territorially contiguous with the colony of Saint-Domingue (present-day Haiti), the Republic's primary concern was to ensure that the population, the Spanish as well as the freed slaves, accepted incorporation into the Republic. See the instructions for a special agent dispatched to carry out this task, signed by the entire Executive Directory: "Mémoire pour servir d'instructions à l'agent provisoire du Gouvernement français à la partie espagnole de St. Domingue," 24 Floréal, Year 5 (May 13 1797), MAE, MD Amérique 14, f. 368–72.

12. "Mémoire et projet présenté au Ministre des Relations extérieurs, ayant rapport à l'établissement d'une colonie," 2 Thermidor, Year 5 (20 July 1797), MAE, MD Amérique 33, f. 210.

13. Sieyès, "Note" on "Espagne, Saint-Domingue, Louisiane, Angleterre," 28 Vendémiaire, Year 4 (20 October 1795), AN, 284 AP 10, d. 11.

little public debate on the topic during the Directory until the Egypt expedition of 1798–99.[14] The invasion, however, was envisioned first and foremost as a strike against England. Largely Bonaparte's personal venture, its leading proponent in the government was Foreign Minister Talleyrand, who was perhaps the day's strongest advocate of overseas expansion in general. Shortly before his appointment to the ministry, he proposed in a speech to the National Institute in 1797 that the Republic prepare for the secession of the American colonies and turn toward establishing commercial colonies along the coast of Africa. Announcing that the end of the Europeans' American empires was afoot, he argued that the new enterprises would have to be semiautonomous, commercially driven settler colonies constructed along the Greek rather than the Roman model.[15] Talleyrand's concern with such questions put him in the minority in post-Terror France, as the debate on foreign policy and the international order tended to focus on expansion within Europe. His modern emphasis on commercial colonies, moreover, set him against the classical-republican wisdom of the day, even if he continued to use classical examples and terms of reference.

This chapter examines the conceptual framework—the way questions were posed, the answers ventured, the very terms of discussion—of the debate on foreign policy and the international order between 1794 and 1799.

The Expansionist Dilemma

Debate about expansion was rooted in the day's political wisdom regarding the nature of the republic as a political form. Republics, it was thought, could not survive expansion. The history of republics and early modern

14. On Napoleon's expedition, see Henry Laurens, *Les origines intellectuelles de l'expédition d'Egypte: l'orientalisme islamisant en France (1698–1798)* (Paris, 1987); Laurens, *L'expédition d'Egypte, 1798–1801* (Paris, 1989); Edward James Kolla, "Not So Criminal: New Understandings of Napoléon's Foreign Policy in the East," *French Historical Studies* 30 (2007): 175–201; and the document collection, Clément de La Jonquière, ed., *L'expédition d'Égypte, 1798–1801,* new edition ed. Jacques Garnier, 6 vols. (Paris, 2003).

15. Talleyrand, *Extrait d'un Essai sur les avantages à retirer de Colonies nouvelles dans les cironstances présentes* (Paris, 1797).

political philosophy both taught that republican liberty and territorial expansion were fundamentally incompatible, that extension would lead inexorably to despotism.[16] This widely held conviction was rooted primarily in the historical example of the Roman Republic, which, it was said, became corrupt and lost its liberty through the extension of territory, the resultant centrifugal forces among citizens, and the rise in power of the armies. Conversely, Sparta, which did not expand, was said to have remained free. Classical history was a lingua franca of eighteenth-century political argument, and the Roman story emerged as a sort of standard narrative.[17] Liberty and virtue, it was thought, could not survive the transformation of a republic into an empire. The story's basic lexicon in Enlightenment and revolutionary France was established in Montesquieu's *The Greatness of the Romans and Their Decline,* which itself was indebted to Machiavelli's telling of Roman history in *The Discourses on Livy.* Chapter 9 of Montesquieu's *Romans,* titled "Two Causes of Rome's Ruin," explained that "when the domination of Rome was limited to Italy, the republic could easily survive." Yet, Montesquieu continued, "when the legions crossed the Alps and the sea," the republic was doomed to be "lost."[18] Montesquieu's analysis was then reiterated by Jaucourt in the *Encyclopédie:* "the Roman Republic had devoured all the other republics, and destroyed all the kings, when it collapsed under the weight of its size and its power. The Romans, in destroying others, destroyed themselves."[19] The Roman story, in short, was a staple feature of eighteenth-century political discourse in France and the early modern Atlantic world. Moreover, the Roman story squared with the commonplace notion, articulated

16. See Armitage, *Ideological Origins of the British Empire,* chap. 5; Armitage, "Empire and Liberty: A Republican Dilemma," in *Republicanism: A Shared European Heritage,* ed. Quentin Skinner and Martin Van Gelderen, vol. 2, *The Values of Republicanism in Early Modern Europe* (Cambridge, 2002).

17. There was a lively early modern debate over Rome's fall, but the different explanations put forward all converged on the same normative lesson: imperial expansion would kill the republic. See J. G. A. Pocock, *Barbarism and Religion,* vol. 3, *The First Decline and Fall* (Cambridge, 2003).

18. Charles-Louis de Secondat, baron de Montesquieu, *Considérations sur les causes de la grandeur des Romains et de leur décadence* [1734], in *Oeuvres complètes,* ed. Roger Caillois, 2 vols. (Paris, 1949–51), 2:116–17.

19. Denis Diderot and Jean Le Rond d'Alembert, eds., *Encyclopédie, ou Dictionnaire raisonné des sciences, des arts et des métiers,* 35 vols. (Paris, 1751–72), s.v. "Romain empire" (article by M. le Chevalier de Jaucourt).

most famously in the eighteenth century by Rousseau, that republics had to be territorially compact.

Anxieties over expansion constituted one part of a wider classical-republican discourse on international affairs. Encompassing a host of diagnoses and prescriptions, this discourse revolved, in its essence, around the corrosive effects of war and diplomacy on domestic liberty and on the tendency of war and the international commercial system to promote despotism. The classical-republican discourse on international affairs was alive and well in eighteenth-century France. It was not, however, the only conceptual framework proffered in the eighteenth century. As in domestic politics, it was obvious to some that the modern world in which they lived was qualitatively new in human history and that political wisdom needed to change to match these wider material and intellectual developments. The miraculous changes of the preceding centuries in commerce, exploration, technology, and knowledge had combined to usher in a brave new world in which the political truths inherited from antiquity were no longer apposite. But in post-Terror France, such "modern" views, while important, would nevertheless remain a minority current in political discourse. Traditional republican wisdom continued to dominate.

The political-philosophical suppositions of the early modern period took on immediate relevance when the French Republic began to occupy increasingly large amounts of territory. The question of what to do with the conquered territories emerged as one of the day's most pressing issues. And the terms of debate were in large part conceptually underpinned, even structured, by classical-republican anxieties about expansion.

These anxieties were voiced in a variety of sites. Petitioners, journalists, and legislators all expressed concern about the corrosive effects of expansion on the health of the body politic. Over and over, it was said that the French Republic had to beware the fate of Rome. For example, an anonymous, untitled petition submitted to the government in late 1794 argued against expansion, warning that "history teaches us the dangers born of size.... Rome was destroyed by its magnitude. Sparta maintained itself by its modesty."[20] The same concerns were also expressed at the highest levels of government. Antoine-Claire Thibaudeau recalled

20. 23 Vendémiaire and 1 Frimaire, Year 3 (14 October and 21 November 1794), MAE, MD Allemagne 117, f. 285–300, 301–12.

in his memoirs that the Commission of Eleven drafting the new constitution in the summer of 1795 struggled with precisely the question of expansion: "We remembered all of the crimes by which the thirst for conquest stained the Roman name, and the mortal blows that it delivered to Rome's liberty. It was feared that one day the same cause would produce the same effects in France. The majority of the Commission sought to prevent this scourge."[21] And François-Antoine Boissy d'Anglas, Thibaudeau's frequent rival within the Commission of Eleven, told the Convention in the summer of 1795 that Rome's "system of conquest... caused its loss."[22] In the prize contest on institutions to found the morality of a people, discussed in chapter 2, the submission that was the most fully and clearly classical-republican in tone also expressed the deepest concern about the effects of expansion on the health of the republic.[23] To give one more example, in 1799 the journalist Pierre Gallet rhetorically asked, "Do we believe that France would adopt so disastrous a system? Do we believe that she would want to imitate the fate of the Romans?"[24] As these different examples, which could be multiplied many times over, all suggest, classical-republican anxieties over expansion were widely, and deeply, felt in post-Terror France. The trope was standard fare in political debate, the anxiety a constituent aspect of the post-Terror political imagination.

The influence of such classical-republican anxieties about expansion can be seen in the elaboration of the two most prominent features of the Republic's foreign policy after 1794: the annexation of territory up to France's so-called "natural frontiers" and the often bewildering policy of establishing sister republics in certain conquered territories. "Natural frontiers" were envisioned as the limit to which the Republic could expand without jeopardizing its republican liberty. Sister republics, in turn, would allow the French Republic to build a "federative system" beyond those frontiers without exposing itself to the expansionist danger.

21. A.-C. Thibaudeau, *Mémoires sur la Convention et le Directoire,* 2 vols. (Paris, 1824), 1:181.

22. Boissy d'Anglas, *Discours sur la situation intérieure et extérieure de la République* (Paris, 1795), 14–15.

23. Roederer, summary of *mémoire* no. 13, n.d., AN, 29 AP 111, f. 359.

24. Pierre Gallet, *Précis sur la paix, contenant le tableau de la situation politique de la France envers les puissances armées et les moyens propres à accélérer l'oeuvre de la pacification, tout en lui donnant une base inebranable* (Paris, 1799), 14–15.

Map 1. The French Republic and Its Sister Republics, early 1799

Natural Frontiers

By 1795 the French Republic possessed, both de jure and de facto, territories extending its borders to France's supposed "natural frontiers": the Atlantic, the Pyrenees, the Mediterranean, the Alps, and the Rhine. These geographical frontiers were imagined to be France's boundaries prescribed by nature—mountains, oceans, rivers. In addition, they were said to be the boundaries assigned to ancient Gaul by Julius Caesar and then delineated by the Greek geographer Strabo. The importance of this model for France's boundaries, underpinned by both nature and history, and disseminated in the schools of the Old Regime, can hardly be overstated. It was, in the words of the historian Denis Richet, part of the revolutionaries' "cultural baggage,... inscribed in their memory."[25] In their vision of France's natural frontiers, the revolutionaries also drew on two additional genealogies, the foreign policy of the Old Regime and the writings of eighteenth-century republicans. In this context, it is important to emphasize that while the natural frontiers foreign policy has normally been associated with long-standing trends in the Old Regime monarchy (especially Richelieu's *Political Testament* and Louis XIV's Rhine policy), the concept also had a distinguished republican lineage. Rousseau, for example, had described natural frontiers as fixing "the number and size" of nations and thus "the political order of the Continent."[26] For republicans such as Rousseau, natural frontiers was an abstract principle dictating a state's ideal size, not a policy legislating conquest and annexation. Nonetheless, the principle could be combined with more traditional ideas within French foreign policy to underpin an expansionist program. In the early Revolution, the concept was trumpeted by the Girondins and invoked to justify the annexations of Avignon and Savoy. Building on and blending these

25. Richet, "Frontières naturelles," in *Dictionnaire critique de la Révolution française: Idées,* ed. François Furet and Mona Ozouf (Paris, 1992), 222. See also Guyot, *Le Directoire et la paix de l'Europe,* 108–20; Peter Sahlins, "Natural Frontiers Revisited: France's Boundaries since the Seventeenth Century," *American Historical Review* 95 (1990): 1423–51; Sahlins, *Boundaries: The Making of France and Spain in the Pyrenees* (Berkeley, 1989), 35–38, 97, 186–92; and Belissa, *Repenser l'ordre européen,* 207–34.

26. Jean-Jacques Rousseau, *Extrait du projet de paix perpetuelle de l'Abbé de Saint Pierre* [1756], quoted in Sahlins, "Natural Frontiers Revisited," 1436. See also Marc Belissa, *Fraternité universelle et intérêt national (1713–1795): Les cosmopolitiques du droit des gens* (Paris, 1998), 97–101.

different pedigrees, the post-Terror republican center envisioned France's natural frontiers as the "natural" limits to which the republic could expand without endangering its republican liberty. Expansion to France's natural frontiers was deemed safe, but beyond was considered dangerous. A natural frontiers policy thus allowed France to annex certain territories while allaying classical-republican anxieties about expansion. As the neo-Jacobin Briot forcefully put it in 1799, France had expanded to "the limits that nature has traced for its territory. We must conserve them intact. But it is essential that we solemnly vow that these limits will never be surpassed.... While conserving them intact, it is of the utmost importance to reject any idea of expansion, which would, inevitably, kill the Republic."[27] This grafting together of classical republicanism and geographical naturalism clearly echoed Montesquieu's take on Rome in *The Greatness of the Romans and Their Decline* and powerfully shaped the post-Terror discourse on foreign policy.

In practice, expansion to its so-called natural frontiers was a priority of the French Republic throughout Thermidor and the Directory. France established the Pyrenees as its border with Spain in the Treaty of Basel, signed on 22 July 1795, and then set securing "the Alps as a barrier" as its goal in negotiations with the King of Sardinia.[28] Expansion to the Rhine, however, was more complicated, for it involved the Austrian Netherlands (modern-day Belgium and Luxembourg), Holland, and the German Rhineland, which was divided among Prussia, Austria, and a host of smaller powers.

Belgium and Luxembourg, for their part, were widely held to fall within France's natural frontiers. The area was originally occupied by French armies in 1792, soon after the revolutionary wars began. The population then voted for "reunion" in January 1793 in a plebiscite organized by the French. Austria temporarily reoccupied the low countries soon afterward, but the French definitively took possession in the summer of 1794 at the battle of Fleurus. France then moved quickly to annex the territories. After assuming control of Dutch territory between the Rhine and the northern edge of Belgium in the Treaty of the Hague of 16 May 1795, the

27. Briot, *Sur la situation intérieure et extérieure de la République* (Paris, 1799), 37, 41.

28. "Rapport de la section des relations extérieurs au Comité de Salut public," Year 3 (1794–95), MAE, MD France 655, f. 18.

National Convention voted overwhelmingly on 1 October 1795 to annex outright "all the lands on this side of the Rhine" comprising the Austrian Netherlands, the Bishopric of Liège, and the area around the Dutch city of Maastricht, declaring them nine new French departments.[29] While Austria did not recognize France's annexation of the erstwhile Austrian Netherlands until the Treaty of Campo Formio, signed on 17 October 1797, the French Republic incorporated the area unimpeded.

The annexation of the German Rhineland proved to be a more contentious issue and provoked a more ardent, longer-lasting debate that flared after the signing of the Treaty of Basel with Prussia in 1795 and again around the Congress of Rastatt in 1798.[30] In fact, France did not formally annex the Rhineland until 1802, after several years of occupation and informal annexation. In diplomatic negotiations, however, it pressed for annexation throughout Thermidor and the Directory. On 5 April 1795 France and Prussia signed the Treaty of Basel, which, in its secret clauses, gave France control of the left bank of the Rhine but postponed formal annexation until peace was reached with Austria. Then, when negotiating with Austria, the Directory instructed its envoys in the spring of 1796 that a minimum condition for peace would be "that the Republic's territory will have all the waters of the Rhine for its borders on the German side" and in the winter of 1796–97 that "the first and most essential" goal was that Austria cede to the Republic "the Austrian Netherlands, the Duchy of Luxembourg, and all of the Empire's possessions on the left bank of the Rhine."[31] Negotiations never settled the status of the Rhineland, which, officially, remained an open question.

As a result, those in favor of annexation of the Rhineland worked to keep the issue alive. Petitions streamed into the Ministry of Foreign Affairs, articles were published, and proannexation politicians pushed their agendas—not least of whom were Sieyès and Jean-François Reubell. Reubell, who sat on the Executive Directory from 1795 to 1799 and was

29. *RM,* 26:122–23.

30. See Ph. Sagnac, *Le Rhin français pendant la Révolution et l'Empire* (Paris, 1917); Biro, *German Policy of Revolutionary France;* T. C. W. Blanning, *The French Revolution in Germany: Occupation and Resistance in the Rhineland, 1792–1802* (Oxford, 1983).

31. Directory to Poteratz, 23 Germinal, Year 4 (12 April 1796), MAE, MD Autriche 8, f. 170–71; Directory to Clarke, 27 Nivôse, Year 5 (16 January 1797), MAE, CP Autriche 367, f. 47–48.

the director most engaged with foreign policy questions, was particularly focused on the issue. A native of Colmar in Alsace, he argued that the annexation of the entire left bank of the Rhine should be the Republic's first foreign policy priority. Outside the halls of government, Reubell maintained close contact with a group of Rhine radicals, centered in Mainz and then Paris, who supported "reunion" with the French Republic as the most effective means to achieve their political goals.[32] Probably more vocal than numerous, proannexation Rhinelanders emphasized the country's philosophical enlightenment, claiming that the *Aufklärung* had prepared the German peoples for political revolution. One essay submitted to the Directory by a Mainz "patriot" claimed that "in general, the rights of peoples are today better known and more widely proclaimed in Germany than in several departments of France."[33] Proannexation Rhinelanders launched public-relations endeavors such as an essay contest in 1795 asking whether France should expand its territorial boundaries to the Rhine. Initiated by Georges-Guillaume Boehmer, a one-time Mainz Jacobin, the contest made no attempt to hide its bias. Its announcement in the *Moniteur* explained that it would be "morally impossible to prove to honest and enlightened judges...that it is in the interest of the republic to let escape this opportune moment to retake its ancient boundaries, drawn by nature herself."[34] The volume in which the essay contest's winning entries were published drove home this message with a frontispiece showing two figures in classical dress approaching a river while examining a map that clearly marked France's border as the Rhine. The caption read, "The descendants of the Gauls reclaiming their ancient limits."[35]

The reasons advanced in support of the annexation of Belgium and the Rhineland, and thus expansion to France's natural frontiers, were diverse.

32. Jacques Droz, *L'Allemagne et la Révolution française* (Paris, 1949), 203–4; Droz, *La pensée politique et morale des cisrhénans* (Paris, 1940).

33. "Observations politiques sur les nouvelles limites de la République française par Metternich, patriote réfugié de Mayence," n.d., BN, Nouv. Acqu. Fr. 23654, f. 76.

34. 5 Fructidor, Year 3 (22 August 1795), *RM,* 25:518. The contest was financed by a manufacturer named List. See Jean-René Suratteau and Alain Bischoff, *Jean-François Reubell: L'Alsacien de la Révolution française* (Steinbrunn-le-Haut, Fr., 1995), 193; and Sagnac, *Le Rhin français pendant la Révolution et l'Empire,* 115–17.

35. Georges-Guillaume Boehmer, ed., *La Rive gauche du Rhin, limite de la République française, ou Recueil de plusieurs dissertations jugées dignes des prix proposés par un négociant de la rive gauche du Rhin* (Paris, 1795).

Théremin argued that it was France's duty to spread liberty and break "the mold of gothic institutions."[36] Similarly, Marc-Antoine Jullien wrote that abandoning the Belgians or the Rhinelanders would constitute an act of "*liberticide.*"[37] François-René Pommereul somewhat absurdly described France's expansion to the Rhine as "the necessary result of the eternal conflict between liberty and slavery." Claiming that the Revolution marked the Gauls' overthrow of fifteen centuries of domination by the aristocratic Franks, Pommereul urged the Republic to reclaim the limits of ancient Gaul (and possibly, he mused, to retake the name "Gaul").[38] Anquetil of the National Institute, who regularly prepared analyses for the Ministry of Foreign Affairs, claimed that Belgium and the Rhineland naturally fell within a greater French economic basin and commercial system.[39] More common was the argument that natural frontiers constituted the most secure form of border and thus a key defensive "barrier" against future invasion. As Karcher, a deputy from Moselle, wrote to the Directory concerning the Rhine: "It is a truth widely acknowledged that the safest barrier, the one that will cost the least to guard and that will be the easiest to defend, is the Rhine."[40] The argument that natural frontiers were militarily the most secure was applied not only to France. Bonaparte noted in a report to Foreign Minister Talleyrand that the Treaty of Campo Formio had secured for the Cisalpine Republic geographical features amounting to "perhaps the most militarily secure frontiers in Europe."[41] Secure borders would, in turn, allow a republic to become a defensive rather than an

36. Théremin, "Discours sur la question: Est-il de l'interêt de la République Française de reculer ses limites jusqu'aux bords du Rhin," in Boehmer, *La Rive gauche du Rhin,* 19.

37. [Marc-Antoine Jullien], "Un mot encore sur la faction des anciennes limites, ou Quelques idées sur les conditions de paix que des prétendus politiques voudraient nous faire accepter," *L'Orateur plébéien ou le Défenseur de la République par une société d'écrivains patriotes,* no. 11 (1795): 3.

38. [Pommereul], "Méditations sur la question proposée: Est-il de l'intérêt de la République française, de reculer ses limites jusqu'aux bords du Rhin?" in Boehmer, *La Rive gauche du Rhin,* 175.

39. Anquetil, "Mémoire sur le commerce d'Allemagne par le Rhin," 23 Fructidor, Year 4 (9 September 1796), MAE, MD Allemagne 117, f. 392–402.

40. Karcher, "Observations sur les limites de la République à l'est," n.d., BN, Nouv. Acqu. Fr. 23654, f. 133.

41. Bonaparte to Talleyrand, 27 Vendémiaire, Year 6 (18 October 1797), in Napoléon Bonaparte, *Correspondance générale,* ed. Thierry Lentz et al., 4 vols. at present (Paris, 2004–), 1:1257, no. 2170 (hereafter cited as *CGN*).

expansionist state. Arguments in favor of expansion to France's natural frontiers were thus made vis-à-vis both specific territories and the abstract principle. Expansion and annexation, it was claimed, would benefit both the French Republic and the peoples of Belgium and the Rhineland.

These diverse claims, however, did not settle the issue. The annexation of Belgium and the Rhineland and thus the question of expansion to France's natural frontiers provoked lively discussion throughout the post-Terror years, even if in the case of Belgium the outcome was never truly in question.[42] Two interrelated issues in particular prompted serious deliberation. The first was the fundamental question of whether expansion was "safe," that is, whether it would jeopardize the health of the French Republic. The second was the problem of incorporating new and different populations into the republic, or the problem of diversity of moeurs. Both issues cut straight to the heart of a host of elemental questions concerning the nature of the republic as a political form. And in both cases classical-republican concerns structured debate. Opponents of annexation played on classical-republican tropes to make their case while supporters had to explicitly respond to classical-republican anxieties about expansion. Among those in favor of expansion, some rejected the relevance of the classical-republican critique to the case in question while others challenged its very conceptual basis. These careful rejections were far from perfunctory. They constituted important justifications or forms of enablement that underline just how deeply classical-republican anxieties were ingrained in the post-Terror political imagination.

One of the most succinct statements of the classical-republican critique of expansion, focusing on the issue of size, was delivered by the deputy Lesage at the outset of the debate in the National Convention on whether to annex Belgium. Lesage urged his colleagues to remember the lessons taught by the republics of classical antiquity. Reprising the standard early modern narrative, he argued that the histories of Athens, Sparta, and Rome all proved that a republic would perish if it succumbed to expansionist ambitions, even expansion to its natural frontiers. "Ambition has destroyed nations and reversed empires," he explained. "Athens was happy and free until the moment...she wanted to govern

42. The decision to annex the Rhineland was not definitively taken until the end of 1797. Belissa, *Repenser l'ordre européen,* 221.

all of Greece, . . . invade Sicily, ruin Sparta, [and] tyrannize her colonies and her allies. . . . The military genius of Rome pushed its warriors and planted its victorious eagles to the extremities of the known world; but all the philosophers agree that Rome's triumphs were the sign of its defeat, and that its own size was a stronger foe than the courage and the fury of the barbarians." Lesage then quoted Rousseau on the dangers of size before laconically summarizing his argument: "It is therefore true that all expansion weakens a state."[43]

Opponents of the annexation of the Rhineland similarly focused on the question of size, repeating the trope that if the French Republic became too large it would rot from within—that, in other words, expansion was not "safe." As an anonymous essay submitted to the Directory argued, "if we want to surpass our former frontiers, we risk losing our liberty."[44] No one, though, suggested a return to the status quo ante. Rather, the primary alternative advocated was an independent state of some form or another along the Rhine's left bank, usually a Cis-Rhénane Republic. Representative of this view was a pamphlet published anonymously in 1797 by Georges Rebmann, a leading Rhine republican.[45] Rebmann played on anxieties about expansion to argue that France should establish a sister republic in the Rhineland rather than annex the territory. A sister republic, he claimed, would inoculate France against exposure to the dangers of expansion.

> One hears that, in expanding, the French Republic would surpass its proper size and that the mélange of several peoples, each with a different language and different character, would undermine its harmony, public spirit, and domestic peace. . . . We admit that these fears, which have been responded to more than once, are well founded. Because of this, . . . nothing would be more advantageous for France than . . . founding a Rheno-Germanic Republic on the basis of the French constitution.[46]

43. *RM,* 26:95.

44. "Quelques Réflexions sur la situation présente du gouvernement français relativement à l'Allemagne," n.d., BN, Nouv. Acqu. Fr. 23654, f. 76.

45. On Rebmann, see Droz, *L'Allemagne et la Révolution française,* 248–59.

46. [Georges Rebmann], *Coup d'oeil sur le Rhin, relativement aux négociations de paix, présenté aux deux pouvoirs suprêmes de la République française* (Paris, 1797), 4. A highly similar argument can be found in *Observations sur cette question, proposée par un Négociant des bords du Rhin: Est-il de l'intérêt de la République française de reculer ses limites jusqu'aux bords du Rhin?* (Lille, 1795).

While the pamphlet was highly tendentious, the fact that Rebmann relied on such classical-republican tropes to make his case speaks to their perceived rhetorical resonance in Directorial debate.

Such arguments did not sway the eventual turn of events, but they resonated strongly enough with the republican wisdom of the day that a host of proannexation speakers felt compelled to respond to the substance of the classical-republican critique. Supporters of annexation of both Belgium and the Rhineland thus took great pains to counter such arguments and demonstrate that expansion to natural frontiers was safe. Stopping at France's natural frontiers, it was claimed, obviated concerns about the Republic's growing too large. During the debate on Belgium, for example, the soon-to-be minister of foreign relations Charles Delacroix, who at this time was making a name for himself as an expert on foreign affairs,[47] described France's natural frontiers as the limits to which France could expand without risking a repeat performance of the Roman tragedy. Significantly, Delacroix did not challenge the veracity of the classical-republican critique of expansion but argued that states have a "natural" size beyond which they expose themselves to the dangers of expansion: "States, like the human body, tend to grow until they have attained the limits that nature has fixed for them. France in particular seems to have eternal limits: the Alps, the Ocean, the Pyrenees, the Rhine. By an irresistible tendency, she tries to reach them. But I would tremble if France ever tried to surpass these limits. Rome would have conserved its force, its glory, its liberty, if, staying in Italy, she had feared to put even one foot on the other side of the Alps." Delacroix here fully accepted the classical-republican forewarning about expansion, repeating almost exactly Montesquieu's analysis in *The Greatness of the Romans and Their Decline*. However, he rejected its relevance to France's annexation of Belgium on the ground that states have a natural size—awareness of which would supposedly have saved Rome.[48] Tellingly, the future minister of foreign relations never challenged the essential conceptual framework of the classical-republican critique of expansion, only its application to the annexation of Belgium.

47. Louis-Marie La Révellière-Lépeaux, *Mémoires de Larevellière-Lépeaux, publiés par son fils*, 3 vols. (Paris, 1895), 1:355.

48. Charles Delacroix, *Opinion sur la réunion de la Belgique et du pays de Liège* (Paris, 1795), 2–3.

At around the same time, J.-J. Derché, an employee in the Ministry of Foreign Affairs, advanced a parallel argument regarding the Rhineland. In a pamphlet that earned a second-place prize in Boehmer's contest, Derché similarly accepted the fundaments of the classical-republican critique but rejected its application to the case in question. After emphasizing at length that the Rhine was France's natural frontier and that only nature, not politics or treaties, could determine the boundaries of a nation, he rebuffed any comparison with Rome. "We should stop frightening ourselves with the example of the Romans, who, because of their conquests, lost the form of their government and finished by succumbing to the most horrible tyranny." The Roman example, while real, did not apply to the French annexation of the Rhineland because of the meager amount of territory in question and because France was extending to its *natural* frontier. Moreover, in practical terms, modern forms of communication rendered the distances in question a fraction of those under the Roman Empire. "The limits France wants to give itself equal only four provinces of the Roman Empire. It is easier for the French to communicate from the Pyrenees to the mouth of the Meuse than it was for the Romans to communicate from one end of Italy to the other."[49] Derché's pamphlet offered a somewhat jumbled set of proannexation arguments, bolstered with a wide range of citations and references, but, importantly, his arguments all proceeded from the premise that the question at issue was whether the classical-republican critique of expansion was germane. And Derché did not challenge its conceptual coherence in the modern world, only its application to France's annexation of the Rhineland.

Not all proannexation pamphlet writers, however, accepted the fundaments of the classical-republican critique of expansion. Some claimed that France was a distinctively modern republic and thus that the received wisdom concerning republics was immaterial. In the debate on Belgium, perhaps the closest statement to a complete dismissal of the classical-republican critique came from Joseph Eschassériaux, who responded directly to the claim that republics could not exist in such large territories. "People advance an objection that derives its force from an old prejudice. People object that France with Belgium added will become too large to

49. J.-J. Derché, *Discours sur la rive gauche du Rhin, limite de la République française* (1795), 19–21.

be governed by a republican system.... The writers who established this maxim saw before them only states without communication, peoples thrown in the desert. It cannot be applied to France, where the speed of communications brings together the most distant lands."[50] Eschassériaux's argument was simple: modern forms of communication and administration had changed the very nature of state practices and thus the basic calculus regarding how large a republic could be. While he did not extend his argument to expansion in all circumstances—he restricted it to the case of France's annexation of Belgium—he nonetheless advanced a powerful challenge to the classical-republican wisdom concerning expansion and the size of republics. France, as a modern nation, he claimed, did not have to worry about the expansionist dilemma.

In the case of the Rhineland, a handful of writers advanced the more novel, even radical, argument that France could expand because the representative system enshrined in the Constitution of the Year III qualitatively changed the nature of the republic as a political form—because, in other words, France was a modern and not a classical republic. This argument was intended to dispel what was taken to be the standard wisdom regarding republics. Théremin, whose essay took first place in Boehmer's contest, simply dismissed the classical-republican critique of expansion as outdated. While discussing possible arguments for and against the annexation of the Rhineland, he explained that "I say nothing about the danger that results from too large an expansion of the empire because we have abandoned the prejudice that a republic should be small and that a large state can survive only as a monarchy." Théremin could write off the traditional "prejudice" against republican expansion so confidently because of the modern institution of representative government. The French Republic could expand yet remain a republic, he admonished his readers, because of "the means that representative government offers for governing even the largest empire."[51] While the majority of his writings urged expansion to the Rhine and the creation of sister republics beyond, he also wrote a few very long ministerial circulars calling for virtually unlimited expansion in the wake of the third partition of Poland: "It would

50. Eschassériaux, *Opinion sur la question de la réunion de la Belgique à la République française* (Paris, 1795), 6.

51. Théremin, "Discours sur la question," 6, 15.

not be good policy for France," he wrote, "to stay within its limits, even its new limits."[52] In Théremin's eyes, representative government changed the basic calculus regarding republics' size and allowed for the modern, expansionist republic.

The importance of representative government in enabling expansion was similarly emphasized by Joseph Hofmann, who had served as president of the short-lived Rheno-German National Convention and strongly supported French annexation of the Rhineland. Hofmann rejected the comparison to Rome and the republics of classical antiquity, protesting what he described as the incessant citations of "the example of Rome's expansion," which those who oppose annexation "never cease to invoke." Sounding slightly exasperated, Hofmann admitted that "I know that the historians and great experts on political affairs are against me." Yet, he continued in a scathing tone,

> I find precisely the opposite of what your authorities claim. Rome did not fall into decline, you say, until she expanded; therefore, expansion is pernicious. I hear a conclusion here, but I do not see a necessary connection between a temporal accident and a tenuous cause. There are a thousand other reasons for Rome's decline; why do you choose only expansion? In the second place, your example proves too much. If the expansion of a state causes its ruin, then not only every province, but also each small village, should remain alone and never enter into political society. If you respond that there is a difference between too much and too little, and that expansion is a relative term, without fixed meaning, then you stipulate for nature's determination and come to my opinion since I regard the Rhine as a natural boundary.

Furthermore, Hofmann charged that revolutionary France and classical Rome were so different that any comparison was baseless. And the crucial feature he pointed to was representative government. If Rome had "a representative government," he even claimed, "the Roman Empire would still exist today."[53]

52. Théremin, "Mémoire raisonné sur la situation actuelle de la République dans ses rapports avec les puissances étrangères," Germinal, Year 4 (March–April 1796), MAE, MD France 655, f. 328.

53. Joseph Hofmann, *Des Nouvelles limites de la République française* (Paris, 1795), 32–36.

Both Théremin and Hofmann claimed that representative government enabled the French Republic to expand without jeopardizing its republican liberty. Their arguments are particularly significant because, taken to their logical extremes, they would enable expansion in a nearly unbridled sense. Neither limited his arguments to the narrower claim that expansion to a certain place under certain conditions is safe. Rather, they both claimed that *expansion itself is safe.* Representative government qualitatively changed the nature of the republic as a political form, creating the "modern republic," which was able to expand yet remain a republic. In both cases, the modern institution of representative government underwrote expansion, engendering a qualitative break with early modern wisdom regarding the republic as a political form.

The possible annexations of Belgium and the Rhineland provoked another, intricately related anxiety: incorporating a new and different people into the French Republic. The diversity of moeurs introduced by expansion, it was feared, would act as a centrifugal force and undermine the collective commitment to the public good necessary for republican political life. Metaphoric space between citizens was threatening in much the same way as literal space between citizens, cities, and institutions. How could the Belgians or the Rhine Germans, different peoples with different traditions and, most important, different moeurs, be integrated into France's republican political culture? Moreover, were they "ready for liberty"? Would they be able to make the transition, which had proven so difficult at home, from subject to citizen?

Such concerns were voiced in typical, if somewhat histrionic, terms by Adrien-Philippe Raoux, a Belgian republican who championed the creation of an independent Belgian republic. In an antiannexation pamphlet published in Paris in 1795, Raoux played on French fears over differences in moeurs, stoking them for argumentative effect. After noting "the opinion of authorities who maintain that the territory of France...is already too vast to form a republic, and that it would be rash to extend it further," which he buttressed with citations to Rousseau's *Social Contract* and *Considerations on the Government of Poland,* Raoux insisted that the Belgian people were too deeply entrenched in their own ways to integrate smoothly into the French Republic. "The Belgians, more than any other people, cling to their ancient customs; one will not undo them in a day." Montesquieu, he stated, had warned against trying to change a people's customs. "'In general,' says Montesquieu, 'peoples are very attached to their customs; taking them away violently will make them unhappy.' "[54] Raoux might have added the rest of the passage from *The Spirit of the Laws,* which squares with the pamphlet's general argument: "therefore one must not change peoples' customs, but engage them to change themselves."[55] Trying to make the Belgians French would be ineffectual at best and counterproductive at worst. In short, he explained with a citation to Rousseau, "moeurs . . . have more influence than laws," a lesson France should take to heart when dealing with foreign peoples.[56] Raoux's pamphlet captured, if for polemical purposes, the widely felt concern that very real differences in moeurs might turn territories subject to annexation into divisive forces within the French Republic.

This line of reasoning and the wider unease it spoke to were countered by a number of proannexation speakers during the debate over Belgium in the National Convention. Boissy d'Anglas argued that the Convention and the French people, in establishing a republican constitution for a nation as large as France, had already disproved both the argument that adding Belgium would make France too large to exist as a republic and the argument that the differences between the French and the Belgians would destabilize the republic from within. "Two principal objections to reunion are introduced," he explained.

> On the one hand, it is said that the French Republic would give too great an extension to its territory. On the other, it is said that the differences between the Belgian nation and the French nation in moeurs, habits, and religious principles will prevent their union from consolidating, that such differences will be a never-ending source of quarrels and discord. . . . It is certain that too great an extension of a state, and especially of a republic, will either weaken it or require an increase in the authority of the government. But you have decided, in creating the constitution that the French people have just accepted, that we do not find ourselves in such a situation. Despite the great size of France, despite its immense population, despite the diversity of moeurs, principles, laws, habits, and characteristics, you have judged that

54. Adrien-Philippe Raoux, *Mémoire sur le projet de réunion de la Belgique à la France* (Paris, 1795), 2, 7.

55. Montesquieu, *De l'esprit des lois* [1748], in *Oeuvres complètes,* 2:565.

56. Raoux, *Mémoire sur le projet de réunion,* 13.

> France could be a republic.... Should the size of Belgium, its population, and its moeurs change your calculations? I am far from believing so.

Significantly, Boissy d'Anglas conceded that size and diversity could destabilize a republic. He did not challenge the basic conceptual claims of the classical-republican critique. Instead, he argued that they were not relevant to France's annexation of Belgium. France was already a large, diverse republic with a constitution to match. Incorporating Belgium would not qualitatively change its nature. The distance, both geographical and cultural, from "Paris to Marseille or Bayonne," he declared, was greater than from "Paris to Maastricht."[57] The classical-republican critique was thus invalid, and the annexation of Belgium would not undermine France's republican constitution.

A different order of response, one that emphasized the ability of politics to change a population's moeurs, was also voiced in regard to the possible annexation of Belgium and the Rhineland. Diversity of moeurs, it was argued, would be overcome in much the same manner that the French population's moeurs would be republicanized—through the hard work of politics, institutions, and time. In regard to Belgium, Joseph Eschassériaux argued that politics and the law would change the Belgians' moeurs. While some "anticipate that the differences in moeurs and institutions, as well as the Belgians' religious prejudices, will be a great obstacle to reunion," he explained, "the experience of time teaches that all of this changes at the will of the government and the law, that a people imperceptibly takes on the character and the moeurs of those to whom it is incorporated, and that this change is rapid for those who come to liberty."[58] Eschassériaux's final point, that the ability of politics and the law to effect change was even more robust when a people was brought to liberty, was made quite frequently. The deputy Garran claimed that living under "institutions... derived solely from the rights of peoples" was as much a novelty for the French as for the Belgians and that both peoples would be transformed and united by "involvement in government and collaborative legislation."[59] An anonymous

57. F. A. Boissy d'Anglas, *Discours sur la réunion de la Belgique à la République française* (Paris, 1795), 6–7.

58. Eschassériaux, *Opinion sur la question de la réunion,* 5.

59. J.-P. Garran de Coulon, *Considérations de droit public sur la réunion de la Belgique à la France* (Paris, 1795), 9.

essay submitted to the Ministry of Foreign Affairs invoked the transformative powers of liberty in similar terms while making the case for annexation of the Rhineland. France should expand to its natural frontiers, the author declared, and "the genius of liberty will warm all the hearts and steer all the wills toward the common good."[60] Eschassériaux, Garran, and the anonymous pamphlet writer all essentially argued that politics and institutions would erase differences in moeurs and create a unified republican population. Living under one government, moved by liberty, differences in moeurs would disappear with time.

In the end, despite the complications and protests, the post-Terror Republic pursued expansion to its natural frontiers by annexing Belgium outright and by de facto annexing the Rhineland. Classical-republican anxieties structured debate around these policies and, in a sense, underwrote the policy. Natural frontiers were seen as the limit, prescribed by nature, to which the French Republic could expand without jeopardizing its republican liberty. Expansion beyond the Rhine, Alps, or Pyrenees, however, was thought treacherous. Beyond its natural frontiers, rather than annexation and expansion, the French Republic thus pursued a very different policy. It established a network of tributary states in Holland, the Italian peninsula, and Switzerland collectively known as sister republics.

Sister Republics

Between 1795 and 1799, the French Republic established eight sister republics: the Batavian (in Holland) in 1795;[61] on the Italian peninsula, from 1796 to 1799, the Cispadane Republic, then the Cisalpine Republic (which the Cispadane joined), the Ligurian Republic (which was really a reorganized version of the Genoan Republic), the Luccan Republic, the Roman Republic, and the Neapolitan (also called the Parthenopaean) Republic; and

60. "Exposé des motifs qui militent en faveur des traités proposés," Pluviose, Year 3 (January–February 1795), MAE, CP Allemagne 667, f. 217.

61. The Batavian Republic presents a special case as its establishment was in many ways akin to intervention in a long-standing civil conflict between Dutch Patriots and Orangists, to refounding the republic after the years of the Stadholder. See Simon Schama, *Patriots and Liberators: Revolution in the Netherlands, 1780–1813* (New York, 1977); Jonathan Israel, *The Dutch Republic: Its Rise, Greatness, and Fall, 1477–1806* (Oxford, 1995), 1119–27.

in Switzerland, the Helvetic Republic in 1798. This experiment in nation building, to use today's political language, was fundamentally informed by classical-republican anxieties about expansion. France did not aim to take possession of lands beyond its natural frontiers, as there was a widespread sense that annexation would prove disastrous for the Republic. Sister republics presented an alternative means to both extend French influence and spread liberty, one that avoided the catalog of perils posed by expansion. La Révellière-Lépeaux recalled in his memoirs that in Italy direct annexations were rejected in favor of sister republics precisely because of concern about the dangers posed by surpassing France's natural limits. As the French army conquered northern Italy, La Révellière-Lépeaux recalled, General Bonaparte proposed the annexation of Genoa, which "I opposed in the strongest terms.... What would happen, I added, if we undertook an excessive extension and left our natural limits? ... When a state like France possesses limits happily traced by nature,... what more can one want? Like households, small states are generally better managed than large ones." Rather, he advocated "a belt of free states attached to France."[62] Such arguments tended to play on standard tropes and anxieties to make their case and thus spoke to an important truism of late eighteenth-century political wisdom and a key feature of the post-Terror political imagination: expansion would jeopardize a republic's political liberty. This anxiety in turn informed the republic's foreign policy as it set about creating sister republics.

Of course, the sister-republic program emerged from a more complicated set of factors than a simple desire to avoid the perceived perils of expansion. If avoiding the dangers posed by expansion were the only concern, the French could have chosen simply to abandon the conquered territories or to trade them away at the peace table. At the moment the sister-republic program was launched, France was almost desperate for peace. Yet it insisted in negotiations with Austria in 1797 that the Cisalpine Republic be recognized as an independent state.[63] Why?

The reasons put forward were various, mirroring in many respects those advanced in support of expansion to France's natural frontiers.

62. La Révellière-Lépeaux, *Mémoires,* 2:35–36.

63. Directory to Clarke, 23 Pluviôse, Year 5 (11 February 1797), MAE, CP Autriche 367, f. 75–76.

Some, such as La Révellière-Lépeaux, argued that sister republics would form a protective belt around France and thus serve as a sort of first line of defense against invasion. Others pointed to the commercial opportunities that would result from such sisters. Another, less common, reason advanced was that a broad program of republicanization would turn the counterrevolutionary forces in Europe on the defensive and help to secure peace at home. François Cacault, apparently renowned for his exceptional knowledge of the Italian peninsula,[64] advised that republicanization was, "of all the plans, that which the Coalition most fears" and could thus be used to bring France's adversaries to the peace table.[65] Fomenting revolution abroad, in other words, would be a potent weapon in the wars and a stick to wield in negotiations.

In addition to such tactical reasons, many believed, as in debate over expansion to France's natural frontiers, in the importance of spreading liberty in an abstract sense. The language used to discuss the sister-republic program frequently referred to liberty as "acquiring" or "winning" a territory or people. Flassan, head of one of the Foreign Ministry's political divisions, wrote that Lombardy had been "acquired" for "Italian liberty."[66] Similarly, General Bonaparte, in a letter to the Directory outlining the Treaty of Campo Formio's likely final form, calculated that between the territories ceded to France and Austria's recognition of the Cisalpine Republic, "liberty gains . . . 7,500,000 inhabitants."[67] While the Treaty of Campo Formio displayed brutal realpolitik in surrendering Venice to the Austrians, Bonaparte's language speaks to the French Republic's very real desire to spread liberty. The Republic's commitment to spreading liberty can also be seen in the fact that it secured amnesty for political prisoners in its peace treaty with the King of Sardinia in 1796 and, likewise, that the Treaty of Campo Formio stipulated that three hundred Venetian patriots be allowed to take refuge in the Cisalpine Republic.[68]

64. Guyot, *Le Directoire et la paix de l'Europe,* 80–81.

65. "Projets sur l'Italie. Extraits de la correspondance du citoyen Cacault, agent de la République en Italie," 26 Pluviôse, Year 4 (14 February 1796), MAE, MD Italie 12, f. 13.

66. Flassan, "Vues générales sur la pacification et la recomposition de divers états d'Italie," Year 4 (1795–96), MAE, MD Italie 12, f. 139.

67. Bonaparte to the Directory, 19 Vendémiaire, Year 6 (10 October 1797), in *CGN,* 1:1248, no. 2153.

68. Belissa, *Repenser l'ordre européen,* 90; Bonaparte to the Directory.

Moreover, the celebratory language used upon the establishment of the various republics always highlighted the progression of liberty in Europe. The creation of sister republics would also be a tonic to republicans in the still-benighted regions of Europe, thereby furthering the cause of liberty indirectly as well. The role played by the desire to spread liberty should not be underestimated.

While the sister-republic program received strong support from certain quarters, it was not universally endorsed and, in fact, was initially rejected. A number of voices questioned the wisdom of establishing small states that would in all likelihood depend on France for survival. Reubell viewed sister republics as virtual parasites. He once jotted in the margin of a report on Geneva that "Brissot...called them little pâtés; but it is with the fat of the meat that pâté is made; and it is at the expense of the great Republic that the little republics fatten themselves."[69] Reubell wanted France to focus on expansion to its natural frontiers, particularly the Rhineland. The Italian campaign, in his eyes, was primarily a means to gain chips to bargain with Austria for the Rhineland, not a beachhead for republicanization. Very much in the same spirit, Flassan proposed in a ministry circular that France should sacrifice the Cispadane Republic—and, more broadly, its "ideas of political perfection"—for peace with Austria. Rather than jeopardize the peace process, Flassan argued, France should establish an independent Lombardy and wait for republics in Italy to proliferate naturally. With inspired rhetorical flourish, he predicted that Lombardy "will grow into a revolutionary *Etna* whose flaming lava, pouring across Italy, will fertilize little by little this soil desiccated by slavery, will purify the air infected by the miasmas of superstition, and will prepare a simultaneous tremor from Florence to Palermo."[70] Flassan's deeper vision, which was typical of those who opposed the sister-republic program, was not to actively forestall the republicanization of Europe but to allow it to proceed organically without sacrificing French interests or entangling the Republic in a quagmire.

In fact, one of the few policy-level treatments of the issue, an untitled working paper on France's Italian policy dated 25 July 1796 plainly rejected

69. 22 Messidor, Year 4 (10 July 1796), AN, AF III 68; quoted in Guyot, *Le Directoire et la paix de l'Europe,* 119.

70. Flassan, "Vues générales," f. 136, 139–40, 142–43.

establishing sister republics in Italy on the grounds that such a policy was not in France's "interests." Drafted by Minister of Foreign Relations Delacroix and signed by four out of five directors, the circular's signature line carefully noted that the piece had been "deliberated"—not decided or decreed—and was "for information and direction only."[71] The circular was drafted while Bonaparte's Italian campaign was still under way, that is, before he had definitively defeated the Austrians and expanded the range of possibilities.[72] It nonetheless stands as an important window into official thinking about foreign policy and why the sister-republic program was rejected in the summer of 1796.

The working paper opens with the statement that "interests" will guide the Republic's Italian policy. "The interests of the republic," Delacroix explained, "should be the basic rule by which we examine and discuss the different [foreign policy] questions. They will dictate the Directory's decision." Thus, at the outset, revolutionary ideals were rejected as the basis of the Republic's Italian policy in favor of "interests," whatever they might be. After establishing this general orientation, the document worked through a series of substantive issues on a point-by-point basis. The first addressed was the question of whether to establish sister republics in Italy: "The first and most important question is this: Should Italy be republicanized? Generally speaking, the question is already decided in the negative." Three reasons were given for this decision. First, "all the information that we have received indicates that the Italian people are not mature enough for liberty." Second, it was important at this point, in the interests of securing a European peace, that France reassure the other European powers that it was not possessed by a "mania...for revolutionizing everything." Third, democratic republics would make less reliable neighbors than would weakened kings. A democratic republic in Piedmont "would be a much more worrying neighbor for us than a king whom we have weakened to the point that he cannot harm us." Similarly, a "nascent republic" in Milan

71. "Italie," 7 Thermidor, Year 4 (25 July 1796), MAE, MD Italie 12, f. 53–62. The only director who did not sign was La Révellière-Lépeaux. Whether this was because he opposed the plan or because he was not present is unfortunately unknown.

72. On 11 June 1796 the Directory had explained to Salicetti that it was waiting to see how the military situation unfolded before committing to a clear policy in either Italy or Germany. "Lettres et instructions du Directoire éxécutif relatives aux operations diplomatiques et militaires depuis le 23 prairial an 4 jusque au 28 thermidor," MAE, MD Italie 12, f. 33[3].

would constantly need support from the French Republic and would turn into "endless seeds of war." "Victorious Rome," it was noted, "did not look to establish republics. It felt that it would always have better deals with kings."[73] Thus, it was concluded, France's interests would in no way be served by republicanization.

The question of whether or not to establish sister republics in Italy at this crucial juncture was thus decided according to a vision of France as an actor in the international arena with interests to be pursued and not one of France as a republic pursuing specifically republican or revolutionary goals. New republics would have to develop organically when their populations were "ready for liberty." They would not be created by the French Republic.

In the end, however, the French Republic embarked on a far-reaching program of republicanization, notably in Italy. The Directory came around to this policy during the spring of 1797, partly in response to Bonaparte's military victories in Italy and partly in response to the strength of the republican movement in Italy, which founded the Cispadane Republic under Bonaparte's aegis. While the working paper from the summer of 1796 decided against republicanization, in April of 1797 the Directory instructed Bonaparte to establish the Cisalpine Republic by joining Lombardy and the nascent Cispadane Republic.[74] By October of 1797, when the Treaty of Campo Formio was being finalized, Bonaparte wrote to Barras of the Executive Directory that he had received the latter's instructions "to revolutionize Italy."[75] The choice to establish sister republics rather than annex the territories in question was decisively influenced by the classical-republican anxiety over expansion. Sister republics allowed France to spread liberty in an abstract sense (to those thought "ready") *and* to extend France's influence—but without territorial annexations and thus without exposing the republic to the potentially corrosive effects of expansion.

Once the Directory embarked upon a policy of republicanization, policymakers had a wide range of strategies on which to draw. Petitions,

73. "Italie," f. 53–54.

74. "Instruction au General Buonaparte sur la maniere dont il devra organiser la partie de l'Italie occupée par les armées francaises," 18 Germinal, Year 5 (7 April 1797), Louis-Marie de La Révellière-Lépeaux Papers, Beinecke Rare Book and Manuscript Library, Yale University, box 6, folder 167.

75. Bonaparte to Barras, 19 Vendémiaire, Year 6 (10 October 1797), *CGN,* 1:1247, no. 2152.

proposals, and plans sketching the formation of sister republics in Italy and Germany circulated within the Ministry of Foreign Affairs and the Executive Directory. Mixing both fanciful and serious ideas, they collectively represented a broad range of possible strategies for the Republic to pursue and demonstrated the types of concerns that characterized the post-Terror political imagination. One of the more aggressive suggestions urged that France "destroy the Germanic constitution," annex the left bank of the Rhine, and then surround France with "a republican belt" by reconstituting the rest of Germany into seven republics and republicanizing the entire Italian peninsula.[76] A more whimsical note was struck by an anonymous petition that advocated turning Rome into "the Republic of Arts" characterized by revivified "republican virtues."[77] Deadly serious in tone was an essay presented to the Directory by a "citizen Link" of Heidelberg. Invoking the population's deep desire for independence and the influence of "the immortal Kant" on public spirit in the region, Link maintained that an independent republic in Swabia was not only the most viable option but also that which would best serve the French Republic. "It would be in France's interests to follow the example of ancient Rome and surround itself with states whose affection and physical power will serve as practically impenetrable boulevards."[78]

In addition to such petitions from concerned citizens, proposals to republicanize both the Italian peninsula and the German states came from agents and analysts within the Ministry of Foreign Affairs. In the spring and summer of 1796, in response to a ministry directive asking whether the Italians were "ready for liberty" and, more broadly, whether France should republicanize the peninsula, a number of French field agents in Italy, albeit a minority, recommended republicanization. Faipault, stationed in Genoa, considered the republicanization of Italy one of France's foremost foreign policy priorities. He advocated the immediate establishment of republics in Milan, Florence, Tuscany, and Bologna and the eventual republicanization of the entire peninsula.[79] Lachèze, also in

76. "Cen Amelin. C. no. 763," n.d., BN, Nouv. Acqu. Fr. 23654, f. 77.

77. "Projet d'échanges" [1796], MAE, MD Italie 12, f. 108.

78. Link, "Mémoire politique sur la rive droite du Rhin," 29 Vendémiaire, Year 5 (20 October 1796), BN, Nouv. Acqu. Fr. 23654, f. 161–76.

79. Faipault to Delacroix, 23 Thermidor, Year 4 (10 August 1796), MAE, MD Italie 12, f. 67–76.

Genoa, advocated establishing republics in Tuscany and Milan. The latter in particular "would then become . . . a *foyer* of liberty for all the other peoples of Italy." While republicanizing the entire peninsula would not be easy, he wrote, because of the influence of the Church, the Italians' natural aversion to the French as conquerors, and "the ignorance of the population, . . . liberty is [nonetheless] from now on inevitable for Italy."[80] Cacault advocated an aggressive program of controlled republicanization. He reported to the Directory that the peninsula would be easy to conquer and that, "as for the manner of governing Italy, we need first of all to bluntly apply our principles and our laws everywhere we go. The people want the humiliation of the upper classes, the abolition of feudalism and titles, the exclusion of nobles from office. It is therefore necessary to sacrifice 200,000 privileged for the 16,000,000 of population."[81] Cacault's reports in particular constituted a clear call for an offensive against the existing institutions of the peninsula and the aggressive republicanization of its peoples.

In regard to the German states, where no sister republic was ever established, the principal advocate of republicanization was Théremin. He proposed in a series of ministerial circulars that France annex the left bank of the Rhine and establish sister republics on its right bank so that eventually it would be "surrounded by republics." It was imperative, he wrote to Foreign Minister Talleyrand in 1799, that the French take the lead in organizing the German lands into republics because the population, "naturally speculative, and who have pushed the theory of liberty quite far, do not know how to act by themselves, do not possess . . . the audacity that characterizes the French republican."[82]

Théremin's proposals for the most part focused on establishing an independent republic in Swabia and the surrounding area. Such a republic, he argued, would serve French interests because it would stand as a third great

80. "Extrait d'une dépêche du C. Lachèze, consul à Gênes," 19 Thermidor, Year 4 (6 August 1796), MAE, MD Italie 12, f. 65–66.

81. "Extrait d'une dépêche du cit. Cacault, Agent de la République en Italie," 28 Germinal, Year 4 (17 April 1796), MAE, MD Italie 12, f. 19.

82. Théremin to Talleyrand, 29 Ventôse, Year 7 (19 March 1799), MAE, CP Allemagne 699, f. 232–234.

power in Germany (alongside Prussia and Austria).[83] The goal of creating a third power in Germany was entertained repeatedly throughout the Directory.[84] Théremin's voice was, however, the loudest within the ministry. One of his circulars, penned in the fall of 1798, spelled out in detail the possible composition of a "Germanic Republic" (*République germanique*) covering most of southwest Germany and extending south and east into contemporary western Austria (the Tyrol and Salzburg) so that it would border the Cisalpine Republic. With 5 million inhabitants, it would be "strong enough to make itself respected by Austria and weak enough to need help from France," thereby guaranteeing France "a perpetual influence in Germany." Moreover, it would push Austria that much further from the Helvetic and Cisalpine republics, helping to secure those republics and to deepen their ties with France. The name "Germanic Republic," Théremin explained, came from Caesar, who named the peoples of this region "*Germains* (men of war)" to differentiate them from the Teutons of northern Germany. The establishment of a distinct "Germanic Republic" would thus reflect the differences in moeurs among the German-speaking peoples.[85] Taken together, Théremin's proposals amounted to a radical program of republicanization in the German lands and a frontal assault on the Holy Roman Empire, the German Constitution, and the influence of Austria west of Bavaria.

Théremin, of all the ministry's agents, was probably the most sanguine about the ability of France to found republics throughout Europe. Most viewed republicanization as a thorny process to be undertaken cautiously and carefully. Moreover, republicanization, actual or potential, raised a number of issues that cut straight to the heart of much eighteenth-century political theory. Could republics be established anywhere the French chose? Or did the local populations need to be somehow predisposed to liberty? More specifically, were the Italian and German peoples ready for

83. Théremin to Talleyrand, Vendémaire, Year 7 (September–October 1798), MAE, CP Allemagne 698, f. 242; Théremin, untitled, 4 Frimaire, Year 4 (25 November 1795), MAE, CP Allemagne, 667, f. 373–74; Théremin, untitled, Year 7 (1798–99), MAE, CP Allemagne 700, f. 187. Théremin's arguments were paralleled in the anonymously published *Développement d'un projet d'alliance de la Souabe avec les Républiques Française et Helvétique* (n.p., [1795]).

84. Belissa, *Repenser l'ordre européen,* 279.

85. Théremin, "Projet pour l'établissement d'une République sur la [rive] droite du Rhin" [September–October 1798], MAE, CP Allemagne 698, f. 247–48.

liberty? And what types of republics would be established? What types of constitutions would they have? Would they be aristocratic or democratic? Small or large? Should a number of small republics be established or fewer large ones? Should they be independent of one another, federated, or even unified? And finally, what would the relationship be between the newly minted republics and the French Republic?

One of the key issues the Directory faced in establishing sister republics, as in expansion to natural frontiers, was whether the peoples in question were "ready for liberty." Once planted by the French, how would a republic take root if the local population's moeurs were not sufficiently republican, if they were "corrupt"? The Directory took this question seriously enough that in the spring of 1796 it asked French agents in Italy to report on the Italians' readiness for liberty. Moreover, the instructions given to General Clarke as he prepared to carry out peace negotiations with Austria in late 1796 enjoined him to investigate whether the population of the Cispadane Republic was "mature enough for liberty" to make securing the republic's existence a priority at the peace table.[86] This quasi-anthropological question reflected both an immediate concern regarding sister republics' ability to sustain themselves and the republican center's more general fixation with the question of moeurs. Liberty, it was thought, was an abstract quality, almost a state, that peoples grew into. A host of factors, from climate to economy to history to politics, determined whether a people was ready for liberty.

When the ministry asked French agents on the Italian peninsula to report on the different populations' readiness for liberty, the responses received were for the most part negative. They painted a picture of an essentially backward population corrupted by the Church and decadent government. Fourcade described the Italians as "debased" and "not in the least ready for liberty." He recommended that "only civil liberty be given to the Italian; political liberty would not agree with his laziness, his indolence." In the margin, Minister Delacroix summarized Fourcade's analysis pointedly: "We must not republicanize Italy . . . because the Italian people are too corrupt." Miot, the French minister in Florence, warned in comparable terms that "establishing liberty . . . and a republican system

86. Delacroix to Clarke, 26 Brumaire, Year 5 (16 November 1796), MAE, CP Autriche 367, f. 6–7.

in Italy... is impossible because the bulk of the population is entirely lacking in enlightenment and, especially, in the noble sentiment and energy that distinguishes the man made for liberty." Faipault, in Genoa, worried that "the Romans are too foolish for a Republic."[87] A few agents noted the rich republican history of the Italian peoples but usually only to observe how far they had fallen.

The negative tone of these reports influenced the working paper of the summer of 1796 that rejected the creation of sister republics in Italy. As quoted above, among the reasons listed for this resolution was the fact that "all of the information that we have received indicates that the Italian people are not mature enough for liberty." The Directory was clearly concerned that the lack of republican sentiment among the population would render any republics established on the peninsula fragile at best. Such weak states would, in turn, become an ongoing drain on France's already overstretched resources. Republicanizing the populations in question through festivals, public instruction, and the like was an obvious option but would amount to an extraordinarily daunting task.[88] As Miot put it, discussing Milan, France had to choose "a *possible* form of government, analogous to the genius of the inhabitants. Amid so many prejudices, entrenched for fifteen centuries, I do not believe in the possibility of a complete change in the principles and the moeurs of a people.... But between the plain and simple adoption of our principles and our constitution, food I find too hardy for the Lombards to digest, and the despotism we have just freed them from, there exist intervals that can deliver a regime suitable for their political existence and for ours."[89] Miot's analysis captures well the wider thinking that underpinned the summer of 1796 decision to forgo republicanization of the peninsula. While the establishment of

87. "Extrait d'une lettre du C. Fourcade, consul de la république à La Canée," 7 Prairial, Year 4 (26 May 1796); "Extrait d'une dépêche du Cn. Miot, agent près le gouv. de Toscane," 9 Thermidor, Year 4 (27 July 1796); Faipault to Delacroix, 23 Thermidor, Year 4 (10 August 1796), MAE, MD Italie 12, f. 24, 64, 73.

88. Another, more extreme, means to republicanize the population was war. In the spring of 1798, Daunou, in Rome, wrote to La Révellière-Lépeaux, then president of the Executive Directory, that a possible benefit of war between the French-controlled Roman Republic and the Kingdom of Naples (which he opposed) would be that it "would excite among the Romans a general enthusiasm and serve as their republican education." 6 Germinal, Year 6 (26 March 1798), BN, Nouv. Acqu. Fr. 21566, f. 190.

89. Miot, "Italie," 10 Prairial, Year 4 (29 May 1796), MAE, CP Toscane 147^{B}, f. 133.

the Batavian Republic the year before had built on the Dutch republican tradition, republics in Italy, it was feared, would fail to take root. The peninsula's proud republican history was buried too far in the past to sustain a republicanization program.

The same considerations, not surprisingly, arose in discussion over whether to establish republics elsewhere in Europe. For example, Delacroix instructed Angelucci, a French agent bound for Corsica, that the Corsicans were more or less ready for liberty, in need only of a push and some guidance from the French.[90] The populations of the western German states, on whose character much ink was spilled, were generally imagined to be rational, enlightened, and thus ready for liberty. Théremin, in his advocacy of a republic in Swabia, pointed to the influence of Kant in the region (as had Link of Heidelberg). "Tübingen University is full of disciples of Kant, speculative philosophers who…could be useful, as liberty is the basis of their speculations."[91] The same characteristics that ostensibly rendered the German peoples ready for liberty, however, led one petitioner to conclude that they are deliberate in their steps and therefore should not be rushed: "cold, difficult to move, but consistent, stable, strong in their movements, serious and ponderous in their course.…It is in the national character to abhor extremes."[92]

Beyond the Italian peninsula, the German states, and Switzerland (which was already a republic at the time the French invaded), the populations were considered more or less beyond the scope of republicanization. France's agent in the Republic of Ragusa (modern-day Dubrovnik) reported that the so-called republic is "governed by an odious aristocracy" that keeps "the peoples of the countryside under the slavery of barbarous times" and corrupts moeurs to the point that sciences and the arts no longer exist.[93] And, in a treatise on the supposedly imminent collapse of the Ottoman Empire, Théremin argued that France should extend its influence to Egypt but should establish "armed trading posts" rather than

90. Delacroix, "Instructions pour le citoyen Angelucci," 21 Floréal, Year 4 (10 May 1796), MAE, MD France 1538, f. 329.

91. Théremin to Talleyrand, Vendémaire, Year 7 (September–October 1798).

92. "Des vrais intérêts respectifs de la France, de la Prusse, et du corps Germanique," n.d., MAE, MD Allemagne 117, f. 350–360.

93. Bruere to Delacroix, 12 Prairial and 14 Thermidor, Year 4 (31 May and 1 August 1796), MAE, MD Autriche (Raguse) 57, f. 82, 86.

either annex Egypt or establish a sister republic "because the French Republic cannot have subjects, and conquest will not make the Egyptians French citizens."[94] Implicit here is that the Egyptians were not ready for liberty—a point Théremin seems to have assumed and did not feel necessary to argue one way or the other.

While such quasi-anthropological analysis affected policy decisions to a point, there were some who objected to this very approach to the issue. In August of 1796, the deputy Massa, for example, wrote to the Executive Directory that the love for liberty lives in all humans, whether or not they display it. Addressing the question of whether to establish a republic in Lombardy, he claimed that the people do not appear "mature enough" for liberty because they have lived under oppressive, denaturing Austrian rule. Given the opportunity, however, they would, as human beings, embrace liberty the moment it was offered to them. "Is this country mature enough for liberty? Mankind would be condemned to eternal slavery if, to possess this maturity, a people has to be composed only of Platos and Brutuses. But any nation that has a well-pronounced hatred for tyranny possesses the maturity in question."[95] Massa professed a more optimistic view of human nature than prevailed within the republican center and maintained that virtually all people are ready for liberty, no matter their behavior or circumstances. This line of reasoning became a staple feature of the neo-Jacobin movement that culminated in the summer of 1799 and pushed, against the policy of the republican center, for an aggressive policy of pan-European republicanization.[96]

Another vital question facing the French Republic as it established sister republics was the constitutional architecture of the republics to be created. The French strove to make sure that the republicans of Italy, Holland, and Switzerland did not repeat the experiments in radical democracy that, it was thought, had led to the Terror. In this regard, the republicans of the rest of Europe were regarded as "minors" in need of supervision from the French, who had just experienced political revolution

94. "Combinaisons pour le cas où l'affaiblissement de l'Empire ottoman entraînerait la destruction en Europe," Pluviôse, Year 6 (January–February 1798), MAE, MD Turquie 15, f. 205.

95. "Extrais de divers mémoires remis au Bureau diplomatique concernant l'Italie," 12 Fructidor, Year 4 (29 August 1796), AN, AF III 71, d. 288, p. 1.

96. See Belissa, *Repenser l'ordre européen,* 332; and Bernard Gainot, *1799, un nouveau Jacobinisme? La démocratie représentative, une alternative à brumaire* (Paris, 2001), esp. 200–208.

in all its extremes.[97] For example, in September of 1795, the outgoing Committee of Public Safety noted that the Dutch should imitate "the civic virtues of the French."[98] Similarly, Reubell explained in a note to Bonaparte in the spring of 1797 regarding Lombardy that "the best policy is to give them an already completed constitution."[99]

While the Dutch were originally allowed a fair amount of leeway in drafting their own constitution in 1795 (which they did not succeed in doing until 1798, and then only after significant French intervention),[100] policy soon changed and the French took an active role in the redaction of the various Italian constitutions and the Helvetic Constitution. The degree of involvement varied from case to case, but French intervention was generally driven by the fear that local democratic movements would unduly influence the constitutional process. For example, in the fall of 1797, soon after the Cisalpine Republic was founded on 9 July 1797 and its first constitution hastily promulgated, Bonaparte wrote to the Directory expressing his concern that in both Genoa and Milan the French Constitution of 1793 had been reprinted and was being cited as a possible model. "The delirium and especially the ignorance are extreme," he warned. To neutralize this democratic delirium, Bonaparte requested that the Directory send three experts "to draft a constitutional plan for Italy." Specifically, he requested Sieyès, Roederer, and Benjamin Constant.[101] The Directory responded that it would find "men capable of fulfilling your requests" and soon thereafter wrote again informing Bonaparte that three prominent intellectuals, "the citizens Daunou, Ginguené, and Cabanis, three members of the National Institute," would "draft a plan for the [second] constitution of the Cisalpine Republic."[102] In fact, Ginguené and Cabanis were never sent, and Daunou was dispatched first to the Roman Republic, along

97. Belissa, *Repenser l'ordre européen,* 303–40.

98. Quoted in ibid., 306.

99. Reubell to Bonaparte, quoted in Raymond Guyot, "Du Directoire au Consulat: les transitions," *Revue Historique* 111 (1912): 11.

100. In 1798 the French launched a coup in the Batavian Republic to break political deadlock there. An analysis of the Batavian Constitution of 1798 as well as a copy can be found in AN, AF III 70, f. 61.

101. The quote is from the summary of Bonaparte's letter prepared for the Directory, AN, AF III 473, plaq. 2906, p. 14.

102. Directory to Bonaparte, 30 Vendémiaire and 23 Brumaire, Year 6 (21 October and 13 November 1797), AN, AF III 473, plaq. 2906, p. 13, and AF III 478, plaq. 2955, p. 16.

with Faipoult, Florent, and Monge, to oversee the implementation of its new constitution on 20 March 1798 before proceeding with Faipoult to the Cisalpine Republic and redacting its second constitution on 10 September 1798. The result was that both constitutions were constructed in the image of the Constitution of the Year III.

These constitutions, as well as the Helvetic of 12 April 1798, were, for all intents and purposes, handed down from Paris. In the case of the Roman Constitution, this was true in the most literal sense. Merlin de Douai wrote it from a desk in Paris, simply going through a pocket edition of the Constitution of the Year III and substituting "Roman" for "French," striking certain articles and adding a few new ones.[103] In this case, the major changes involved restricting the activities of political clubs and strengthening the executive. The French commissioners in Rome were then charged with "executing the constitutional project for the Roman Republic decreed by the Executive Directory."[104] In general, perhaps no other issue provoked the degree of direct intervention by the French into the affairs of the sister republics. The Directory was determined that its new sisters not repeat the experiments in radical democracy that the French had undertaken. The new republics were to be Thermidorian but with a few key changes—notably the strengthened executive—that pointed ahead to the Consulate.[105]

Among the urgent questions facing the Directory was whether the new republics established on the Italian peninsula would be amalgamated into an overarching political body or remain independent of one another. If they were to be joined together, would it be a unitary republic or a "federative republic" in which the constituent republics retained a measure of autonomy? Those in favor of some sort of amalgamated Italian political body, federative or unitary, argued that if the individual sister republics were joined, the resultant larger republic would be better suited to defend

103. The copy he worked through is in the French National Archives. AN, AF III 78, d. 322, plaq. 2.

104. 12 Pluviôse, Year 6 (31 January 1798), AN, AF III 498, plaq. 3135.

105. The Batavian Constitution of 1798, drafted primarily by Daunou, was also marked by a stronger executive. The constitution of the Consulate is discussed in the next chapter. Guyot highlights those changes that foreshadowed the Consulate in "Du Directoire au Consulat"; see also Marcel Gauchet, *La Révolution des pouvoirs: La souveraineté, le peuple, et la représentation, 1789–1799* (Paris, 1995), 207–12.

itself militarily. Advocates of a specifically federative republic worried that a unitary republic could turn aggressive on the international stage and held up the federative republic as a peaceful alternative. The federative republic, they claimed, often with reference to the Swiss example, was unaggressive by nature and thus less likely to begin a war that might embroil France. As a result, it was repeated time and again, federative republics made strong but defensive allies and thus good neighbors.[106] Moreover, they argued, the federative republic was better able to resist the internal corruption born of size than a large single republic would be. In *The Spirit of the Laws,* Montesquieu, in a passage Jaucourt repeated nearly word for word in the *Encyclopédie,* had established these qualities as constitutive of the federative republic as a political form. "If a republic is small, it is destroyed by a foreign force; if it is large, it destroys itself by an interior vice.... [There exists, however,] a kind of constitution that possesses all the internal advantages of republican government and the external force of monarchy. I speak of the federative republic."[107] Those opposed to the establishment of a larger Italian political body, unitary or federative, did not deny such considerations but claimed simply that smaller, independent, and isolated republics would be less likely to pursue policies independent of French influence. The key issue for them was French control of the peninsula. The latter position won the day as the Directory quashed the various efforts to create a larger Italian Republic. While this sometimes caused tensions with the Cisalpine Republic, whose leaders often harbored ambitions of unifying the peninsula under the Cisalpine flag, the Directory remained steadfast in its belief that a divided Italy would better serve French interests and better withstand the corruption born of size. The question was nonetheless seriously discussed throughout the Directorial period.

Even before France embarked on the sister-republic program in Italy, there were already significant murmurings about the possible creation of

106. E.g., the anonymous pamphlet calling for a federative republic on the Rhine's right bank, *Dissertation sur une question intéressante, relativement aux nouvelles limites de la France* (n.p., [1797]).

107. Montesquieu, *De l'esprit des lois,* 2:369. *Encyclopédie,* s.v. "République fédérative." Intellectuals at the National Institute remained interested in the nature of the federative republic. For example, on 13 September 1799 the historian De Sales recommended to the Class of Moral and Political Sciences that *Du gouvernement fédératif dans les anciennes Républiques* by a certain Cit. Sainte Croix be recommended to the government as worthy of public recognition. AI, SMP, A2.

a unified Italian republic encompassing one part or another of the peninsula. In August of 1796, Faipault recommended that a "confederation" of "the republics of Milan, Florence, Tuscany, and Bologna be organized" to which Genoa and Venice would eventually be admitted as well.[108] Faipault's plan would thus have created a large federative republic in the north and part of the middle but did not extend south past Tuscany. In March of 1796, Foreign Minister Delacroix sounded extremely ambitious notes in writing to Cacault, "Let the boundaries separating the various states disappear so that only one shall be formed. Let the peoples woken by the tocsin of liberty . . . feel the desire to unite and form a single people strong enough to defend the rights that the powerful arms of the Republic will have reconquered for them."[109] Delacroix, it seemed, was calling for an Italian Republic that spanned the entire peninsula. Cacault, for his part, then forwarded to the Ministry of Foreign Affairs (and to Sieyès) a treatise penned by François-René Pommereul that called for the establishment of a federative league in Italy. Pommereul, serving in the French legation in Florence at the time, outlined in great detail a potential federation of Italian republics to be called the "Italian League."[110] Pommereul's essay circulated widely during these months before being published in the fall of 1796 and stands as one of the more cogent plans for a federative republic in Italy.

Pommereul outlined a sweeping reorganization of the Italian peninsula that would permanently banish Austria, end the temporal power of the papacy, abolish the Inquisition, and keep Italy in "its divided state" because if united it "would be too formidable." More specifically, he advocated carving Italy into three principal zones: in the north, the Kingdom of Sardinia (pushed from Piedmont into Lombardy so France could

108. Faipault to Delacroix, 23 Thermidor, Year 4 (10 August 1796), MAE, MD Italie 12, f. 73–74.

109. Delacroix to Cacault, 27 March 1796. Quoted in Godechot, *La grande nation: L'expansion révolutionnaire de la France dans le monde de 1789 à 1799,* 2d ed. (Paris, 1983), 245.

110. Pommereul's term, *ligue italique,* used the adjective *italique* rather than *italienne; italique* carried a reference to classical Italy that *italienne* did not. The manuscript, "Vues générales sur l'Italie dans ses rapports politiques avec la République française à l'époque du mois de floréal de l'an 4," sits in the files of the Executive Directory, AN, AF III 71, d. 288, p. 1. It was then printed in F. Pommereul, *Vues générales sur l'Italie, Malte, etc. Dans leurs rapports politiques avec la République française, et sur les limites de la France à la rive droite du Rhin, suivies d'un mémoire sur les Beaux-Arts, et les institutions propres à les faire fleurir* (Paris, 1796). Citations here are to the manuscript.

expand to the Alps); in the south, the Kingdom of Two Sicilies; and in the broad middle, a federation called the Italian League composed of a host of small republics, including, among others, a Roman Republic, an Appenine Republic, and a Gallocisalpine Republic. In addition, a seat would be held for a possible future Lombard Republic. These different republics would be "united by a federative bond along the lines of the United States or the Swiss Cantons" such that the Italian League would be republican in nature but would "not form a single republic, because it would then soon devour its monarchical neighbors." The French Republic would be its "guarantor and perpetual ally." The league would have a "Senate" in which each republic and France would hold one seat. While the individual republics retained their basic legislative and executive powers, the Senate would have complete control for the entire league over foreign policy, the military, weights and measures, and public instruction. "This Italian League," Pommereul argued, "founded by France, would become, like the Batavian Republic, France's natural and perpetual ally." Furthermore, it would "assure the French Republic political and commercial preponderance in Italy" and turn the Mediterranean into a "French lake." It was important, Pommereul wrote, that the league remain a federation of autonomous republics because a unified republic would pose too strong a counterweight to French hegemony in the region.[111] Indeed, the summary of the essay written for the Executive Directory concurred with Pommereul that a federative state was preferable to a unified state because "we would not have to fear the spirit of conquest, which can never take hold of federative states."[112] While Pommereul's plan was not followed by the Directory, it garnered significant support, was discussed in the ministry, and captured in broad contours the general argument for federation on the Italian peninsula.[113]

Yet the Directory refused the establishment of a federative republic in Italy. The working paper authored by Foreign Minister Delacroix in the summer of 1796 that decided against the creation of sister republics

111. Pommereul, "Vues générales sur l'Italie."

112. "Extrais de divers mémoires remis au Bureau diplomatique, concernant l'Italie," AN, AF III 71, d. 288, p. 1.

113. In addition to Cacault, Miot endorsed the plan. "Italie," 10 Prairial, Year 4 (29 May 1796), MAE, CP Toscane 147^B, f. 139–40; summarized in "Extrait d'un mémoire du Miot à Florence," 26 Prairial, Year 4 (14 June 1796), MAE, MD Italie 12, f. 34–35.

in Italy paused over the question of whether to create "a sort of federative republic" on the peninsula but opted against such a plan. Referring in all likelihood to Pommereul's essay, Delacroix wrote, "Among the numerous propositions regarding the future of Italy that I have carefully collected for the benefit of the Republic, there is one that merits the Directory's attention: turning Italy, as it is today or as we propose to make it, into a sort of federative republic, governed by a Diet or Council." Delacroix analyzed the issue in light of France's interests and concluded that a federative republic would benefit France primarily because it would be better able to resist future Austrian aggression than would a host of individual states. Moreover, he wrote, citing the Swiss example, "a federative power is naturally disposed to peace and becomes dangerous only with difficulty." France would then be surrounded by republics, "by friendly peoples, tied to the Republic by either need, interest, or concern for their safety." Finally, France would be able to influence the federation and, as a result, would enjoy "a decided preponderance" on the peninsula. In contrast, the only negative reason Delacroix adduced was that "the proposed establishment . . . could become embarrassing for France without providing any real benefit for Italy." Delacroix's analysis within the working paper did not resolve the question, concluding with the statement that the "Directory is invited to weigh, in its wisdom, the reasons for and against just invoked, and to plot for me the line that I should follow." However, at the very end of the document it was noted without explanation that "to form a league of all the powers of Italy" was not in France's interests.[114] Thus the Directory, when it rejected the republicanization of Italy, also rejected the establishment of a federative republic on the peninsula.

Once the Directory did decide to pursue a policy of republicanization it was nonetheless still concerned to ensure that any Italian republic would not be too weak to defend itself. In April of 1797 the Directory instructed Bonaparte to join the nascent Cispadane Republic, centered in Bologna, with Lombardy. Both the Cispadane and Lombardy, it was feared, were too small and hence too vulnerable to survive on their own. It was "extremely important in the eyes of the Directory to place under the same government the territories on both sides of the Po River. Separate, the two

114. "Italie," 7 Thermidor, Year 4 (25 July 1796), MAE, MD Italie 12, f. 61–62.

entities are too weak to defend themselves.... Their union will assure for the French Republic a barrier strong enough to shelter it from any harassment by the Emperor without, however, forming a power capable of alarming us."[115] The result was the Cisalpine Republic, spanning both sides of the Po, proclaimed on 9 July 1797 precisely so that there would be a formidable republic in northern Italy but not one so formidable as to alarm France.

The creation of the larger Cisalpine Republic, however, provoked concern that a rivalry between Bologna and Milan would turn into a seed of corruption. The directors proposed a creative solution, instructing Bonaparte to remove the capital from either big city to "a small, central location" along the lines of the Dutch and American examples. Detached from the cities, "the legislature and the government would be more free, less influenced, less subject to corruption, less delivered to intrigue." If the capital were to remain in either city, "the families of the citizens who sit in the legislature and the Executive Directory as well as those citizens themselves... would become accustomed to all the artificial and fashionable pleasures of big cities, lose the taste for domestic life and for the peaceful but occupied life. They would all squeeze into a capital city where they will become corrupted and scheme because there one needs power and gold, always more, to satisfy the passions and temptations that remain before one's eyes."[116] The fact that La Révellière-Lépeaux and the Directory, in a letter instructing General Bonaparte on Italian policy, placed such emphasis on negating the corrupting influences of the city speaks volumes about the extent to which classical-republican anxieties shaped the post-Terror discussion of foreign policy.[117]

While the Cisalpine Republic was created so that it would be strong enough to defend itself against external aggression, the Directory remained adamant that it stay within the borders prescribed and not grow into a true peninsular power. The only moment of hesitation on this front occurred in

115. "Instruction au General Buonaparte sur la manière dont il devra organiser la partie de l'Italie occupée par les armées francaises," 18 Germinal, Year 5 (7 April 1797), Louis-Marie de La Réveillère-Lépeaux Papers, Beinecke Rare Book and Manuscript Library, Yale University, box 6, folder 167. For similar concerns about Lombardy, see, e.g., "Nécessité de décider le sort de la Lombardie," 11 Pluviôse, Year 5 (30 January 1797), AN, AF III 71, d. 289, plaq. 2.

116. "Instruction au General Buonaparte."

117. In fact, though, the Cisalpine capital was established in Milan.

the immediate aftermath of the signing on 17 October 1797 of the Treaty of Campo Formio, which secured Austrian recognition of the Cisalpine Republic. The Directory, it seems, had considered allowing the Cisalpine to serve as the basis for a unified republic in Italy but reversed itself after hearing Bonaparte's objections to such a plan. The general wrote, "It appears that the Directory wants to make Italy a great republic, but does it not fear making the republic too strong?" Moreover, added Bonaparte, the Directory should remember the ingratitude of the United States, "our cruelest enemy in a war for liberty." Next to his comment, Reubell, seemingly influenced by Bonaparte's argument, scrawled in the margin that "Genoa should remain as it is and the south of Italy should not form a single state with the north."[118] Then the Directory's formal response to Bonaparte, signed by all five directors, encouraged the further republicanization of the peninsula but announced that it was opposed to a single, strong republic in Italy: "As for the establishment in Italy of a single large Republic, or of several independent states, the Executive Directory believes it should explain its views to you. It wants, without doubt, that the Cisalpine Republic be able to offer sufficient resistance, but without enveloping Genoa, which can and should remain as it is. Moreover, the south of Italy should not form a single state with the north. But it is nonetheless desirable that liberty penetrate the entire south and that free governments, moved by interest in a common cause, drive Austrian influence out of this country and furnish security for the French Republic."[119]

The Directory maintained its opposition to a unified or federative republic in Italy even as the republicanization program gained steam and France established the Roman and the Neapolitan (also called the Parthenopaean) Republics on 15 February 1798 and 26 January 1799, respectively. Just as before, the Directory feared that a large republic, however constituted, might emerge as a rival rather than a partner. On 2 July 1798, Talleyrand repeated that the different Italian republics should be prevented from unifying because "this republic would become too powerful and France would have to fear that it forgets the benevolence of its

118. Bonaparte's words are from a summary of his letter prepared for the Directory; Reubell's comment is in the margin. AN, AF III 473, plaq. 2906, p. 14.

119. Directory to Bonaparte, 30 Vendémiaire, Year 6 (21 October 1797), AN, AF III 473, plaq. 2906, p. 13.

creation, that it would want to rival the mother republic. It has been said for a long time that gratitude is not a virtue of peoples."[120] While there continued to be isolated challenges to this way of thinking—Bignon, a former secretary in the French legations to the Helvetic and Cisalpine Republics, called for the establishment of two large, robust republics in Italy, and a certain Rincheval advocated the creation of a single "Italian Republic"[121]—the Directory maintained a steadfast opposition to the creation of a single Italian republic, federative or otherwise. The sister republics were to remain both small and isolated from one another, free from the corruption born of size and under French authority.

A Federative System

In addition to the question of whether the sister republics would be linked with one another in national federations or stand as independent entities, there was also the question of whether they would be linked to the French Republic in a transnational "federative system." If so, just how closely would they be tied to France? Would the sister republics have the autonomy to make their own decisions or would they simply answer to Paris? Moreover, would such a federative system be intrinsically republican? Would it be a great republican confederation working for specifically republican aims or would it serve French interests in a more narrow sense?

In practice, the sister republics were largely under French control. While official proclamations and treaties struck a high-minded tone of partnerships of equals working for a common republican cause, the actual relationship between the French Republic and its so-called sisters was generally one-sided. Coups were launched, legislation decreed, and decisions made at the behest of commissioners who reported to Paris. The state of affairs

120. Talleyrand, "Rapport au Directoire sur la situation de la republique francaise considerée dans ses rapports extérieurs avec les autres puissances," 14 Messidor, Year 6 (2 July 1798), MAE, MD France 656, f. 153.

121. Ed. Bignon, *Du Système suivi par le Directoire exécutif relativement à la République cisalpine et quelques détails sur les derniers événements qui ont eu lieu dans cette République* (Paris, 1799), 68–69; A.-V. Rincheval, *De la nécessité de réunir en une seule toutes les Républiques d'Italie, pour l'intérêt mutuel des Républiques Italienne et Française* (n.p., [1799]).

was captured well by Reubell in his personal jottings: "Whoever governs the Cisalpine Republic,... the most important thing is that the acts of the French Executive Directory are executed, regardless of whether they are good or bad. All is lost if, once, the [French] government were demeaned and not obeyed."[122] An official account of the Italian situation prepared for the Directory in June of 1799 corroborated Reubell's musings, explaining that in the Roman Republic "the true exercise of sovereignty [is] in the hands of France."[123] Such pronouncements notwithstanding, however, the sister republics should not be viewed simply as French puppet states. Indigenous republican movements did exercise influence and local politicians did wield power.[124] Moreover, there were significant variations among France's relations with the different sister republics. The Batavian and the Cisalpine tended to retain a greater degree of independence while the Roman was particularly controlled by France. The historian Marc Belissa describes the international federation created by the Directory as "not an Empire nor an absolute domination, but a form of aggregation" centered on "the interests of the hegemonic power."[125] The Directory sought to steer the various indigenous republican movements but did not simply control them. The relationship might be characterized as a "soft imperialism."

The sister republics were to fit into a federative system centered on the French Republic. As the French armies occupied more and more territory, calls for such a system became quite frequent. In late summer 1794, an unnamed official—probably Emmanuel-Joseph Sieyès—drafted an "Outline of the French Republic's relations with the powers of Europe" for the Committee of Public Safety that argued for the creation of an entirely new international order based on a federative system centered around the French Republic.[126] Describing the creation of a federative system as "the

122. Reubell, untitled, undated jottings, BN, Nouv. Acqu. Fr. 23654, f. 378.

123. "Rapport au Directoire Exécutif sur la situation actuelle de l'italie," 21 Prairial, Year 7 (9 June 1799), MAE, MD Italie 12, f. 154–56.

124. Among historians, R. R. Palmer has emphasized more than any other the intensity and self-sufficiency of the various indigenous republican movements in *The Age of the Democratic Revolution: A Political History of Europe and America, 1760–1800,* vol. 2, *The Struggle* (Princeton, 1964).

125. Belissa, *Repenser l'ordre européen,* 310–11.

126. "Apperçu des rapports de la République française avec les Puissances de l'Europe," Fructidor, Year 2 (August–September 1794), AN, 284 AP 10–11, and MAE, MD France, 652, f. 72–88.

best use of our conquests," the author explained that the essence of such a system inhered in attaching the interests of other nations to those of France, which would require a series of individualized policies vis-à-vis the specific polities in question. On the whole, this is exactly what France did over the following five years. Opinion was divided, however, on whether such a system was to be strictly republican. The prominent Italian republican Matteo Galdi advocated a great republican confederation, possibly including the nascent American Republic, with ideology as the principal binding tie, while a multilingual edition of the French, Ligurian, and Cisalpine constitutions and the American Declaration of Independence also suggested such a panrepublican affiliation.[127] Others imagined a federative system based on nonideological interests in which nonrepublics would be included. A certain J.-M. Bertrand petitioned the Directory in January of 1796 to buttress the Republic's "federative power" through alliances based on "natural interests" with Spain, Prussia, the Ottoman Porte, and certain smaller powers. While such an alliance clearly smacked of pre-1756 French foreign policy, the old alliances were reimagined by Bertrand under the category of federative power.[128] Similarly, Marie-Louis Descorches, a ministry authority on Ottoman affairs, wrote to Talleyrand in January of 1799 that France should work to prevent the destruction of the Ottoman state and incorporate it into "the Republic's federative system," thus augmenting "the only power that remains for us to acquire in order to complete our political organization, *our federative power.*"[129]

The piece is unattributed, found today both in Sieyès's papers and in the archives of the Ministry of Foreign Affairs. The author is clearly a high-ranking official, as the text refers to Prussia's then-secret overtures to open negotiations with France. The theoretical approach and language of the document, notably the clear influence of Physiocracy, suggest Sieyès's influence and probable authorship. Fortoul, an early editor of Sieyès's papers, thought the piece composed either by Sieyès or Cambacérès.

127. E.g., Galdi, *Discours sur les rapports politiques-économiques de l'Italie libre avec la France et les autres états de l'Europe* [1797], trans. L.-P. Couret-Villeneuve (Paris, 1798); *Constitution des républiques française, cisalpine et ligurienne; avec l'acte d'indépendance des États-Unis d'Amérique, dans les quatres langues française, anglaise, allemande, et italienne* (Paris, Year 7 [1798–99]).

128. J.-M. Bertrand, "Mémoire sur les Alliances qui conviennent à la République française," Nivôse, Year 4 (December–January 1795–96), MAE, MD France 652, f. 138–145. A second copy, dated 17 Prairial, Year 4 (5 June 1796), can be found in MAE, MD France 655, f. 358–365.

129. Descorches to Talleyrand, 5 Pluviôse, Year 7 (24 January 1799), Louis-Marie de La Révellière-Lépeaux Papers, Beinecke Rare Book and Manuscript Library, Yale University, box 1, folder 25.

For all, regardless of whether the federative system was to be ideological in character, the French Republic would stand as the dominant power. The creation of a federative system offered a means to project French influence without subjecting the Republic to the dangers of expansion.

A federative system along these lines can be understood as having two distinct conceptual lineages. First, and most important, the idea of a republican federation had a distinctly classical-republican legacy. Early modern political philosophers all associated the creation of federative systems with republics, and the term "federative republic" encompassed large-scale leagues between republics, such as the Achaean League, or the Roman model, as well as smaller federations such as Holland and Switzerland. Montesquieu's definition of a federative republic in *The Spirit of the Laws* did not stipulate any criteria regarding size and specifically referenced the Greek and Roman leagues. The definition of a federative republic, he wrote in a passage Jaucourt used in the *Encyclopédie,* was "a society of societies that make a new one, which can be enlarged by new partners that join with it.... It was such associations that made Greece flourish for so long. By using them, the Romans attacked the universe; and by them alone the universe defended itself from the Romans."[130] Moreover, the establishment of such a federative system was widely viewed in the early modern period as a solution to the expansionist dilemma. In his *Discourses on Livy,* Machiavelli had recommended the Roman method of creating "partners" while keeping "the rank of command" within the system, warning that "a republic that wishes to expand" should not "take another mode."[131] James Harrington had similarly called for the creation of "unequal leagues" rather than the direct annexation of conquered territories in his *Oceana* precisely in response to the dangers posed by expansion. As David Armitage explains, "Harrington's solution was, like Machiavelli's, based upon the Roman model of unequal leagues, in which the metropolitan state retained the leadership, rather than the subordination of conquered territory."[132] The creation of a Europe-wide federative

130. Montesquieu, *De l'esprit des lois,* 2:369; *Encyclopédie,* s.v. "République fédérative" (article by Jaucourt).

131. Niccolò Machiavelli, *Discourses on Livy,* trans. Harvey C. Mansfield and Nathan Tarcov (Chicago, 1996), 136–37.

132. Armitage, *Ideological Origins of the British Empire,* 137.

system with France at the helm could thus find conceptual resources in the classical-republican tradition. The Roman model of the federative system was explicitly cited during the Directory, such as in an analysis prepared for the Ministry of Foreign Affairs by the historian Anquetil of the National Institute in the summer of 1796. Anquetil counseled the institution of a federative system along the lines of the Roman version, under which, according to Anquetil, "almost all" of Rome's conquests were "conserved as free states, as tributary allies of the republic, and only became subjects under the emperors."[133] In an important sense, the post-Terror republic did in fact pursue the establishment of a classical-republican "unequal league." In the conquered territories, it created subordinate republics and, at the same time, did not enter into federative relationships with nonrepublican states. While it signed peace treaties with Prussia, Spain, and Austria, those monarchies were never included in a federative relationship.

The second conceptual framework the post-Terror republic could look to was the Kantian vision of "perpetual peace," also centered on a great, hegemonic republic. Drawing on the abbé de Saint-Pierre's conception of perpetual peace, which itself looked to Henry IV's "grand design" of fewer, larger European states, Kant called for a positive international juridical order resembling a federation or "international republic" with the French Republic as its nodal point and guarantor.[134] In *Perpetual Peace: A Philosophical Sketch,* Kant famously labeled his new international order a "*ius cosmopoliticum*" (*Weltbürgerrecht,* cosmopolitan law) or "universal state of mankind." Kant's new order would ideally take the form of an international republic, which served as both a metaphor to describe the new order and a normative description for the legal form it should ultimately take. In contrast to the classical-republican conception of an "unequal league," the Kantian ius cosmopoliticum would work toward an international republic

133. Anquetil, "Extrait d'un Mémoire sur l'Italie," 24 Messidor, Year 4 (12 July 1796), MAE, MD Italie 12, f. 40.

134. See Pierre Laberge, Guy Lafrance, and Denis Dumas, eds., *L'année 1795: Kant, Essai sur la paix* (Paris, 1997); Belissa, *Fraternité universelle et intérêt national,* 42–49; Richard Tuck, *The Rights of War and Peace: Political Thought and the International Order from Grotius to Kant* (Oxford, 1999), esp. chaps. 6 and 7; Michael Sonenscher, *Before the Deluge: Public Debt, Inequality, and the Intellectual Origins of the French Revolution* (Princeton, 2007), 112–15; and Belissa, *Repenser l'ordre européen,* 371–411.

and positive international law. The Kantian version was therefore much more universalist in its ambitions, seeking to create a universal, perpetual order rather than a network of individual alliances. But if that proved to be impossibly utopian, it would at least become what Kant called a "Federation of Free States." Kant wrote that states

> must renounce their savage and lawless freedom, adapt themselves to public coercive laws, and thus form an *international state (civitas gentium),* which would necessarily continue to grow until it embraced all the peoples of the earth. But since this is not the will of the nations, according to their present conception of international law (so that they reject *in hypothesi* what is true *in thesi*), the positive idea of a *world republic* cannot be realized. If all is not to be lost, this can at best find a negative substitute in the shape of an enduring and gradually expanding *federation* likely to prevent war.

Kant made it clear that an international republic could be founded in the absence of consent between nations if "one powerful and enlightened nation," as he put it in an obvious reference to the French Republic, would take the lead.[135] Kant wrote *Perpetual Peace* in the immediate aftermath of the Treaty of Basel, at the very moment when France seemed to be establishing a new international order in Europe based on the new geopolitical map created by its armies. He thought that France could play the role of "an international Leviathan," to take Richard Tuck's term. In Kant's view, as Tuck argues, "If states did not voluntarily recognize the principles of international and cosmopolitan right,...international relations would have to be conducted on Hobbesian and not Pufendorfian lines." Kant's *Perpetual Peace* was received in France as an endorsement of the "powerful and enlightened nation" acting to end the state of war between nations.[136] Within French political circles, the Kantian model was articulated most fully by Théremin, who, in his various essays, sketched a view of international affairs that plainly paralleled Kant's.[137] For Théremin, in the tracks

135. Kant, *Political Writings,* ed. H. S. Reiss and trans. H. B. Nisbet (Cambridge, 1991), 98–99n, 102, 105, 104.

136. Tuck, *Rights of War and Peace,* 220–23.

137. Théremin used the term "perpetual peace" in only one of his treatises, *De la Situation intérieure de la République*. Elsewhere he used the phrases "eternal peace," "constant peace," and "permanent peace."

of Kant, the new European order would be centered around a hegemonic French Republic that both furthered its own interests and worked toward the creation of an international republic based on positive international law.

Théremin's Kantian conception of the international order led him to formulate some of the most audacious proposals found in the files of the Ministry of Foreign Affairs. In addition to advocating the republicanization of the German states, in February of 1798 he put forward a bold plan for French penetration into the eastern Mediterranean in the face of the Ottoman Empire's apparently impending dissolution. In the wake of the partition of Poland and the ongoing reorganizations of the German and Italians lands, Théremin argued that the trend in Europe was toward fewer, larger states. "In following this system necessitated by the current circumstances, the French Republic should consider . . . some form of territorial expansion in order to keep pace with others." As a result, the French Republic should move eastward and establish a republic in the Balkans while annexing key port cities. "All the peoples who inhabit the right bank of the Rhine down to and including the Greek archipelago will form a free nation, and the Greek Republic will be, like the Batavian and the Cisalpine, under the direct protection of the mother Republic and tied to her by an intimate alliance." At the same time, France would "conserve" several ports and armed trading posts within the newly formed Greek Republic, notably Varna and Constantinople. "In this way, the French Republic will be sovereign, so to speak, in all the west and south of Europe from the mouth of the Elms in the North Sea to the mouth of the Danube in the Black Sea. It will see in this immense space almost solely representative republics such as the Batavian, the Helvetic, the Ligurian, the Cispaline, the Greek, etc., etc." Finally, France would "establish armed trading posts" in Egypt. As mentioned earlier, Théremin did not recommend annexation of Egypt "since the French Republic cannot have subjects, and conquest will not make the Egyptians French citizens." Rather, he wrote, the Egyptians "would continue to be governed by their own laws but with a form of government more sensible and less debased than that of the Mamluks."[138]

138. "Combinaisons pour le cas où l'affaiblissement de l'Empire ottoman entraînerait la destruction en Europe," Pluviôse, Year 6 (January–February 1798), MAE, MD Turquie 15, f. 204–5.

Théremin's proposal amounted to an extraordinary projection of French influence, especially when coupled with his ministerial circulars on the German states. If Théremin's plans were followed, France would radically reorganize the eastern Mediterranean and turn enormous swaths of Europe into a French-dominated system of allied republics punctuated by French strongholds. The French Republic would dominate both the Mediterranean and all of continental Europe to the south and west of a line running from "from the mouth of the Elms in the North Sea to the mouth of the Danube in the Black Sea." To Théremin, establishing a sister republic and annexing certain territories was fairly simple stuff. His writings show none of the anxieties that so clearly mark classical-republican thinking about the international order. The establishment of a ius cosmopoliticum was to Théremin not just an abstraction but a real possibility to be actively and aggressively pursued. An even more extreme version of Théremin's vision was in fact pursued only a few years later as Napoleon Bonaparte transformed the Republic's federative system into a continental empire.

From Federation to Empire

The federative system envisioned by so many during these years never really came to fruition. A report penned by Talleyrand in July 1798 summarized the state of affairs: "The Republics that we have created, with the exception of the Batavian,...are in a state of infancy and unrest that makes them a burden on us....The time following a war as widespread and extraordinary in its results as that which has just ended is not a moment when it is easy to construct a federative system, especially for a nation that has given itself a government that is new in the history of the world."[139] Talleyrand's report underscores the fact that France was engaged in the creation of a federative system and simultaneously highlights its failure. With the renewal of continental war in 1799 and then the rise of Napoleon Bonaparte in France later that year, the federative system of

139. Talleyrand, "Rapport au Directoire sur la situation de la République française considérée dans ses rapports extérieurs avec les autres puissances," 14 Messidor, Year 6 (2 July 1798), MAE, MD France 652, f. 231.

the post-Terror Republic would definitively collapse and give way to the Napoleonic Empire. As Marc Belissa writes, "the 'federative' and republican hegemony of the Directory gave way to an authoritarian hegemony in which the dependent states were no longer 'sisters,' even dominated ones, but tributary allies."[140] Moreover, France soon annexed huge swaths of territory, eventually directly ruling the entire Netherlands, parts of northern Germany and northern Italy, the former Papal States, and the Dalmatian coast—not to mention the several "dependent states" ruled by members of Napoleon's family. Empire had displaced federation.

In an important sense, Napoleon's new hegemony built on the "modern" position in post-Terror debate. While more classical visions of the republic advocated cautious expansion and the establishment of sister republics in a relationship analogous to Machiavelli's and Harrington's "unequal league," the more modern version might involve aggressive expansionism. The political theorist Judith Shklar has suggested that the crucial difference between classical and modern republicanism was size. "The modern state was large, its culture diffuse, while the ancient republic had to be small and governed by a shared civic ethos." For modern republicans, the republic as a political form "would have to be imaginatively recreated or to be explicitly replaced by a new expansive republicanism to fit the modern political world."[141] The modern position during the post-Terror years is best exemplified by the writings of Charles-Guillaume Théremin, whose political pamphlets and ministerial circulars taken together advocated a foreign policy program that constituted nothing less than a frontal assault on both the extant international order and the day's received wisdom. For Théremin, the modern republic would be able to expand yet remain a republic in ways that the received, classical wisdom judged impossible. Théremin's thinking points to a broader conceptual pairing of modern republicanism and expansionism that can be said to have existed throughout the Revolution. While the relationship should not be exaggerated, it is noteworthy that those in favor of the republic's extension were most

140. Belissa, *Repenser l'ordre européen,* 247.

141. Shklar, "Montesquieu and the New Republicanism," in *Machiavelli and Republicanism,* ed. Gisella Bock, Quentin Skinner, and Maurizio Viroli (Cambridge, 1990), 266–67. See also Jacob T. Levy, "Beyond Publius: Montesquieu, Liberal Republicanism, and the Small-Republic Thesis," *History of Political Thought* 27 (2006): 50–90.

often those who championed a modern republicanism. During the Revolution's early years, Brissot and the Girondins were consistently prowar and proexpansion, denounced as such by Robespierre, who was himself consistently antiannexationist, in what Keith Baker has convincingly argued were classical-republican terms.[142] And Camille Desmoulins, one of the most outspoken critics of the revolutionary wars, condemned the war by drawing on Tacitus's account of the Roman republic's decline into empire.[143] The same conceptual mapping continued through the post-Terror period. Taking a broader, Atlantic view, *The Federalist* no. 10, penned by James Madison in 1787 and arguably the most distinctly modern political-philosophical text of the age of revolutions, lent conceptual support to expansion with the astonishingly radical argument that republics function most effectively when large.[144]

None of this is to say, of course, that a modern political-philosophical outlook necessarily resulted in an expansionist foreign policy. Many eighteenth-century advocates of doux commerce, for example, believed that the advent of commercial society would lead to the obsolescence of warfare. Diderot even thought commerce would obviate expansionism.[145] And Benjamin Constant would later write against Napoleonic conquest and expansionism in *The Spirit of Conquest and Usurpation and Their Relation to European Civilization.* Nonetheless, it is significant that modern republicans such as Théremin claimed the republic could expand without jeopardizing its health specifically because of its modernity. The very traits that modern republicans trumpeted to dispel the age-old claim that a republic could survive only in a small territory, notably representative government, enabled territorial expansion. Here we see one aspect of the importance

142. Keith Baker, "Transformations of Classical Republicanism in Eighteenth-Century France," *Journal of Modern History* 73 (2001): 47–48. Consider as well Robespierre's famous statement that "the most ridiculous idea that can arise in the head of a politician is to believe that it is enough to invade a country to make it adopt your laws and your constitution. No one likes armed missionaries."

143. On Desmoulins's debt to the classical-republican tradition, see Rachel Hammersley, "Camille Desmoulin's *Le Vieux Cordelier:* A Link between English and French Republicanism," *History of European Ideas* 27 (2001): 115–32.

144. Madison was indebted to Hume for this argument. See Douglass Adair, "'That Politics May Be Reduced to a Science': David Hume, James Madison, and the Tenth Federalist," in *Fame and the Founding Fathers* (Indianapolis, 1998).

145. Sankar Muthu, *Enlightenment Against Empire* (Princeton, 2003), chap. 3.

of the modern conviction that representative government is, as Pierre Rosanvallon puts it, "a *positive philosophical vision* with its own virtues,...an original and specific political form."[146] In political-philosophical terms, modern republicanism could enable new avenues for expansion and thus helped to elaborate the conceptual bridge from federation to empire.[147] Conversely, those who were the most classical in their republicanism continued to voice anxieties about expansion. And, ironically enough, those classical-republican anxieties gained credence as France followed the Roman script and the Republic became the Empire. When introducing the legislation that would make Napoleon Bonaparte hereditary emperor in 1804, Pierre-Louis Roederer explained, with a citation to Montesquieu, that "a vast empire can be governed only by a single man."[148]

The post-Terror years witnessed the French Republic expand its borders to its natural frontiers, establish a complex of sister republics, and attempt to institute a version of a federative system in Europe. As these issues were debated, discussion turned, to a significant degree, on the differences between classical and modern visions of the republic as a political form. Debate on foreign policy thus paralleled domestic political debate and further highlights the significance of the post-Terror period as a watershed in the transition from classical to modern republicanism. The next chapter will take up the influence of modern republicanism in a very different context, that of Napoleon Bonaparte's rise to power.

146. Rosanvallon, *La démocratie inachevée: Histoire de la souveraineté du peuple en France* (Paris, 2000), 12. See also Bernard Manin, *The Principles of Representative Government* (Cambridge, 1997).

147. A growing literature has explored the relationship between liberalism and European nineteenth-century overseas empire. See Uday Singh Mehta, *Liberalism and Empire: A Study in Nineteenth-Century British Liberal Thought* (Chicago, 1999); and Jennifer Pitts, *A Turn to Empire: The Rise of Imperial Liberalism in Britain and France* (Princeton, 2005).

148. Pierre-Louis Roederer, "De l'hérédité du pouvoir suprême" [1804], reprinted in *Œuvres du comte P.-L. Roederer,* ed. Antoine-Marie Roederer, 8 vols. (Paris, 1853–1959), 7:268. Roederer went on to explain that, contra Montesquieu, "a large state can be governed monarchically and not despotically" (269). On Roederer's use of Montesquieu in this text, see Sonenscher, *Before the Deluge,* 349–50.

5

Liberal Authoritarianism and the Constitution of the Year VIII

[After Brumaire] we spoke much less of liberty and equality. It was a question only of liberal ideas. And soon the liberals succeeded the republicans just as the republicans had succeeded the patriots.

Jean Jacques Régis de Cambacérès, *Mémoires inédits*

On 18 Brumaire of the Year VIII (9 November 1799) a group of disaffected political, intellectual, and military elites overthrew the Directorial regime. The coup's primary organizer was Sieyès, who famously declared, "I'm looking for a sword" and turned to Bonaparte only after his first choice, General Joubert, died in battle and his second choice, General Moreau, suggested Bonaparte in the wake of Bonaparte's daring return from Egypt in October of 1799.[1] Sieyès's and Bonaparte's "joint venture" aimed to put an end to the turmoil of the preceding years, the seemingly endless coups and crises, the lawlessness and brigandage engulfing France's countryside, and the rise of neo-Jacobinism in 1799.[2] "The days of 18 and

1. Albert Meynier, *Les coups d'état du Directoire,* vol. 3, *Le dix-huit Brumaire an VIII (9 Novembre 1799) et la fin de la République* (Paris, 1928), 94–95; Thierry Lentz, *Le Grand Consulat, 1799–1804* (Paris, 1999), 51.

2. "Joint venture" is Isser Woloch's term in *Napoleon and His Collaborators: The Making of a Dictatorship* (New York, 2001), chap. 1.

19 Brumaire," explained P.-J.-G. Cabanis, one of the leading Brumairians, were launched "against a cruel and absurd system that was rapidly leading the Republic to its inevitable ruin."[3] The men who led the coup sought not only to end the Directory but also to realize their vision of the new order they hoped to erect in its place. As Bonaparte explained on the day following the coup, "Conservative, tutelary, liberal ideas have regained their rights."[4] Unlike the coup against Robespierre carried out on 9 Thermidor of the Year II, the coup of Brumaire was anything but an event in search of its meaning.[5] Its organizers sought to establish a modern regime "founded upon the true principles of representative government, upon the sacred rights of property, equality, and liberty."[6] Property had replaced fraternity in the revolutionary trinity. The new regime would embody the political-philosophical principles of the modern, rationalist wing of the republican center, most notably those of Emmanuel-Joseph Sieyès and Pierre-Louis Roederer. Sieyès and Roederer were the progenitors of the Constitution of the Year VIII established in the wake of the coup, both in its literal drafting and in providing its conceptual inspiration. The new constitution, the fourth of the revolution, actualized their political-philosophical principles, thus signaling the triumph of "liberal authoritarianism" in the French Revolution.

I take the term "liberal authoritarianism" from the historian Howard Brown, who has described the emergence of a liberal authoritarianism in juridico-military practices during the years of the Directory and the Consulate.[7] Liberal authoritarianism constituted not a rejection of liberal principles but, rather, an attempt to maintain them through the establishment of a Hobbesian sovereign and the concomitant rejection of democratic

3. Cabanis, *Quelques considérations sur l'organisation sociale en général et particulièrement sur la nouvelle constitution,* in *Oeuvre philosophiques de Cabanis,* ed. Claude Lehec and Jean Cazeneuve, 2 vols. (Paris, 1956), 2:460.

4. *Proclamation du général en chef Bonaparte, le 19 brumaire, onze heures du soir,* in Vincent Lombard de Langres, *Le dix-huit brumaire ou tableau des événements qui ont amené cette journée; des moyens secrets par lesquels elle a été préparée; des faits qui l'ont accompagnée, et des résultats qu'elle doit avoir* (Paris, Year 8), 377.

5. To allude to Bronislaw Baczko's elegant description of the coup of Thermidor in *Ending the Terror: The French Revolution after Robespierre,* trans. Michel Petheram (Cambridge, 1994).

6. *Moniteur,* 25 Frimare, Year 8 (16 December 1799), 335.

7. Howard G. Brown, *Ending the French Revolution: Violence, Justice, and Repression from the Terror to Napoleon* (Charlottesville, Va., 2006).

practices. Another apt term for this system would be "legal despotism," the phrase coined by the Physiocrat Pierre-Paul Le Mercier de la Rivière in his *L'ordre naturel et essentiel des sociétés politiques (The Natural and Essential Order of Political Societies),* and attached to Physiocracy more generally, which Rousseau famously equated with "the most perfect Hobbesism."[8] Liberal authoritarianism was instantiated in political-philosophical terms in the Constitution of the Year VIII, thereby marking an important rupture in the political-constitutional realm. This characteristic of the Constitution of the Year VIII and its connections with liberal political theory were recognized in a law thesis submitted to the University of Paris in 1939 by Jean Bourdon: "Sieyès estimated that if individual rights were respected and the domain of the State restricted, this domain could and even should be governed in an authoritarian manner. This combination of elements, often considered contradictory, was not the fantasy of a lone figure but the doctrine of an entire part of the liberal school."[9] Bourdon's perspective, however, has remained occluded from the vast majority of scholarship on the Constitution of the Year VIII and the political culture of the Consulate. While the final version of the constitution, after Bonaparte's revisions, was perfectly true to neither Roederer's nor Sieyès's prescriptions, it nonetheless reflected their collective vision and squared well with Bonaparte's own antipoliticism.[10] The Constitution of the Year VIII furthermore laid the groundwork for the eventual consolidation of the Napoleonic system. If Napoleon's rule should be understood as an offshoot of "enlightened despotism,"[11] then the logic of that regime was given its preliminary institutional articulation in the Constitution of the Year VIII at the hands of Roederer and, especially, Sieyès.

Liberal authoritarianism was predicated on the fundamentally liberal notion that the freedom to pursue individual ends is the touchstone of the polity and is best protected by a strong central authority restricting political activity to only the most confined spaces. In this, it was true to modern liberalism. "The liberty of the moderns" was placed above all else, and

8. Jean-Jacques Rousseau to the marquis de Mirabeau (1767), in Rousseau, *The Social Contract and Other Later Political Writings,* ed. Victor Gourevitch (Cambridge, 1997), 270.

9. Jean Bourdon, *La Constitution de l'an VIII* (Rodez, 1941), 109.

10. For Bonaparte's distrust of politics, see Steven Englund, *Napoleon: A Political Life* (Cambridge, Mass., 2004), chap. 7, esp. 142–50.

11. E.g., Louis Bergeron, *France Under Napoleon,* trans. R. R. Palmer (Princeton, 1981), 4.

democracy sacrificed to liberalism. This turned out to be disastrous in practice, as Napoleon Bonaparte slowly erected a police state and dismantled virtually all civil liberties, but it needs to be emphasized that liberal authoritarianism was not a priori an illogical construction. In formal terms, an authoritarian regime is fully capable of preserving civil liberties. Indeed, support for an absolutist state was very much part of the early liberal tradition. One of modern liberalism's most prominent genealogical strands, which arose in response to the brutal wars of religion in the sixteenth and seventeenth centuries, called explicitly for an absolutist state committed to preserving civil liberties. In addition, Enlightenment figures such as Voltaire advocated an enlightened absolutism configured on this model. The price paid for this solution, however, was the extirpation of the political as such. The system erected by Sieyès and Roederer aimed to expunge politics by creating a state that stood outside and above political activity. This characteristic of the liberal-authoritarian mind found historical antecedent in what Pierre Rosanvallon has called the antipolitical strain of early modern political thought. Rosanvallon delineates two principal early modern counterpolitical currents, Hobbesian voluntarism and rationalist liberalism, both of which aimed to suppress the political in the name of social harmony.[12] Building on Rosanvallon's argument, we can add Sheldon Wolin's insight that both Hobbes and the rationalist liberals of the eighteenth century sought to reduce politics to a science of administration or theory of organization, thereby eliminating politics.[13] The liberal-authoritarian mind of Sieyès, Roederer, and the Constitution of the Year VIII stands as the French Revolution's preeminent example of such antipolitical thought. In a certain sense, Roederer and Sieyès brought together the Hobbesian and the rationalist liberal strands of thought and created what could be called a rationalist, liberal sovereign.[14] The reorganization of France's political architecture by the Brumairians was more than the establishment

12. Rosanvallon, *Le capitalisme utopique: Histoire de l'idée de marché,* 3d ed. (Paris, 1999).

13. Sheldon Wolin, *Politics and Vision: Continuity and Innovation in Western Political Thought* (Boston, 1960), esp. 388–93.

14. Both Roederer and Sieyès were serious readers of Hobbes. Sieyès wrote a short piece on Hobbes, now republished in Pasquale Pasquino, *Sieyès et l'invention de la constitution en France* (Paris, 1998), 165–66. Revealingly, in 1791 Dominique Garat published an article in the *Journal de Paris* that located the origins of Sieyès's political theory in Hobbes's thought. Michael Sonenscher, introduction to *Political Writings,* by Emmanuel-Joseph Sieyès (Indianapolis, 2003), xlv–xlvii. Roederer, for his part, undertook a translation of Hobbes's *De Cive* while in hiding during the Terror.

of a new central authority. It was the elimination of politics in the name of a different vision of society and the human subject living in that society.

This liberal-authoritarian antipolitics was made patently clear in the official discourse justifying the coup and explaining the new constitution. The Brumairians placed social order above all else, sounding the theme again and again as they vindicated the coup and the new regime. In the government's official introduction to the Constitution of the Year VIII, Boulay de la Meurthe placed social order at the center of the new government's priorities.[15] Dominique Garat likewise exclaimed that with the strong central power created, "the French Republic will no longer be an arena constantly open to factions" and that "social order" and "stability" would soon be achieved.[16] Cabanis justified the new constitution by pointing to the civil liberties and increased individual happiness a strong government would provide, arguing that "all good government should be strong, because otherwise it cannot effectively protect the liberty of individuals."[17] While making these arguments, however, the Brumairians did not abandon the rhetoric of republicanism. To the contrary, they portrayed the coup of Brumaire as a veritable new dawn for republicanism. They argued that only a strong central government could effectively guarantee the public good, which they claimed was the essence of republicanism. For example, one pamphlet celebrating the new regime explained that "whenever . . . the government renders to each citizen the liberty, safety, protection, and happiness to which he is entitled, the *public good,* the *Republic,* exists in the government, whatever its form."[18] This line of reasoning limited the definition of the republic, and the purpose of the state, to concern with the public good and thereby radically decoupled the republic as a political form from any specific constitutional architecture.

The triumph of such antipolitical liberal-authoritarianism sounded the death knell of classical republicanism in France's political center. Roederer

15. Antoine Boulay de la Meurthe, *Manuel portratif, contenant la constitution française de l'an VIII* (Paris, 1800), 21.

16. Garat, *Discours prononcé par Garat dans la séance du 23 frimaire, après la première lecture de la résolution relative à l'acceptation de l'acte constitutionnel,* in Lombard de Langres, *Le dix-huit brumaire,* 426, 428.

17. Cabanis, *Quelques considérations,* 2:463.

18. Nicolas-Pierre Gilbert, *Du Pacte social, ou Examen raisonné de la Constitution de l'an VIII* (Paris, 1799), 4–5.

and Sieyès were among the leading critics of classical republicanism throughout the Revolution—recall their criticisms of the Constitution of the Year III, discussed in chapter 1. Their ascension and the triumph of their ideas in the Constitution of the Year VIII signaled a political-philosophical shift in the republican center. While the institutions of the Constitution of the Year VIII made use of nomenclature taken from republican Rome (Consuls, Tribunate, and a Senate), the speeches and political discourse around the constitution were largely devoid of the Revolution's typical references to classical antiquity. More important, classical-republican precepts were clearly spurned. The Brumairians sought to end the cycle of coups and crises not through the reestablishment of constitutional balance or the promotion of virtue among the active citizenry but through the creation of a rational political order with a single overarching power. Classical-republican fears about combining liberty and power and about a strong executive were cast aside in favor of a quasi-Hobbesian sovereign. In addition, the Brumairians rejected more democratic forms of republicanism. While they still referred to the sovereignty of the people, this sovereignty was to be enacted only in plebiscites and extremely limited elections—what the historian Jean-Yves Coppolani calls "the Napoleonic electoral comedy."[19] As Cabanis explained, by breaking with the model of "the anarchic democracies of antiquity," the new French order would establish "democracy purged of its inconveniences. There is no more rabble to incite in the forum or in clubs. The ignorant classes no longer exercise any influence on either the legislature or the government."[20] The Brumairians' seizure of power and promulgation of the Constitution of the Year VIII was not a return to the constitutional monarchy of 1789–92, the democratic republicanism of 1792–94, or the classical republicanism of the post-Terror period. Rather, it announced a seismic shift in the organization of France's polity, the establishment of a liberal-authoritarian regime.

The Constitution of the Year VIII realized the political-philosophical programs of Sieyès and Roederer. While their styles were utterly different—Sieyès was a philosopher by temperament, Roederer a journalist—their intellectual and political programs were closely parallel and the two were loosely associated throughout the Revolution. In 1789, reports Michael

19. Jean-Yves Coppolani, *Les élections en France à l'époque napoléonienne* (Paris, 1980).
20. Cabanis, *Quelques considérations,* 473–75.

Sonenscher, Roederer was "in Sieyès's entourage," and the two advocated similar solutions to the debt crisis of 1787–89, each rejecting the principle that only landed property could confer a stake in the nation's sovereignty.[21] In the early years of the Revolution they were both close to Condorcet, sharing his commitment to developing a science of politics and society. Both went into hiding during the Terror and emerged to find their political sympathies more or less aligned. The two discussed collaborating in their journalistic endeavors, apparently agreeing in February of 1795 that Roederer would contribute to a journal Sieyès and Julien Duhamel were starting entitled the *Journal d'instruction morale et politique.*[22] Since this journal seems to have been something of an attempt to relaunch the *Journal d'instruction sociale* that Duhamel, Sieyès, and Condorcet had published in 1793, Roederer, it appears, was to replace Condorcet (who had committed suicide during the Terror). The day after making this agreement, however, Roederer wrote to Sieyès that he had to renege because of a prior commitment to Pierre-Louis Ginguené and the *Décade philosophique.* Roederer proposed that instead of launching the *Journal d'instruction morale et politique,* Sieyès and Duhamel should join him at the *Décade.*[23] Sieyès never wrote for the *Décade,* but their near-alliance testifies to the fact that they perceived each other as sharing a common intellectual and political program.

The alignment of their political views was further proven during the constitutional debates of the summer of 1795, when both were critical of the Commission of Eleven's proposed constitution, notably its more classical-republican features.[24] Then, when the Directory first convened in the fall of 1795 and Sieyès declined the seat he was offered, Roederer urged Sieyès to reconsider his decision. "I hear, my dear friend, that you are refusing the seat conferred to you. I beg you, I beseech you in the name of the patrie and of liberty to take a few more days to examine your conscience

21. Michael Sonenscher, "The Nation's Debt and the Birth of the Modern Republic: The French Fiscal Deficit and the Politics of the Revolution of 1789, part II," *History of Political Thought* 18 (1997): 286, n. 175, 303, 306.

22. The *Journal d'instruction morale et politique,* however, apparently never got off the ground. I have not been able to find any issues or references to it, but the contract between Duhamel and Sieyès, dated 29 Pluviôse, Year 3 (17 February 1795), is in Sieyès's personal papers. AN, 284 AP 9–5.

23. Roederer to Sieyès, 23 Pluviose, Year 3 (11 February 1795), AN, 284 AP 9–5.

24. Discussed in chapter 1.

about what you have the right to do. Do not abandon us to perversity and stupidity. I see only you between the enlightened friends of liberty, especially its honest friends, and the most terrible calamities. . . . If you leave, it is an inestimable loss."[25] Roederer continued to admire Sieyès during the Directory, even penning a fictional dialogue in his *Journal d'économie publique* that had Sieyès explaining the true principles of government—to "conserve and protect . . . liberty and property"—to Bayle, Locke, Hobbes, Helvétius, Montesquieu, Rousseau, and Voltaire, all of whom are embroiled in an irresolvable dispute until Sieyès enters the scene and enlightens them.[26] During the planning for the coup of 18 Brumaire, Roederer along with Talleyrand passed messages between Sieyès and Bonaparte so that no one would see the latter two in communication with each other.[27] Their shared itinerary then culminated in the aftermath of the coup, when Sieyès set about drafting the new constitution and Roederer worked closely with him both in drafting the constitution and in hammering out compromises between Sieyès and Bonaparte.

Pierre-Louis Roederer

Pierre-Louis Roederer was one of the Revolution's great survivors, staying at or near the center of action in revolutionary France from the calling of the Estates General in 1788 through the July Revolution of 1830. An industrialist from Metz, he sat in the National Assembly, was close to Condorcet, Lafayette, and Sieyès, and then spent the Terror in hiding. He reemerged immediately after 9 Thermidor as an important journalist, penned Tallien's famous speech on the Terror, and in 1795 took a seat in the Political Economy section of the Institute's Class of Moral and Political Sciences. Roederer supported the Directory at its outset, despite having been a critic of the Constitution of the Year III during its redaction but

25. Roederer to Sieyès, 11 Brumaire, Year 4 (2 November 1795), AN, 284 AP 11–5.

26. Roederer, "Entretien de plusieurs philosophes célèbres, sur les gouvernements républicain et monarchique," *Journal d'économie publique,* 20 Prairial, Year 5 (8 June 1797), reprinted in Pierre-Louis Roederer, *Œuvres du comte P.-L. Roederer,* ed. Antoine-Marie Roederer, 8 vols. (Paris, 1853–1959), 7:61–71 (hereafter cited as *OR*).

27. François Auguste Mignet, "Roederer, sa vie et ses travaux," *Revue des deux mondes* 13 (1838): 90. See also, Lentz, *Le Grand Consulat,* 55.

fiercely criticized both the Directory and its intellectual supporters during the events leading up to, during, and after the coup of 18 Fructidor, Year V.[28] Following the coup of Brumaire, he was an enthusiastic supporter of the Napoleonic regime, serving first on the Council of State and then in the Senate. After Napoleon's defeat in 1814–15, Roederer managed to avoid proscription and counted as an important member of the liberal political opposition during the Restoration before taking office after the July Revolution of 1830. If nothing else, his intellectual and political career was a testament to staying power and longevity.[29]

Roederer's political-philosophical program was undergirded by a science of society, or "social science," that was indebted to the Physiocrats and Condorcet.[30] His social science involved a reworking of the economic principles of Physiocracy and its "social art," a reworking that rejected the Physiocrats' claim that land is the sole source of wealth. Roederer agreed with the Physiocrats that property constituted the basis of the social-political order and should be legally inviolable, but unlike them, he celebrated property in all its forms—landed, industrial, and commercial. This modification of what was arguably Physiocracy's core principle should not, however, obscure the extent to which Roederer's ideas remained within the Physiocratic paradigm.[31] He retained the Physiocratic confidence that society and politics could be rationalized and mastered according to a single and complete system. In his eyes, there was a formula, a system, that could rationalize France's economic, social, and political life and thus bring the

28. E.g., Roederer attacked Benjamin Constant for what he considered Constant's abandonment of liberal principles in the name of blind loyalty to the Republic. Roederer, review of *Des Réactions politiques,* by Benjamin Constant, *Journal d'économie publique,* 10 Floréal, Year 5 (29 April 1797), reprinted in *OR,* 5:5–10.

29. Despite this extraordinary career, Roederer has remained surprisingly neglected by historians. See Kenneth Margerison, *P.-L. Roederer: Political Thought and Practice During the French Revolution* (Philadelphia, 1983); Thierry Lentz, *Roederer* (Metz, 1989); Ingrid Rademacher, "La science sociale républicaine de Pierre-Louis Roederer," *Revue française d'histoire des idées politiques* 13 (2001): 25–56; Ruth Scurr, "Social Equality in Pierre-Louis Roederer's Interpretation of the Modern Republic, 1793," *History of European Ideas* 26 (2000): 105–26; Scurr, "Pierre-Louis Roederer and the Debate on Forms of Government in Revolutionary France," *Political Studies* 52 (2004): 251–68; Sonenscher, *Before the Deluge: Public Debt, Inequality, and the Intellectual Origins of the French Revolution* (Princeton, 2007).

30. Rademacher, "La science sociale républicaine de Pierre-Louis Roederer," 25–56; Margerison, *P.-L. Roederer.*

31. Scurr, "Social Equality," 110.

Revolution to a close without returning to the Old Regime. The result of his system was a liberal authoritarianism in many ways all but indistinguishable from Physiocratic legal despotism. Roederer's thought is best understood as a reworking of the Physiocratic economic system and an extension of its political program.

The system that Roederer advocated required the proper organization of the economy along resolutely modern and procommercial lines. He had no patience for his contemporaries' fixation with classical models, which he derided in his *Cours d'organisation sociale* of 1793 as "l'antiqu'archie."[32] Elsewhere, in an unpublished speech on China delivered to the Class of Moral and Political Sciences in three parts during the spring and summer of 1796, he complained, "We never cease talking about the Greek republics and the Roman republic; it is from there that we take our lessons and our examples of morality and of politics" even though "such clouds hang over their history! Such a blend of greatness and barbarism is found in what we know of their actions! Such alternatives of peace and unrest, of shame and glory, of prosperity and misfortune at the heart of their existence! Such prompt decline, such rapid fall, such a short existence...." He delighted in pointing out the faults and failures of classical Rome and, especially, Sparta. "Examining the constitutions of Sparta and Rome,... I recognized that there was a military tyranny, patrician and even royal, precisely where our rhetoricians show us only perfect liberty."[33] In a series of published and unpublished fragments on Xenophon's histories, Roederer portrayed Sparta as "an oligarchy, almost a monarchy," in which the population was denatured and debased by Lycurgus's tyrannical laws. "These Greeks and these Romans," he wrote, "were in their political and moral existence only barbarian peoples, without knowledge of the social art, without guarantees of man's natural rights, and as a result without the pleasures that nature wanted to compose true happiness."[34] When Roederer did have positive

32. Quoted in Richard Whatmore, "Adam Smith's Role in the French Revolution," *Past and Present* 175 (2002): 85.

33. Roederer, "Mémoires sur le gouvernement de la Chine, sur la langue des Chinois, et particulièrement sur leur écriture," AN, 29 AP 109, f. 2–66, reprinted in *OR,* 8:98–99. The records of the Class of Moral and Political Sciences show the speech as delivered on 7 Floréal, 17 Floréal, and 7 Thermidor, Year 6 (26 April, 6 May, and 25 July 1798). AI, SMP, A1.

34. "La République d'athenes par Xenophon. Constitution," n.d., AN, 29 AP 110, f. 777; and Roederer, *Journal de Paris,* 10 Floréal, Year 3 and 7 Frimaire, Year 4 (29 April 1795 and 28 November 1795), reprinted in *OR,* 5:180–82.

things to say about the ancient world, they were usually reserved for Athens, the commercial city-state that in eighteenth-century argument sometimes served as a code word for promodern and procommercial positions. In Roederer's eyes, the classical world was consigned to endless warfare because it knew nothing of the benevolent effects of commercial interaction, of the increasingly dense layers of interdependence produced by exchange. Indeed, Roederer argued for the benevolent effects of commerce throughout the revolutionary era. The historian Richard Whatmore describes Roederer's *Cours* of 1793 in terms that could be extended to virtually any of Roederer's economic writings: his "overriding concern was to prove that the love of wealth could serve the public good."[35] This economic vision provided the purpose for Roederer's political system. In his eyes, the political structure of the nation was there to ensure that individuals could pursue their economic desires. Politics was subservient to commerce.

Roederer's celebration of commerce rested on an understanding of the human personality in which self-interest was taken to be the primary human motivation. He mocked the notion that a republic could be founded on virtue and rejected as unrealistic and outmoded the classical-republican imperative to subject private to public good in the name of a higher virtue.[36] In notes composed on the Jansenist Pierre Nicole, Roederer approved of Nicolés claim that even charity is motivated by self-love.[37] "Self-interest," he explained in a report to the National Institute on moral catechisms, "is the strongest guarantee that one can give to morality. One can wish to see the chain of duties attached higher, but one cannot see it attached more solidly."[38] Furthermore, Roederer found thoroughly unpersuasive the notion of sympathy espoused by the Scottish moral philosophers Hutcheson and Smith, which had numerous adherents among French intellectuals at the time.[39] Sympathy, Roederer argued, could not exist on its own and had to be explained by a prior motive, which he identified as self-interest.[40]

35. Whatmore, *Republicanism and the French Revolution: An Intellectual History of Jean-Baptiste Say's Political Economy* (Oxford, 2000), 102; see also Margerison, *P.-L. Roederer,* chap. 6.

36. Roederer, "Collection et analyse des éléments moraux de la société," n.d., AN, 29 AP 89.

37. Roederer, "Essais de morale de Nicole," n.d., AN, 29 AP 110, f. 27.

38. Roederer, "Rapport à l'Institut sur le catéchisme universel de Saint-Lambert," [1798], in *OR,* 5:112.

39. See James Livesey, *Making Democracy in the French Revolution* (Cambridge, Mass., 2001).

40. See Roederer's "Théorie des Sentiments Moraux," *Journal de Paris,* 21 Messidor, Year 6 (9 July 1798), reprinted in *OR,* 4:496–98; Roederer, "Des Lettres de la citoyenne Condorcet sur la

While Roederer seems to have misread Smith on this front,[41] his criticism of Smith casts his own views into sharp relief. In the brave new world of the late eighteenth century that Roederer described and advocated, self-interest would underpin commercial society and cause men to be "joined tightly together."[42]

For such a commercial society to flourish, Roederer maintained, public order was essential. Repeated calls for order were perhaps the most salient feature of his Thermidorian and Directorial journalism.[43] "Order, order," Roederer exclaimed in the first article of the first issue of his *Journal d'économie publique, de morale et de politique,* "this is the object of all constitutions, the task of all governments, the principle of all prosperity." Order was essential for liberty: "The republic gives it to us; *order* secures it."[44] In his unpublished speech to the Class of Moral and Political Sciences on China, he urged that France take the government of China as a present-day model. He told his colleagues, in an astonishingly erroneous representation of Chinese history, that "China has existed powerful, peaceful, happy, always the same, for four thousand years.... If, from what I said of China, it does not follow that stability is a fruit of liberty, it will be necessary to conclude that liberty is the happy fruit of stability."[45]

To guarantee this order and stability, Roederer prescribed several key supports. In keeping with the Directorial discourse of moeurs discussed in chapter 2, he aimed to change public opinion and, more radically, to change people's habits, which he described as the true task of "the moralist."[46] In political-institutional terms, he emphasized the need to erect a strong

---

sympathie," *Journal de Paris,* 26 Messidor, Year 6 (14 July 1798), reprinted in *OR,* 4:498–501; his untitled, undated fictional dialogue between Helvétius and Adam Smith about whether interest or sympathy is "l'unique mobile des actions humaines," *OR,* 5:391; and his "Definitions diverses de la vertu," n.d., AN, 29 AP 110, f. 231.

41. Sympathy, for Smith, was more an extension of self-interest to another person than a rejection of self-interest.

42. Roederer, quoted in Thomas Kaiser, "Politics and Political Economy in the Thought of the Idéologues," *History of Political Economy* 12 (1980): 149.

43. See Thierry Lentz, "La presse républicaine modérée sous la Convention thermidorienne et le Directoire: Pierre-Louis Roederer, animateur et propriétaire du *Journal de Paris* et du *Journal d'économie publique,*" *Revue historique* 292 (1994): 297–313.

44. Roederer, "Introduction," *Journal d'économie publique, de morale et de politique,* 10 Fructidor, Year 4 (27 August 1796), 3–4, 15.

45. Roederer, "Mémoires sur le gouvernement de la Chine," 8:98, 112.

46. Roederer, "Du traité *des devoirs* du Cicéron," 1798, AN, 29 AP 110, f. 495.

"governing power" that would enable people to live together peacefully.[47] In this vein, he was critical of the Constitution of the Year III because of its weak executive, writing at the time of its redaction that "the enlightened citizens who fix their eyes on the goal to which all governments should tend want a republic organized such that strength and rectitude are united in its executive power."[48] Throughout the years of the Directory, he demanded repeatedly that the executive be strengthened in order to prevent the recurrent crises that plagued the Directorial regime. For example, in an otherwise unsympathetic review of Necker's *De la Révolution française* of 1796, Roederer praised Necker's criticisms of the weak executive established in the Constitution of the Year III.[49] The strong governing power that Roederer advocated would be modeled on the "patriarchal authority" of the family, which, in turn, would be more than a model for the state—it would also be one of the fundaments of the entire order, "the best foundation of the Republic."[50] Reflecting this emphasis on patriarchal authority, citizenship would be restricted to men. "The *heads of family* alone are citizens; one should understand by this phrase, as in the Roman paterfamilias, not only the father of the family, but also anyone who *can be one.*"[51] Moreover, citizens would be men of wealth and property. In his 1788 *De la députation aux États généraux,* Roederer claimed that "the man without property is a mere passenger in the state."[52] In late 1795 he chided the creators of the Constitution of the Year III for not following rigorously enough the principle that "the degree of power should be proportional to the degree of wealth."[53] It is important to note, however, that, extending

47. Roederer, "Est-il possible d'unir si parfaitement les hommes en société qu'ils n'aient pas besoin de chefs et de lois coactives pour vivre ensemble en bonne intelligence?" *Journal d'économie publique,* 30 Messidor, Year 5 (18 July 1797), reprinted in *OR,* 5:153–54.

48. Roederer, "Du Gouvernement," originally a series of articles in the *Journal de Paris* in August 1795; reprinted in *OR,* 7:28.

49. His review, originally published in the *Journal d'économie publique, de morale et de politique* in several parts over the winter of 1796–97, is reprinted in *OR,* 4:559–90. See esp. 590.

50. Roederer, "De l'autorité Patriarchale et de l'autorité Paternelle," n.d., AN, 29 AP 109, f. 167.

51. Roederer, "Réflexions sur l'ouvrage du citoyen Guiraudet, intitulé: *De la famille, considérée comme l'élément des sociétés,*" *Journal d'économie politique,* 20 Thermidor, Year 5 (7 August 1797), reprinted in *OR,* 5:98. See also Anne Verjus, *Le cens de la famille: Les femmes et le vote, 1789–1848* (Paris, 2002), 64–78.

52. Quoted in Sonenscher, "The Nation's Debt and the Birth of the Modern Republic," 286, n. 175.

53. Roederer, review of *Oeuvres politiques de J. Harrington, contenant la République d'Océana, les aphorismes et les autres traités du même auteur, Journal de Paris,* 15 Fructidor Year 3 (1 September 1795), reprinted in *OR,* 4:525–26.

his critique of Physiocracy, he did not limit his definition of property to land. He insisted that in order to vote one must "possess a property, either landed, mobile, or industrial.... Those are the circumstances that guarantee the *interest* of the individual in the social order."[54]

Roederer's limited definition of who possessed a genuine interest in the social order led him to divide the population into "citizens" and "inhabitants."[55] As he explained elsewhere, "the political association is not contracted between all the individuals that it contains, that it protects, and who have an indirect interest in its conservation. It is composed of those who...have taken a direct interest, an *action* in the social enterprise."[56] Only those with sufficient "interest"—that is, wealth—would be able to participate in political decision making. All other political activity would be confined to highly restricted spaces. For this reason, Roederer advocated that political associations of more than twelve to fifteen people be outlawed.[57] Roederer's distrust of political participation or activity led him in the summer of 1795, in an important anticipation of the Napoleonic system, to advocate the establishment of a plebiscitary system in which the political activity of the general population would be limited to simple yes or no votes.[58] These measures were aspects of Roederer's general prejudice against political activity as such, which can also be seen in a response he penned to Toussaint Guiraudet after Guiraudet published a new translation of Machiavelli's *Oeuvres* in 1799 that placed paramount emphasis on Machiavelli's *Discourses on Livy*.[59] Roederer railed against Machiavelli, comparing him to Marat and claiming that "I do not find a single fertile thought in Machiavelli, a single great idea, a single salutary view." Roederer particularly objected to Guiraudet's favorable treatment

54. Roederer, "Constitution," *Journal de Paris,* 8 Germinal to 19 Messidor, Year 3 (28 May to 7 July 1795), reprinted in *OR,* 6:96.

55. Ibid., 95.

56. Roederer, "De la majorité nationale, de la manière dont elle se forme, et des moyens auxquels on peut la reconnaître, ou Théorie de l'opinion publique" (1797), reprinted in Lucien Jaume, *Échec au Libéralisme: les Jacobins et l'État* (Paris, 1990), 99.

57. Roederer, *Des Sociétés particulières, telles que clubs, réunions, etc.* (Paris, 1798), 18.

58. Roederer, "Constitution," 6:88–89.

59. Guiraudet, "Discours sur Machiavel," in *Oeuvres de Machiavel; traduction nouvelle par T. Guiraudet,* by Niccolò Machiavelli, 9 vols. (Paris, 1799), vol. 1. Guiraudet sent Roederer a copy of his translation upon its publication. Guiraudet to Roederer, 6 Floréal, Year 7 (25 April 1799), AN, 29 AP 110, f. 465.

of Machiavelli's *Discourses,* criticizing Machiavelli's ideas about constitutional balance and labeling the *Discourses* "an instruction manual for coups d'état" that promoted factionalism and provided "a lesson for conspiracies to succeed."[60] Machiavelli, of course, was the early modern *political* thinker par excellence.[61] Roederer's stress on public order led him to a decisively antipolitical stance.

The exact form that Roederer's orderly society would take was not of particular importance to him. Sweeping aside centuries of political-philosophical debate, Roederer thought that a good government could be either a republic or a monarchy as long as it successfully maintained order, guaranteed civil liberties, and promoted commerce. In an unpublished fragment titled "Voltaire: If he was a republican," Roederer noted that Voltaire, whom he greatly admired, "constantly vacillates in his opinion about the principles of government" but that the important point was that Voltaire "loved liberty." "One can change political opinions; one cannot arbitrarily change moral affections."[62] This, in essence, captured Roederer's own stance: he favored certain principles, not forms of government.[63] This preference was also demonstrated in his talk to the National Institute on the Chinese political system: "I would venture that China is not a republic, but a government in which all the great qualities that characterize republican government surmount those that belong to despotism, and where the purest elements of the representative system tower over those of tyranny."[64] In other words, China demonstrated that all of a republic's positive features could be spawned without creating an actual republic, confirming Roederer's conviction that a strong, central state based on limited suffrage but focused on the public good was the answer to France's cycle of political crises. This position proved fateful in 1799 when he collaborated with Sieyès and Bonaparte to overthrow the Directory and establish a liberal-authoritarian regime.

60. Roederer, "Sur Machiavel, à Tuissant Guiraudet," [1799], AN, 29 AP 110, f. 465–73.

61. See Claude Lefort, *Le travail de l'oeuvre Machiavel* (Paris, 1972).

62. Roederer, "Voltaire: S'il a été Républicain," n.d., AN, 29 AP 110, f. 329.

63. Elsewhere, Roederer more or less agreed with Montesquieu that virtue is necessary for republics, which, given his repeated skepticism about people's ability to maintain virtue, would seem to imply doubts about the sustainability of republics. Roederer, "Querelle de Montesquieu et de Voltaire sur les deux principes du gouvernement monarchique et du gouvernement républicain," *Journal d'économie publique,* 10 Nivôse, Year 5 (30 December 1796), reprinted in *OR,* 7:55–57.

64. Roederer, "Mémoires sur le gouvernement de la Chine," 8:100.

Emmanuel-Joseph Sieyès

Emmanuel-Joseph Sieyès has long been one of the Revolution's most famous figures. His celebrated *What Is the Third Estate?* was the single most important political pamphlet of 1788–89, his exhortations to the Third Estate to declare itself the National Assembly can be said to have ended the society of orders in France, and in 1799 he organized the coup of Brumaire. This résumé, to give only a few examples from a much longer list, has led the historian Jean-Denis Bredin to dub Sieyès "the key to the Revolution."[65] In recent years scholarly attention has focused less on his strictly political role in the Revolution and turned more to his originality as an economic and political thinker.[66] He is now credited with being a liberal voice in the Revolution, one muffled by the political excesses of Jacobinism.[67] Such an interpretive line, however, risks understating the authoritarian and antidemocratic aspects of Sieyès's thought. Sieyès was the preeminent theorist of liberal authoritarianism.

Over the course of the Revolution, in a series of published works and unpublished manuscripts, Sieyès articulated an original if enigmatic political philosophy.[68] As a political actor as well as a theorist, he considered his work to have a hard-edged realism that precluded utopian or excessively optimistic programs. In an undated piece, he remarked, "If something distinguishes me from ancient and modern publicists, it is the importance that I attach to a politics of [constitutional] organization and how infrequently I use... eternal phrases drawn from morality and philosophy when it is a case of constructing machinery and making them work together to

65. Jean-Denis Bredin, *Sieyès: La clé de la Révolution française* (Paris, 1988).

66. See in particular Pasquino, *Sieyès et l'invention de la constitution en France;* Murray Forsyth, *Reason and Revolution: The Political Thought of the Abbé Sieyès* (Leicester, 1987); William H. Sewell, *A Rhetoric of Bourgeois Revolution: The Abbé Sieyès and* What Is the Third Estate? (Durham, N.C., 1994); Jacques Guilhaumou, *Sieyès et l'ordre de la langue: L'invention de la politique moderne* (Paris, 2002); and the series of works published by Michael Sonenscher: "The Nation's Debt and the Birth of the Modern Republic"; introduction to Sieyès, *Political Writings;* and *Before the Deluge.*

67. E.g., Pasquino, "The Constitutional Republicanism of Emmanuel Sieyès," in *The Invention of the Modern Republic,* ed. Biancamaria Fontana (Cambridge, 1994), esp. 110–11.

68. According to Christine Fauré, Sieyès's political philosophy remained at its core essentially unchanged across the revolutionary decade, an interpretation Michael Sonenscher's recent *Before the Deluge* reaffirms. Fauré, introduction to *Des Manuscrits de Sieyès, 1773–1799* by Emmanuel-Joseph Sieyès, ed. Fauré, Jacques Guilhaumou, and Jacques Valier (Paris, 1999), 32.

produce a real impact."[69] Furthermore, Sieyès developed his ideas in complete confidence that he was on the path to advancing political philosophy and politics itself to a state of near perfection, to a "science," as he called it. As he wrote in a review of his own work that he intended to publish anonymously in order to draw attention to his writings, "I have always thought that political morality... forms a true science."[70] Moreover, Sieyès is reported to have declared on one occasion that he had succeeded in "completing" the science of politics.[71]

At the core of his science of politics stood the rationalist belief that politics and France's political life could, if only organized correctly, run with complete efficiency, free of conflict. In this, Sieyès, like Roederer, was very much an heir to the Physiocrats, who wished to expunge politics from governance, to establish an apolitical society.[72] Over the course of the revolutionary decade, as he observed and participated in the disorder and tumult of French politics, Sieyès's desire to construct a rationalist solution to the vagaries of political life only deepened. He thought that such a perfectly organized society was possible because of the discovery or invention of the division of labor. For Sieyès, the division of labor would allow for a seamlessly efficient ordering of society, the economy, and public administration so that politics would become increasingly unnecessary. To use Simone Meyssonnier's and Bernard Manin's metaphors for the great divide in eighteenth-century liberal and protoliberal political thought, Sieyès was an advocate of "rules" and "clockwork" over "balance."[73] His extraordinary confidence in the division of labor stemmed from a more general admiration for modern commercial society and from his immersion in the nascent discipline of political

69. AN, 284 AP 5–1/5, quoted in Pasquino, *Sieyes et l'invention de la constitution en France,* 100. Insertion by Pasquino.

70. AN, 284 AP 4–8, quoted in Pasquino, "The Constitutional Republicanism of Emmanuel Sieyès," 111.

71. Quoted in Sonenscher, "The Nation's Debt and the Birth of the Modern Republic," 284, n. 168.

72. Sieyès wrote extensively on the Physiocrats. See in particular his *Grand cahier métaphysique,* composed initially during the 1770s and then continued in the early nineteenth century, AN, 284 AP 2–2, reprinted in *Des Manuscrits de Sieyès, 1773–1799,* 75–166. On the piece's date of composition, see Guilhaumou's presentation, ibid., 51–72.

73. Simone Meyssonnier, *La balance et l'horloge: La genèse de la pensée libérale en France au XVIIIe siècle* (Montreuil, 1989); and Bernard Manin, "Les deux libéralismes: La règle et la balance," in *La Famille, la loi, l'État: De la Révolution au Code civil,* ed. C. Biet and I. Théry (Paris, 1989).

economy.[74] Indeed, Sieyès was among the Revolution's leading partisans of the modern commercial world, and, like Roederer, he considered the obsession with classical antiquity displayed by so many of his contemporaries to be little short of ridiculous. He took economic interests to be the primary motivation of modern populations, in 1789 telling the National Assembly that "modern European peoples bear little resemblance to the ancients. Among us it is always a question of commerce, agriculture, manufactures, etc."[75] Sieyès, in short, was a procommercial rationalist and a modern.

The basis of Sieyès's political thought throughout the revolutionary decade was the claim that the nation, and only the nation, is sovereign. He famously articulated this doctrine in *What Is the Third Estate?* deploying it for the revolutionary purpose of arrogating sovereignty to the Third Estate as the sole true locus of "the nation." Sieyès envisioned the nation not only as sovereign but also as unified, an undivided source of sovereignty with a single general interest. This claim entailed the rejection of both an "English-style" division of sovereignty and Physiocratic notions of anchoring a unified sovereignty in landed property or in a contract.[76] It is hard to overstate the radicalism and historical importance of Sieyès's claims in this regard. They were the capstone of the prerevolution and the prelude to the Third Estate's dramatic declaration, at Sieyès's urging, of itself as the sovereign National Assembly on 17 June 1789. It is important to realize, though, that in Sieyès's construction, "the nation" was not "the people." For all of Sieyès's radicalism in 1789, the analytic decoupling of nation and people could lead to antidemocratic conclusions. This limitation was implicitly highlighted in an ironic neo-Jacobin anti-Directorial pamphlet published in 1799 composed of excerpts from *What Is the Third Estate?* in which the words "the people" were substituted for "the Third Estate" (and "men of the Government" for "privileged men of the Old Regime")—ironic because at that time Sieyès was president of the very Executive Directory that the pamphlet attacked.[77] Sieyès justified his distinction between nation

74. The most important studies of this aspect of Sieyès's thought are Sewell, *A Rhetoric of Bourgeois Revolution;* and Sonenscher, *Before the Deluge.*

75. Sieyès, *Dire de l'Abbé Sieyès sur la question du veto Royale,* quoted in Sewell, *A Rhetoric of Bourgeois Revolution,* 72.

76. Sonenscher, "The Nation's Debt and the Birth of the Modern Republic," 303, 312.

77. *Qu'est-ce que le peuple considéré dans ses rapports avec ceux qui le gouvernent et l'administrent* (Paris, 1799). See as well the letter from the bookseller Aubry to Sieyès explaining the pamphlet's intention, 13 Messidor, Year 7 (1 July 1799), AN 284 AP 15–3.

and people by pointing to the fact that the nation endured in a way that the mortal people could not. In his personal notes, he compared this relationship to that between a species and an individual. "A nation should be considered as is a species in natural history. The individual grows, withers and dies; the species endures. Similarly, those who are citizens today will die; but there will be others who will be replaced by yet others; and this civil *species* is immortal if you allow its laws to mutate."[78] Another analogy would be that between the king's immortal and mortal bodies, between the enduring monarchy and the succession of individual kings. Regardless of the metaphor, the effect of Sieyès's attribution of undivided sovereignty to the nation and of his strong distinction between the nation and the people was the potential displacement of the affairs of government from democratic institutions to more elitist ones that had been designated the guardians of the nation and its interest. And in Sieyès's practical proposals, that is exactly what he did. Vesting sovereignty in the nation, Sieyès effectively removed it from the people.

Sieyès's concept of the nation was, as the historian Michael Sonenscher describes it, "not a body, but an abstraction represented by a body."[79] Thus, the question of what type of body would represent the nation became a matter of crucial importance. The body in question would of course be a government of some kind, and Sieyès devoted a great deal of attention to thinking through just how the government represented the nation. In so doing, he put forth the essentially Hobbesian notion that the nation could become a political body only through representation—that is, that the nation did not exist as a political body prior to its representation in a government. For Sieyès, as for Bodin and Hobbes before him, a people is transformed from a multitude into a single entity through the act of submission to a sovereign. The nation did not delegate its sovereign will to the government but had that will *formed* through the sovereign government. Sieyès's notion of political representation was in fact but one aspect of a sweepingly broad concept of representation he employed to describe virtually all forms of human activity in modern society. As he put it in his constitutional speech of 1795, "All is representation in the social state. It is found everywhere in the private order as in the public order.... I would even

78. AN, 284 AP 3–2/1, quoted in Sonenscher, "The Nation's Debt and the Birth of the Modern Republic," 313.

79. Sonenscher, "The Nation's Debt and the Birth of the Modern Republic," 314.

say that representation is confounded with the very essence of social life."[80] In Sieyès's eyes—as Sonenscher renders it, drawing on one of Sieyès's own examples—"the person who makes your shoes is your representative in exactly the same sense as the person who makes your laws" because both carry out functions that fulfill your needs and thus "represent" your will.[81] This idea of representation was conceptually underpinned by Sieyès's fascination with the division of labor as an all-encompassing mode of organizing society. Indeed, for Sieyès the two concepts were practically coterminous. As he put it in a paper found in his notes titled "Bases of the social order," "The division of labor, of professions, etc. is simply the representative system establishing itself spontaneously."[82] Furthermore, Sieyès held that the complex differentiation inherent in the division of labor would cause the will of the nation to be represented in plural channels that prevented its unitary and thus potentially despotic incarnation. "In representation, the plenitude of power cannot be exercised anywhere," he noted, "Only representation can guarantee liberty entirely."[83] Thus, contrary to the received wisdom of the republican tradition in Europe and, especially, to Rousseau, Sieyès thought that large nations, because they were forced to employ the division of labor and representation, were in fact optimal for creating good constitutions and free peoples. In addition to safeguarding freedom, the division of labor and the multiplication of paths of representation would lead to greater efficiency in government. As he put it in 1795, "One of the effects of the representative system on the political order is to put each function in the hands of experts."[84] As a result, in Sieyès's eyes, the more complex the differentiation and representation, the better. Once again, though, Sieyès's ideas on this front established a radical disjuncture between the nation and its representatives, with the practical consequence that representative institutions might be established on an antidemocratic basis.

80. Quoted in Sewell, *A Rhetoric of Bourgeois Revolution,* 93.

81. Sonenscher, "The Nation's Debt and the Birth of the Modern Republic," 316. See also Keith Michael Baker, *Inventing the French Revolution: Essays on French Political Culture in the Eighteenth Century* (Cambridge, 1990), chap. 10.

82. "Bases de l'ordre social," [1794–95], AN 284 AP 5–1/6, reprinted in *Des Manuscrits de Sieyès, 1773–1799,* 510.

83. AN, 284 AP 4–4, quoted in Sonenscher, "The Nation's Debt and the Birth of the Modern Republic," 318.

84. "Classe disponible vue politiquement," AN, 284 AP 5–1/4, reprinted in *Des Manuscrits de Sieyès, 1773–1799,* 488.

Sieyès's conception of representative government led him to define the term "republic" in the strictest of senses. What made a government a republic for Sieyès was not the actual form of government but its animating principle. And Sieyès limited the animating principle of a republic to dedication to the public good or "public thing"—the literal meaning of "republic," or *res publica.* The result of this narrow definition was to leave tremendous latitude in the actual form of government, so much that in his private notes Sieyès at one point referred to his model of France's government as "a republican monarchy or a monarchical republic."[85] Indeed, in his famous debate with Thomas Paine in 1792 Sieyès defended such a configuration, in which the republic's executive would be a permanent and unelected monarch standing above personal ambition and thus able to protect the public good in a disinterested fashion. In Sieyès's eyes, the amount of virtue required to set aside personal ambition would be impossible in an elected assembly. For all his emphasis on the public good, however, Sieyès also stressed that it should never become all-encompassing. As he wrote in 1795 in his unpublished "Bases of the social order," the commission drafting France's new constitution should not "create a *Ré-totale* ["total thing"], but only a *Ré-publique* ["public thing"]."[86] Four years later, in a note found in his personal papers and filed with his theoretical reflections from the time of the drafting of the Constitution of the Year VIII, he echoed this same line of thought while sketching just what he thought France's status as a republic entailed. "France is a republic," he wrote.

> That means: the French citizens established a republican *government.*... France *self*-governs as a republic [and] governs its social and political state as a *ré-public* ["public thing"], not as a *ré-individuelle* ["individual thing"] or *ré-royale* ["royal thing"]. That does not mean a free *constitution:* the constitution and the republic are two different ideas.... There is no *government* of the mass of citizens, of individuals, or of families, there is no government of the totality; there is not even government of the legislature; there is only government of the means of executing the law; government of the public good.[87]

85. AN, 284 AP 2–15, quoted in Sonenscher, "The Nation's Debt and the Birth of the Modern Republic," 307.

86. "Bases de l'ordre social," 511.

87. "La France est une république," [1799], AN, 284 AP 5–2/3, f. 11.

While Sieyès's jottings here are somewhat elliptical, there is nonetheless an unmistakable overarching meaning: being a republic implied only an emphasis on the public good, no more. In his hands, and contrary to so much of the pamphlet literature of the Revolution and especially his neo-Jacobin adversaries at the time he drafted this note,[88] the word "republic" was shorn of its radical connotations if not its very meaning. It did not mean popular participation in politics, increased opportunities for individual self-determination, or even the illustrious but nebulous notion of "free government." Rather, it meant only a government that placed priority on the public good.

The only way that the public good could be preserved, Sieyès argued, was through the proper organization of the government. "If one seriously wants to reestablish order in France, it would be necessary to give a constitution—not the metaphysical, moral, literary, etc. constitution—but... the true constitution, that is, *the organization of the central institution.*"[89] To accomplish this goal, he devised a constitutional structure by which the government would act as a single entity, which he named "the system of unity." This somewhat cryptic plan would integrate several governmental powers so that they acted in a unified fashion. He urged a system of unity before the National Convention during the constitutional debate of 1795 and continued to elaborate its premises in his personal notes throughout the Directory. On the most basic level, Sieyès's system of unity signaled a rejection of any balance-of-powers type of constitutional arrangement. As a good rationalist, Sieyès considered the "system of *balance,*" which he described as a "suspensive state of *tension* or counteraction," to be little more than a redundancy of function that would necessarily lead to constitutional blockage and even hostility between the different branches of government.[90] Indeed, he mocked the English constitution as "gothic."[91] But Sieyès also rejected the establishment of a single branch of government, what he called a "system of *unique action,*" because it would create "despotism."[92]

88. See esp. Isser Woloch, *Jacobin Legacy: The Democratic Movement under the Directory* (Princeton, 1970); and Bernard Gainot, *1799, un nouveau Jacobinisme? La démocratie représentative, une alternative à brumaire* (Paris, 2001).

89. "Constitution à établir, les limites de la Constitution," [1799], AN, 284 AP 5–2/3, f. 29.

90. "3 systêmes," [1799], AN, 284 AP 5–2/3, f. 16.

91. Untitled note, n.d., AN, 284 AP 5–1/7.

92. "3 systêmes," f. 16.

Elsewhere in his notes he described "all the dangers,... all the adversity," of the Revolution as the "inevitable consequence" of establishing "a single and unique body" in 1789, "of this organizational defect."[93] His system of unity, to the contrary, would coordinate multiple branches of government so that they would act in unison without clashing with each other. He defined his system of unity in the following terms:

> It is not uniqueness [*unicité*] of action, of an *organization* of several actions; all the actions are there without confusion, without dissociation, without counteraction. But all the parts are *organized* to form a whole; since there is *unity* of *purpose,* there should be unity of *operation,* unity of *will;* before the moment of will or of decision, it is irrelevant whether there is *unity....* *Unity* of action does not signify that there is *one* action but that the action is *one.*[94]

Sieyès's advocacy of a unified republic in which the nation and no other agency was sovereign led him to question the necessity of a declaration of rights. In notes he composed upon reading the French translation of the *Federalist Papers,* Sieyès reflected on the very notion of a sovereign body's declaring rights and, consequently, limiting its own sovereignty. Historically, he noted, rights have been established in opposition to the sovereign by a population or corporate body seeking to bind that sovereign's will. Analytically, this implied the existence of two distinct agencies:

> If one consults the history of declarations of rights, one sees that they are, under this name or that of *charters,* only an *arrangement* between masters and their insurrectionary subjects. There were for the moment two powers that wanted to demarcate their rights on both sides, as if the duties of authority could be *rights,* prerogatives.... The general and common character of all declarations is always the *implicit recognition* of a lord, a suzerain, a master toward whom one is naturally obligated, and of some type of oppression of which one wants to be free. All of these are reduced to the following words: "You promise not to renew the bonds of our chain."

The American and French revolutions, he observed, posed the historically novel situation of a single agency choosing to bind itself. "The American

93. Untitled note, [1799], AN, 284 AP 5–2/4, f. 32.
94. "3 systêmes," f. 16.

Revolution is the first to have assumed a different character because it decisively and entirely shook off the yoke of its despot. But the Americans conceived the future authority that they were going to establish just as one had until then conceived the governing power; they wanted to protect themselves against the excesses of authority." The impulse guiding the Americans' declaration, Sieyès decided, must have been "the memory of wrongs suffered." In Sieyès's opinion, there was a certain absurdity to a sovereign people declaring rights against itself.

> It is ridiculous for a people who retake their full sovereignty to give themselves a declaration of rights.... In this case, a declaration of rights should completely change in spirit and in nature. It ceases to be an arrangement, a transaction, a condition of a treaty, a contract, etc. between authorities. There is only *one* power, only *one* authority.[95]

In this passage, Sieyès mocks as nonsensical the idea that Bruce Ackerman would later dub "self-binding."[96] Rather than restrict the government and the sovereign will of the nation, a declaration of rights, he thought, should play a strictly didactic role. It should educate both the people and the government without establishing formal constraints. Sieyès's pronounced hostility to a declaration of rights along the lines of those formulated in the Revolution's previous constitutions highlights the extent to which he thought the sovereign state should remain unbound.

Sieyès's misgivings about establishing individual rights against the sovereign government did not, however, lead him to reject the classical liberal notion of individual liberties protected by the law. Rather, his thought was marked by the impulse to create a unified sovereign that would establish and protect individual liberties. In a scrap titled "Liberty," Sieyès declared plainly that "the law offers to all individuals not only an *equal* protection, but a *complete* protection.... Its true nature is to *guarantee* completely the

95. "Fausses déclarations," n.d., AN, 284 AP 5–1/5, reprinted in *Des Manuscrits de Sieyès, 1773–1799,* 499–500. Later in this piece, Sieyès explained that when he drafted a declaration earlier in the Revolution he was forced by public opinion to add articles in "the American style." Ibid, 500. On this fragment, see also Keith Michael Baker, "The Idea of a Declaration of Rights," in *The French Idea of Freedom: The Old Regime and the Declaration of Rights of 1789,* ed. Dale K. Van Kley (Stanford, Calif., 1994), 158–59.

96. Bruce Ackerman, *We the People,* 2 vols. at present (Cambridge, Mass., 1991–).

liberty of each individual."[97] Here Sieyès articulated in unambiguous terms a position akin to the classical liberal doctrine of universal and equal protection before the law. The genesis of such rights, he explained elsewhere, is the fact that people have needs that exist in nature that are then simultaneously limited and extended in the social state. One of his scraps was titled "The need of society is respect for individual liberty," which argued, as the title suggests, that the "social state" should be organized "to protect and perfect *individual liberty*."[98] In another note, Sieyès explained that "in nature, all that have needs (and everything alive has needs) possess the right to satisfy those needs, and, as a result, the right to the means necessary to satisfy those needs." Yet, he continued in Hobbesian terms, in nature the fulfillment of one's needs can lead to brutality. In the social state, however, possessing rights involves "an exchange," a compact "to not force others, to leave them free.... The rights of man are thus reduced to the *equality* that reconciles the two compromisers (the social state guarantees this equality)." He thus considered membership in a political community to involve a certain sacrifice of raw freedom, which, in turn, enabled a far more complete freedom to act free from the interference of others. "Imperfect rights," he continued, "belong to the state of nature." "In society," to the contrary, there exists "perfect right."[99] The most important point in the present context is the fact that Sieyès did place significant emphasis on outlining a program of rights guaranteed by the law, even if he placed limits on how far they should extend.

While Sieyès thought it important to establish a basic set of civil liberties, he stopped short of advocating a society of politically autonomous individuals. He feared that too much individual autonomy would lead to disorder. Just how far Sieyès took this fear can be seen in the marginal notes he made in his copy of Condorcet's *De la nature des pouvoirs politiques dans une nation libre (On the Nature of Political Powers in a Free Nation)* at around the same time as he drafted the Constitution of the Year VIII. Sieyès chastised Condorcet for granting too much individual liberty and for

97. "Liberté," [1799], AN, 284 AP 5–2/5, f. 100.

98. "Besoin de la société = respect de la liberté inidividuelle," AN, 284 AP 5–1/2, quoted in Sonenscher, introduction to Sieyès, *Political Writings,* xvii.

99. "Droits de l'homme," [1794–95], AN, 284 AP 5–1/5, reprinted in *Des Manuscrits de Sieyès, 1773–1799,* 497–98.

not placing enough emphasis on order. Condorcet, in an important passage of the text, had argued,

> Reason in accord with nature puts but one limit on individual independence, adds but one sole social obligation to those of morality: the necessity and the obligation to obey in those of one's actions that should follow common rules, not one's own reason but the collective reason of the greatest number. I say its reason and not its will because the power of the majority over the minority should not be arbitrary, does not extend to violating the rights of a single individual, to obliging submission even when evidently contradicting reason. This distinction is not trivial. A collection of men, as well as an individual, can and should distinguish what it wants from what it finds reasonable and just.

In response to Condorcet, Sieyès jotted in the margin: "What is your intention! Do you want to give a lesson to the legislature? Or do you want to provide the governed with an enduring pretext to rebel? Does the legislature express itself other than by its *will,* the product of its *reason?* Do you want everyone, before obeying, to *judge?* Is the law the work of reason or of will? Marat! Where are you?"[100] Sieyès's objection to Condorcet here entails an uncompromising rejection of virtually any sense of individual political autonomy in a nation's political life. He plainly stated that individuals should not judge before obeying, and went so far as to compare Condorcet's rather moderate position to Marat. While Sieyès thought a nation's population should be economically active and productive, he allowed no room for parallel activity in the political sphere.

The disorder that Sieyès feared would stem from granting too much individual autonomy can also be seen in his ambivalence about, and distrust of, democracy. He viewed the extension of both rights and democracy as potential threats to public order because they both strengthened individuals against the state. Roederer approvingly highlighted this aspect of Sieyès's thought in the fictional dialogue he wrote between Sieyès and the great figures of early modern European political thought mentioned at the outset of this chapter. In the dialogue, Sieyès explains,

100. The text with Sieyès's notes can be found in Sieyès's personal papers at the French National Archives in a dossier titled "Notes concernant la Constitution de l'an VIII." [1799], AN, 284 AP 5–2/3, f. 15; pages 1–2 of Condorcet's text.

"I do not accept Montesquieu's distinction between corrupt and healthy democracies.... One of the fundamental questions is whether there is in democracy a principle of imminent corruption, and if this is not one of its misfortunes."[101] Sieyès, as William Sewell notes, "profoundly distrusted the people."[102] Yet Sieyès also saw great productive potential in democracy. In a scrap found in his papers bearing the simple title "Democracy," he wrote, "Democracy is a vast field of fermentation and political possibility. It is where man is worth all that he can be, and where the state achieves all that it can achieve." Life under a "monarchy cannot be compared to this harvest." But, Sieyès, continued, "the public establishment is not democracy, it is a body erected by democracy, upon democracy, for the public need.... Democracy is in the citizens and in their mass; in the public establishment, to the contrary, there can be only *unity* and/or *organization*." "Tell me," he asked rhetorically, "what is the idea of those who want to democratize every political action in the body of the public establishment? That would be like democratizing every civic or industrial action in the mass of citizens, democratizing justice, the police, war, finances."[103] While Sieyès credited democracy with positive potential, he clearly thought that it could pull a nation down into chaos. As a result, he sought to ensure that the actual exercise of political power remained divorced from democracy. His political-philosophical program during the revolutionary decade and especially the Directorial period was, in essence, a form of liberal authoritarianism. This was to profoundly shape the constitutional blueprint that Sieyès hastily put together in the wake of the coup of Brumaire.

The Constitution of the Year VIII

The political-philosophical programs of Roederer and Sieyès came to fruition in the Constitution of the Year VIII established following the coup of 18 Brumaire, Year VIII (9 November 1799). The coup, it bears repeating, was not simply a power grab. In fact, there was very little change in personnel. In the post-Brumaire government 90 percent of the legislative body

101. Roederer, "Entretien de plusieurs philosophes célèbres," in *OR,* 7:70.

102. Sewell, *A Rhetoric of Bourgeois Revolution,* 192–93.

103. "Démocratie," [1799], AN, 284 AP 5–2/3, f. 30.

and 70 percent of the Tribunate had held seats in either the Council of Five Hundred or the Council of Elders.[104] Rather, the coup was an attempt to establish a new political order, one that would put an end to the instability of the Directory. The Constitution of the Year VIII, which was to structure the new regime, was the brainchild of Roederer and, especially, Sieyès.

The redaction of the new constitution began immediately after the coup. Emergency decrees passed on 10 November established two commissions, one drawn from the Council of Five Hundred and the other from the Council of Elders, charged with, among other tasks, promulgating a new constitution.[105] The constitutional subcommittees of the commissions included a number of the republican center's preeminent figures, men such as Boulay de la Meurthe, Cabanis, Chénier, Daunou, Garat, and Lenoir-Laroche. However, the real work was done by Sieyès, who set about drafting the new constitution on 11 November, dictating his ideas to Boulay de la Meurthe in several installments.[106] Roederer was also intimately involved in this process. As Boulay de la Meurthe informed him in a note, "Sieyès was delighted" about "the arrangement by which you would work on the redaction of the constitutional articles.... See him as soon as possible. He will give you all the materials pertaining to this matter."[107] Roederer and Boulay were then responsible for communicating the content of Sieyès's drafts to Bonaparte, who was quickly becoming the most powerful figure on the political scene. No constitution could be completed without his sanction. Tensions arose, however, as Bonaparte grew dissatisfied with aspects of Sieyès's work. While the general orientation of Sieyès's constitutional proposals matched his own views on politics, Bonaparte was displeased with the amount of power assigned to the future executive, the position reserved for him. Constitutional negotiations soon reached something of an impasse.

During this time, rumors of the new constitution's content circulated widely, and journals speculated about what kind of political order it would institute. For example, the *Diplomate* reported on 20 November that Sieyès had prepared a constitution establishing the constitutional jury he had

104. Irene Collins, *Napoleon and His Parliaments, 1800–1815* (London, 1979), 19–20.

105. *Moniteur,* 21 Brumaire, Year 8 (12 November 1799), 200.

106. François-Joseph Boulay de la Meurthe, *Boulay de la Meurthe* (Paris, 1868), 112.

107. Boulay to Roederer, November 1799, AN, 29 AP 10, f. 141.

proposed in the summer of 1795, "national representation based on property, an executive power along the lines of that in the United States, [and] mentioning neither *common good,* nor *equality,* nor *unity.*" Similarly, the *Journal des Hommes libres* of 4 December treated in unflattering terms "the oligarchic code coming from the cavernous brain of the abbé Sieyès."[108] Amid these rumors and reports, the quasi-official *Moniteur* threw up its hands and announced on 3 December that the "constitutional plans vary from day to day and journal to journal.... We will no longer speak about the constitutional project except to report its genuine redaction."[109] In the end, the essential features of the Constitution of the Year VIII were hammered out during the night of 8–9 December among Sieyès, Bonaparte, Roederer, Boulay, and the constitutional subcommittees in a meeting that, Roederer reported in the *Journal de Paris,* lasted until five in the morning.[110] While Daunou served as the redactor in this session, it was Sieyès's draft that functioned as the starting point of the negotiations.[111] Over the ensuing nights modifications were made, but the essentials of the final product had already been established. Once the constitution was completed, Boulay de la Meurthe began presenting it to the rump councils on 12 December but did not finish until the fourteenth because a final round of negotiations occurred during the night of 12–13 December during which "changes were made."[112] The constitution was then ratified in a popular referendum on 7 February 1800, with Lucien Bonaparte's Ministry of the Interior fixing the results to ensure overwhelming approval.[113]

The Constitution of the Year VIII was first and foremost the product of Sieyès's fertile mind. In a piece Roederer drafted that was intended "to present the theory of the new constitution" and "to show clearly the spirit

108. Alphonse Aulard, ed., *Paris sous le Consulat: Recueil de documents pour l'histoire de l'esprit public à Paris,* 4 vols. (Paris, 1903), 1:14–15, 37; for other examples, see 1:31, 33–34, 38–39, 41, 43, 45, 48, 55–56.

109. *Moniteur,* 12 Frimaire, Year 8 (3 December 1799), 284.

110. *Journal de Paris,* 19 Frimaire, Year 8 (10 December 1799), 359.

111. Boulay de la Meurthe, *Boulay de la Meurthe,* 114. See also Bourdon, *La Constitution de l'an VIII,* 29, n. 42.

112. *Moniteur,* 22 Frimare, Year 8 (13 December 1799), 325–26; 23 Frimaire, Year 8 (14 December 1799), 330; 24 Frimaire, Year 8 (15 December 1799), 334. See also the "Minute originale de la Constitution de l'an VIII," with the final changes written in, dated 22 Frimaire, Year 8 (13 December 1799), in AN, AF IV 991.

113. Claude Langlois, "Le Plebiscite de l'an VIII, ou le coup d'état du 18 Pluviôse an VIII," *Annales historiques de la Révolution française* 207 (1972): 43–65, 231–46, 390–415.

that motivated it," he explained that "the new ideas presented in the constitution were part of Sieyès's plan."[114] Sieyès's leading role should not, however, obscure the significance of Roederer's influence.[115] The final version of the constitution bore important traces of his thinking, and, on a more abstract level, the new constitution very much embodied Roederer's ideas and reproduced a number of his specific theories. Thus the Constitution of the Year VIII is best described as the joint product of Sieyès's and Roederer's political philosophies.[116]

The principal goal of both Sieyès's draft constitution and the actual Constitution of the Year VIII was to institutionalize Sieyès's "representative system." As he put it in his draft, "the French nation constitutes itself neither as a monarchy, nor a republic, an aristocracy, democracy, nor despotism. These denominations are all vague, slavish, corrupt, and lend themselves to all kinds of abuses. They are foreign to the true nature of a good government and proper order.... France constitutes itself in a public *association*.... If one looks at those who hold public power, it is a *representative regime.* If one considers the spirit of the constitution, it is a veritable *social order.*"[117] While the constitution was being drafted, Roederer wrote a series of articles in his *Journal de Paris* outlining a theory of representative government essentially parallel to Sieyès's and insisting that the representative system had never been established in France.[118] Upon the completion of the actual Constitution of the Year VIII, the official pronouncement marking its passage declared that it was "founded upon the true principles of representative government."[119] As explained above, Sieyès considered

114. Roederer, "De la Constitution française," [1799], AN, 29 AP 79, f. 3.

115. Accounts of the Constitution of the Year VIII typically underplay the influence of Roederer (and overestimate Daunou's role). Two exceptions are Bourdon, *La Constitution de l'an VIII,* 22; and Margerison, *P.-L. Roederer,* 149.

116. My reconstruction and analsyis are based on a rough draft of the constitution in Sieyès's hand ([1799], AN, 284 AP 5–2, folders 2, 3, 4, 6, 7); notes composed by Roederer during the drafting process (AN, 29 AP 79); notes made by the Brumairian Antoine Boulay de la Meurthe, to whom Sieyès dictated his constitutional ideas in several meetings between 11 and 21 November 1799 ("Observations constitutionnelles," AN, 284 AP 5–2/7, reprinted in *Des Manuscrits de Sieyès, 1773–1799,* 519–26); the very final draft of the constitution ("Minute originale de la Constitution de l'an VIII"); and a number of memoirs, pamphlets, journals, and the like.

117. AN, 284 AP 5–2/4, f. 37.

118. Roederer, "Du gouvernement représentatif" and "Système représentatif de la nouvelle constitution," *Journal de Paris,* 17 and 18 Frimaire, Year 8 (8 and 9 December 1799).

119. *Moniteur,* 25 Frimare, Year 8 (16 December 1799), 335.

his representative system to be anchored in democratic legitimacy while simultaneously improving upon and rejecting the practices of democracy. He explained this principle to Boulay de la Meurthe while composing his draft constitution: "Raw democracy is absurd, were it even possible. The representative system is far superior, it alone is capable of enabling the enjoyment of true liberty and of improving mankind. Democracy being the base of the representative system and the public establishment, the government erected on this base should not resemble it; the government is necessarily representative."[120] Representative government guaranteed that political power would be placed in the hands of those most qualified to exercise that power, which, in turn, enabled that power to function efficiently and thus in the best interests of the nation. A key feature of this system was a carefully attuned "ladder" of hierarchies.[121] Sieyès envisioned the constitution and France's political structure as a pyramid—all his constitutional jottings from 1795 to 1799 take the form of pyramids—with intersecting hierarchies calibrated to maximize the efficiency of government.[122] Sieyès stated the matter bluntly: "Confidence comes from below and authority from above." Or, as Cabanis explained in surprisingly candid terms, "In the true representative system, everything is done in the name of the people and for the people; nothing is done directly by the people. The people are the sacred source of all powers, but do not exercise any of them."[123]

One of the foremost priorities of Sieyès's representative system as established in his constitutional draft was the protection of civil liberties. To achieve this, however, he sacrificed political liberty. Sieyès articulated these goals in the opening section of his draft constitution, entitled "Preliminary articles. *Spirit of the French constitution.*" Expansive in their scope, these articles amounted to a succinct statement of the political-philosophical principles that Sieyès thought should undergird the French polity in 1799. While this section was not included in the final version of the Constitution of the Year VIII, it nonetheless throws into relief the ideas underpinning the final redaction. Article 1 declared, "All the French feel the need for civil liberty; everyone wants to enjoy it. But experience and

120. "Observations constitutionnelles," 519.
121. AN, 284 AP 5–2/4, f. 57.
122. E.g., AN, 248 AP 5–1/7, 1/11, 2/5.
123. Cabanis, *Quelques considérations,* 2:481.

good sense demonstrate equally that civil liberty is ensured and guaranteed only by political liberty. Organizing political liberty for ensuring civil liberty, that is the object of the constitution."[124] Sieyès thus began his constitution by subordinating political liberty to civil liberty. The former was to be "organized" in order to guarantee the latter. Political liberty was not established as an important end in itself but only as a means to the prior end of "enjoying" civil liberty. By opening the constitution with this declaration, Sieyès placed it squarely within the tradition of "the liberty of the moderns" over that of "the liberty of the ancients." His admission that some form of political liberty is necessary to guarantee civil liberty points to a nuanced account of how civil liberty works, but his proposed opening declaration nonetheless placed political liberty below civil liberty among the nation's political priorities.

Sieyès's distrust of political liberty led him to write his draft's opening section on the constitution's "spirit" as a set of didactic articles rather than as a declaration of rights. The purpose of such an opening section, Sieyès had written four years earlier in his notes on the *Federalist Papers,* was to instruct both legislators and the population on the principles organizing France's political life. A legally binding declaration of rights, he noted, would limit the power of the sovereign while simultaneously furnishing the population with a potentially revolutionary tool.[125] A statement of general principles, however, would fulfill the primary purpose of a declaration of rights—guiding legislators in making laws and apprising the population of its rights—without opening the door to insurrection. Sieyès rejected the notion of a social contract on similar grounds in article 3 of this preliminary section, charging that "a so-called contract between the mass of citizens and one or several masters is a false idea, a political and moral monstrosity."[126] The actual Constitution of the Year VIII reflected Sieyès's thinking on this front and did not contain a declaration of rights, the first constitution of the French Revolution without one. Rather, it ended with a set of "general measures" limited to the articulation of a handful of important but extremely specific rights, the spirit of which Roederer

124. AN, 284 AP 5–2/4, f. 37. For the order of the different articles, see f. 47.

125. "Fausses déclarations," n.d., AN, 284 AP 5–1/5, reprinted in *Des Manuscrits de Sieyès, 1773–1799,* 499–500. Discussed above.

126. AN, 284 AP 5–2/4, f. 37.

captured well in his copy of the Constitution of the Year VIII, crossing out the title "general measures" and replacing it with "particular matters of the constitution."[127]

The most important way in which Sieyès set about limiting political liberty was through a complex electoral process designed to generate what he termed "lists of notables" from among the population. Antoine-Claire Thibaudeau later described this system as "a mysterious religion with a secret goal, and Roederer was its high priest," to which the historian Jean-Yves Coppolani has added the remark that Sieyès was its "prophet."[128] In 1795, Roederer had proposed generating communal lists from which local officials would be chosen by the executive branch of government, and it seems clear that his ideas on electoral procedures influenced Sieyès during the drafting of the Constitution of the Year VIII.[129] Sieyès delineated this procedure in a section of his draft titled "Foundations of the political order," which was then replicated in the actual constitution in the section "On the exercise of political rights."[130] This electoral procedure began with local assemblies that would designate one in ten among themselves as local notables, a process that in the actual constitution was referred to as generating "a list of confidence." These local notables would, in turn, repeat this procedure in order to designate one-tenth of their number departmental notables. The departmental notables would then repeat this process yet again and choose one-tenth of their number for a final list of national notables. The final list, designed to include six thousand names, comprised a pool of national notables eligible to hold office from which an unelected body (the College of Guardians in Sieyès draft; the *Sénat conservateur* or Senate-Guarantor in the actual constitution) would then choose to fill vacancies in the legislative branch of government. As the *Moniteur* summarized this procedure, "This jury will carry out all the elections ascribed to the people."[131] These men were to be France's new "notability," a painstakingly winnowed list of France's best and brightest. Sieyès,

127. AN, 29 AP 79, f. 2.

128. A. C. Thibaudeau, *Mémoires sur le Consulat, 1799 à 1804, par un ancien conseiller d'Etat* (Paris, 1827), 69; Coppolani, *Les élections en France,* 8.

129. See Margerison, *P.-L. Roederer,* 150.

130. AN, 284 AP 5–2/4, f. 44; Jacques Godechot, ed., *Les constitutions de la France depuis 1789* (Paris, 1979), 152.

131. *Moniteur,* 10 Frimare, Year 8 (1 December 1799), 276.

Roederer, and the leading Brumairians all thought that political stability could be achieved only by severely constraining popular participation in the nation's political life. As a result of this organization, Cabanis chortled, "The ignorant classes no longer exercise any influence."[132] Boulay de la Meurthe retrospectively defended this aspect of Sieyès's system by arguing that France needed to be governed by its elites. "What is the need, and therefore the true and constant wish, of a people? It is most certainly, not being capable of governing itself, to be governed by those men who are the most upright, educated, and enthusiastic about the people's well-being. In a word, by those men who most have its confidence."[133] The electoral system designed by Sieyès and incorporated into the Constitution of the Year VIII aimed to place power in the hands of a notability, or representative elite, and thereby emasculate democracy in France.

There was, however, one crucial difference between the electoral system in Sieyès's draft constitution and that in the final version. In Sieyès's version, the first round of elections would take place in "primary assemblies" comprised of "primary citizens" who had met strict financial and social conditions. These were detailed in article 7 of part 2 of his draft constitution:

> Any resident Frenchmen, twenty years old and above, can become a primary citizen on condition of demonstrating interest, capacity, and good will toward the public good. That is to say, 1. He should possess some type of property in France bearing a value of at least 3,000. 2. He should obtain a written certificate, signed by 8–10 primary citizens of his canton, attesting that they know him personally, that he is a man of honor, and that he is educated enough to exercise the "primary functions" [i.e., the functions of the primary assemblies]. 3. He willingly pays the tribute of the private citizen, called the voluntary social tribute, as a demonstration of his good will and of the interest that he takes in the liberty of his patrie.

Only those who could fulfill these requirements would be able to exercise political power, even at this lowest of levels. As he put it in his draft,

132. Cabanis, *Quelques considérations.*

133. Antoine Boulay de la Meurthe, *Théorie constitutionnelle de Sieyès, Constitution de l'an VIII: Extraits des mémoirs inédits de M. Boulay de la Meurthe* (Paris, 1836), 14.

"*political rights* can be exercised only by *primary citizens.*"[134] Similarly, Roederer's "Organization of a Representative Government," written in conjunction with Sieyès's draft, stipulated that only those "who pay a tax equal to three days of work . . . are *French citizens.* These men govern the other inhabitants, who are women, children, servants and *compagnons,* and simple workers."[135] The division between those eligible to sit in such assemblies and those who could not amounted to a division between those who constituted the nation's political body and those who did not. Sieyès's draft stipulated that "The French nation, considered as a *civil society,* is composed of the universality of the French. Considered as a *political association,* it is composed of the universality of primary citizens who, by themselves or by their representatives, are responsible for the formation of the law and the exercise of political functions." And, in another section of his draft, Sieyès explained that the "primary citizens spread out across the area of France should be considered the true shareholders [*actionnaires*] of the social order, and the primary assemblies the foundation of the political structure."[136] For Sieyès and Roederer, in short, the primary citizens alone constituted the true citizens of the nation.[137]

In the final version, however, there were no such property requirements (although domestics and those without domicile were still denied the right to vote). How this came about is something of a mystery. The *Moniteur* reported during the drafting of the constitution that under the new constitution "the number of active citizens is greatly reduced. To exercise any kind of function, it will be necessary to pay a tax worth twelve days of work."[138] Yet, at some point during the constitutional negotiations, the tax was dropped. While the reasons for this are unknown—perhaps the democratic legitimacy accorded by wider eligibility at the primary level was considered important—I would speculate that the filtering system described above was deemed rigorous enough to render the tax unnecessary.

134. AN, 284 AP 5–2/4, f. 44. Sieyès also considered requiring that only primary citizens could hold public office (f. 48).

135. "Organisation d'un gouvernement représentatif," [1799], AN, 29 AP 79, f. 81.

136. AN, 284 AP 5–2/4, f. 44, 57.

137. For many years, while Sieyès's notes were "lost," it was assumed that he was against property requirements. See, e.g., Bourdon, *La Constitution de l'an VIII,* 66–70, and Jacques Godechot, *Les institutions de la France sous la Révolution et l'Empire,* 3rd ed. (Paris, 1985), 554.

138. *Moniteur,* 10 Frimaire, Year 8 (1 December 1799), 276.

Cambacérès would later remember the "system of notability" as the "basis of the plan."[139] Moreover, the senators who would select new legislators from among the list of notables were certain to be Sieyès and his allies since it was written into the final version of the Constitution of the Year VIII—added during the final night of negotiations—that Sieyès was in the Senate-Guarantor, and that he, Roger-Ducos, Cambacérès, and Lebrun would name the remaining senators (article 24).[140] Finally, new senators in the future would be chosen by the Senate itself, so there was little danger of the ruling clique's losing control of the government.[141] Thus the final version of the constitution built in sufficient procedures to obviate the voting tax.

This baroque electoral system was only the first step in the effort to guarantee public order. Roederer was so concerned with order that in one of his notes, titled "On the redaction of the new constitution," he even suggested "we must not call it a *constitution* . . . because the idea of stability is no longer attached to this word."[142] To establish order and stability, Sieyès revived his system of unity, which was to bring together the different powers that, reflecting Sieyès's and Roederer's writings, were carefully separated but not balanced. There were no horizontal balancing functions between the branches of government, only hierarchies. Sieyès affirmed these principles in article 8 of his proposed opening section on the spirit of the constitution: "The political unity of the French nation is of a fundamental necessity. The separation of public powers is a need no less essential, no less fundamental." His deep-seated adherence to the doctrine of unified government was also made clear in article 2 of his proposed opening principles, which stated that "there is no political power in France other than the national power."[143] That is, there would be no federalist or corporatist structures to, in Sieyès's eyes, potentially fracture the nation. France, in other words, was to have a fully unified and unquestioned political center. While the two articles just quoted were not in the final version of the Constitution

139. Jean Jacques Régis de Cambacérès, *Mémoires inédits: Éclaircissements publiés par Cambacérès sur les principaux événements de sa vie politique,* ed. Laurence Chatel de Brancion, 2 vols. (Paris, 1999), 1:453.

140. *Les Constitutions,* 154. Article 24 was added to the "Minute originale de la Constitution de l'an VIII," dated 22 Frimaire, Year 8 (13 December 1799), in the middle of Boulay's presentation. AN, AF IV 991.

141. *Les Constitutions,* 153.

142. "De la rédaction de la nouvelle Constitution," [1799], AN, 29 AP 79, f. 91.

143. AN, 284 AP 5–2/4, f. 37.

of the Year VIII, they nonetheless articulated the political-philosophical principles that structured the political architecture of the Consulate. As Cambacérès put it in his memoirs, the Brumairians sought "a form of government that, while retaining the name and forms of the republic, would, however, possess all the unity of action demonstrated by a monarchy."[144]

The capstone of Sieyès's system of unity was a College of Guardians (*Collège des Conservateurs*) made up of one hundred unelected members serving lifetime appointments. The College's mandate was to "conserve" the entire political edifice. This institution was in effect a modified version of—Sieyès thought an improvement upon—the constitutional jury he had proposed in 1795. He envisioned the College as a power standing above, almost outside, the government. As Sieyès explained it to Boulay de la Meurthe, "This college has no presence in the executive order, in the government, or in the legislative order."[145] The College was assigned three principal functions. First, it performed the semiregular task of choosing new members of the legislature from the list of notables described above. Second, it was to be a "constitutional magistracy" that would adjudicate disputes among the different branches of government and conserve the constitution by deciding whether laws were constitutional and by pronouncing on proposed constitutional changes.[146] It would not, however, be able to modify the constitution on its own, and individual citizens would not be able to bring constitutional complaints to the College but would have to go through designated channels.[147] The College's power was thus carefully circumscribed to prevent its taking any initiative. Third, the College was to play the role of a "censor" and work to maintain public morality. In the notes that Sieyès dictated to Boulay de la Meurthe, he explained:

> In all states sufficiently constituted to preserve their existence, there is in the public establishment, and above all at the highest level of this establishment, a moral power that, by its influence on moeurs, minds, and even fashion, keeps all the particular movements within a circumscribed sphere and prevents the disruptions caused by disorderly ambitions.

144. Cambacérès, *Mémoires inédits,* 1:451.

145. "Observations constitutionnelles," AN, 284 AP 5–2/7, reprinted in *Des Manuscrits de Sieyès, 1773–1799,* 524.

146. Boulay de la Meurthe, *Théorie constitutionnelle de Sieyès,* 32.

147. AN, 284 AP 5–2/4, f. 40.

> In monarchies this power is the monarch, the princes of the blood, the grandees of the crown. In the ancient republics, it is a hereditary and aristocratic mass.
>
> It is in the College of Guardians that we want to place this great influence of moeurs, virtue, service, names and even property.

For the College to carry out its mission, Sieyès thought, it had to be immune from political pressures. He thus stipulated that its members serve lifetime appointments and that each be provided with a substantial rent-generating property. He anticipated the objection that the College would be an essentially aristocratic institution, "an oligarchy," and countered that such an establishment was in fact "the only way of countervailing the natural aristocracy of wealth . . . and of destroying the old aristocratic influence."[148] His protestations notwithstanding, Sieyès's College certainly smacked of oligarchy and was, at the very least, deeply antidemocratic. His intention was to create a group of unelected men who would stand above the noise and din of France's political life, who could conserve the state. In 1792 he had argued that the monarchy should play such a role; in 1795 he called for a constitutional jury; and in 1799 he proposed the creation of a College of Guardians.

Sieyès's conviction that such a "conserving power" was necessary to prevent constitutional crises had gained in popularity among France's intellectual and political elites since he first proposed it and the National Convention unanimously rejected it in 1795. During the intervening four years, as the Directory suffered crisis after crisis, calls for the establishment of such a conserving institution became increasingly common. As discussed earlier, Germaine de Staël's unpublished *On the Current Circumstances That Could End the Revolution and the Principles That Should Found the Republic in France* called for a Conserving Body based on Sieyès's constitutional jury of 1795 as the only way to save the republic. And in 1799 Benjamin Constant wrote that under the Constitution of the Year III those in power "are continuously reduced to crumpling up, evading, and even openly violating it." Something, he wrote, had to be done.[149] Similarly, the important

148. "Observations constitutionnelles," 524.

149. Benjamin Constant, *Des suites de la contre-révolution de 1660 en Angleterre* [1799], in *Oeuvres complètes de Benjamin Constant,* vol. 1, *Écrit de jeunesse (1774–1799),* ed. Lucia Omacini and Jean-Daniel Candaux (Tübingen, Ger., 1799), 676.

journal *La Décade philosophique* editorialized on the eve of the Brumaire coup that "everyone in France of right mind recognized the need for a *conserving* power, which, like the key to a vault, would keep each part of the constitutional edifice in its place." Only such an institution, opined the *Décade,* could put an end to "the dangers brought on by this perpetual struggle between the executive power and the two councils, which, by the nature of things, will carry on almost continuously."[150] As the quote from the *Décade* suggests, the reason for this growth in support for Sieyès's idea was the continued confrontations between the executive and the legislative during the Directory and the several coups that resulted. Thus, when Sieyès proposed the College to the committees in late 1799, he almost certainly found a sympathetic audience. Yet the version of the College found in the actual Constitution of the Year VIII, renamed the Senate-Guarantor, was pared of its most important conserving functions, which were largely reassigned to the executive "First Consul."[151]

The First Consul, which the text of the Constitution of the Year VIII expressly assigned to Bonaparte, grew out of the idea of a "Great Elector." Roederer had proposed the creation of a Great Elector in 1795 in his pieces on the Constitution of the Year III,[152] and Sieyès then adopted Roederer's idea into his draft of the Constitution of the Year VIII. In Sieyès's plan, however, the Great Elector would be selected by the College of Guardians from the list of national notables, serve a nonhereditary lifetime appointment, and possess the authority to "name, direct, and revoke the members of the government" but "without being able to give orders, . . . without commanding resolutions."[153] Thus the actual power held by the proposed Great Elector would have been purely reactive. He could not have taken

150. *La Décade philosophique, littéraire, et politique,* 10 Brumaire, Year 8 (1 November 1799), 249. This article appeared in three parts in the foreign affairs section of *La Décade,* dated 20 Vendémiaire and then 10 and 20 Brumaire, Year 8 (12 October and 1 and 11 November 1799). The author is unattributed, but Raymond Guyot suggested in 1912 that it was Daunou ("Du Directoire au Consulat: les transitions," *Revue Historique* 111 [1912], 8), which has become the standard attribution.

151. *Les Constitutions de la France,* 153–58.

152. "Du Gouvernement," in *OR,* 7:24–46.

153. AN, 284 AP 5–2/4, f. 56. In another proposal, however, Sieyès limited the scope of the Great Elector's power to naming the two consuls (one for the interior, the other for the exterior) that headed the executive branch of government. Boulay de la Meurthe, *Théorie constitutionnelle de Sieyès,* 26.

any initiative. The historian Mignet, based on conversations with Daunou, described the Great Elector as "incapable of governing."[154] The Great Elector was meant to stand over the entire executive branch of government, "to oversee the government and the executive power," and to intervene if conflict should arise within the executive. The Great Elector would be, wrote Sieyès, "*the guardian of the social order.*"[155] In the notes that Sieyès dictated to Boulay de la Meurthe, he explained the Great Elector's role:

> Government and execution of the laws take place under his name. An account is rendered to him. He watches over, but he does not govern. His signature is affixed by a clerk. He is not responsible.
>
> He is the representative of the national majesty at home and abroad and, as the people do not exercise any executive right, he does not exercise any himself. He is represented by his ministers. He conveys movement to the executive machine and gives it unity. Being independent and placed above particular passions and the interests of factions, *he chooses* and *dismisses* those in the government, the ministers, etc., under the sole influence of his reason and properly observed public opinion. He prevents or neutralizes by his existence alone all dangerous ambition within the government or in any other citizen.[156]

So that the Great Elector would be "surrounded with splendor," he would have a substantial revenue that would also serve to guarantee his independence.[157] The pomp and circumstance attached to the office would bestow a certain authority on the entire government in domestic affairs, and "With regard to foreigners, he represents the nation and assures it against their influence."[158]

In the actual Constitution of the Year VIII, the Great Elector was replaced by a First Consul. There is no way of knowing exactly when the title was changed. Two weeks before the constitution was completed, the *Moniteur* of 1 December reported that the new constitution would have a

154. François Auguste Mignet, *Histoire de la Révolution française, depuis 1789 jusq'en 1814,* 2 vols. (Paris, 1824), 2:640.

155. AN, 284 AP 5–2/4, f. 55.

156. "Observations constitutionnelles," AN, 284 AP 5–2/7, reprinted in *Des Manuscrits de Sieyès, 1773–1799,* 525.

157. Boulay de la Meurthe, *Théorie constitutionnelle de Sieyès,* 30–31.

158. AN, 284 AP 5–2/4, f. 56.

Great Elector, while the draft made by the historian Mignet in the early nineteenth century using Daunou's notes on Sieyès's plan (not Daunou's own plan) calls the figure a *Proclamateur-Électeur.*[159] The *Journal des Hommes libres* of 5 December reported, "Rumor has it today that a number of those who have examined the proposed constitution no longer want a Great Elector," and then on 6 December that "there will not be a Great Elector."[160] More important than the change in title was a change in function. The First Consul stood at the head of the government or executive rather than outside and above it. The distinction is crucial. Rather than a sort of conserving power of the executive, the First Consul was the actual head of the executive and thus endowed with a host of executive prerogatives. Furthermore, the First Consul possessed many of the conserving powers that Sieyès had originally assigned to the College of Guardians. In his draft, Sieyès had clearly subordinated the Great Elector to the College of Guardians, endowing the College in at least one draft of the constitution with the ability to recall the Great Elector by "absorbing" him into the College.[161] In the final version of the constitution, however, the First Consul stood at the summit of the political order, above all other bodies of government.

This change came about because Bonaparte was unhappy with the largely ceremonial functions of the Great Elector (which was clearly designed for him), reportedly responding to Sieyès's proposals with the statement that he had no interest in becoming "a fattened pig."[162] He particularly objected to the fact that the College would be able to recall the Great Elector.[163] Indeed, during the drafting process the *Moniteur* reported that there was a dispute over whether "the Great Elector will be dismissible. Will

159. *Moniteur,* 10 Frimaire, Year 8 (1 December 1799), 276. Mignet, *Histoire de la Révolution française,* 2:640. In Roederer's notes, the terms "Great Elector" and "First Consul" are found in different, undated pieces. "Organisation d'un gouvernement représentatif," [1799], AN, 29 AP 79, f. 81; and "Pouvoir exécutif," [1799], AN, 29 AP 79, f. 93.

160. Aulard, *Paris sous le Consulat,* 1:39, 41.

161. Boulay de la Meurthe, *Boulay de la Meurthe,* 111–12. Mignet also describes the College as possessing "the right of absorption." *Histoire de la Révolution française,* 2:643. And Roederer, in one piece he drafted on the constitution, wrote that "the Great Elector can be called into the body of conservators and from this moment his functions cease." "Organisation d'un gouvernement représentatif," f. 81. Similarly, a chart in Roederer's hand (most likely a diagram of Sieyès's proposals) clearly places the College of Guardians at the zenith. [1799], AN, 29 AP 79, f. 83.

162. Quoted in Woloch, *Napoleon and His Collaborators,* 30.

163. Boulay de la Meurthe, *Boulay de la Meurthe,* 112.

death alone bring an end to his term? Opinions are divided between those who fear the abuses of a power without responsibility, and those who want to foil from above all the efforts of factions."[164] At one point, Bonaparte swept aside Sieyès's proposals and ordered Daunou to prepare a constitution on short notice. Daunou had considerable experience in this area. He had been the principal architect of the Constitution of the Year III and, in the meantime, had played a prominent role in writing the constitutions for several sister republics. Daunou obliged, but Bonaparte was also dissatisfied with the restrictions Daunou would have placed on the power of the executive.[165] Bonaparte's insistence on a strong executive stemmed both from the fact that he would hold the office of executive and from a prior belief that, as he wrote to Talleyrand in 1797, the executive "ought to be considered the true representative of the nation."[166] Bonaparte's insistence on creating a strong executive was undoubtedly bolstered by a growing sentiment among France's political elites, especially Roederer and Talleyrand, that only a strong executive could end the ongoing cycle of political crises.[167] While Roederer had urged the creation of a strong executive numerous times during the preceding five years, he was not alone. The second installment of the above-quoted *Décade* piece calling for a conserving power also demanded "monarchical efficiency" from the constitutional revisions it proposed.[168] And Cambacérès later remembered that the prevailing sentiment was to establish "a great figure who would be the head of the new edifice."[169] These calls resonated with a vibrant strand of Directorial thought, encompassing a diverse group of figures from Germaine de Staël to Bertrand Barère, which the historian Pierre Serna has provocatively dubbed "the extreme center." These figures argued that a robust liberal republic could be realized only if the executive was endowed with extraordinary powers capable of guaranteeing the republic's

164. *Moniteur,* 10 Frimaire, Year 8 (1 December 1799), 276.

165. Daunou's draft constitution can now be found in his personal papers, BN, Nouv. Acqu. Fr. 21891, f. 74–190, and was reprinted by Alphonse-Honoré Taillandier in the mid-nineteenth century. Taillandier, *Documents biographiques sur P.-C.-F. Daunou,* 2d ed. (Paris, 1847), 174–88.

166. Quoted in Englund, *Napoleon: A Political Life,* 169.

167. On Talleyrand's support for a strong executive, see his letter of 14 Messidor, Year 7 (2 July 1799) to Lacuée of the National Institute, found in MAE, MD France 652, f. 256–63.

168. *La Décade philosophique,* 20 Brumaire, Year 8 (11 November 1799), 315.

169. Cambacérès, *Mémoires inédits,* 1:450.

survival.[170] Furthermore, important precedent for a strong executive had been set by the constitutions of the sister republics, drafted principally by Daunou and Merlin de Douai.[171] Thus Bonaparte, between his growing political strength and the preexisting theoretical support for a strong executive, was able to carry the day. While the constitution included a version of the College of Guardians—the Senate-Guarantor was designed to play an important role as something of a safeguard for liberty; one pro-Brumairian pamphlet called it "the key to the whole edifice"—its powers nonetheless paled in comparison to those of the First Consul.[172]

The First Consul, with Bonaparte named to the post in the text of the constitution itself, was invested with a remarkable amount of power. The extent of this power is captured in article 44 of the Constitution of the Year VIII, which stated that the executive (called "the government" in the constitution) "proposes the laws and enacts the regulations necessary to assure their execution."[173] In other words, the executive would be able to enact whatever regulations it deemed necessary to ensure the integrity of previously established laws—an extraordinarily expansive "regulatory power."[174] Originally the article had limited the regulatory power so that "these regulations obligate public functionaries and not citizens. They cannot thwart or modify any law." But this more limited version of the regulatory power was changed in the final version, and again in all likelihood during the final round of negotiations during the night of 12–13 December.[175] The

170. Pierre Serna, "Barère, penseur et acteur d'un premier opportunisme répûblicain face au Directoire exécutif," *Annales historiques de la Révolution française* 332 (2003): 101–28; and Serna, *La République des girouettes: 1789–1815... et au-delà: Une anomalie politique, la France de l'extrême centre* (Paris, 2005), chap. 9.

171. See chapter 4; Guyot, "Du Directoire au Consulat"; and Marcel Gauchet, *La Révolution des pouvoirs: La souveraineté, le peuple, et la représentation, 1789–1799* (Paris, 1995), 207–12.

172. For the quote see Boucher-la-Richarderie, *La Régénération de la République d'Athènes, fragment historique, traduit du grec* (Paris, 1799), 22. This humorous tract, supposedly a long-lost Greek manuscript found in Naples by an officer in Bonaparte's army, told the story of how Athens was saved by a general "Nobaterap" and a citizen "Ysiès" (i.e., the letters of Bonaparte and Sieyès rearranged), who together gave Athens "a new constitution, better coordinated and more vigorous."

173. *Les Constitutions de la France,* 156.

174. See Michel Verpeaux, *La naissance du pouvoir réglementaire, 1789–1799* (Paris, 1991), 406–12.

175. The change is visibly written into the "Minute originale de la Constitution de l'an VIII," 22 Frimaire, Year 8 (13 December 1799), AN, AF IV 991. The original wording can be found in both this copy and in the draft in Daunou's papers, BN, Nouv. Acqu. Fr. 21891, f. 120. See also Bourdon, *La Constitution de l'an VIII,* 48.

final version removed the restrictions stipulated in the original version and gave Bonaparte great power to pass emergency decrees, which he of course soon did. The importance of assigning such an expansive regulatory power was noted by Roederer in his piece clarifying the new constitution. After noting the great power that "this constitution establishes" and "confides" to Bonaparte, Roederer explained that "the regulatory articles [are] necessary to maintain" the smooth functioning of government, "the regularity of movement."[176] Some sort of regulatory power was necessary in a constitution, Roederer suggested, and the branch of government that possessed it was de facto the most important because it could enact regulations that were not subject to oversight by any other governmental authority.

The extreme power concentrated in the executive was noted by more than one commentator. For example, a pamphlet published by a certain Hyacinthe Martin explained in great detail that the office of the First Consul established in the Constitution of the Year VIII possessed far more power than did the king in the Constitution of 1791—which he worried might be abused, so he said, by a "successor" to Bonaparte. Going through the constitution article by article, Martin showed that the Constitution of 1791 "gave to the *King* powers infinitely less expansive than those possessed by the *republican Consul*" in the Constitution of the Year VIII, which he described as "too powerful for a constitutional *King*."[177] Another pamphlet acknowledged that "the makeup of the executive power in republics has always been the most difficult problem of political economy to solve," but it took a much more favorable view of these same developments, arguing that only such a strong executive could guarantee the public good.[178] Similarly, the *Décade* editorialized that "this new social pact [the constitution] offers characteristics of stability" such as "an executive power endowed with great strength."[179]

176. Roederer, "De la Constitution française," [1799], AN, 29 AP 79, f. 4. See also Roederer, "De la rédaction de la nouvelle Constitution," [1799], AN, 29 AP 79, f. 91.

177. Hyacinthe Martin, *Comparaison de la constitution monarchique de 1791 avec le projet de la constitution républicaine de l'an VIII* (Blois, 1799), 9, 17.

178. Gilbert, *Du Pacte social,* 41. For a similar set of claims, see Charles-Louis Cadet-Gassicourt, *Cahier de réformes, ou Voeux d'un ami de l'ordre adressés aux consuls et aux commissions législatives* (Paris, 1799).

179. *La Décade philosophique,* 30 Frimaire, Year 8 (21 December 1799), 570–71.

The decision to establish an overarching power in the First Consul represented an important departure from the classical-republican tradition, with its profound distrust of executive power and attendant emphasis on constitutional balance. In this regard, Sieyès's plan to assign preeminent authority to the College of Guardians would also have amounted to an important departure from the classical-republican tradition's obsession with balance. Thus, regardless of whether the College or the Great Elector, the Senate-Guarantor or the First Consul, was to be the government's conserving power, the very attempt to erect such an overarching power signaled a profound shift in France's political order. The idea of the balance of powers, "the game of these so-called balances," as Cabanis put it, was displaced by Sieyès's system of unity.[180] The Brumairians opted for a single central sovereign. In so doing, they foreshadowed the consulate for life enacted in the Constitution of the Year X (1802) and the subsequent declaration of the Napoleonic Empire in the Year XII (1804).

In sum, both Sieyès's proposed constitution and the actual Constitution of the Year VIII outlined a liberal-authoritarian political edifice. While the final version of the constitution assigned the executive significantly more power than Sieyès would have liked, there is an important sense in which his (and Roederer's) principles were more modified than betrayed. The Constitution of the Year VIII was antidemocratic and antipolitical, vesting final authority in an unelected body that disempowered the population in the name of preserving their civil liberties through order and unity. Whether that body was an individual or a group of one hundred notables is a difference of degree, not kind. The animating spirit is the same, captured by Sieyès's famous statement that "confidence comes from below, authority from above." The end result of both Roederer's and Sieyès's ideas was a version of liberal authoritarianism that was institutionally instantiated in the Constitution of the Year VIII. Sieyès later highlighted the connections between his ideas and the constitution actually promulgated when he scrawled across the top of the notes he dictated to Boulay de la Meurthe during the drafting process that "it was according to these ideas that the constitution was written, [and] adopted with apparent satisfaction."[181] And

180. Cabanis, *Quelques considérations,* 2:469–70.

181. The full quote, referring to the several changes made during subsequent years, reads: "It was according to these ideas that the constitution was successively written, adopted with apparent

Roederer, for his part, became one of Bonaparte's most faithful acolytes. By creating a constitution that stood above politics and forswore any kind of democratic accountability, Sieyès and Roederer could be said to have paved the way for Bonaparte's eventual usurpation of all forms of political power. In the end, Sieyès's desire to displace sovereignty from the people and ensure that authority came from above and only confidence from below led, as Georges Lefebvre noted, "to abolishing the electoral regime and, as a result, to instituting dictatorship. Not a provisional dictatorship like that desired by the Revolutionary Government, but one that was thoroughly permanent."[182]

---

satisfaction, subsequently changed, altered more and more, and finally abolished." "Observations constitutionnelles," AN, 284 AP 5–2/7, reprinted in *Des Manuscrits de Sieyès, 1773–1799,* 519.

182. Georges Lefebvre, *La France sous le Directoire, 1795–1799,* 2d ed. (Paris, 1984), 711. It should be pointed out that there was classical precedent for a temporary dictatorship on the Roman model. Sieyès once scribbled notes on the possible need for what "the Ancients" called "a dictator." "Urgence," [1794–95], AN, 284 AP 5–1/3, reprinted in *Des Manuscrits de Sieyès, 1773–1799,* 480. Similarly, in 1797, on the eve of the coup of 18 Fructidor, one supporter of the republican center sent a pamphlet to the Directory urging, in Albert Meynier's paraphrase, the establishment of "a temporary dictatorship, justified by the example of Rome. It would be enough for the magistrates of the Republic to invoke the famous words of Cicero: '*Salvatam a me patriam juro*!' [I swear that I saved the fatherland]." Quoted in Meynier, *Les coups d'état du Directoire,* vol. 1, *Le dix-huit Fructidor an V (4 Septembre 1797)* (Paris, 1927), 120.

6

Liberal Republicanism and Dissent against Bonaparte

The official proclamation upon the passage of the Constitution of the Year VIII declared that "the Revolution is established on the principles that began it: It is finished."[1] Bonaparte and his collaborators then set about establishing a liberal-authoritarian political order and finishing the Revolution, but a significant schism developed over just what that meant. While Bonaparte and Minister of Police Fouché emphasized social order and turned the Consulate in an increasingly authoritarian direction, Brumairians such as P.-C.-F. Daunou and Marie-Joseph Chénier sought to uphold the liberal side of the Brumairian settlement and envisioned a robust program of civil liberties in the new order. The ensuing rift over how to finish the Revolution was a cardinal feature of the political culture of the Consulate.

The fissure manifested itself almost immediately. On 11 January 1800, a mere two months after the coup of Brumaire and less than one month

1. "Procès verbal de la séance des Consuls," 24 Frimaire, Year 8 (15 December 1799), AN, AF IV 911.

after the promulgation of the new constitution, the *Gazette de France* accused Chénier, J.-P. Chazal, and Benjamin Constant of forming "a metaphysical faction" and "seeking to divide France into two factions."[2] There was a degree of truth to this charge, as Chénier, Constant, Daunou, and their allies had formed what Germaine de Staël would describe in May of 1800 as "the sort of small opposition which the present state of things allows."[3] Those who led the opposition to Bonaparte, for the most part, came out of the republican center. Highlighting the long-standing ties between these figures, police reports sometimes referred to them as "the Thermidorians."[4] In their efforts to prevent Bonaparte's Consulate from drifting into unfettered authoritarianism, several of these figures began to articulate a liberal-republican political philosophy that anticipated the key traits of French Liberalism.

The Consulate's drift toward unchecked authoritarianism was by no means foreordained. As Tocqueville observed in his notes on the Consulate, "Among those who favored 18 Brumaire a very large number did not think they were being pushed into despotism."[5] The process occurred on a range of fronts. Perhaps foremost among these was the gradual obliteration of civil liberties and emasculation of the rule of law. The rule of law was suspended almost immediately in wide areas of the French countryside that were plagued by brigandage, lawlessness, and counterrevolution. While the Directory had engaged harsh measures to deal with brigandage, Bonaparte's Consulate "made even greater use of exceptional justice," in the words of Howard Brown, the leading historian of the government's pacification campaigns. In Brittany the constitution was formally suspended from 16 January 1800 to 21 April 1800, and in the region around Avignon Bonaparte personally authorized General P.-M.-B. Férino to use "extraordinary powers," including

2. Alphonse Aulard, ed., *Paris sous le Consulat: Recueil de documents pour l'histoire de l'esprit public à Paris,* 4 vols. (Paris, 1904), 1:102.

3. Staël to Du Pont de Nemours, 2 May 1800, in Germaine de Staël and Pierre Samuel Du Pont de Nemours, *De Staël-Du Pont Letters: Correspondence of Madame de Staël and Pierre Samuel Du Pont de Nemours and of Other Members of the Necker and Du Pont families,* ed. and trans. James Fred Marshall (Madison, Wis., 1968), 21.

4. Aulard, *Paris sous le Consulat,* 2:188, 192.

5. Alexis de Tocqueville, *Oeuvres complètes,* ed. J.-P. Mayer, vol. 2, pt. 2, *L'Ancien Régime et la Révolution: Fragments et notes inédites sur la Révolution* (Paris, 1953), 311.

on-the-spot executions of brigands caught with arms in hand.[6] Brown quotes General Calvin, in charge of pacifying the Vaucluse, as representative of the wider program: "The reign of factions is over, that of order is beginning. The Government detests the wicked, and I declare in its name that I will make open war on the brigands.... Soon,... with the Revolution ended, all Frenchmen will enjoy, under a strong and just government, peace, liberty, and public security, without which there is no happiness."[7] General Calvin's pronouncement captured the emphasis on order, and the willingness to use harsh measures to attain it, that characterized Bonaparte's rule.

Bonaparte's assault on the rule of law accelerated in the wake of the royalist assassination attempt against him on 12 December 1800. Although Fouché knew well that it was royalists who had tried to kill Bonaparte, the government used the episode as an excuse for a wide-ranging crackdown on enemies real and potential. First, the Parisian left was targeted and then the royalist right. Hundreds were deported or executed without trial. In addition, the military units operating in the south and west had their already broad mandates expanded.[8] Bonaparte's brutal response was a major turning point in the nature of the Consulate. It was, writes Isser Woloch, "from the standpoint of legality, his first truly transgressive act as first consul. In turn, this arbitrary and brutal repression affected the spirit and equilibrium of the consular regime.... The joint venture of Brumaire was becoming a forced merger."[9] While the Consular Terror of 1800–1801 was eventually curbed, Bonaparte continued to chip away at the rule of law and turn the Consulate into a reflection of his personal will alone. Fouché's police grew in strength and numbers, and, buoyed by his military successes, Bonaparte became increasingly brazen. Germaine de Staël observed in June of 1801 that "there is only one man in France in the first rank, in the second rank, and in the third rank. One notices a fog called the nation, but one can distinguish nothing in it. He alone is in the front of the

6. Howard G. Brown, *Ending the French Revolution: Violence, Justice, and Repression from the Terror to Napoleon* (Charlottesville, Va., 2006), 308.

7. Quoted in ibid., 302.

8. Ibid., 316–24.

9. Isser Woloch, *Napoleon and His Collaborators: The Making of a Dictatorship* (New York, 2001), 80.

picture."[10] Brown, directing attention to the regime's use "of surveillance and regulatory control in maintaining public order," coins the neologism "security state" to describe Bonaparte's Consulate.[11] Legal forms would be respected when possible, but those forms would be highly elastic. The rule of law would always be subservient to Bonaparte's sovereign will.[12]

The result of the increasingly authoritarian nature of Bonaparte's regime was the betrayal of the French Revolution. The ideals of 1789 were definitively quashed. Precisely when this occurred, when the liberal side of the Brumairian settlement was abandoned, is an unsettled question. One might choose Bonaparte's Concordat with the Catholic Church of April 1802 as the date the Revolution ended. Germaine de Staël, for example, wrote to Dupont de Nemours that the Concordat was part of Bonaparte's plan "to start a fourth dynasty, to imitate Charlemagne."[13] And, relates Tocqueville, Lafayette interpreted the Concordat as an attempt by Bonaparte to form an "alliance with [the Church] against the liberal mind, the common enemy."[14] Alternatively, one might view Bonaparte's taking the title Consul for Life in August 1802 as the end of the Revolution.[15] Certainly, the Revolution ended no later than December 1804, when Bonaparte was crowned Napoleon I, Emperor of the French. Whether in 1799, 1802, 1804, or in between, the Revolution was betrayed by Bonaparte's authoritarian dictatorship during the Consulate.

The efforts of Bonaparte and his collaborators to sacrifice liberty before the altar of order were resisted by a liberal-leaning minority that grew out of

10. Staël to Du Pont de Nemours, 10 Messidor, Year 9 (29 June 1801), in *De Staël-Du Pont Letters,* 94.

11. Brown argues that the "security state" in fact began during the Directory and was fully achieved during the Consulate in "From Organic Society to Security State: The War on Brigandage in France, 1797–1802," *Journal of Modern History* 69 (1997): 693, and in *Ending the French Revolution,* esp. chap. 12.

12. While the Senate Commission on Individual Liberty was meant to ensure that people were not illegally imprisoned, it was thoroughly co-opted. See Michael Sibalis, "Arbitrary Detention, Human Rights and the Napoleonic Senate," in *Taking Liberties: Problems of a New Order from the French Revolution to Napoleon,* ed. Howard G. Brown and Judith A. Miller (Manchester, U.K., 2002); and Sibalis, "Napoleonic Police State," in *Napoleon and Europe,* ed. Philip Dwyer (London, 2001).

13. Staël to Du Pont de Nemours, 25 April 1802, in *De Staël-Du Pont Letters,* 129.

14. This is Tocqueville's summary of Lafayette's analysis in his *Fragments et notes inédites sur la Révolution,* 317.

15. E.g., Brown, *Ending the French Revolution,* 357–58.

the post-Terror republican center. These figures formed a dissident current emphasizing the importance of liberty, the rule of law, and the preservation of juridical liberties in the face of Bonaparte's increasingly authoritarian rule. In short, they made civil liberty the touchstone of their opposition to him. These former Thermidorians articulated liberal political values not in response to the Terror but only when confronted with Bonaparte's "security state."[16] The liberty they defended tended to be extremely abstract, a somewhat vague principle that took definite form only in relation to specific issues. It was not defined with prior reference to natural rights or utilitarian principles but was simply asserted to be a good in itself. This defense of liberty, however indistinct, would go on to constitute the essential core of French Liberalism. Ironically, the emergence of a liberal opposition to Bonaparte was the culmination of the same developments that had led so many members of the republican center to support the coup of Brumaire in the first place: a shift toward liberal values in the principles underpinning politics. Key elements of the classical-republican constellation that had so decisively informed the political culture of Thermidor and the Directory continued to cede pride of place to more liberal concerns. Yet even as these dissidents articulated a liberal critique of Bonaparte, their liberalism remained deeply inflected by classical-republican precepts. Most important among these precepts was the conviction that liberty is best preserved by republican constitutional forms. More specifically, they came to believe that liberty could be preserved only in a republic with an active political life, with a substantial degree of political liberty confined to virtuous political elites. Liberty would always be in jeopardy if the polity was subservient to the arbitrary, potentially despotic, will of a single individual. The result was a blend of these two political-philosophical languages, not always perfectly coherent, that is best described as liberal republicanism. In schematic terms, the liberal critique of Bonaparte articulated by these figures rejected the liberal authoritarianism of the Brumairian settlement and broke with the classical republicanism of Thermidor and the Directory while, however, remaining decisively informed by classical-republican principles.

This liberal-republican critique of Bonaparte can be seen emerging in three crucial moments during the Consulate. First was a debate in the

16. In a note, Isser Woloch comments in passing that "the term 'liberal' began to have a certain currency only in the Napoleonic years." *Napoleon and His Collaborators,* 271, n. 61.

Tribunate in 1801 over establishing extrajudicial tribunals to deal with brigandage in France's countryside. During the debate, key liberal-leaning members of the erstwhile republican center resisted the proposed legislation in the name of the rule of law. This debate was the single most important example of parliamentary opposition to Bonaparte, an avenue that was eventually closed off when Bonaparte purged the Tribunate in 1802. Second was an essay contest sponsored by the Class of Moral and Political Sciences in 1802 asking, "What was the influence of Luther's Reformation on the political situation of the different European states and on the progress of Enlightenment?" along with the winning response by Charles de Villers, *Essay on the Spirit and Influence of Luther's Reformation.* Villers's text used the genre of history to advance a liberal-republican criticism of Bonaparte's regime. Third was Benjamin Constant's *On the Possibility of a Republican Constitution in a Large Country.* Constant's text, which remained unpublished until 1991 and has been largely neglected in Constant scholarship, elaborated a liberal-republican constitution that both captured the liberal-republican critique of Bonaparte and articulated the central kernel of French Liberalism.

The Debate over Military Tribunals

On 7 January 1801 a law establishing special criminal tribunals was presented to the Tribunate by J.-E.-M. Portalis, speaking in the name of the First Consul. The law was the third of three bills presented by the government that day, the first of which trimmed the number of elected justices of the peace and the second of which transferred the investigation and prosecution of crime from justices of the peace to government-appointed "security magistrates." While all three were offensive to the liberal opposition, it was the third, establishing special criminal tribunals, that provoked serious opposition. The bill would enable the government to establish special eight-person tribunals whenever and wherever it saw fit as a response to the brigandage in France's countryside. While the government had already deployed military units to quell the brigandage, the proposed special tribunals were to incorporate the pacification strategies into a broader legal framework. The tribunals would be charged with hearing cases involving serious threats to public order such as brigandage, arson, and armed rebellion as well as more minor offenses along the lines of vagrancy and begging. The tribunals' eight members would be drawn from both the military and civilian spheres, with five of them appointed directly by the First Consul. The tribunals would replace normal criminal courts, which used trial by jury, and their judgments could not be appealed. Furthermore, the special tribunals would bypass the normal grand jury system and take cases directly from officers of the gendarmerie and magistrates.[17] The law clearly circumvented the established system of justice and reversed the legacy of 1789 in the sphere of criminal justice. As the nineteenth-century French legal scholar Adhémar Esmein noted, the proposed tribunals resurrected Old Regime notions of extraordinary justice and established "two justices; one ordinary, the other exceptional; for some the jury, for others special tribunals."[18] The liberal dissenters deemed this two-track system unacceptable and fought the government's proposal tooth and nail. The ensuing debate was the single most contentious in the brief history of the Tribunate and was instrumental in provoking Bonaparte's purge of that body one year later. In the end, the bill passed by a vote of forty-nine to forty-one, a remarkably thin margin by the standards of the Tribunate.

The debate was a defining moment in the elaboration of a liberal critique of Bonaparte. The opposition was led by veterans of the republican center, such as Daunou, Chénier, Ginguené, and Constant, some of whom would go on to become Restoration liberals. In addition, Sieyès, who was not in the Tribunate, was reported by the police to be "furious" about the law and to have helped plan the opposition within the Tribunate.[19] Their opposition and the ensuing debate constituted a literal and symbolic divorce between the liberal and authoritarian vectors that had been joined in the Brumairian settlement. The two elements came into conflict over the issue of the government's ability to pass measures of exception. The opposition centered their arguments on a defense of the rule of law underpinned by a universalist, liberal logic. Their celebration of the rule of law was furthermore freighted with memories of the Terror and the tradition

17. *Archives parlementaires de 1787 à 1860, recueil complet des débats législatifs et politiques des chambres françaises. Deuxième série (1800 à 1860),* 127 vols. (Paris, 1862–1913), 2:70–71 (hereafter cited as AP_2).

18. Adhémar Esmein, *Histoire de la procédure criminelle en France, et spécialement de la procédure inquisitoire depuis le XIIIe siècle jusqu'à nos jours* (Paris, 1882), 471, 474.

19. Aulard, *Paris sous le Consulat,* 2:155.

of exceptional justice under the Old Regime. For the opposition, more was at stake than the interpretive question of whether or not the bill violated the letter of the constitution. At stake was the deeper issue of whether France would be a constitutional, law-governed order, whether ultimate sovereignty would lie in Bonaparte or in the law.

The significance of the bill and the debate over it was widely perceived. Chénier, speaking for the opposition, declared that no less than "a question of the social pact, civil liberty, honor and the life of the citizenry" hung in the balance. "It is thus for the principles of all free states, for the dignity of the Tribunate and the legislative body, for the national interest, that we are specially charged with rejecting it."[20] The government, for its part, interpreted the liberals' opposition as aiding and abetting the very brigands the law was directed against and, more seriously still, as disloyalty to Bonaparte and the Consulate. During the debate over the tribunals, Fouché's inspectors described regular gatherings between the liberal-leaning members of the Tribunate and other high-ranking figures, notably Sieyès, as the meetings of an organized opposition.[21] On 31 January 1801, at the height of the debate, the prefect of the Parisian police identified Sieyès and Chénier as leading the opposition to the bill and, moreover, as plotting a coup d'état.

> Secret meetings of Tribunes and Legislators are becoming more frequent. It is in these meetings that they formulate the opinions on the propositions of the government that they then put forward in public. It is remarked not indifferently that several Tribunes have already openly thrown off their masks and...certain people think they should be regarded as the forerunners of a storm. Chénier in particular is mentioned. Other sources also say he is not a friend of the government and that he is put in front by people who hate the government even more.
>
> One adds that Sieyès, remaining behind the curtain as he always does, is the soul of this clique; that he is consulted in the shadows and in secrecy, and that nothing is done without his participation. These rebellious men are counting on a crisis, and do not conceal their hopes from their

20. Marie-Joseph Chénier, *Opinion de M. J. Chénier contre le projet de loi concernant l'établissement de tribunaux criminels spéciaux* (Paris, 1801), 1–2.

21. Aulard, *Paris sous le Consulat,* 2:137, 139, 150, 154–55, 159, 161–62, 165, 171–72, 175, 178–79, 188, 192–93.

> friends.... Moreover, it is agreed among all those who openly divide the Legislative Body and the Tribunate that a coup d'état is needed and should be brought about no matter the cost.

This was not the only police report that accused the liberal opposition of plotting a coup. On 3 February, immediately after the bill passed, one police informer filed a report that Ginguené had exclaimed, "I would rather lose my name than see France oppressed. There are generals who will not view all of this with a kind eye; we have friends in the army."[22] Cambacérès would repeat the fundaments of this charge in his memoirs, ascribing "the obstinacy of the Tribunate" over the proposed tribunals to the desire of certain individuals "to weaken the government."[23]

The liberal-leaning deputies who opposed the law took umbrage at the government's accusations and fashioned themselves a loyal opposition, which was something of a novelty in the political dynamics of the revolutionary years.[24] They repeatedly declared their allegiance to Bonaparte and the Consulate and resisted the government's efforts to define the debate in terms of loyalty and disloyalty, opposition to or support for brigandage. Rather, they sought to keep the debate focused on questions of the rule of law and legality. The ever-eloquent Benjamin Constant complained that the government's attacks did nothing to address the substantive issues at hand and warned against perversely conflating reservations about the bill with support for those the bill targeted:

> It is easy to say that those who oppose this proposed law plead the brigands' cause, obstruct the reestablishment of order and public security, and impede the necessary action of swift justice against the enemies of the social state.... But precisely because we want the brigandage to be repressed, we cannot want the innocent to be confused with the guilty; because our existence depends on respect for national properties, we cannot agree to a law

22. Ibid., 2:146, 150. See also ibid., 2:155.

23. Jean Jacques Régis de Cambacérès, *Mémoires inédits: Éclaircissements publiés par Cambacérès sur les principaux événements de sa vie politique,* ed. Laurence Chatel de Brancion, 2 vols. (Paris, 1999), 1:548.

24. The neo-Jacobins of 1798–99 had previously fashioned themselves a loyal opposition, perhaps the first true political party of the Revolution. See Isser Woloch, *Jacobin Legacy: The Democratic Movement Under the Directory* (Princeton, 1970); and Bernard Gainot, *1799, un nouveau Jacobinisme? La démocratie représentative, une alternative à brumaire* (Paris, 2001).

> that gives them an illusory guarantee, one that is arbitrary; because we are tied to the government, we should look after the maintenance of the constitution, in which alone the government finds legal measures and a solidity beyond all attack.[25]

Constant's speech encapsulates the rhetorical-political position the opposition tried to stake out: a loyal opposition that agreed with the spirit of the proposed legislation but could not accept the specific mechanisms it proposed; a loyal opposition seeking to save France from a grievous error that would undermine the liberal accomplishments of the Revolution and return France to the dark days of the Old Regime.

The government also claimed to act in defense of the Revolution. It argued that only the establishment of such tribunals could guarantee the achievements of the Revolution in the face of persistent and potentially deadly attacks from the Revolution's enemies. France was under siege from all sides, the progovernment deputies explained. If the government did not act swiftly and decisively, monarchists, brigands, and English gold would bring about the demise of the Consulate and restore the Old Regime. The government conceded that the bill violated those articles of the Constitution of the Year VIII that protected the rights of the accused and guaranteed trial by jury. Notable among these was article 46, which prohibited as "arbitrary detention" holding those accused of "conspiracy against the state" for more than ten days without bringing formal charges. However, the government argued, article 92 allowed for the partial suspension of the constitution in the face of the threat posed by brigandage. The article stated that "in the case of armed revolt, or of unrest that threatens the security of the state, the law can suspend, in the times and places it determines, the empire of the constitution."[26] The brigandage afflicting France's countryside, claimed the government, was a form of armed revolt. It furthermore contended that the implicit logic of the article allowed for the partial suspension of the constitution under the maxim "He who can do more can do less." That is, the government claimed it could choose to

25. Benjamin Constant, *Opinion de Benjamin Constant sur le projet de loi concernant l'établissement de Tribunaux criminels spéciaux* (Paris, 1801), 3.

26. Jacques Godechot, ed., *Les constitutions de la France depuis 1789* (Paris, 1979), 156, 161.

suspend certain articles of the constitution without actually suspending its entire "empire."

The crux of the government's justification, however, did not depend on the text of the Constitution of the Year VIII or the subtleties of constitutional interpretation. The government instead appealed to what it viewed as a transcendent principle: its responsibility to maintain order, even if that involved the suspension of juridical liberties. The logic of the government's argument was stated clearly a few months before by Fouché: "The Police of a free people no doubt must clothe itself in the many forms of Justice; but Justice itself must sanction and adopt the rapidity of the Police when it acts against brigands who make war on this people's freedom."[27] The Consulate's legitimacy at this point rested primarily on its ability to preserve order, so its move in this regard was no surprise. Progovernment deputies appealed to the Brumairian orthodoxy and extolled the necessity of order for the preservation of liberty. The deputy Trouvé asked what kind of political association would tie its hands such that it would not be able to guarantee its population "the preservation and enjoyment of its possessions, the safety and liberty of its person." Likewise, J.-A. Perreau argued that liberty demands a "truly protective authority" to "reassure society against the audacity of crime," against actions "that tend to nothing less... than the reversal of the social order." In similar terms, Gary declared that "the only goal that unites men in society, the goals of any polity" are "its preservation [and] the safety and security of the people who form it and of the properties it protects.... If this goal is attained, the association has arrived at the highest degree of perfection." Gary maintained that there was no one ironclad path to achieve this end and that governments therefore needed a significant degree of flexibility in their efforts. "To refuse a government a measure necessary for public security under the pretext that it could be led astray by its agents in the application of this measure, is, essentially, to refuse a government the means to govern." Moreover, he argued, no one set of rules could possibly apply to all peoples in all times and places, an argument that was a pointed challenge to the liberal, universalist logic of those who criticized the bill. "There is not a people that, as a result of the diverse circumstances in which fortune and time has placed it, was not obliged

27. Quoted in Brown, *Ending the French Revolution,* 325.

to change its principles and its laws.... In the final analysis, are principles made for men or men for principles?"[28]

Perhaps the most succinctly Brumairian defense of the bill was offered by the political chameleon Jean Debry. A veteran of virtually every stage of the Revolution with a particular knack for falling in step with the dominant political ideology, Debry was at pains to point out that "the true goal of all political association is security, liberty, and the protection of property; that is what every individual stipulates, formally or tacitly, when he subjects himself to the obligations that the law imposes on him." The only way security, liberty, and property could be guaranteed, Debry argued, was if the government placed the survival of the social and political body above all other considerations, even if that entailed exceptional or extraordinary measures: "The principle of public security, the interest of liberty, the need for domestic peace, and the necessity to put an end to all that might bring about a new revolution or a counterrevolution compel the legislator to leave the normal path and establish a force capable of preventing and punishing the disorders that afflict us; to follow this law anterior to positive laws, this law that far-sighted nature has imposed on all beings, and from which political bodies are not exempt, the law of self-preservation."[29] Only through robust and concerted action to ensure order, argued Debry, could the Revolution be brought to a close.

The opposition objected vociferously to the government's appeal to public safety as a transcendent principle, accusing it of rekindling the ideology and rhetoric of high Jacobinism. Ginguené, in a passage that, following the objections of several progovernment deputies, was struck from the official account in the *Moniteur,* explicitly equated the government's justification of the bill to that of the Terror. Some of those who supported the bill, he explained, claimed that "the bad, the gravity of which no one is tempted to deny, can only be cured by the most violent remedies, only by the infringement of principles and, if necessary, even of the constitution. I most certainly respect the intentions of these orators, but they either do not know or do not remember where such maxims lead. They would themselves be shocked by the similarity between these assertions... and those of the most frenetic demagogues of 1793." The proposed law, Ginguené charged, was

28. *AP*$_2$, 2:230, 176–77, 199–200, 201, 200.

29. Ibid., 2:189. See also, e.g., Caillemer, ibid., 2:241; Laussat, ibid., 2:256.

"imprinted with all the revolutionary signs and symptoms."[30] Against the government's recourse to public safety, the opposition argued for the sovereignty of the constitution and the law. While they repeated constantly that the bill violated the Constitution of the Year VIII, the deeper issue was whether France would be a constitutional, law-governed polity. In the eyes of Parent-Réal, the very nature of France's political order and the legacy of the Revolution were at stake. "The proposed law," he argued, "is contrary to the constitution, subversive of individual security, and dangerous for public liberty.... It is not your duty, nor is it in the interest of the polity, that the constitution be violated."[31]

Beyond such high-minded principles, the crux of the opposition's technical constitutional argument was that the law would violate article 92 of the Constitution of the Year VIII. The liberal-leaning deputies challenged the government's interpretation of article 92, insisting that the letter of the article be followed strictly. They rejected the axiom "He who can do more can do less" and asserted that if part of the constitution were to be suspended, the entire constitution would have to be suspended. Garat-Maillia, posing the matter as the choice between constitutionalism and despotism, derided the government's interpretation of article 92 and insisted that "a constitution and its empire exist in the ensemble and interaction of all of its parts.... It is absurd to say and impossible to prove that one-half, that one-quarter of a single one of these institutions can be deprived of its effect or that this effect is a danger.... One cannot calculate at what point the suspension of one of these constitutional institutions would halt or deprave the action of all the others."[32] Daunou, who had helped draft the constitution, also challenged the government's reading of article 92. The real danger of the government's interpretation, he argued, was that such a specious interpretation—a "preliminary fiction," as he put it—would open the door to extraconstitutional government. If the bill were to pass, he worried, "you would, from now on, no longer have to investigate if a proposal agrees with the fundamental law of the Republic. It would suffice that, by a preliminary fiction, you place yourself under the hypothesis of article 92,

30. P.-L. Ginguené, *Opinion de P. L. Ginguené sur le projet de loi relatif à l'établissement d'un tribunal spécial* (Paris, 1801), 29, 2.

31. AP_2, 2:283.

32. Ibid., 2:289.

and that you conceive of the proposal as demanding less than this article authorizes demanding." For Daunou, the special tribunals themselves, as odious as he found them, were far less dangerous than the long-term implications of such a reading of article 92 and, in effect, enabling extraconstitutional government.

> Citizen colleagues, special tribunals can without doubt seem frightening. In my eyes, they are a thousand times less frightening than the demonstration being given to us of their possibility. Indeed, by this demonstration, it is no longer only special tribunals that are possible. All the results of extraconstitutional government are equally possible. A law could establish all that the constitution prohibits: suspension of individual rights, of all the social guarantees; military taxes; arbitrary arrests; indefinite detentions; [and] arbitrary inquisitions.[33]

The fears of the liberal-leaning deputies concerning the legitimation of extraconstitutional government were summarized by Benjamin Constant, who contended that more dangerous than the law itself was the constitutional theory justifying it. For Constant, if the spirit of the constitution were allowed to override its specific, written rules, then the word "constitution" would have no meaning: "Either I have no understanding of the word *constitution,* or a constitution is only the ensemble of rules wanted by the people who adopt it for its government and its administration. These rules are particular in as much as each applies to a specific object; but they are general in as much as their application is obligatory." Constant phrased his speech in careful language, showing his support for Bonaparte's government by saluting the government's intentions. Yet he reminded his colleagues in the Tribunate that a single system of justice was the great issue in 1789 and, he claimed, what the French people still desired in 1801. "The entire nation has always objected to the creation of tribunals different from ordinary ones. . . . It is the most national opinion that has ever existed among the French people."[34] A single system of justice was, for the liberal-leaning deputies, the most important legacy of the Revolution and the foundation of their political-philosophical program.

33. P. C. F. Daunou, *Opinion de Daunou, Tribun, contre un projet de loi tendant à établir des tribunaux spéciaux* (Paris, 1801), 4, 3–4.

34. Constant, *Opinion,* 1–4, 29, 35.

The opposition's argument for the rule of law did not rest only on grand principles. They also advanced much more practical arguments, asserting that the peace, stability, and social order the government desired could be attained only through the consistent application of constitutional principles and the rule of law. Political and social stability, they argued, would be impossible without public spirit and popular loyalty to the government, which, in turn, could be engendered only by the rule of law. As Daunou put it, "How do you expect citizens to become attached to that which guarantees them nothing,...to the stability of the whole, when there is no consistency?" Constitutional order, he argued, was what "the public interest demands." And "unconstitutional projects" such as that proposed by the government "are exactly the most contrary thing to this interest that one can conceive....The proposal that you are discussing is not beneficial for increasing the true strength of the government, nor, certainly, for maintaining the constitution, nor for public tranquillity." More problematical still, Daunou argued, was the fact that such measures of exception sowed the seeds of future disorder because they undermined faith in constitutional government: "What a strange amalgam, this coexistence of two regimes opposed by their nature, the one constitutional and the other revolutionary; the one made of appearances, the other of realities; but the two so confused in the eyes of a large part of the people that it becomes natural to impute to the first the abuses one receives from the second.... I would not hesitate to label all of these extraordinary, revolutionary, special laws—laws of circumstance, of public security, of public safety—*secrets for perpetuating unrest and preventing order from reemerging under the empire of constitutions.*"[35] The deputy Garat-Maillia voiced a similar set of claims, contending that "public spirit...alone is the true support of states. It can develop and strengthen only with the stability of the law."[36] Thus, for the opposition, the rule of law was desirable not only because of political-philosophical principle but for long-term practical considerations as well. Only the rule of law, they held, could underpin the long-term construction of a stable polity.

In addition to their deep concerns about the long-term and somewhat abstract effects of legitimating extraconstitutional rule, the opposition was

35. Daunou, *Opinion,* 27, 24–25, 28–29.
36. AP_2, 2:297.

also worried that the proposed law would lead to the near-total effacement of individual liberties in France. The deputy Isnard described the proposed law as potentially "fatal to individual liberty."[37] Specifically, the opposition feared that the law violated constitutional safeguards for the accused. For the men of the opposition, criminal rights constituted an uncompromisable liberal aspect of the Brumairian settlement. Just as those who gathered at Versailles in August of 1789 had placed the rights of the accused at the center of their agenda and promulgated articles 7, 8, and 9 of the Declaration of the Rights of Man and of the Citizen of August 1789,[38] the liberal opposition of 1801 considered juridical safeguards for the accused an essential aspect of a liberal polity. To highlight the proposed bill's backwardness, they frequently compared it to the most notorious examples of Old Regime criminal justice and argued that its passage would be tantamount to a return to such dark times. The proposed legislation, they warned, would eliminate the independence of the judiciary, deny the accused any right of appeal or recourse to a body outside the tribunals, and, most important, eliminate trial by jury.

Without question, the proposed law undermined the independence of the judiciary. Five out of the eight judges would be appointed by the First Consul, rendering the tribunals little more than an extension of Bonaparte's will. In the eyes of the opposition, this posed a profound threat to individual liberty in all its forms. They held an independent judiciary to be an indispensable prerequisite for the impartial justice that alone could guarantee individual liberty and the rule of law. Garat-Maillia voiced the opposition's conviction that "a judicial order . . . can alone guarantee the rights and the existence of citizens." The deputy Chazal gave one of the most impassioned pleas on this point, objecting that if the proposed measure were to pass, the government would become both prosecutor and judge. This was, he claimed, nothing less than the gravest of threats to individual liberty. "With regard to the citizen, the government is only, and can be only, a claimant and never a judge. Between the government and the citizens

37. Ibid., 2:173.

38. On these articles and their prehistory, see David A. Bell, "Safeguarding the Rights of the Accused: Lawyers and Political Trials in France, 1716–1789," in *The French Idea of Freedom: The Old Regime and the Declaration of Rights of 1789,* ed. Dale K. Van Kley (Stanford, Calif., 1994).

there should always stand a judge."[39] Chénier voiced a similar concern, insisting that the "independence of tribunals is one of the principal foundations of liberty.... What becomes of this guarantee in a tribunal where five out of eight judges can be dismissed? Who doesn't see that such a tribunal is, in point of fact, really a commission controlled by the government?" Chénier also feared that, if the bill were to pass, the civil judiciary would be subsumed by the military, which he described as nothing less than "declaring public servitude,... consecrating tyranny."[40]

The second major threat to the rights of the accused that the opposition saw in the law was the fact that there would be no mechanism for appeal. Under the proposed law, the tribunal's judgments would stand as final. The accused would have no recourse to any other body. In Ginguené's words, the law assumed "that the special tribunal can never make a mistake in the application of the law." Given the law's broad descriptions of "crimes," seasonal workers and others, he feared, could be arrested without the ability to appeal their arrests.[41] The deputy Desrenaudes also worried about the accused's inability to appeal to a body beyond the tribunals. He professed his faith in the government but was concerned, he said, that "if the law remains this vague, who can tell me that the judges appointed by the government will not one day, despite the government, make a dire use of the law?" Appealing to his colleagues' memories of the Revolution, Desrenaudes pointed to what the historian Charles Walton has recently termed the Revolution's "culture of calumny" and argued that human nature was far too capricious to abandon rigorous legal structures and to allow the tribunals' decisions to stand as final.

> There is, in the depths of men's souls, a frightening tendency that moral philosophers have not even suspected, and that the Revolution alone revealed to us: it is this disposition that leads all, more or less, to regard as guilty of bad intentions, and often as criminal, those who profess, as they are free to do, opinions different from our own. Over the course of the Revolution we have frequently seen the gentlest, most trusting, most perfectly tolerant men

39. *AP*$_2$, 2:292, 212.
40. Chénier, *Opinion,* 4, 3. Garat-Maillia, *AP*$_2$, 293–94, and Ginguené, *Opinion,* 10, also voiced concerns about the bill's effects on the relationship between the military and civilian spheres.
41. Ginguené, *Opinion,* 26, 14, 18–19.

> forget in a moment their generous instincts and, following political dissent, blacken with the most odious charges men whom they had until that moment held in the highest esteem. We have seen friends, as the result of political disagreements, renounce forever, without regret, a friendship that until that moment nothing had troubled. This genre of fanaticism, no less terrible than religious fanaticism, is certainly not extinguished.... Today, we find it everywhere it can be awoken, and it does not appear to have lost anything of its strength.[42]

The specific objection the opposition voiced most frequently, however, was that the proposed law would destroy the system of trial by jury. There was no single issue about which they were more resolute. The deputy Chazal, achieving rhetorical heights not out of step with the speeches of his colleagues, declared, "Citizen tribunes, it has been said, repeated thousands and thousands of times, that the institution of the jury is the judgment of God, the judgment of the people, and the palladium of liberty."[43] The liberal opposition held the jury to be the key institution guaranteeing procedural consistency for all and thus the central axis of the legal and political culture they hoped to foster. It represented the polar opposite of arbitrariness. Their commitment to the jury followed from a prominent strand of Enlightenment thought exemplified by Beccaria[44] and from the reformers of 1789, for whom criminal justice had been of paramount importance. As Isser Woloch puts it, speaking of 1789, "For what greater form of liberty could there be than securing a citizen's right to a fair trial and protecting the innocent?"[45] In the eyes of the liberal opposition of 1801, trial by jury was an indispensable legacy of the Revolution, a non-negotiable feature of the new regime.

The opposition's defense of the jury highlights its deeper political-philosophical commitment to the rule of law. Daunou claimed the jury was the linchpin of the Constitution of the Year VIII's judicial system and

42. *AP_2*, 2:196; Charles Walton, *Policing Public Opinion in the French Revolution: The Culture of Calumny and the Problem of Free Speech* (Oxford, 2008).

43. Ibid., 2:204; see also, Isnard, ibid., 2:171.

44. See esp. Franco Venturi, *Utopia and Reform in the Enlightenment* (Cambridge, 1971), chap. 4.

45. Isser Woloch, *The New Regime: Transformations of the French Civic Order, 1789–1820s* (New York, 1994), 356.

essential to guaranteeing civil liberty in France.[46] Chénier referred to juries as "this wise and beneficent institution . . . that the immortal Montesquieu declared, more than a half-century ago, the chef-d'oeuvre of the legislation of a free people."[47] The deputy Desrenaudes depicted juries as the "institution that those peoples who are most in love with their rights regard as the final rampart of their civil liberty," while Parent-Réal declared that "the jury is one of the strong columns of the constitution. If you dislodge it," he continued, "even temporarily, beware that the social edifice . . . will soon wobble on its base; beware that it will crumble into all of its parts, and that it will sweep away with it the last altars of liberty."[48] Benjamin Constant also sang the praises of the jury, calling it "the best means to discern the innocent from the guilty." His defense of the jury encapsulated the liberal opposition's larger claims about the importance of the law and impartial justice. Constant pleaded for the value of juries by stressing the importance of forms and procedures. The proposed law, he explained, implied "that there are external and infallible signs according to which one can distinguish, before judgment, before instruction, the innocent and the guilty, those who should enjoy the prerogative of juries and those who should be denied them, those to whom this institution belongs and those to whom it does not." He urged his fellow tribunes to reject such reasoning and heed the importance of forms and procedures.

> If such signs existed, we would have need for neither ordinary tribunals nor special tribunals. It is because such signs do not exist that forms are necessary. It is because the institution of the jury has appeared the best means to discern the innocent from the guilty that all the free and humane peoples have demanded it. . . . Forms are a safeguard. The abbreviation of forms is the reduction or the loss of this safeguard. The abbreviation of forms is therefore a punishment.[49]

The deep-seated rift between the opposition and the government was manifested nowhere more clearly than in the latter's justifications for suspending the jury system. The bill's supporters acknowledged the concerns

46. Daunou, *Opinion,* 9.
47. Chénier, *Opinion,* 6.
48. AP_2, 2:193, 283.
49. Constant, *Opinion,* 33, 32–33, 33.

of the opposition but objected that the crisis in those areas of France assailed by brigandage had rendered the jury system inadequate. The crimes in question, they contended, stood beyond the purview of normal governance. In fact, they argued, only by recourse to exceptional justice could the institution of the jury, and society itself, be saved.[50] According to the deputy Savoye-Rollin, France was besieged by "the types of offenses that attack the very life of the social body,... offenses against the political order" that "can only be suppressed... [by] a judiciary system contrary to the institution of the jury." Similarly, Depierre effusively praised juries but asked whether "this mode of administering criminal justice, essentially protective of society and its members, is equally suitable for a people in all circumstances?" For the bill's opponents, however, such an argument was intrinsically flawed, if not unintelligible. According to their universalist logic, the rule of law was always superior to arbitrary rule, no matter the circumstances. While the government argued that institutions and the legal system existed for society, Garat-Maillia and the liberal opposition questioned the very coherence of this line of argument: "Society *for which civil and political institutions exist*—does society therefore exist other than by these institutions? Is the nature of these institutions immaterial?"[51] In other words, in the eyes of the liberal opposition, it was nonsensical to speak of society as distinct from its institutions. The rule of law could be established only through institutions that incarnated that principle.[52]

Liberty as a Historical Question

"The war of books is an issue of no small importance."[53] So wrote Pierre-Louis Roederer in the pages of the *Journal de Paris* in 1801 as the liberal

50. Esmein, *Histoire de la procédure criminelle en France,* 477–79.

51. AP_2, 2:283, 216, 289.

52. Chénier was the only member of the opposition to appeal openly to republicanism as the form of government that could best incarnate such liberal principles, probably because it was so politically provocative to do so. He voiced this sentiment as he finished his speech, urging his colleagues to keep alive the republican spirit of the Revolution: "Let the government rally ever more to republican principles, to republican institutions, to republican opinion.... Let the reins of administration everywhere be confided in republican hands." *Opinion,* 12.

53. Roederer, review of *Histoire de la Révolution de France, pendant les dernières années du Règne de Louis XVI,* by A. F. Bertrand de Moleville, *Journal de Paris,* 1 Pluviôse, Year 9 (21 January 1801), 731.

opposition contested Bonaparte's increasingly authoritarian regime not only in parliamentary debate but also in the domain of intellectual production. The government took such intellectual production extremely seriously and moved to silence a range of books and journals. In an internal report in January of 1800, just two months after the coup of Brumaire and a few weeks after the promulgation of the Constitution of the Year VIII, the Ministry of Police noted that "journals have always been the tocsin of revolutions"[54] and reduced the number of political journals in Paris from sixty to thirteen.[55] The official decree announcing the closure of over three-quarters of the capital's political journals sounded a Brumairian justification, explaining that "the government is specially charged by the French people to look after its security."[56]

This shrinking of public political discussion was felt acutely by those in the opposition. In 1801, Benjamin Constant wrote to Sismondi that he could not find a publisher in France for Sismondi's *Recherches sur les constitutions des peuples libres* (*Researches on the Constitutions of Free Peoples*) because of fears about censorship.[57] The following year, moreover, Germaine de Staël dedicated her novel *Delphine* to "the silent but enlightened France."[58] In addition to imposing censorship, Bonaparte purged liberal-leaning figures from the halls of government and drove certain individuals into exile. Staël was expelled from Paris and forbidden to come within forty miles of the city. She explained in a letter to Dupont de Nemours that she had suffered for her beliefs and would now "not concern myself with anything. I shall not write about anything, I shall even try not to speak about anything. But never have my heart and my mind been more penetrated with and earnest in the love of liberty."[59] With the space for the expression of critical ideas increasingly constricted during the Consulate, opposition-minded authors had to find indirect avenues for political expression.

54. Aulard, *Paris sous le Consulat,* 1:96.

55. André Cabanis, *La presse sous le Consulat et l'Empire, 1799–1814* (Paris, 1975), 11–14.

56. Decree of 27 Nivôse, Year 8 (17 January 1800); reprinted in ibid., 319.

57. Constant to Sismondi, 25 October 1801, in Constant and Sismondi, *La Correspondance de Benjamin Constant et de Sismondi (1801–1830),* ed. Norman King and Jean-Daniel Candaux (Geneva, 1980), 89.

58. Quoted in Martyn Lyons, *Napoleon Bonaparte and the Legacy of the French Revolution* (London, 1994), 141.

59. Staël to de Nemours, 5 November 1802, in *De Staël-Du Pont Letters,* 144.

One of the primary indirect forms was the writing of history.[60] Historical narrative was charged with political stakes. Revealingly, Roederer's statement about the "war of books" was made in a review of A. F. Bertrand de Moleville's *History of the French Revolution during the Final Years of the Reign of Louis XVI.* History as a medium for political expression, of course, was not new in the Consulate. It was in many regards the lingua franca of eighteenth-century political argument.[61] While the political discourse of the Revolution's early years often rejected historically based arguments, the post-Terror period witnessed a decided upswing in historical consciousness. During the Directory, numerous figures in the republican center turned to history in their reading and writing, and historical narrative was a politically charged subject. For example, Necker's *De la Révolution française* provoked a critical, extremely detailed review from Ginguené in 1797, and in 1798 and 1799 Boulay de la Meurthe and Benjamin Constant wrote dueling histories of the English Revolution and Restoration that transparently addressed the political situation in France.[62] France's leading intellectuals and politicians regularly made use of comparative historical perspective for assessing and arguing about France's own situation. F.-A. Boissy d'Anglas, while jotting down his reflections on the Revolution during the later years of the Directory, filled his manuscript with quotes from Robertson's *History* and Machiavelli's *Discourses* that were meant to make sense of the Revolution by historicizing it.[63] In the same vein, the Class of Moral and Political Sciences at the National Institute invited French intellectuals in 1799 to reflect on the politically charged question,

60. Literature also emerged as an important political medium, as Tocqueville observed in his notes on the Consulate and the Empire: "Literature had become the only weapon with which old political enemies could still attack each other." Tocqueville, *Fragments et notes inédites sur la Révolution,* 328.

61. See Keith Michael Baker, *Inventing the French Revolution: Essays on French Political Culture in the Eighteenth Century* (Cambridge, 1990), pt. 1; and Jean-Marie Goulemot, *Le règne de l'histoire: Discours historiques et révolutions, XVIIe–XVIIIe siècle,* 2d ed. (Paris, 1996).

62. P. L. Ginguené, *De M. Necker et de son livre intitulé* De la Révolution française (Paris, 1797); Antoine-Jacques-Claude-Joseph Boulay de la Meurthe, *Essai sur les causes qui, en 1649, amenèrent en Angleterre l'établissement de la République, sur celles qui devaient l'y consolider, sur celles qui l'y firent périr* (Paris, 1798); Benjamin Constant, *Des suites de la contre-révolution de 1660 en Angleterre* [1799], in *Oeuvres complètes de Benjamin Constant,* vol. 1, *Écrits de jeunesse (1774–1799),* ed. Lucia Omacini and Jean-Daniel Candaux (Tübingen, Ger., 1998).

63. Boissy d'Anglas, "Pensées diverses et anecdotes sur la Révolution française," 28 Prairial to 3 Thermidor, Year 7 (16 June to 21 July 1799), AN, 175 AP 4, 2, f. 8, 10, 18–19, 28.

"By what causes has the spirit of liberty developed in France from François I to 1789?"[64] And in 1800, as part of a series of republican manuals that had been launched in 1799 under François de Neufchateau, the Ministry of the Interior published a "handbook" made up of excerpts from the histories of Dubos and Mably that was to teach the French about the evils of its deposed monarchy.[65]

History continued to be a political genre during the Consulate. Chénier, one of the leaders of the liberal opposition, spelled out the importance of history in a speech on 17 August 1801 in which he described the study of history and legislation as "the principal studies of man and citizen."[66] Chénier's praise for historical knowledge was echoed in early 1802 by Mercier, who extolled the importance of learning from history in a report to the National Institute titled *Appreciation of Ancient History*.[67] And Pierre-Charles Lévesque wrote what could be termed "Brumairian history," which, in analyzing the histories of Sparta and Athens, emphasized the importance of order and warned of the disarray and chaos democracy could bring about.[68] Official recognition of the political stakes of history writing can be seen in government censorship records. For example, in the summer of 1803 a book by the historian Jean de Sales, who was a member of the National Institute, was censored for portraying Louis XVI too sympathetically and the Revolution too negatively.[69] Bonaparte himself took notice

64. *Mémoires de l'Institut National des sciences et arts: Sciences Morales et Politiques,* vol. 4 (Paris, 1802), 12. The author Nicolas Ponce took first place. 7 Vendémiaire, Year 9, AI, SMP, A3.

65. *Abrégé des révolutions de l'ancien gouvernement français. Ouvrage élémentaire, extrait de l'abbé Dubos et de l'abbé Mably, par Thouret, membre de l'assemblée constituante; pour l'instruction de son fils* (Paris, 1800); briefly discussed in chapter 2.

66. Marie-Joseph Chénier, *Discours sur les progrès des connaissances en Europe, et de l'enseignement public en France* (Paris, 1801), 44. Chénier pointed to a genealogy of great—often republican—authors that ran from classical writers such as Livy, Tacitus, and Cicero through Machiavelli and Guicciardini, Fénélon, and, in the eighteenth century, Montesquieu, Rousseau, and Voltaire. Ibid., 7–32.

67. P. C. F. Daunou, *Notice des travaux de la classe des sciences morales et scientifiques durant les mois de nivôse, pluviôse et ventôse, an X* (Paris, 1802), 15.

68. Lévesque, "Mémoire sur la constitution de la république de Sparte," "Premier mémoire sur la constitution de la république d'Athènes," "Second mémoire sur la constitution de la république d'Athènes," and "Troisième mémoire sur la constitution de la république d'Athènes," in *Mémoires de l'Institut National des sciences et arts: Sciences morales et politiques,* vols. 3 and 4 (Paris, 1801 and 1802).

69. 12 Fructidor, Year 11 (30 August 1803), AN, F 18 39, f. 97.

of de Sale's tract, writing to the police, "I request Consul Cambacérès to inform himself about this brochure, to know why this madman was not prevented from writing, and if there is not a way to stop this publication; and to know if one could not exclude from the Institute a man who writes against the state."[70] Historical narrative was a primary medium for the expression of political argument during the Consulate and was often a political minefield.

The most important example of the use of historical narrative in political argument during the Consulate was an essay contest sponsored by the Class of Moral and Political Sciences in 1802, which asked, "What was the influence of Luther's Reformation on the political situation of the different European states and on the progress of Enlightenment?" The question seemed to invite respondents to criticize the Catholic Church, which was tantamount to inviting them to comment negatively on Bonaparte's Concordat with the Church. The question was announced on the same day in April 1802 that Councilor of State Portalis presented the Concordat to the legislative body.[71] While on one level criticism of papal infallibility might serve Bonaparte in his dealings with the Church, the official discourse around the Concordat never condemned the papacy in the manner that the class's question seemed to invite. In other words, the question was political provocation.[72] The Class of Moral and Political Sciences, it should be noted, had used prize contests as political provocation before. For example, on the eve of the debate about extrajudicial military tribunals, the class proposed a prize contest on the question, "By what means may the institution of the jury be improved in France?"[73] Frustration with the Class of Moral and Political Sciences' political views and activities eventually led Bonaparte to disband it as part of a reorganization of the National Institute in January of 1803.

70. Bonaparte to Cambacérès, 5 Messidor, Year 11 (24 June 1803), in *Correspondance de Napoléon Ier, publiée par ordre de l'empereur Napoléon III,* 32 vols. (Paris, 1858–1870), 8:374, no. 6855.

71. It had, however, been decided earlier, on 3 March 1802. 12 Ventôse, Year 10, AI, SMP, A3.

72. "Provocation" is Martin Staum's term, although Staum interprets the contest on the Reformation as less politically provocative. *Minerva's Message: Stabilizing the French Revolution* (Montreal, 1996), 73–75. Staum, in my opinion, underplays the political stakes of inviting respondents to broadly criticize the Church, given the extreme sensitivity of the Concordat.

73. 12 Nivôse, Year 9 (2 January 1801), AI, SMP, A3.

The Concordat was a highly charged topic among France's political and intellectual elites, provoking one of the deepest fractures in the Brumairian coalition.[74] Many figures in the republican center were deeply hostile to the papacy and viewed Bonaparte's compromise with it as nothing short of a betrayal of the Revolution. Moreover, the Concordat came at a time when the issue of Catholicism was even more charged than usual. Chateaubriand's deeply Catholic *Atala* (1801) had recently provoked "the battle of Atala," with Marie-Joseph Chénier's mocking *Les nouveaux Saints* (1801) leading the secularist counterattack and Chateaubriand responding with his *Génie du Christianisme* (1802).[75] Staël articulated the dissatisfaction with the Concordat in a letter to Dupont de Nemours after Dupont defended it as an example of Bonaparte's genius. Bonaparte, Dupont claimed, had no intention of making France more Catholic, only of appeasing public opinion and of smoothing over a rift dividing the nation: "You think that I am heartbroken. Not at all. I see the thing in another light. Pythagoras and several other philosophers or legislators had a public doctrine and a secret doctrine. My confidence in the genius of Bonaparte is still such that he did not betray it at all by this apparent retreat to the manure of theology."[76] Staël replied that Dupont's reading of the situation was wildly optimistic. Rather, she wrote to him, Bonaparte had "a more direct goal: . . . to start a fourth dynasty, to imitate Charlemagne, etc.; and in order to imitate him better, must we not bring our minds back to the time when he lived?"[77] The class's question, when viewed against the backdrop of such outrage over the Concordat and coupled with wider concerns about the increasingly authoritarian bent of Bonaparte's rule, appears as political provocation.

The winning submission in the Institute's contest was a book by Charles de Villers titled simply *Essay on the Spirit and Influence of Luther's Reformation*. Villers, an important intellectual in his own day who has received relatively little attention from historians, was born in Lorraine in 1765, emigrated to Germany during the Revolution, and settled in Göttingen, where he enrolled in the university and published a series of articles on

74. See Thierry Lentz, *Le Grand Consulat, 1799–1804* (Paris, 1999), chap. 13.

75. Ibid., 420.

76. Du Pont de Nemours to de Staël, 3 December 1801, in *De Staël-Du Pont Letters,* 121 (translation modified).

77. Staël to Du Pont de Nemours, 25 April 1802, in *De Staël-Du Pont Letters,* 129 (partially quoted above).

Kant in the journal *Le Spectateur du nord.*[78] He was reasonably well known in French intellectual circles at the time and was especially close to Germaine de Staël and Benjamin Constant.[79] Villers had gained some fame in 1801 for a treatise on Kant that he presented to the National Institute, which, however, was rejected because of the anti-Kantianism that predominated in the Institute at the time.[80] Villers's *Essay on the Spirit and Influence of Luther's Reformation* nonetheless won first prize in the class's contest and was printed twice in 1804, the second edition with a new preface responding to some of his critics and an appendix outlining the history of "the Christian Church from its founder until the Reformation."[81] The text was reprinted multiple times in subsequent years and was translated into English and German, going through multiple printings in those languages as well.

Villers's *Essay* argued in emphatic terms that the Reformation was the single most decisive turning point in human history since the establishment of the Christian religion. In his estimation, "the results of this revolution offer a surplus of good for humanity.... It should be counted as one of the major events that has most powerfully contributed to the progress of civilization and Enlightenment, not only in Europe but in all the parts of the earth where Europeans have brought their culture."[82] Depicting the Reformation as a return to the original principles of Christianity from a corrupt Catholic Church, Villers claimed that the defining feature of the Reformation was the demand for freedom of thought and for civil liberty. Through this portrayal, Villers's book advanced an important political argument against both the Concordat and Bonaparte's increasingly authoritarian

78. See James Mitchell Lee, "Charles Villers and German Thought in France, 1797–1804," *Proceedings of the Annual Meeting of the Western Society for French History* 25 (1998); and Louis Wittmer, *Charles de Villers, 1765–1815: Un intermédiaire entre la France et l'Allemagne et un précurseur de Mme de Staël* (Paris, 1908).

79. See Madame de Staël, Charles de Villers, and Benjamin Constant, *Correspondance,* ed. Kurt Kloocke (Frankfurt am Main, 1993); and the numerous entries that refer to Villers in Constant, *Oeuvres complètes de Benjamin Constant,* vol. 6, *Journaux intimes (1804–1807),* ed. Paul Delbouille and Kurt Kloocke (Tübingen, Ger., 2002).

80. Charles de Villers, *Philosophie de Kant, ou, Principes fondamentaux de la philosophie transcendentale* (Metz, Fr., 1801).

81. Citations here are to the second edition: Charles de Villers, *Essai sur l'esprit et l'influence de la réformation de Luther,* 2d ed. (Paris, 1804).

82. Ibid., 384.

rule.[83] Its attack against the Catholic Church was so withering that the Concordat could only appear to be a compromise with an utterly debased institution. Benjamin Constant was astonished that the Institute awarded Villers's treatise first prize. The book was "excellent," Constant wrote in his journal, but it "is inexplicable... that the Institute has crowned it. It is the most hostile work against Catholicism that may ever be published."[84] Its unrestrained anti-Catholicism set off a minicontroversy in the press, with pro-Catholic journals attacking Villers and the Institute.[85] Roederer, who may have been Bonaparte's single most zealous supporter, had his *Journal de Paris* commend aspects of the book but disapprove of Villers's excessive criticism of Catholicism.[86] While Bonaparte was no great friend of the Church, the severity of Villers's criticisms cast the Concordat in a harshly negative light. Furthermore, the book praised both republicanism and an abstract notion of liberty, thereby presenting a liberal-republican political vision thoroughly incompatible with Bonaparte's increasingly authoritarian rule.

Villers, following the structure of the question proposed, discussed the intellectual and political repercussions of Luther and the Reformation in running parallel sections of his book. The two categories, however, frequently blended in his analysis. Intellectual and political developments were shown to mutually influence each other and to have caused a two-pronged sea change in European history. For Europe's intellectual life, in Villers's account, the Reformation "began a philosophical period during which interest in truths of a higher order, in the discussion of the highest rules of logic, metaphysics and morality, gained a level of activity that had not been seen for many centuries." He noted the importance of the Renaissance in paving the way for the Reformation but claimed unambiguously that it was only with Luther that Europe's true intellectual revolution

83. Villers's book thus used religious history as a vehicle for political argument, following in the steps of ecclesiastical histories such as Paolo Sarpi's 1619 *History of the Council of Trent* (which Villers cited several times).

84. Constant, *Journaux intimes (1804–1807),* 105. Similarly, Constant wrote to Villers that he admired the book greatly and that the ideas expressed were very similar to his own. Constant to Villers, 6 Prairial, Year 12 (26 May 1804), in Staël, Villers, and Constant, *Correspondance,* 91–92. Like Villers, Constant and Staël both professed the superiority of Protestantism in the modern world.

85. Wittmer, *Charles de Villers,* 216–71.

86. Ibid., 227–28.

began. The Reformation, in his narrative, fundamentally advanced humanity on its path to perfection.[87] Villers also argued that the Reformation revolutionized Europe's political landscape. "A new political order" emerged from the Reformation and reintroduced to Europe political principles such as republicanism, freedom of conscience, and, more generally, an abstract notion of liberty. Thus, for Villers, the Reformation redirected the course of European, and world, history.

The single most important outcome of the Reformation, Villers argued, was to put the issue of liberty at the center of European political and intellectual life. This was a momentous development, he wrote, as liberty was necessary for the "the human spirit" to strive toward perfection. He used the term "liberty" as a broad, somewhat abstract, catchall that encompassed religious liberty, freedom of expression, civil liberty, and finally political liberty. This political and intellectual earthquake was, however, an unintended consequence of Luther's actions. In the beginning, Villers explained, "the intention of the reformers was to free themselves from the despotism and infallibility of the popes." As a result of their efforts, however, there was a flowering of "freedom of thought, so precious to man, and the foundation of his civil liberty." This newfound liberty then fostered a wide range of creative developments in science, philosophy, and politics, furthering both the progress of reason and the human spirit's march toward perfection. From this wider vantage, Villers passionately declared in Kantian terms, "the Reformation was, in its essence, nothing other than the act by which reason declared itself emancipated from the yoke of arbitrary authority." Reason's self-emancipation, Villers asserted, would have been impossible under the pre-Reformation Catholic Church: "the old system of Roman Catholicism was diametrically opposed to the progress of enlightenment." More deeply, he claimed, the full and active development of reason was antithetical to Catholicism, which he described as telling people, "Submit to authority without examination" while "the Protestant church says: 'Examine, and submit only to your convictions.'"[88] Villers thus depicted the Reformation and Protestantism as the beginning of the Enlightenment as Kant had famously defined it—as "man's emancipation

87. Villers, *Essai sur l'esprit et l'influence de la réformation de Luther,* 272, i. Villers, in Kantian terms, treated perfection as a heuristic that "will never be the fate of mortals" but as a goal to aspire toward much like "the geometrical phenomenon of the asymptote." Ibid., 15.

88. Ibid., 240–41, 326, 237–38, 248.

from his self-incurred immaturity" and having the "courage" to use one's own reason and understanding.[89]

In Villers's narrative, the progress of Enlightenment and reason, liberated by the Reformation, precipitated widespread demands for "liberty in the political order." As a result, he alleged, liberty developed more fully in Europe's Protestant countries than in those that adhered to Catholicism. Furthermore, he provocatively claimed, the French Revolution would never have had to occur in a Protestant country. The ideals of 1789 were only the political incarnation of Protestantism's inherent rationality:

> The Reformation, which was at first only a return to liberty in the religious order, became...a return to liberty in the political order as well....The Protestant sovereigns adopted a different language toward their peoples than their Catholic counterparts, they professed different principles of liberty and humanity. For a long time, the Protestant peoples have been familiarized with the language and the principles of reason; they know that this is the basis of their governments and they are accustomed to discussion of their interests and their rights: such discussion does not cause the slightest stir. The liberty to think and to write is as natural to them as the air they breathe. All of this might make one think, correctly, that a political revolution like the one in France could never have occurred in the non-Catholic states; the most essential results of such a revolution were already established.

Yet for all his praise of liberty, Villers cautioned against "absolute liberty." He equated the "enthusiastic sects born of the Reformation, such as the Anabaptists," with "the excesses of the Jacobins in France." Both were characterized by "the same pretensions to absolute equality and liberty."[90] Mainstream Protestantism and the ideals of 1789 were, in Villers's analysis, the religious and political incarnations of reason and the proper extension of liberty. The political implications of his analysis stood in pointed contrast to contemporaneous developments in the nature of Bonaparte's regime. Villers's praise of liberty and his argument that Protestantism nurtured it implicitly criticized Bonaparte's general rolling back of liberties and his Concordat with the Catholic Church. Bonaparte, Villers tacitly charged, was betraying the ideals of 1789.

89. Kant, *Political Writings,* ed. H. S. Reiss and trans. H. B. Nisbet (Cambridge, 1991), 54.
90. Villers, *Essai sur l'esprit et l'influence de la réformation de Luther,* 139, 141.

The political implications of Villers's analysis were further driven home by a number of passages in which he equated the Reformation with republicanism and the Catholic Church with "universal monarchy" or "despotism." The true principles of Christianity—by which he meant Protestantism, liberty, and republican government—emerge in his analysis as thoroughly intertwined. "The calm and solemn sentiment of the highest dignity of man is the only worthwhile foundation of a true republicanism, and it is only by such a sentiment that the equality of rights, the reciprocity of duties, is established. Christianity, in its pure essence, inspires this sentiment."[91] Villers contrasted this liberty-engendering republicanism with the "despotism" of the papacy. The popes were "the emperors of a new Western Empire" set on "universal monarchy." In the sixteenth century, the pope and Charles V sought the "subjugation" of Europe under "the yoke of universal monarchy" but were stopped by those "who enjoyed a republican constitution and nourished the penchant for liberty." The term "universal monarchy" was a critical one throughout the eighteenth century, associated with despotism in writers such as Montesquieu, Mably, Voltaire, and Raynal. Villers's use of it to describe the Church was a damning rebuke. The contrast between the despotic Church and republican-inclined Protestantism was further drawn through the mobilization of familiar tropes of early modern republican writing: Villers described the Church as corrupted by luxury, while Protestants and republicans presented a virtuous and austere counterpoint.[92]

Villers also linked Protestantism, liberty, and republicanism in a handful of comments about conciliarism's representing the true spirit of Christianity. He praised the councils of Pisa, Constance, and Basel for having resisted the papacy's despotic tendencies and defending "this long-forgotten principle...'*that the council is above the Pope.*'" His book was peppered with praise for figures associated with conciliarism, such as Paolo Sarpi, and even the most radical currents within "the courageous Gallican Church," notably Gerson and Richer. More pointedly, Villers claimed that the early Church was essentially a republic and that it was the conciliar tradition that preserved this republican heritage in the face of the popes' gradual usurpation of all forms of power, spiritual and temporal. In Villers's

91. Ibid., 133; see also 49, 56, 138–39, 201–2.
92. Ibid., 359, 3, 91, 56, 71–72.

telling, the history of Christianity was one of decline from a republic to a despotic empire.[93] It was only with the Reformation that the republican principles at the heart of Christianity, kept alive through the conciliar tradition and other antipapal dissidents, were revivified. Villers's celebration of the conciliar tradition and concomitant claims that the early Church was a republic amounted to the historical legitimation of republicanism as a form of government and thus an implicit criticism of the antirepublican direction of Bonaparte's rule. Villers assigned final political authority to the councils and equated liberty with republicanism, a formula that could only stand in contrast to Napoleon's increasingly authoritarian regime. Furthermore, his praise for republican government in contrast to empires could only be read as a critique of Bonaparte's assuming the title Consul for Life in 1802.

Villers was not the only respondent whose narrative held such political implications. J.-J. Leuliette, who won second place in the contest, also inscribed the Reformation within the longer-term history of republicanism, liberty, and the progress of reason. Leuliette celebrated "the civil and political independence" stemming from the Reformation and credited the desire for liberty it provoked with rekindling "the disinterestedness and the virtues of the ancient republics.... Will we forget that, in the middle of the discord, one saw born political ideas, ideas of religious independence, that struck a chord even during the Enlightenment?" Leuliette went on to explicitly tie the seventeenth- and eighteenth-century republican tradition, and authors such as Harrington and Sidney, to the cycle of events set off by Luther and the Reformation. Furthermore, and like Villers, he celebrated the historical role of conciliarism as a counterpoint to the power of the papacy.[94] Thus, the political implications of Leuliette's narrative were extremely close to those of Villers. Similarly, the respondent who took third place, Nicolas Ponce, who had won the prize contest on the historical development of liberty in France a few years before, echoed Villers and Leuliette in comparing Holland's defense of its religious liberty and its commitment to

93. Ibid., 448–49, 125–26, 385–456. Similarly, earlier in the text Villers wrote, in deeply classical-republican terms, that all political constitutions decline toward despotism via oligarchy and monarchy. Ibid., 28–29.

94. J.-J. Leuliette, *Discours qui a eu la mention honorable sur cette question proposée par l'Institut national: Quelle a été l'influence de la Réformation de Luther sur les lumières et la situation politique des différens États de l'Europe?* (Paris, 1804), 102–4, 149–50, 127.

"liberal ideas" to "the glorious days of Sparta." Ponce's tract, which commended the Concordat for permanently weakening the papacy vis-à-vis Europe's temporal powers, staked a more neutral overall position in regard to Bonaparte's rule than did either Villers's or Leuliette's.[95] Yet Ponce extolled the idea of liberty, however imprecisely, thereby tacitly censuring the direction of the Consulate. The political moral of Leuliette's and Ponce's histories, in short, echoed that of Villers's.

Villers's account of the Reformation and its influence on the politics of Europe and the progress of Enlightenment advanced a liberal-republican critique of Bonaparte's increasingly authoritarian regime. Villers, like many authors of his day, mobilized historical narrative as a tool for political critique. His book took first place in the National Institute's prize contest, which amounted to an endorsement of his analysis by France's foremost intellectual institution. In the face of Napoleon's growing authoritarianism, a liberal-republican alternative was thus put forward and endorsed, however obliquely. Villers's *Essay* helped to inaugurate the emergent liberal-republican critique of Napoleon, a critique that positioned an abstract notion of liberty as the first principle of political life while also holding that liberty is best fostered and safeguarded by republican forms of government. The text furthermore constituted an important chapter in the genre of history writing as a tool to celebrate liberty in opposition to Napoleonic rule.[96] Other texts in this genre included Sismondi's *Histoire des républiques italiennes du moyen âge (History of the Italian Republics of the Middle Ages)* and Daunou's anonymously published *Essai historique sur la puissance temporelle des papes (Historical Essay on the Temporal Power of the Popes).*[97] Finally, Viller's *Essay* had an important influence on Benjamin

95. Nicolas Ponce, *Essai historique sur cette question proposée par l'Institut national: Quelle a été l'influence de la Réformation de Luther sur la situation politique des différens États de l'Europe, et sur le progrès des lumières* (Paris, 1804), 60–62, 98–99.

96. While scholars have noted the importance of history writing during the eighteenth century and the Restoration, the continuity of this genre through the Napoleonic period has been missed by, e.g., Stanley Mellon in his classic *The Political Uses of History: A Study of Historians in the French Restoration* (Stanford, Calif, 1958). An important exception is June K. Burton, *Napoleon and Clio* (Durham, N.C., 1979).

97. Jean-Charles-Leonard Simonde de Sismondi, *Histoire des républiques italiennes du moyen âge,* 8 vols. (Zurich, 1807–9); [Daunou], *Essai historique sur la puissance temporelle des papes, sur l'abus qu'ils ont fait de leur ministère spirituel, et sur les guerres qu'ils déclarées aux souverains, spécialement*

Constant, who wrote about the book in his journal on 5 September 1804 and then on 6 September noted his own plans to write a book about religion.[98] Before turning to that topic, however, Constant remained engaged with a text he had been working on for several years, his *De la possibilité d'une constitution républicaine dans un grands pays (On the Possibility of a Republican Constitution in a Large Country).*

Benjamin Constant's Liberal Republicanism

Benjamin Constant's *On the Possibility of a Republican Constitution in a Large Country* stands out as the Consulate's single most important articulation of the nascent liberal-republican political philosophy that would later constitute the central kernel of French Liberalism.[99] Penned over an extended period, from as early as 1798 and until as late as 1806 but primarily between 1801 and 1803,[100] the text went unpublished until 1991 and has remained understudied in Constant scholarship. *On the Possibility of a Republican Constitution in a Large Country* stands out in Constant's oeuvre both as his first effort at a systematic discussion of political-philosophical principles and as his first foray into constitutional architecture. The central goal of the text was to outline a constitution for a liberal republic. Constant had labeled his political views "liberal" in 1797—and was, along with

à ceux qui avaient la prépondérance en Italie; ouvrage traduit de l'espagnol (Paris, 1810). Daunou's authorship of the anonymously published book is confirmed by a manuscript in Daunou's hand in BN, Nouv. Acqu. Fr. 21906; and in correspondence between Daunou and the ministry of police dated February–March 1811 in AN, F7 6615, d. S 1070. Daunou's text, like Villers's, combined a criticism of papal usurpation of temporal power with a celebration of republicanism and conciliarism.

98. Constant, *Journaux intimes (1804–1807),* 204–5.

99. I have followed the title used in Constant's complete works: *De la possibilité d'une constitution républicaine dans un grands pays, Fragments d'un ouvrage abandonné (1800–1803),* in Constant, *Oeuvres complètes de Benjamin Constant,* vol. 4, *Discours au Tribunat; De la possibilité d'une constitution républicaine dans un grands pays (1799–1803),* ed. María Luisa Sánchez-Mejía and Kurt Kloocke (Tübingen, Ger., 2005). Citations to the text, however, are to Constant, *Fragments d'un ouvrage abandonné sur la possibilité d'une constitution républicaine dans un grand pays,* ed. Henri Grange (Paris, 1991).

100. Sánchez-Mejía, introduction to Constant, *De la possibilité d'une constitution républicaine dans un grands pays,* 364.

Germaine de Staël, notes K. Steven Vincent, "the first in France to use this term to define a political stance"[101]—but *Republican Constitution* was his first attempt to sketch a liberal constitutional order.[102] It is, however, a liberal-*republican* text. It advanced the central thrust of Constant's mature thought, as articulated in his 1819 lecture on "The Liberty of the Ancients Compared with That of the Moderns:" a constitutional order that put civil liberty first while also demanding an active political life in order to thwart despotism. If civil liberty was the baseline, political liberty, even if confined to virtuous elites, could not be sacrificed. Political liberty, republican institutions, and what might be termed republican energies were necessary to preserve a healthy polity. The two forms of liberty had to be combined. As the first French Republic died at the hands of Bonaparte, Constant's *Republican Constitution* outlined both the justification and the constitutional architecture for a liberal republic.

Constant's *Republican Constitution* was indelibly marked by the Napoleonic experience. Constant was an active politician during the years he worked on the manuscript, and his experiences in the Tribunate clearly informed his more speculative deliberations. He had been wary of the Brumairian experiment to begin with, and his encounter with Bonaparte's growing authoritarianism only deepened his conviction that a republic alone could guarantee liberty.[103] As a result, *Republican Constitution* exhibited a fuller commitment both to republicanism as a form of government and to liberalism as a first-order political principle than had his Directorial

101. Vincent, "Benjamin Constant, the French Revolution, and the Origins of French Romantic Liberalism," *French Historical Studies* 23 (2000): 622.

102. The question of when Constant became a full-fledged liberal is a matter of some dispute in Constant scholarship. Etienne Hofmann and Marcel Gauchet both argue that he cannot be considered a liberal until 1806, when he composed the *Principles of Politics Applicable to All Governments,* a text that provided political-philosophical support for either a moderate republic or a constitutional monarchy. Hofmann, *Les "Principes de politique" de Benjamin Constant: La genèse d'une oeuvre et l'évolution de la pensée de leur auteur, 1789–1806,* 2 vols. (Geneva, 1980); Gauchet, "Constant," in *A Critical Dictionary of the French Revolution,* ed. François Furet and Mona Ozouf (Cambridge, Mass., 1989). Vincent, however, argues for Constant's Directorial writings as the crucial moment in defining his liberalism, "Benjamin Constant," esp. 609, while James Lee's dissertation "reasserts the importance of 1806" and the *Principles of Politics* because it was then that Constant "adopted the economic history of civilization" in his analysis. "Benjamin Constant: The Moralization of Modern Liberty" (PhD diss., University of Wisconsin, Madison, 2003), 50–51.

103. See his well-known letter to Sieyès on 19 Brumaire warning that Bonaparte posed a threat to liberty. AN, 284 AP 16, d. 3.

writings. The text's argument that a republic was the best form of government to guarantee the liberty of the individual challenged the Brumairian line that modern social and economic forms demand a government providing order, basic civil liberties, and little more. Whereas key Brumairians such as Roederer and Sieyès believed that the modern world made political liberty irrelevant, even an irritant, Constant feared that such a perspective could enable dictatorial rule.

On the Possibility of a Republican Constitution in a Large Country was Constant's first attempt at a methodical political-philosophical treatise. All his previous writings were composed in relation to a specific political dispute or issue and lacked the work's systematicity and scope. While his political pamphlets of the Directory dealt with questions of sovereignty, arbitrary authority, and constitutional government and at moments seemed to reveal an underlying political-philosophical position, they tended to jumble together a range of political arguments and never approached the scale, ambition, or overall coherence of *Republican Constitution.* The project furthermore stands out in Constant's oeuvre as his first attempt to outline a specific institutional project, to engage, as Lucien Jaume puts it, with "the more institutional side of the search for 'guarantees.'"[104] Constant's ambition in the text is clear. He delineates a full-blown constitutional structure for a republic in a large country and strikes an ongoing dialogue with three principal references: Aristotle's *Politics,* Machiavelli's *Discourses on Livy,* and Montesquieu's *Spirit of the Laws.*[105] However, Constant's *Republican Constitution* is best read as an extension of the problems Staël had posed in *On the Current Circumstances That Could End the Revolution and the Principles That Should Found the Republic in France,* perhaps even as an extension of the text itself.[106] As James Livesey perceptively observes, Constant was prone to "a kind of shallow eclecticism" and "was rescued from these dead ends by Germaine de Staël's sharper appreciation of the connection

104. Lucien Jaume, *L'individu effacé ou le paradoxe du libéralisme français* (Paris, 1997), 64. See also Stephen Holmes, *Benjamin Constant and The Making of Modern Liberalism* (New Haven, 1984), chap. 5.

105. Sánchez-Mejía, introduction to Constant, *De la possibilité,* 372.

106. As discussed in chapter 3, Constant had edited Staël's text. See Lucia Omacini's introduction to *Des circonstances actuelles qui peuvent terminer la révolution et des principes qui doivent fonder la république en France,* by Germaine de Staël, ed. Omacini (Geneva, 1979), lxvii–lxx, lxxxii–lxxxiv.

between moral plurality and the health of a modern republic, and of the need to defend moral plurality and the republic in principle, rather than pragmatically."[107] Both Staël's and Constant's texts took up the problem of institutionalizing liberal guarantees in a republican political order, the only kind, in their eyes, that could prevent those guarantees from disappearing at the hands of a tyrant. Both Staël and Constant urged in uncompromising language the establishment of republican constitutional government as the only alternative and antidote to despotism.

Constant was unwavering in *Republican Constitution* that the republic was the only form of government capable of guaranteeing liberty. In the constitution he laid out, "the citizens govern themselves."[108] He reinforced this claim and challenged the antirepublican drift of the Consulate by refuting the commonplace argument that monarchies are more peaceful and stable than republics. Although Bonaparte was not a monarch, the justifications for his rule and for his becoming Consul for Life and then Emperor increasingly echoed the standard early modern arguments for a monarchy over a republic—namely, that monarchies provide peace and prosperity while republics are permanently plagued by political turmoil.[109] Constant charged those who made such claims with a "basic fallacy" in their comparisons: "One examines monarchy only when it is gentle. When it is violent, one does not have the ability to examine it. Monarchies oppress in quiet, in detail, without noise, without upheaval. Republics oppress with popular movements, in storms and en masse, which renders their calamities more noteworthy." The quiet oppression of monarchies, he continued, is no less serious than the more noisy injustices of republics. "When monarchical government is violent, it kills public spirit. It follows that individual injustices, provoking no opposition, make no noise. But the tragedy is no less for the objects of these injustices." Furthermore, Constant explained, when republics are violent it is always the literate classes and other eminent figures who are harmed, while in a monarchy it is the general population who suffers. Because republics hurt those who tend to be remembered by

107. James Livesey, *Making Democracy in the French Revolution* (Cambridge, Mass., 2001), 82.

108. *Fragments,* 449.

109. See Lentz, *Le Grand Consulat, 1799–1804,* chap. 14; Woloch, *Napoleon and His Collaborators,* chap. 4.

posterity, a sort of class-informed bias against republics has been fashioned. In a republic, he wrote,

> Under the despotism of factions, in the middle of the turmoil of anarchy, eminent figures are in greater danger. Under monarchies, oppression hangs, irreparably, over those who are little known.
>
> The tyranny of governments that call themselves republican is directed against the enlightened classes, those who speak, who write, who dispute. Monarchy strengthens its yoke over the mute and resigned classes.[110]

For Constant, then, a monarchy was by nature a deeply violent and oppressive polity. He argued that a republic, by contrast, if properly organized with a good constitution, would provide more peace, tranquillity, and liberty than even the best of monarchies.

Constant further bolstered his argument for the republic as the best form of government by undermining the traditional claim that a republic could exist only in a small territory—hence the title of his manuscript, *On the Possibility of a Republican Constitution in a Large Country.* Constant argued that a republican constitution could thrive in France, despite the country's great size, because of the institution of representative government. To choose the nation's representatives, Constant outlined two distinct voting procedures, one for the nation's bicameral legislature and the other for its multiheaded executive (the legislature and executive will be described in detail below). Both procedures were carefully calibrated to prevent the undue influence of either "the people" or organized factions. The representatives in the legislature would be chosen in what Constant termed "popular elections." However, he stipulated, only "men possessing a fully independent revenue" would be eligible to vote. In each district, those who qualified to vote would decide on a slate of fifty candidates. One hundred large-property holders would then choose five of those fifty to stand for election. The original group of eligible voters would finish the procedure by electing the actual representative from among those five. He devised this procedure to ensure that the small group of large-property holders would carry more weight—he plainly rejected direct popular election—but also to make sure that those property holders would not

110. *Fragments,* 217–18.

dominate the electoral procedure. For the executive, he devised a parallel but substantially more restrictive procedure: the large-property holders of each department would name "a certain number" of candidates; one house of the legislature would reduce the number of candidates; the large-property holders would then reduce the number again; and, finally, the second legislative house would choose from among those left.[111]

Despite the obvious restrictiveness of Constant's schema, he strongly believed that popular political participation was necessary in a republic. The recent experiences of the Revolution, he feared, had discredited popular election despite the fact that "all the ancient writers and modern experiences testify in its favor." The people, he noted with reference to Machiavelli and Montesquieu, whom he referred to as "the two leading political philosophers of modern times," possess an "admirable instinct" for choosing representatives who will convey their will and defend their interests. Moreover, he argued, popular participation would help the people feel connected to their representatives and to the decisions of their government. "Popular election alone can invest the national representation with true strength and give it deep roots in opinion.... Without popular election, the citizens of a country will never have the sentiment of their own importance, which presents to them the glory and the liberty of their patrie as the most precious portion of their individual patrimony. Without popular election, the representative system is only miserable parody." More deeply still, Constant believed that a certain amount of political activity was necessary to prevent a nation from sliding into despotism. Sounding some of the most republican notes of his entire oeuvre, Constant praised the effects of political activity on a nation's population. At one point in *Republican Constitution* he even suggested, in a comment on Montesquieu's *The Greatness of the Romans and Their Decline,* that factions are "useful" in a republic as long as they stem from the ambitions of individuals and not from hereditary corporations. Here he agreed with Montesquieu that, as Constant paraphrased it, when a republic is too "tranquil...one can be sure that liberty does not exist." In a passage that was clearly penned in reaction to Bonaparte's utter evisceration of France's political life, Constant argued

111. Ibid., 318, 251–52.

that active politics, even if they produce some disorder, are necessary to save a nation from despotism-enabling torpor.

> For the sentiment of liberty to enter into the soul of the people, it is perhaps necessary that liberty sometimes take comprehensible forms, vulgar, angry, and loud forms. I prefer that a few unexpected accidents result than, if by the absence of such forms, the nation were to become indifferent and disheartened. When the nation loses interest in its rights, the executive power frees itself from its limits and launches nonsensical wars, gets away with illegal persecutions. If you object that some men will suffer misfortune or perish, crushed by the mob or in an unexpected brawl, I would ask if those who are deported to far-off, deserted beaches, those that the whim of a single man sends across the seas for murderous expeditions, those that cram the prisons, do not perish.
>
> These things can be stopped only by a freely elected national representation.[112]

The tribute to active politics in this passage speaks volumes about the extent to which Bonaparte's rise and consolidation of power affirmed for Constant the importance of promoting political life and thus caused him to reprise key themes of the republican tradition. Without an active political life, he ventured, a nation would always be susceptible to a Bonaparte.

Constant thought that active politics could best preserve liberty if structured by a republican constitution. In other words, just as a healthy republic required an active political life, political life required the proper institutional framework to prevent it from becoming destructive. A balance between politics and institutions was crucial for Constant. Also crucial was balance within the republic's institutional architecture. Toward this end, the republican constitution that Constant designed had three powers: a legislative, an executive, and a "preserving power" (*pouvoir préservateur*) to keep the first two in a state of balance.[113] Constant considered the legislative power the most important, calling it "the first in rank and dignity." Its function was to "express the national will." Like the Council of Five Hundred and the Council of Elders under the Directory,

112. Ibid., 291–92, 300, 301, 143, 319–20.
113. Constant explicitly argued that the judicial power was not a political power. Ibid., 149.

there would be two legislative chambers, one charged with proposition and discussion and the other with "the sanction of laws." The function of the executive power, in turn, was "the realization of this national will, as expressed by the legislative power." The executive power, again like under the Directory, was to be a multiheaded "complex" power. Such complexity, argued Constant, would inoculate the executive power against falling prey to the machinations of any given individual. Moreover, it would transport the principle of constitutional balance inside the executive power; Constant claimed that unity within the executive would sacrifice the more general principle of balance. Unlike under the Directory, however, the executive power would be able to propose and veto legislation and thus balance the legislative power to a significant degree. This advocacy of a complex executive power demonstrates the extent to which the experience of Bonaparte's rule reaffirmed for Constant the danger of the executive and caused him to reprise the long-standing republican critique of executive power. It also differentiated him from Staël and so many others in and around the republican center who had come to feel, after the years of the Directory, that a strong executive was needed to provide political stability. In Constant's eyes, a unified executive posed a far greater threat to the nation's liberty than any complex executive ever could. While the executive power Constant advocated in *Republican Constitution* would possess more authority than the Executive Directory, there was no doubt that Constant feared the excesses of the executive power far more than he feared those of the legislative. An entire book of the text is titled "Of the natural abuses of the executive power" (book VII). Commenting on contemporary "distrust of the legislative power," he accused his contemporaries of overlearning the lessons of "our recent misfortunes." Despite the history of the National Convention, the legislative power, in his eyes, was the true bastion of people's liberty:

> These days, people are disposed to deny in theory and in practice this supremacy of the legislative power over the executive power.... Among us, the inversion of everything that has existed until now has often made the legislative power the oppressor, and sometimes the executive power has seemed to be a safeguard against oppression.... It is necessary, without doubt, to give great strength to the executive power; but it is no less indisputable that, according to the principles of liberty, that is, in all constitutions that identify

> their origin in the national will, the legislative power and the assemblies that are its agent are the first of the powers.[114]

In this passage, we can clearly see the extent to which Constant's *On the Possibility of a Republican Constitution in a Large Country* was marked by the experience of Bonaparte's usurpation of power and the extent to which it remained within the republican tradition.

Perhaps the most innovative aspect of Constant's constitution was a "preserving or neutral power" that was meant to be an improvement on Sieyès's constitutional jury of 1795 and the Senate of the Constitution of the Year VIII. The idea for an institution of this type had been in the air for some time, and in *On the Current Circumstances That Could End the Revolution and the Principles That Should Found the Republic in France* Staël had advocated a variation, to be called the Conserving Body. The preserving power that Constant proposed in *Republican Constitution* would keep the peace between the legislative and executive powers. "It is essential," Constant wrote, "to create a power with interests distinct from those of the legislative power and the executive power, and organized such that its own need will be not to undermine these two eternal rivals but to maintain equilibrium and harmony between them."[115] The preserving power points to one of Constant's central concerns in *Republican Constitution:* the abuse of power by the respective branches of government. Indeed, the manuscript is riddled with anxieties about the abuses to which the various powers of government are naturally prone. In the words of Marcel Gauchet, the text displays "a defensive systematicity. The problem of the organization of powers is envisaged exclusively under the angle of the *abuses* that they are likely to commit and the *guarantees* that can oppose them."[116] In this regard, Constant organized the government in a largely negative fashion, more concerned with thwarting the possible abuse of power than with the positive, potentially edifying, functions a government might be able to carry out.

The liberal underpinnings of Constant's *Republican Constitution* can be seen most pronouncedly in the declared overriding purpose of the

114. Ibid., 151, 447, 151, 231–36, 244, 151–53.

115. Ibid., 375.

116. Marcel Gauchet, *La Révolution des pouvoirs: La souveraineté, le peuple, et la représentation, 1789–1799* (Paris, 1995), 243.

constitutional architecture Constant proposed: the preservation of individual liberties. He stated plainly at the end of the manuscript that "everything done by a government organized in this way is on behalf of the individual."[117] His concern with the preservation of individual liberties is present throughout the text. For example, among three "natural abuses" of executive power that Constant outlined, he included "arbitrary attacks on the liberty of citizens." "Partial oppressions" of citizens' liberties, he wrote, "are in the nature, in the personal interest of the individuals who exercise executive power." As a counterbalance, Constant proposed an independent judiciary and absolutely inviolable trial by jury.[118] The reason for such an overarching emphasis on civil liberties was that by the time he composed *On the Possibility of a Republican Constitution in a Large Country,* Constant felt that the purpose of the republic was to allow individuals to pursue their own ends—what he later dubbed "the liberty of the moderns." He did not explore in any depth questions of individual ends in *Republican Constitution*—he assumed both their priority and their plurality without delving into the matter—but did so at length in his *Principles of Politics Applicable to All Governments,* which was conceived as something of a companion to the work and composed beginning in 1806. Notable among these individual ends was commerce. Not only was commerce one of the great intellectual and political questions of the day, but Constant, it is worth remembering, spent 1783–85 in Edinburgh, where he was certainly exposed to procommercial ideas among the famous Scottish thinkers of the day.[119] A revealing window into Constant's thinking about commerce at this time is provided by a description in his diary of a discussion he had with August Wilhelm Schlegel on 27 May 1804 about "commerce and its consequences." Schlegel, he wrote, "is one of those men who, never having had to engage with real life, believe that everything is done by prescriptions and laws without thinking of the struggle that persecutory laws provoke between citizens and authority." Such "Spartan ideas," he continued, "are crazy in modern civilization where needs have become part of our existence.... If they governed, Robespierre would begin again, with the best intentions in

117. *Fragments,* 449; see also 451–52.

118. Ibid., 323–25, 333–40, 401.

119. The Scottish influence is emphasized by Biancamaria Fontana, *Benjamin Constant and the Post-Revolutionary Mind* (New Haven, 1991); and Lee, "Benjamin Constant."

the world."[120] In this diary entry from 1804 we can see almost fully enunciated the critique of emphasizing ancient liberty at the expense of modern liberty that would constitute one-half of Constant's famous analysis in 1819 and that Théremin and Staël had each articulated before him.

In the final analysis, Benjamin Constant aimed in *Republican Constitution* to conceive a republican form of government in which individual, modern liberty would flourish. The manuscript outlines a constitutional architecture for a liberal republic. Much of its language of balance and advocacy of an active political life reprised key features of the early modern classical-republican tradition. *Republican Constitution,* however, was clearly not a classical-republican text. The text's overriding emphasis on the individual, specifically individual civil liberty, places it squarely within the developing liberal tradition.[121] Yet Constant's liberalism at this time was deeply inflected with republican principles. It was, in other words, a liberal republicanism. Penned largely in response to Bonaparte's growing authoritarianism, Benjamin Constant's *On the Possibility of a Republican Constitution in a Large Country* limned the central kernel of the liberal-republican political philosophy that would flower in France during the first half of the nineteenth century.

120. *Journaux intimes,* 134.

121. In addition, the text's strong underlying commitment to the possibility of collective human perfectibility broke with the classical-republican tradition. Constant viewed perfection not as an individual trait but as a collective one. An entry in his diary describing a conversation with Villers is revealing in this regard. "Spoke with Villers for two hours.... How he believes in the influence of books and the possibility of improving men! I also believe in perfectibility, but not so individually. The centuries passing lead to it, but each individual man contributes only in an imperceptible manner." Ibid, 311–12.

Epilogue

The Fate of French Liberal Republicanism

Liberalism, in a now familiar story, suffered a tragic fate in modern France, never gaining intellectual or political hegemony as it did in the Anglophone world. Following the demise of the First Republic, French history was marked by a series of nonliberal political regimes ranging from the Restoration monarchy to the radical republicanism of the Second Republic to the Bonapartist regime of the Second Empire to the cautious republicanism of the Third Republic. This story of liberalism's failure, however, was punctuated by towering intellectual achievement, especially during the first half of the nineteenth century.[1] Benjamin Constant, Pierre-Paul Royer-Collard, François Guizot, and Alexis de Tocqueville, to cite just the most prominent names, articulated a rich array of liberal political principles during these years. Liberal republicanism in particular reached its peak in Constant's "The Liberty of the Ancients Compared with That

1. On liberalism in nineteenth-century France, see in particular Lucien Jaume, *L'individu effacé ou le paradoxe du libéralisme français* (Paris, 1997).

of the Moderns" (1819) and, shortly after the Restoration, in Alexis de Tocqueville's *Democracy in America* (1835 and 1840). The respective efforts of Constant and Tocqueville constituted the culmination of French liberal republicanism as well as two of the most profound and celebrated attempts in the history of political philosophy to articulate liberal political principles.

Liberalism's crowning moment in nineteenth-century France came during the Bourbon Restoration, when a loosely united liberal school published a series of brilliant treatises, took up seats in the Chamber of Deputies, and even helped to lead the July Revolution of 1830. Restoration liberals, in both parliament and in the press, fought the resurgent ultraroyalists on the key issues of the day, such as the status of the Church, freedom of the press, suffrage, trial by jury, and the very nature of the Constitutional Charter.[2] Between 1817 and 1820, they even managed to implement important aspects of their legislative agenda.

In fact, not one but two competing liberal traditions emerged in Restoration France, paralleling the two competing strands of liberalism that had materialized at the end of the Directory. Post-Terror liberal republicanism enjoyed a second life in the writings of Constant, Daunou, and Lanjuinais, while the liberal authoritarianism of Roederer and Sieyès, and of the Physiocrats before them, issued in the rationalist liberalism of Guizot, Royer-Collard, and the Doctrinaires. The liberal republicans continued to articulate a liberalism deeply marked by classical republican values as they feared a renewed evisceration of politics of the sort that had happened under Napoleon. Guizot and the Doctrinaires, conversely, valorized "the sovereignty of reason" over and above politics.[3] The two schools could agree on a number of specific issues, but their most basic political values

2. Promulgated by Louis XVIII upon his return to the throne in 1814, the *Charte constitutionnelle* established full civil equality and a division of powers among the king, a hereditary Chamber of Peers, and a Chamber of Deputies elected by France's upper echelon of property holders (strict tax thresholds both to hold a seat and to vote meant that only ten thousand French citizens qualified to sit in the chamber and but one hundred thousand to vote). However, the charter assigned to the king full executive power, the right to dissolve the Chamber of Deputies, and the dominant share of legislative power as the monarch alone could propose laws, the two chambers subsequently voted on the proposed legislation, and then the king ratified the law in question.

3. On Guizot and the Doctrinaires, see Pierre Rosanvallon, *Le moment Guizot* (Paris, 1985); and Aurelian Craiutu, *Liberalism under Siege: The Political Thought of the French Doctrinaires* (Lanham, Md., 2003).

diverged substantially. The two competing strands of early nineteenth-century French liberalism thus had direct roots, both personal and intellectual, in the post-Terror years.

In some ways, the divide between the two schools was generational. The "new" liberals of the nineteenth century, those who had not experienced the Revolution at first hand, gravitated toward Guizot and the Doctrinaires. The veterans of the Revolution, specifically of the post-Terror years, for the most part remained committed to a liberalism inflected by republican themes. Having lived through or witnessed the liberal Revolution of 1789–91, the crisis years of 1792–94, the failed attempts to refound the republic from 1794 to 1799, and, finally, the Napoleonic disaster that ended once and for all at Waterloo on 18 June 1815, these revolutionary veterans remained committed to both liberal principles and the republic as a political value. As Constant professed to Daunou, his "dear former colleague," when sending him a copy of the fourth edition of his *On the Spirit of Conquest and Usurpation and Their Relation to European Civilization* in July of 1814, he had remained true to "my old principles."[4]

In practical political terms, liberal republicanism lost out to rationalist liberalism as the years 1814–48 came to be dominated by the towering figure of François Guizot (and as Guizot drifted to the political right, ultimately leading to his immortalization in the opening lines of Karl Marx's *Communist Manifesto*). Liberal republicanism nonetheless remained an important political idiom in the writings and parliamentary speeches of those liberals grouped around Constant, Daunou, and Lanjuinais. Although not always in agreement with one another, Restoration liberal republicans sought to protect individual liberties and preserve a minimally active political life. Given the political realities of the day, they had to assume a more modest or "negative" stance and focus on the preservation of individual liberties rather than the construction of a more robustly political polity. Openly calling for a republic or reforming the monarchy too far along republican lines was illegal, so the liberal republicans advocated constitutional monarchy with full liberal guarantees and significant republican overtones. Restoration liberal republicanism was thus, on the whole, more liberal than republican. However, while their first priority during the

4. Constant to Daunou, 8 July 1814, BN, Nouv. Acqu. Fr. 21881, f. 222.

Restoration was a strong and inviolable program of individual liberties, the liberal republicans simultaneously retained a strong faith in politics and institutions. They repeatedly invoked the importance of regular elections, constitutional balance, and other staple features of liberal republicanism. The result was an admixture often more liberal than republican but nonetheless distinctly liberal republican in nature. This is most clear in three prominent tracts published by Pierre-Claude-François Daunou, Jean-Denis Lanjuinais, and Benjamin Constant in 1818 and 1819, the years when liberals enjoyed the most influence and passed important legislation concerning electoral law, the organization of the military, and the freedom of the press.

Along the spectrum of Restoration liberal republicanism, perhaps the farthest to the liberal end was Daunou's *Essai sur les garanties individuelles que réclame l'état actuel de la société (Essay on the Individual Guarantees That the Current State of Society Demands).* Originally published as a series of articles in the journal *Le Censeur européen* in 1818 and then in book form in 1819, Daunou's text constituted a forceful defense of what he called "individual guarantees" against the potential abuse of power by the state. In making his argument, Daunou rejected any recourse to natural rights or what he referred to as "abstract principles," instead simply claiming that such "guarantees" were embedded in contemporary language and thus "the ideas and sentiments of civilized humanity." "Guarantees," for Daunou, meant civil liberty. He explicitly placed political liberty secondary to civil liberty, writing that citizen participation in the formation of the law mattered only as a defensive "means necessary to prevent the state of the subject from being transformed into servitude." In other words, political liberty was important only as a safeguard for civil liberty, that is, for instrumental reasons rather than as a good in itself. However, Daunou also sounded more republican notes in stipulating that a regularly elected legislature was indispensable to the preservation of individual guarantees and that the population itself should vigilantly resist any attempt to undermine those guarantees.[5] Calling for citizen participation and responsibility in this way was significantly more republican than anything Guizot and the Doctrinaires, for example, would have allowed. Daunou also revealed more

5. Pierre-Claude-François Daunou, *Essai sur les garanties individuelles que réclame l'état actuel de la société* [1819] (Paris, 2000), 63, 68, 162, 171–72.

republican instincts in his private notes, in which, at one point during the Restoration, he drafted a constitution that would have established a considerably more republican political order in France.[6] Daunou's draft constitution located sovereign authority in the nation and not the monarchy—the preamble read "the French nation, exercising its sovereign rights, gives itself the following constitution"—and substantially reduced the powers of the king by placing legislative power almost entirely in an elected legislative body and Senate. A critical feature of Daunou's draft constitution was that legislation could be passed over and above monarchical authority, as the king could not veto a law but only suspend it for one year, after which the Senate could then overrule the king and ratify the legislation.[7] The king's real sovereignty would be limited to executive power, which he possessed fully. Daunou's proposed constitution would have made Restoration France, like the England described by Montesquieu, "a nation where the republic hides under the form of a monarchy"—but even more so.[8] Daunou, while clearly more liberal than republican at this point, nonetheless continued to adhere to certain core republican values.

A more republican example of Restoration liberal republicanism was Lanjuinais's *Constitutions de la nation française (Constitutions of the French Nation).* Published in 1819, the text advanced a liberal-republican interpretation of the charter intended to bolster legislative authority as well as enshrine more traditional liberal concerns such as freedom of the press and trial by jury. Lanjuinais argued that all legitimate governments recognize the "national will" as their "fundamental and constituent principle" and that "representative and constitutional... mixed governments" are the highest form of the state. The key for Lanjuinais was that governments be "mixed" rather than "simple" because in the latter power is by definition "absolute" and thus turns into "despotism." Lanjuinais essentially effaced the distinction between monarchy and republic, writing that "the determination of republic suits any constitutional and representative government." Thus, the best form of government, the highest form of the

6. N.d., BN, Nouv. Acqu. Fr. 21907, f. 270–71.

7. In Daunou's draft constitution, legislation would be proposed by either the king or a tribune drawn from the legislative body and then passed by both the legislative body and the Senate. The king could then exercise the one-year "suspension" in question.

8. Charles-Louis de Secondat, baron de Montesquieu, *De l'esprit des lois* [1748], in *Oeuvres complètes,* ed. Roger Caillois, 2 vols. (Paris, 1949–51), 2:304.

evolution of the state, is one that resembles a republic: a mixed, representative constitution. After this potentially provocative analysis, Lanjuinais argued later in the text that the charter was in fact a mixed, representative constitution composed of two "sovereign powers," the legislative and the executive, which "must never be combined in the same individual or the same body, being destined to reciprocally balance and watch over one another.... Without the separation of these two powers, without the surveillance of one by the other, [and] without the division of the legislative power into several branches, there will be despotism."[9] This was clearly a tendentious interpretation intended to alter the spirit of the charter, which had expressly combined the entire executive power and a substantial share of legislative power in the person of the king. Earlier, in 1816, Lanjuinais had similarly attempted to increase legislative authority by insisting in the Chamber of Peers that the legislative power should have the prerogative to propose laws.[10] Lanjuinais's goal, it seems, was to republicanize the charter by strengthening legislative authority. At the same time, Lanjuinais also remained committed to liberal principles, devoting over one hundred pages of *Constitutions of the French Nation* to discussing the "individual rights or 'private rights' of the French." If followed, Lanjuinais's interpretation of the charter would have rendered France a liberal-republican state.

The most striking example of Restoration liberal republicanism, however, was undoubtedly Benjamin Constant's lecture given to the Athénée royal de Paris in February of 1819, "The Liberty of the Ancients Compared with That of the Moderns." Reprising the Directorial arguments of Théremin and Staël, Constant devoted the bulk of his lecture to explaining that, with the advent of commercial civilization, modern liberty had superseded ancient liberty. The latter, which he defined as "the sharing of social power among the citizens of the same patrie," was simply unsuitable

9. Jean-Denis Lanjuinais, *Constitutions de la nation française, avec une essai de traité historique et politique sur la Charte, et un recueil de pièces corrélatives,* 2 vols. (Paris, 1819), 1:13, 16, 14, 182–83. Lanjuinais was remarkably consistent in championing "mixed government," having done so in 1795 on the Commission of Eleven that drafted the Constitution of the Year III and, before then, in 1788 when he wrote that "we cherish that mixed form [of government] so desired by the ancient political writers, so applauded by the moderns." Quoted in G. A. Kelley, "Liberalism and Aristocracy in the French Restoration," *Journal of the History of Ideas* 26 (1965): 518.

10. As quoted in Jean-Paul Clément, *Aux sources du libéralisme français: Boissy d'Anglas, Daunou, Lanjuinais* (Paris, 2000), 121.

for the modern, commercial world. "The aim of the moderns is security in the enjoyment of private pleasures; and they call liberty the guarantees accorded by institutions to these pleasures." In the modern world, "individual existence is less absorbed in political existence" and "we can no longer enjoy the liberty of the ancients." However, after his seemingly unequivocal argument in favor of modern liberty, Constant then announced that "far from renouncing either of the two types of liberty,... we must... learn to combine the one with the other," and, in conclusion, all but reversed course with an arresting paean to the liberty of the ancients.[11]

While the modern, commercial world had introduced novel wants and desires, Constant explained, this new focus on "private pleasures" involved danger and loss. It was dangerous because exclusive preoccupation with the liberty of the moderns would allow the power of the government to grow unchecked. "The danger of modern liberty is that, absorbed in the enjoyment of our private independence, and in the pursuit of our particular interests, we would relinquish too easily our right to share in political power." Those in power, "the trustees of authority," as Constant called them, are only too eager to "to urge us to do so." It involved loss, Constant continued, because the pursuit of individual happiness alone would neglect "the better part of our nature." Modern people must treasure political liberty because only the liberty of the ancients can foster the moral improvement of humanity. "Political liberty is the most powerful, the most vigorous means of improvement that heaven has given us." Moreover, "political liberty," by compelling citizens to "examine and study their most sacred interests, enlarges their spirit [and] ennobles their thoughts."[12] Constant even goes on to say, with reference to his friend Sismondi's *Histoire des républiques italiennes du moyen âge (History of the Italian Republics of the Middle Ages),* a text that emphasized the importance of political institutions in history, that institutions alone can achieve the moral improvement of humanity.[13] "Institutions... must accomplish the destiny of humankind. They can best achieve their purpose by elevating the largest possible number of citizens

11. Benjamin Constant, "De la liberté des anciens comparée à celle des modernes" [1819], in *Écrits politiques,* ed. Marcel Gauchet, 2d ed. (Paris, 1997), 603, 603, 615, 602, 618.

12. Ibid., 616–17.

13. See Jean-Charles-Leonard Simonde de Sismondi, *Histoire des républiques italiennes du moyen âge,* 8 vols. (Zurich, 1807–9).

to the highest moral dignity." And it is the duty of the legislator to ensure that they do so.

> The work of the legislator is not complete when he has simply made the people peaceful. Even when the people are happy, there remains much to do. Institutions must achieve the moral education of the citizens. While respecting citizens' individual rights, looking after their independence, and not disturbing their work, institutions must nonetheless consecrate citizens' influence over public affairs, call them to contribute to the exercise of power by their determinations and by their votes, and guarantee them a right of control and surveillance by the expression of their opinions. Institutions, by forming citizens in this way, by practical experience, give them both the desire and the ability to fulfill these noble functions.[14]

Constant's lecture thus reached a stunning conclusion. While the march of history has turned people to the liberty of the moderns, the liberty of the ancients in fact reflects "the better part of our nature," public and not private considerations are people's "most sacred interests," and the citizenry's "influence over public affairs" should be purposely, even didactically, cultivated. Politics is necessary to fulfill human nature, and it is the duty of the legislator to form citizens who will not neglect their political liberty and "the exercise of power." Constant's lecture to the Athénée royal in 1819, so often described as the apogee of liberalism in France, in fact reprised the republican currents that ran so strongly through *On the Possibility of a Republican Constitution in a Large Country.* It advanced a robustly republican version of liberal republicanism.[15]

French liberal republicanism culminated, and perhaps ended, in Alexis de Tocqueville's *Democracy in America,* published in two volumes in 1835 and 1840.[16] Arguably France's greatest liberal political philosopher, Tocqueville combined a commitment to modern liberty with a steadfast belief in the importance of a vigorous political life in a manner that strongly echoed

14. Constant, "De la liberté des anciens," 618–19.

15. On the broader series of lectures Constant gave to the Athénée royal de Paris, others of which emphasized the importance of an active political life, see Alain Laquièze, "Benjamin Constant et les lectures à l'Athénée royal consacrées à la Constitution anglaise," *Annales Benjamin Constant* 23–24 (2000): 155–71, esp. 160.

16. Jean-Fabien Spitz's recent *Le moment républicain en France* (Paris, 2005), however, argues for a vital liberal-republican "moment" at the end of the nineteenth century.

the central concerns of post-Terror liberal republicanism. In this context, it is worth noting that Tocqueville, as a historian, was particularly interested in the post-Terror period. His notes for the never completed second volume of *The Old Regime and the Revolution* devoted a great deal of attention to the years after the Terror, and he was particularly interested in Benjamin Constant's political pamphlets from the time.[17] Tocqueville, perhaps even more than Constant, represents a bridge between the classical-republican and the modern liberal traditions. His principal concerns were the lurking menace of despotism and the threat posed to individual liberty and distinctiveness by the age of equality, but the antidotes he recommended were drawn from an older, more political tradition of thinking about the polity. In an important sense, Tocqueville stands as the last classical thinker while also introducing a new set of concerns to the Western political-philosophical tradition.

That Tocqueville was a liberal, if a "strange" one, all but goes without saying.[18] By virtually any set of criteria, Tocqueville professed liberal political values.[19] Less commonly appreciated, however, is his status as a *political* thinker. Tocqueville judged a robust political life the antidote to modern despotism, both the more visible despotism of a Napoleon and the "soft despotism" he thought Guizot and Louis-Philippe had created in July Monarchy France by effacing "political life itself."[20] The individualism and privatization he so feared were to be countered through the deliberate and pointed stimulation of politics. The political philosopher Sheldon Wolin has even argued that "the abiding concern of Tocqueville's thinking . . . was the revival of the political: in his phrase, *la chose publique*."[21] Wilhelm Hennis has similarly claimed that the principal question animating Tocqueville's

17. Alexis de Tocqueville, *L'Ancien Régime et la Révolution: Fragments et notes inédites sur la Révolution,* vol. 2, pt. 2 of *Oeuvres complètes,* ed. J.-P. Mayer, 17 vols. at present (Paris, 1951–); Robert Gannett, *Tocqueville Unveiled: The Historian and His Sources for* The Old Regime and the Revolution (Chicago, 2003), 32–35.

18. Roger Boesche, *The Strange Liberalism of Alexis de Tocqueville* (Ithaca, 1987).

19. E.g., Jack Lively, *The Social and Political Thought of Alexis de Tocqueville* (Oxford, 1962), esp. 10–11.

20. Quoted in Melvin Richter, "Tocqueville on Threats to Liberty in Democracies," in *The Cambridge Companion to Tocqueville,* ed. Cheryl B. Welch (Cambridge, 2006), 249. On Tocqueville's conception of "soft despotism," see Laurence Guellec, "L'énigmatique douceur du despotisme démocratique," *The Tocqueville Review/La Revue Tocqueville* 27 (2006): 103–17.

21. Sheldon Wolin, *Tocqueville between Two Worlds: The Making of a Political and Theoretical Life* (Princeton, 2001), 5.

thought was "the relationship between man and citizen,...the disjunction between the private and the public," which Hennis judges the central problem "for all truly political thought."[22] As Wolin and Hennis suggest, Tocqueville believed deeply in the value of politics itself. Near the end of *Democracy in America,* he states plainly that "my principal goal in writing this book has been to combat" the "penchants" of people in "democratic times" to immerse themselves in "private life" and thus abandon "public affairs" and "political life."[23] The weight Tocqueville accorded an active political life is precisely what made him a strange liberal. While Wolin argues that Tocqueville chose liberalism as "the vehicle...for realizing the political," a choice Wolin labels a "halting one,"[24] it would be more accurate to say that Tocqueville wanted to balance the two. Tocqueville thought politics and liberalism needed to realize each other—an equally halting choice and one that reflects the broader French liberal-republican tradition inaugurated during the post-Terror years and its debt to the early modern classical-republican tradition.

Tocqueville's enduring concern with politics and political life grew out of his basic diagnosis of the modern age, which, he famously wrote, was defined by democracy and equality. Equality and democracy were not a choice. Their age had arrived, by the hand of God. "The gradual development of the equality of conditions is therefore a providential fact....It is universal, it is durable, it every day eludes human power. Every event, like every individual, contributes to its development." Faced with this "providential fact," Tocqueville set out to understand democracy and the modern age. "The entire book," he explains, "was written in the grip of a kind of religious terror produced in the soul of the author by the sight of this irresistible revolution." There was no point in resisting democracy—"To want to stop democracy would appear...to struggle against God himself." Rather, the task facing Tocqueville's generation was to study democracy and, hopefully, "educate democracy."[25]

22. Wilhelm Hennis, "In Search of the 'New Science of Politics,'" in *Interpreting Tocqueville's* Democracy in America, ed. Ken Masugi (Savage, Md., 1991), 36. For analogous suggestions, see Gannett, *Tocqueville Unveiled,* 160; and Françoise Mélonio, *Tocqueville et les Français* (Paris, 1993).

23. Alexis de Tocqueville, *De la démocratie en Amérique,* vol. 1 of *Oeuvres complètes,* pt. 2, 300 (hereafter cited as *DA*).

24. Wolin, *Tocqueville between Two Worlds,* 6.

25. *DA,* pt. 1, 4–5.

Tocqueville's journey to America taught him that modern democracy was defined first and foremost by individualism and privatization. "Individualism," which Tocqueville contrasted to the older "egoism" or "selfishness" (*égoïsme*), he deemed to be a specifically modern phenomenon, "democratic in origin, and it threatens to develop as conditions become equal." The crucial, and arresting, fact about individualism was that it resulted in privatization and, consequently, the death of the polity. Citizens became immersed in their own private worlds and turned their back on public affairs. They focused exclusively on themselves and entrusted public matters to the government alone, which, in turn, became impersonal, abstract, and disconnected from the citizenry. Tocqueville defined individualism as "a considered and peaceful sentiment that disposes each citizen to isolate himself from the mass of his fellow citizens and to withdraw into a circle of family and friends, so that, after having created a little society for his own use, he gladly abandons society at large to itself."[26] In his draft notes for *Democracy in America* Tocqueville wrote, "Individualism—the habit of living isolated from one's fellows, of not concerning oneself with anything that is common business, of abandoning this care to the sole, clearly visible representative of common interests, which is the government."[27] Democracy itself was the root cause of this process, of individualism, privatization, and the collective abandonment of public affairs: "Democracy . . . constantly leads man back to himself and ultimately threatens to imprison him entirely in the loneliness of his own heart." In addition, the epoch's general drift toward privatization was amplified by the appetite for material well-being that characterized modern commercial societies. The end result of democracy's privatizing tendencies, Tocqueville warned, would be either "license or tyranny, anarchy or despotism. Both are equally to be feared and both can arise equally easily from one and the same cause, which is *general apathy,* the fruit of individualism."[28] Just as Constant and the post-Terror liberal republicans before him worried that the modern pursuit of private pleasures would result in widespread depoliticization, so Tocqueville feared the politically sedating effects of modern individualism and privatization.

26. *DA,* pt. 2, 105. See Jean-Claude Lamberti, *La notion d'individualisme chez Tocqueville* (Paris, 1970).

27. Quoted in James T. Schleifer, *The Making of Tocqueville's* Democracy in America (Chapel Hill, N.C., 1980), 253.

28. *DA,* pt. 2, 106, 348.

Tocqueville's analysis of individualism and privatization was in essence an analysis of democratic moeurs. It encompassed the panoply of habits, customs, morals, and manners—in short, the moeurs—that characterized modern democracy. Tocqueville was explicit in *Democracy in America* that he considered moeurs to be a society's foundational level, ahead of climate, laws, institutions, or any other factor. Moeurs were therefore to constitute the first level of analysis in any effort to understand a given society.[29] Moeurs, however, do not signify a prepolitical realm in *Democracy in America.* To the contrary, they are politically saturated. In this regard, his analytic approach shows his debt to the classical-republican tradition and to post-Terror liberal republicanism. His emphasis on moeurs and their fundamentally political character distinctly echoed the claims of the Directorial discourse of moeurs and its early modern classical-republican antecedents such as Rousseau, who avowed in his *Confessions* that "everything fundamentally depend[s] on politics."[30] At the same time, however, Tocqueville's understanding of the political nature of moeurs significantly modified that of Rousseau and the dominant strand of post-Terror thinking, as Tocqueville did not place the same emphasis on the role of the state in didactically forming moeurs (the passage from Rousseau's *Confessions* continues, "no people would ever be anything other than what its Government made of it").[31] Indeed, part of Tocqueville's genius was to see the politically saturated character of society and culture as separate from the state and thereby avoid a definition of politics as government. For Tocqueville, politics was everywhere, even prior to the state. Yet because moeurs were so deeply political for Tocqueville, he also avoided the base-superstructure type of relationship between a prepolitical culture or society and a differentiated level of politics that characterized so much of modern liberalism. In *Democracy in America,* moeurs and the state exist in a mutually interactive relationship, each influencing the other. Thus culture, while anterior to the state, is not anterior to politics but is itself deeply political.

29. "The importance of moeurs is a common truth that study and experience constantly return to. . . . I find it occupying a central place in my thinking, I notice it at the end of all my ideas." *DA,* pt. 1, 322–23.

30. Quoted in David A. Bell, *The Cult of the Nation in France: Inventing Nationalism, 1680–1800* (Cambridge, Mass., 2001), 145.

31. Ibid.

For all his pessimism about the deadening effects of individualism and privatization on the body politic, Tocqueville did think that their burgeoning weight could be offset by vigorous citizen commitment to public life—by the liberty of the ancients, in Constant's vocabulary. As Tocqueville bluntly put it, "To combat the evils that equality can produce, there is only one effective remedy: political freedom." Just as Constant believed the liberty of the moderns had to be offset by a renewed dedication to the liberty of the ancients, so Tocqueville thought that individualism and privatization had to be checked by robust civic politics. Specifically, Tocqueville believed that the institutions and practices he witnessed in America created an engaged citizenry that did not forsake public affairs. The townships and local government, the jury system, and the associational life he described, to take three prominent examples, all promoted civic consciousness; they "continuously remind each citizen, in a thousand ways, that he lives in society."[32] In other words, they collectively served as a powerful counterpoise to modern privatization. "Communal institutions," he wrote in his notes, "not only teach the *art to make use of liberty,* they also form the *genuine taste for liberty.*"[33] And, writing of "communal spirit" in New England, Tocqueville praised the "care" taken "to *scatter* power in order to interest more people in public affairs" and promote "political existence." As a result, "the life of the community makes itself felt, in a way, at every instant. It manifests itself every day by the fulfillment of a duty or by the exercise of a right."[34] Tocqueville's belief in the importance of political freedom can also be seen in *The Old Regime and the Revolution,* in which he suggested that the monarchy was able to impose its despotism on France precisely because the nobility turned inward and failed to resist the centralizing absolutist state—because, in other words, the nobility became the very picture of mediocrity and acquiescence and thereby abandoned its own form of civic engagement.[35]

Tocqueville did not believe that citizen commitment to public life demanded civic virtue in the classical sense of individuals consciously

32. *DA,* pt. 2, 112.

33. N.d., Tocqueville Manuscripts, Beinecke Rare Book and Manuscript Library, Yale University, C.V.e.8.

34. *DA,* pt. 1, 66–67.

35. *L'Ancien Régime et la Révolution* [1856], vol. 2, pt. 1 of *Oeuvres complètes.*

sacrificing their own interests for the greater good. Rather, it necessitated a more modern understanding of political virtue that focused on the effects of behavior rather than the cause. In an important passage in his notes, Tocqueville mused that Montesquieu's famous dictum that virtue is the "principle" and thus the lifeblood of republics did not require the motives of the population to be virtuous, only that the effects of their behavior be virtuous.

> Americans do not form a virtuous people and yet they are free. This does not prove absolutely that virtue, as Montesquieu thought of it, is not essential to the existence of republics. One must not take Montesquieu's idea in a narrow sense. What this great man wanted to say is that republics can survive only by the action of society on itself. What he understands by virtue is the moral power that each individual exercises on himself and that prevents him from violating the rights of others. When this triumph of honor over temptation is the result of the weakness of temptation or the calculation of personal interest, it does not constitute virtue in the eyes of the moralist. But it fits with Montesquieu's idea, who spoke of the effect much more than its cause.

The essence of Tocqueville's reflections here is that the category political virtue should not be defined narrowly, but can be understood as a description of people's actions without worrying about their motives. Political virtue can be a mode of behavior, not a deeper moral stance. "In America," Tocqueville continued, "it is not virtue that is great, it is temptation that is small, which amounts to the same thing. It is not disinterestedness that is great, it is interest that is well understood, which amounts to almost the same thing. Montesquieu was therefore right, although he spoke of ancient virtue, and what he said of the Greeks and Romans applies as well to the Americans."[36] Tocqueville thus believed, following Montesquieu and the received wisdom of the classical-republican tradition, that virtue was necessary for republics, including the American republic, but he redefined the principle of virtue in what might be thought of as more modern terms (and attributes this definition to Montesquieu). Moreover, for Tocqueville, modern virtue, like classical, has to be fashioned by political institutions and legislation.

36. N.d., Tocqueville Manuscripts, C.V.e., 12–13.

Americans were led to step outside their narrow private worlds, take up public matters, and imagine issues from others' perspectives by the deliberate creation of a shared political life. America's legislators, to counteract the encroaching effects of individualism and privatization, had virtually forced the population to become public citizens rather than private individuals. "When citizens are forced to concern themselves with public affairs, they are unavoidably pulled out of the sphere of their own interests and, from time to time, torn away from the sight of themselves. From the moment common affairs are treated in common, each man perceives that he is not as independent of his fellow men as he had initially imagined." The fabrication of collective political life thus broke down people's isolation from one another and compelled them to inhabit a shared world. Tocqueville applauded the successes of the Americans in creating such institutions and thus public-minded citizens who bucked the privatizing tendencies of the modern age. In fact, he wrote,

> The Americans have used liberty to combat the individualism born of equality, and they have defeated it. The legislators of America did not believe that, to cure a disease so natural to the social body in democratic times, and so fatal, it would suffice to accord to the nation as a whole a representation of itself [that is, political representation]. They thought that, in addition, it was appropriate to foster political life in each portion of the territory in order to multiply indefinitely for the citizens opportunities to act together and to make them feel every day that they depend on one another. This was done wisely.[37]

In one draft of *Democracy in America,* Tocqueville continued this passage with the comment that the "great object of legislators in democracies should therefore be to create common *affairs* that *force* men to enter into contact with one another."[38] The American example taught Tocqueville that legislators in democracies would have to play a quasi-pedagogic role, reorient people's self-interest to encompass others and the public good, and promote an active political life. Otherwise, liberty would wither and despotism rise in its stead. In essence, the array of institutions established

37. *DA,* pt. 2, 109, 110.

38. Alexis de Tocqueville, *De la Démocratie en Amérique,* ed. Eduardo Nolla, 2 vols. (Paris, 1990), 2:101.

in America to counteract the atrophying effects of individualism all worked toward the promotion of politics itself. Tocqueville's concern with privatization and the apathy that would result and his prescription of political virtue and a shared political life as the antidote speak to his status as a political thinker—and to his debt to post-Terror liberal republicanism.

Politics thus emerges in *Democracy in America* as the cure to democracy's ills. Just as democracy created the disease, however, it also created the remedy. The shared political life Tocqueville so prized depended on modern democratic vitality. An active political life in modern democracy, he thought, would result from channeling into civic participation the dazzling energy democracy produces. "Democracy does not give the people the most skillful government, but it does what the most skillful government is often powerless to create: it spreads a restless activity through the whole social body, a superabundant strength, an energy that never exists without it, and which . . . can bring forth marvels."[39] Democracy thus had to combat its privatizing tendencies by guiding its own "restless activity" and "superabundant strength" into a shared political life. In so doing, democracy generated the cure to its own disease. For Tocqueville, as for Rousseau, the antidote was in the poison.[40] It was in this spirit that Tocqueville wrote some of the most moving words of his entire oeuvre: "Far from reproaching equality for the unruliness it inspires, I for one praise it principally for that. I admire equality as I see it deposit that obscure notion and instinctive penchant for political independence at the bottom of the mind and heart of every man, thus preparing the remedy for the evil that it brings forth." Or, as he put it elsewhere in the text, "It is by the enjoyment of a dangerous freedom that the Americans learn the art of rendering the dangers of freedom less formidable."[41]

39. *DA*, pt. 1, 255. On this point, see Claude Lefort, *Democracy and Political Theory,* trans. David Macey (Minneapolis, 1988), 169.

40. To take Jean Starobinski's phrase from *Le remède dans le mal: Critique et légitimation de l'artifice à l'âge des lumières* (Paris, 1989).

41. *DA,* pt. 2, 296, 126. Tocqueville considered the participatory politics and associational life he saw in America to have a distinctively aristocratic genealogy as well. The very notion of political freedom, according to Tocqueville (and echoing Montesquieu), was rooted in the various particular liberties Europe's feudal aristocracy had erected against the central monarch (e.g., *DA,* pt. 1, 41). Democracy, he thought, would have to internalize aristocracy's emphasis on particular rights against the centralizing, homogenizing tendencies of central authority.

Tocqueville's enduring concern with politics and political life led him to a number of surprisingly republican declarations for a thinker so frequently placed squarely within the liberal tradition. At numerous points in *Democracy in America,* Tocqueville states clearly that he considers the tumult and disorder of political life in a democracy superior to the tranquillity of more "stable" forms of government. His belief on this front thoroughly broke with the liberal authoritarianism of Sieyès and Roederer as well as the rationalist liberalism of Guizot and the Doctrinaires. For example, in a striking passage Tocqueville echoed Constant's *On the Possibility of a Republican Constitution in a Large Country* (which he could not have read) by claiming that political life, even if unruly and disorderly, should not be sacrificed before the altar of public peace. To do so, Tocqueville warned, was to write the epitaph of freedom and pave the way for tyranny.

> I will easily admit that public peace is a great good. However, I do not want to forget that it is by way of good order that all peoples have arrived at tyranny. It does not follow, assuredly, that people should scorn public peace. But it must not suffice for them. A nation that asks no more of its government than the maintenance of order is already a slave at the bottom of its heart. It is a slave to its well-being, ready for the man who will put it in chains.

Tocqueville's thinking is unambiguous. If people turn to their personal interests alone, if "the mass of citizens only concerns itself with private affairs," as he phrased it two sentences later, then tyranny will surely follow. Put differently, if the liberty of the modern is all that matters, despotism is all but a fait accompli. While despotism may be easy, so easy that "peoples are lulled to sleep in the bosom of its temporary prosperity," and while "there is nothing harder than the apprenticeship of liberty," Tocqueville was adamant that "there is nothing more prolific in marvels than the art of being free."[42]

Tocqueville considered an active political life necessary not only for staving off despotism but for the moral fulfillment of humanity as well. Politics, for Tocqueville, as for Constant, was essential for human beings to fulfill their nature. On this front, his conception of the human subject sounded almost Aristotelian at points. Jean-Fabien Spitz argues that in

42. *DA,* pt. 2, 147–48; pt. 1, 250.

Tocqueville's eyes "political virtue should be pursued for its own sake, for the effects that it produces on the nature of the individual, on the richness and quality of his or her personality, on his or her morality.... Only political liberty allows man to be what he should be."[43] To be sure, Tocqueville did not consider everyday political participation the sole path to moral improvement. Perhaps the primary means in his eyes was the pursuit of individual distinctiveness, whether in art, poetry, politics, or some other potentially aesthetic realm. Nonetheless, he also placed great importance on the moral improvement attainable through active engagement with quotidian political life. Political activity forces individuals to interact with each other and thus fulfill the intersubjective side of their being. In Hennis's words, for Tocqueville the social interaction of political engagement counteracts democracy's "loneliness," which otherwise "weakens and destroys spiritual strength and the soul of man if he is not torn from behind the walls of his ego into constant social and brotherly responsibility."[44] Or, as Tocqueville put it when writing of associations, "Feelings and ideas are renewed, the heart expands, and the human spirit develops only through the reciprocal action of men upon one another."[45] Simply put, the isolated individual of modern, democratic societies lives a morally impoverished existence. For Tocqueville, politics is necessary both for the health of the polity and to promote the moral improvement of individuals.

Tocqueville thus placed great value on politics itself both to counteract the individualizing and privatizing tide of modern democracy and to fulfill human nature. The central status politics occupied in his thinking distinctly echoed the early modern classical-republican tradition and its reverberations in post-Terror political culture, liberal republicanism, and the thought of Benjamin Constant. Tocqueville's debt to the classical-republican tradition, however, was not confined to his thoughts on the importance of politics. His analysis of America and modern democracy more generally employed a host of tropes and themes redolent of classical-republican writings, or, at the least, of the general early modern wisdom about the nature of republics. For example, his various diagnoses of threats to the body politic sounded characteristically classical-republican notes.

43. Jean-Fabien Spitz, *La liberté politique: Essai de généalogie conceptuelle* (Paris, 1995), 475–76.

44. Hennis, "In Search of the 'New Science of Politics,'" 49.

45. *DA,* pt. 2, 115–16.

In addition to his trepidations about privatization and citizen abandonment of public affairs, Tocqueville feared the corrosive effects of luxury and was concerned that the sheer size of the American republic might doom its future.[46] He also warned against a powerful executive and advocated keeping government powers in a careful state of balance.[47] Perhaps more than any other trope, Tocqueville's overarching concern that freedom and independence were intrinsically fragile and constantly at risk of being subsumed by encroaching despotism if not vigilantly guarded echoed the trademark classical-republican anxieties about the essential contingency of liberty and the republic. Finally, the influence of the classical-republican tradition, and Tocqueville's status as a fundamentally political thinker, can be seen in his very analytic style. Unlike Comte, Marx, Durkheim, and other quintessentially nineteenth-century thinkers who placed society or economy at the center of their analyses, Tocqueville viewed a nation's essential characteristics through the prism of politics. His very starting point for analyzing America was a political category: democracy, not capitalism, social infrastructure, or the like. While the latter features figure in his discussion, sometimes prominently, they are emphatically secondary to democracy itself. Moreover, they are secondary to democracy studied primarily at the level of politically saturated moeurs.[48] In this regard, Tocqueville was heir to the early modern tradition of Machiavelli, Montesquieu, and Rousseau. Indeed, he once remarked that he read Montesquieu and Rousseau (as well as Pascal) every day. As a result, not surprisingly, a handful of scholars have noted the importance of classical-republican themes in *Democracy in America.*[49] None of this is to say, however, that Tocqueville should be interpreted as a straightforwardly classical-republican political philosopher. Instead, he is best understood as a transitional figure whose thinking remained rooted in the early modern classical-republican tradition at the same time that he so eloquently articulated liberal and other more modern sentiments. Rather than

46. On luxury, see, e.g., *DA,* pt. 1, 3; on size, pt. 1, 163–64.

47. Ibid., pt. 1, 130–33.

48. While Tocqueville sometimes understood democracy in more social terms, especially in volume one of *Democracy in America,* I contend that the political sense of the term predominated.

49. See Melvin Richter, "The Uses of Theory: Tocqueville's Adaptation of Montesquieu," in *Essays in Theory and History: An Approach to the Social Sciences,* ed. Richter (Cambridge, Mass., 1970); Boesche, *Strange Liberalism,* 213, n. 8; Alan Kahan, *Aristocratic Liberalism: The Social and Political Thought of Jacob Burckhardt, John Stuart Mill, and Alexis de Tocqueville* (Oxford, 1992), chap. 4; Spitz, *Liberté politique,* chap. 12.

simply defending classical republicanism or modern liberalism, Tocqueville sought to find a balance between them. His particular brilliance resided in his stunning analyses of a new political phenomenon, the mass individualization and privatization that characterized modern democracy, but his diagnosis was made in large part with an understanding of politics rooted in the classical-republican tradition. The persistence of classical-republican tropes, categories, and concerns in Tocqueville's writings perhaps represents the last major gasp of that tradition. In this vein, Wolin suggests that Tocqueville's "formulation" of political liberty "can be read as a late and beleaguered expression of the republican tradition of civic virtue" and that "Tocqueville might be the last influential theorist who can be said to have truly cared about political life."[50] Tocqueville's thinking was neither liberal nor republican in any simple sense. Tocqueville stood with one foot in each tradition, representing both the culmination and the concluding act of French liberal republicanism.[51]

Constant and Tocqueville both thought that modern polities would need to strike a balance between the liberty of the moderns and the liberty of the ancients. As Constant put it, "far from renouncing either of the two types of liberty,... we must... learn to combine the one with the other." For both, however, such an amalgamation amounted to a balancing act that would forever remain precarious. Constant, while professing the importance of political liberty to stave off the depoliticization of modern liberty, also argued that an excessive devotion to the liberty of the ancients had led to the Terror. Ancient liberty, he claimed, denatured modern individuals and always threatened to turn murderous in the modern world.[52] Similarly, Tocqueville's belief in the importance of an active political life led him in *The Old Regime and the Revolution* to profess a deep admiration for the "idea of political liberty" that he thought characterized the revolution

50. Wolin, *Tocqueville between Two Worlds,* 559, 5.

51. My analysis here places Tocqueville's political philosophy in a very different context from three important recent accounts of his thought. Craiutu argues for the influence of the Doctrinaires, *Liberalism under Siege,* chap. 4; Eric Nelson's *The Greek Tradition in Republican Thought* (Cambridge, 2004) locates Tocqueville's thought in a specifically "Greek" republican tradition focused on the just distribution of property; and Annelien de Dijn argues for the importance of a wider discourse centered on the role of intermediary powers, "Aristocratic Liberalism in Post-Revolutionary France," *Historical Journal* 84 (2005): 661–81.

52. E.g., Constant, *De l'esprit de conquête et de l'usurpation dans leurs rapports avec la civilisation européenne* [1814], in *Écrits politiques,* 211–23.

of 1789 at the same time as he despaired of its antiliberal transformations.[53] For both Constant and Tocqueville, modern and ancient liberty constantly threatened to negate each other, the former by causing the latter to fall into neglect and the latter by dissolving the former in its devouring intensity. Constant and Tocqueville thus, each in his own way, left a great paradox at the heart of French Liberalism.

Yet, faced with this paradox, their writings assumed very different tones. Constant, with his inveterate faith in human perfectibility, retained an optimistic vision of liberty's, and democracy's, future. The balance, he seemed to believe, could be struck, however fragile it might be. Tocqueville, to the contrary, felt the paradox intensely, especially in his later works. *The Old Regime and the Revolution* in particular frequently breathes with despair, even a sense of tragedy, as Tocqueville contemplated in the wake of the trauma of 1848–51 the downward spiral political freedom had just taken and might again take in the modern world. The balancing act, he feared, always threatened to collapse in the democratic age's version of the Polybian cycle. For Tocqueville, it sometimes seems, there was no way out of modernity's maze. Yet, modern democratic polities, faced with this dilemma, must still try, however imperfect the balance may be.

Constant's and Tocqueville's shared conviction that modern liberty was insufficient and needed to be counterbalanced by a steadfast commitment to the liberty of the ancients points to the distinctive character of French liberal republicanism. Unlike both the rationalist liberals in France and the mainstream Anglo-American liberal tradition, French liberal republicans believed that a robust political life was necessary to stave off the deadening torpor and potential despotism that stems from modern privatization. Moreover, they held that a vigorous engagement with politics was necessary to fulfill individual human potential, "the better part of our nature" in Constant's terms. In addition, both Constant and Tocqueville considered political institutions to play a critical role in inculcating such civic commitment and thus fulfilling human potential, a stance Anglo-American liberals would never countenance. These common core beliefs animating Constant's and Tocqueville's political philosophies highlight the extent to which French Liberalism was determinately shaped by a host

53. See Gannett, *Tocqueville Unveiled,* 158–59; quote at 158.

of classical-republican concerns and themes. They thus underscore the unique trajectory taken by French liberal republicanism as it emerged contingently, even haphazardly, from the post-Terror period.

From a political-philosophical point of view, the history of post-Terror classical republicanism and the origins of French Liberalism cannot be separated from an analysis of the relative strengths and weaknesses of these political languages. This book has been written from a perspective strongly influenced by the work of Sheldon Wolin and Pierre Rosanvallon.[54] While I have tried to avoid the language of moral judgment, the terms of my analysis and the questions I have put to the material unavoidably speak to my own normative biases. One such question, which stands at the heart of this book, is the status of politics or the political and of democratic practices in the political discourses studied. Although "the political" and "democratic practices" are not the same thing, there is nonetheless an important relationship between the two. Without a commitment to the political, there can be little space for democratic practices. As Wolin and Rosanvallon have both argued, modern liberalism typically circumscribes the political and, with it, more robust forms of democracy. However, an emphasis on politics is by no means sufficient to ensure a deep commitment to democracy. As the examples of classical republicanism and French Liberalism both attest, an active political life can be envisioned as central to the health of the polity and, simultaneously, as exclusionary. In both cases, politics itself was not rejected but democratic practice was as the citizenry was imagined in exclusivist terms. In evaluative terms, I would argue that this characteristic of both classical republicanism and French Liberalism presents too high a cost to uncritically celebrate either of these political languages. Yet in today's world, marked by the atrophy of the political, the impulse to emphasize politics as such may be salutary. Any revival of French Liberalism would, however, need to correct for its antidemocratic tendencies. As a political philosophy, French Liberalism presents a potentially rich starting point but not a terminus.

54. Especially Sheldon Wolin, *Politics and Vision: Continuity and Innovation in Western Political Thought* (Boston, 1960); and Pierre Rosanvallon, *Le capitalisme utopique: Histoire de l'idée de marché,* 3d ed. (Paris, 1999).

Index